Postmodern Interpretations of the Bible

Also from Chalice Press:

Handbook of Postmodern Biblical Interpretation
A. K. M. Adam, Editor

Postmodern Interpretations of the Bible

–A Reader

A.K.M. ADAM, Editor

Chalice Press®
St. Louis, Missouri

Bible quotations, unless otherwise marked, are author's translation.

Bible quotations marked NRSV are from the *New Revised Standard Version Bible*, copyright 1989, Division of Christian Education of the National Council of the Churches of Christ in the United States of America. Used by permission. All rights reserved.

Biblical quotations marked (JPS) are taken from *the TANAKH, the new JPS translation according to the traditional Hebrew text,* copyright © 1985 by the Jewish Publication Society. All rights reserved. Used by permission.

Cover art: Bob Watkins
Cover design: Mike Foley
Interior design: Elizabeth Wright
Interior photograph: Sir Edward Coley Burne-Jones, "The Song of Songs which
    is Solomon's," (stained-glass window at St. Helen's Church, Darley
    Dale, England). Photograph: W. John Lyons
Art direction: Michael Domínguez

This book is printed on acid-free, recycled paper.

Visit Chalice Press on the World Wide Web at
www.chalicepress.com

10 9 8 7 6 5 4 3 2 1   01 02 03

Library of Congress Cataloging–in–Publication Data

Postmodern interpretations of the Bible : a reader / edited by A. K. M. Adam.
        p.   cm.
    Includes bibliographical references and index.
    ISBN 0-8272-2970-4
    1. Bible–Hermeneutics.   2. Postmodernism–Religious aspects–Christianity.
I. Adam, A. K. M. (Andrew Keith Malcom), 1957–
    BS476   .P675   2000
    220.6–dc21

                                                    00–010816

Printed in the United States of America

Contents

Preface

Any number of witnesses testify that the Bible is the Book *par eminence:* the derivation of its conventional name from the Greek ὁ βίβλος, the fact that some editions of this text are simply called "The Book," and the common knowledge about numbers of copies sold. But if the Bible is *the Book,* what are you now holding in your hands?

This book, *Postmodern Interpretations of the Bible—A Reader,* is not a substitute for the Bible, or its successor, though one might deem it a supplement. The *Reader* presents works from a variety of scholars in order to offer examples of what happens when interpreters whose conversations have been inflected with the accents of postmodern thinking approach the biblical texts. Here our skeletal claims about history, gender, truth, class, culture, reading, and writing (as expounded in *Handbook of Postmodern Biblical Interpretation*) take flesh and walk. Here "talking about postmodernity" yields its place to "talking postmodern-ly." Here we show some of the ways that the fruits of the discipline of biblical studies might taste when one prepares interpretive feasts with the unfamiliar seasonings of postmodern theory.

So imagine a coffee shop or bar with twenty or so tables at which animated discussions are taking place. At each table one of our colleagues holds forth, urging our attention to ways of considering these familiar admonitions and stories, but with unaccustomed emphases. Some are wearing the obligatory black attire of nonconformity and rebellion; others model fashions so au courant that one wonders how an academic fit into them; others are in T-shirts and cut-offs; and still others dress with suspicious decorousness. Survey the varying hairstyles and colors, peer around voyeuristically to see whether anyone sports a tattoo or outlandish body piercing. Order a cup of coffee (or, if you must, one of the fancified variations thereof), find a vacant seat, and come listen. Think of it as an Interpretation Slam.

Why assemble such a plaza of discussions?

—Because not every interested reader has ready access to journals such as *Biblical Interpretation* or *Semeia.* Whereas one can wander down to any mega-bookstore to obtain numerous conventional guidebooks to the Bible, and one can go to most decent theological libraries to examine issues of the *Journal of Biblical Literature,* the sources for imbibing postmodern biblical interpretations are rarer and, often, more expensive. They likewise often focus on one particular gesture from the postmodern repertoire or on one portion of the biblical canon. Here one-and-twenty readers hold forth on what excites them about pursuing their interpretive work on postmodern premises, without restriction to one topic, theme, or canonical division.

—Because scholars who practice postmodern biblical interpretation do not always have ready access to the most prominent venues for promulgating biblical interpretations, and because the politics of interpretative association make those venues uncomfortable places even when they open themselves to postmodern interpreters. Here we are among *copains,* collaborators.

—Because even though postmodern-ly inclined scholars are becoming somewhat more visible in the public spaces of biblical interpretation, we still generate more ideas than there are opportunities to work them out in print. Poof! We just made room for twenty-one more good ideas.

—Because publication and hiring are the two social gestures by which institutions validate, celebrate, propagate, and promote biblical interpreters— and because we couldn't arrange for an en masse elevation of these colleagues to named professorial chairs at an Institute for Postmodern Biblical Interpretation. (If you are aware of an opportunity to establish and fund such an endeavor, please do not think that this volume preempts that admirable plan.)

—Because we are restlessly imaginative and can't just stop at writing reports about what other theoreticians of postmodernity have thought and done. Because a collection of topical essays represents an appetizer for the main course of textual interpretations; the heart of the matter lies in the *doing* of interpretation. All right: Here's a sampling of what we do.

—Because that's what the publisher suggested, thinking that a pair of books such as the *Handbook of Postmodern Biblical Interpretation* and this one would reinforce each other's sales. We're not innocents in the domain of material considerations or the means by which knowledge is produced and reproduced. Academic publishing constitutes an uncanny site in the complex of transactions that fuel a market economy, with businesses that range from the arrogantly exploitative to those that demonstrate respect and cooperation; our publisher has clearly stood among the latter, and if they want to produce two coordinated volumes of essays, we have ample ideas with which to fill them.

—Because once you start writing about postmodernism, it's hard to stop. This volume gives us an occasion to read and to think hard about the theories and arguments about history, narrative, evidence, communication, humanity, theology, and meaning (among countless other topics) that excite us and fascinate us. While all these contributors are quite capable of ordinary exegesis, and many have demonstrated this in long catalogs of books, articles, and scholarly papers, we revel in the chance to explore, to gambol, to present a different array of possibilities to readers.

—Because we wanted to be *together,* presenting *together* our various divergent notions of what postmodern interpretive practice might be. Because however much the participants in this project disagree—and take my word, we sustain a broad array of sharp, sometimes fierce disagreements—we recognize a sense in which this is still our interpretive neighborhood, in which we belong together, no matter how wrongheaded our colleague's appropriation of Derrida may be. In this volume and its companion, we pitch a tent where curious wanderers may come for edification, entertainment, instruction, perhaps for companionship, or eventually for participation. We're delighted to extend the hermeneutical hospitality by which some, after all, have entertained angels unaware.

The Chalice Press *Handbook of Postmodern Biblical Interpretation* is dedicated to our forerunners and to our successors in the enterprise of demanding more of interpretation than fourteen steps to an exegetical conclusion. Perhaps this book may serve as a sign of gratitude to one another, to what we learn from friends and colleagues by persisting with one another, listening to one another, debating one another, helping one another, irritating one another, appreciating one another. In a complicated world wherein limits, disappointments, frustrations, hostilities, and ignorance taint the satisfaction that our joys bring us, such friendship and solidarity may be among our strongest earthly resources.

A. K. M. Adam
August 2000

List of Contributors

Jon L. Berquist–Chalice Press, St. Louis, Missouri

Fiona C. Black–University of Alberta, Edmonton, Alberta, Canada

Walter Brueggemann–Columbia Theological Seminary, Decatur, Georgia

John Dominic Crossan–DePaul University (Emeritus), Chicago, Ilinois

Musa W. Dube–University of Botswana, Gaborone, Botswana

Danna Nolan Fewell–Drew University, Madison, New Jersey

Stephen Fowl–Loyola College, Baltimore, Maryland

Teresa J. Hornsby–Drury University, Springfield, Missouri

David Jobling–St. Andrew's College, Saskatoon, Saskatchewan, Canada

Catherine Keller–Drew University, Madison, New Jersey

Deborah Krause–Eden Theological Seminary, St. Louis, Missouri

Peter D. Miscall–Aurora, Colorado

Tania Oldenhage–Temple University, Philadelphia, Pennsylvania

Dennis T. Olson–Princeton Theological Seminary, Princeton, New Jersey

David Penchansky–University of St. Thomas, St. Paul, Minnesota

Donald C. Polaski–College of William and Mary, Williamsburg, Virginia

Sandra Hack Polaski–Baptist Theological Seminary at Richmond, Richmond, Virginia

Hugh S. Pyper–University of Leeds, Leeds, United Kingdom

Erin Runions–McGill University, Montreal, Quebec, Canada

Mary E. Shields–Trinity Lutheran Seminary, Columbus, Ohio

R. S. Sugirtharajah–University of Birmingham, Birmingham, United Kingdom

Building Babel

Danna Nolan Fewell

The tower of Babel is a cultural icon in Western society.[1] Theories of language,[2] philosophy,[3] politics,[4] and ethics;[5] architectural innovations;[6] critiques of technology;[7] visions of empires; denunciations of urbanization; images of postmodern life;[8] arguments for ethnic diversity and segregation;[9] and condemnations of human arrogance[10] have all looked to Babel for symbolic shade and shelter.[11] We only have to speak its name, and a structure

---

[1]This work began in 1996 as a contribution to a larger collaborative exploration of Babel and Pentecost (Acts 2) by the Bible and Culture Collective. Participants in that discussion were George Aichele, Fred Burnett, Elizabeth Castelli, Tamara Eskenazi, David Jobling, Tina Pippin, Gary Phillips, Ron Schleifer, and I. The members of the group explored not only the multiple dimensions of Genesis 11 and Acts 2 but also the various ways "Babel" has manifested itself in Western culture. My investigation of Babel here, greatly enriched by this interchange, attempts to engage many of the insightful questions raised by my colleagues who will no doubt hear echoes of our earlier conversations in the pages that follow. I would like to dedicate this piece to them in gratitude for the rich conversation and interpersonal connection in the summer of 1996.

[2]E.g., George Steiner, *After Babel. Aspects of Language and Translation* (Oxford: Oxford University Press, 1975); Umberto Eco, *The Search for the Perfect Language,* trans. James Fentress (Oxford, U.K./Cambridge, Mass.: Blackwell, 1995).

[3]E.g., Jacques Derrida, "Des Tours de Babel," *Semeia* 54 (1991): 3–34. Repr. from *Difference in Translation,* ed. and trans. J. F. Graham (Ithaca, N.Y.: Cornell University Press, 1985).

[4]E.g., David Hertzberg, "Genesis of the Polity–An Analysis of the Sin of Babel" in *Porat Yosef,* ed. Bezalel Safran and Eliyahu Safran (Hoboken, N.J.: Ktav, 1992), 43–47.

[5]E.g., Jeffrey Stout, *Ethics after Babel: The Languages of Morals and Their Discontents* (Boston: Beacon, 1988/Edinburgh: James Clarke, 1990).

[6]E.g., the work of artist/architect Robert Smithson.

[7]See Edna St. Vincent Millay's poetry, *Conversation at Midnight* (New York: Harper & Row, 1937), 100.

[8]Depictions of Babel in Western artistic tradition illustrate these three foci well. See the extensive collection of paintings, engravings, drawings, and sculptures in Helmut Minkowski, *Vermutungen uber den Turm zu Babel* (Freren: Luca Verlag, 1991). My thanks to Tina Pippin for bringing this work to my attention.

[9]See G. D. Cloete and D. J. Smit, "Its Name was Called Babel" *Journal of Theology for Southern Africa* 86 (1994): 81–87; Stephen Haynes, *Noah's Curse: Race, Slavery and the American Imagination* (New York: Oxford University Press, forthcoming).

[10]See particularly the Christian commentary tradition.

[11]On the many ways that Babel has been utilized culturally, see Hubert Bost, *Babel: Du texte au symbole* (Genève: Éditions Labor et Fides, 1985).

1

appears in our imaginations, an archaic skyscraper ascending toward, but never reaching, the heavens, conjuring images of confusion, scattering, and failed ambition. In the post-Holocaust world, the tower has taken on even more sinister dimensions as it has been portrayed as the feat of death-camp workers, many of whom found release only by way of its chimneys.[12] In his memoir of his days in the *Lager,* Primo Levi would come to write:

> The Carbide Tower, which rises in the middle of Buna and whose top is rarely visible in the fog, was built by us. Its bricks were called *Ziegel, briques, tegula, cegli, kamenny, mattoni, téglak,* and they were cemented by hate; hate and discord, like the Tower of Babel, and it is this that we call it: *Babelturm, Bobelturm;* and in it we hate the insane dream of grandeur of our masters, their contempt for God and men, for us men.
>
> And today just as in the old fable, we all feel, and the Germans themselves feel, that a curse—not transcendent and divine, but inherent and historical—hangs over the insolent building based on the confusion of languages and erected in defiance of heaven like a stone oath.[13]

In the Bible itself, the story of Babel offers little by way of detail. The tower is minimally described, and the story's participants are collective and stereotypical, without depth or nuance or any of the intense emotional reflection of a Primo Levi. It is perhaps this sparsity of both story and tower that magnetically attracts the multiple and varied significations, much like the plain of Shinar lured the ancient Babelians.

It is perhaps also this sparsity that encourages biblical scholars to look to contextual and intertextual connections as they build their interpretations of Babel. In biblical studies, Babel is rarely allowed to stand alone; rather, the story is seen to be both the crowning episode in the longer story of Genesis 1–11 and the transition into, indeed the necessity for, the call of Abraham in Genesis 12. Babel's meanings then are not inherent in its own bricks and mortar, but are contingent on how the introductory chapters of Genesis are seen to bear their semantic load.

What follows is a description of two prominent ways that Babel, within the context of Genesis 1–12, has been understood and some reflection on how two such incompatible interpretations may have, in a postexilic world, found their homes in the same text.

---

[12]This connection has been made most profoundly by Gary Phillips, "Babel Lives On: Speaking Many Languages, Producing Many Texts," a paper delivered to the Canadian Society of Biblical Studies, June, 1997. It is with his permission and encouragement that I reproduce some of his observed connections here.

[13]Primo Levi, *Survival in Auschwitz: The Nazi Assault on Humanity,* trans. Stuart Woolf (New York: Simon & Schuster, 1996), 72–73.

Genesis 1—11: Falling from Eden

A characteristically Christian interpretation of Genesis 1–11 starts from and emphasizes "the fall."[14] In Eden the first couple "falls" away from God and "falls" from paradise because of their desire to be like gods. Every succeeding episode in Genesis 1–11 demonstrates humanity's insatiable desire to transcend their creaturely lot and become divine. Various narrative elements are called on to support this thesis: for example, Eve's claim at Cain's birth, "I have acquired/created a man [with the help of] Yʜᴡʜ" (4:1), the violence dramatized in the story of Cain and Abel (4:1-16), Lamech's boast of violence (4:23-24), and the evil and the violence blamed for the flood (6:5-6, 11-12). All of these are used to illustrate how humanity, from its very inception, wanted godlike power over life and death. Even the enigmatic report about the "sons of the gods" and the "daughters of men" in Genesis 6:1-4 becomes an occasion to blame humans for attempting, through seduction, to co-opt divinity. Babel, accordingly, becomes the crowning act of hubris: the attempt of humankind to storm the heavens and to make a monument and a name for themselves in rebellion against, or at the very least in total disregard for, God.[15]

This act of rebellion and self-exaltation is understood to be in keeping with all human action thus far in Genesis,[16] and God's response is thus seen as swift and fitting punishment. The builders want to make a name for themselves; but the name becomes Babel, a name that, in the context of the story, means "confusion," a satire on its (Babylonian) meaning as "gate of God." Their desire for honor and glory ends in ridicule. Their eagerness to stay together is met with divinely ordained dispersal.

---

[14]Ellen van Wolde ("The Tower of Babel as Lookout over Genesis 1–11," in her *Words Become Worlds: Semantic Studies of Genesis 1–11*, Biblical Interpretation Series, vol. 6 [Leiden: Brill, 1994], 84–109) has characterized this reading as "Christian" and the subsequent one as "Jewish." This, to a large extent, seems to reflect some of the differences between current Christian and Jewish theologies. A Jewish reading that emphasizes a "fall" is, however, present since early on (Paul being a notable example), though these sources could be identified as reflecting "sectarian" rather than mainstream Judaism. See Gunther Plaut, *The Torah. A Modern Commentary* (New York: Union of American Hebrew Congregations, 1981).

[15]There are, of course, more tempered versions of this line of reading. See, for example, Gerhard von Rad (*Genesis: A Commentary* [Philadelphia: Westminster Press, 1972]), who has argued more enthusiastically than anyone that Genesis 1–11 is a story "characterized on the human side by an increase in sin to avalanche proportions" (152):

> That men wanted to storm heaven, God's dwelling place, is not said. Rather, one will observe a subtlety of the narrative in the fact that it does not give anything unprecedented as the motive for this building, but rather something that lies within the realm of human possibility, namely, a combination of their energies on the one hand, and on the other the winning of fame, i.e., a naive desire to be great. Jacob points also to the underlying motive of anxiety. These are therefore the basic forces of what we call culture. But in them, in the penetrating judgment of our narrator, is rebellion against God, a concealed Titanism, or at least…the first step in that direction. (149)

[16]For an overview of commentators reading in this vein, see van Wolde, *Words Become Worlds*.

At this point in the primeval story, God despairs that humankind will ever live the way that God intended. Enter Abraham and a new divine tactic to bring "salvation" or, in the words of the text, "blessing" to all the other families of the earth. Thus, we begin a "salvation history" that is seen to run uninterrupted through the last pages of the book of Revelation.

Genesis 1—11: Filling the Earth

A somewhat different set of readings, more popular among Jewish readers and other readers resistant to traditional Christian interpretation, see the move from Eden as a natural process of creation. God has created human beings "to fill the earth" (Gen. 1:28) and "to till the ground" (Gen. 2:5). Although the first human beings are "born" in the garden of Eden, they are destined to grow up and leave the garden eventually in order to get on with the business of filling the earth and tilling the ground. Eventually, they must learn about sexuality and mortality and to discern between what is good and what is not. Eating from the tree of the knowledge of good and evil is the first step toward maturity. Like children, they test their boundaries and assert their independence. In this reading, a divine parent and human children negotiate their newly assigned roles through trial and error, trying to balance relationship and independence, care and control.[17]

Jonathan Magonet nicely captures the theological spirit of this interpretation:

> It is as if God, like an over-protective father, had accidentally achieved the very thing He wanted to avoid. By trying to keep the children from the pain of knowledge, God led them to seek it; in trying to keep them in the Garden of Eden, in the paradise of childhood, God had given them the impetus to step outside and once outside, there was no way back. When a certain innocence is lost, it cannot be recaptured, except by wilfully denying the new reality.
>
> So did they fall, or were they pushed? And is the 'Fall' the cataclysm that some theologies see it as, or is it a first, necessary step towards emancipation of humanity, the first liberation from the slavery of the womb? Because if it is only a 'fall,' then the journey back to God is either enmeshed in guilt, or so dependent on some external source of salvation that human creativity, generosity and goodness are reduced to mere irrelevances or successful strategies for a return to divine favour. But if it is a liberation, however bitter and painful it

---

[17]Representatives of this interpretive tradition, despite their quite distinctive readings, would include Umberto Cassuto (*A Commentary on the Book of Genesis. Part Two: From Noah to Abraham* [Jerusalem: Magnes, 1974]), Gunther Plaut and Carol Meyers (*Discovering Eve: Ancient Israelite Women in Context* [New York: Oxford University Press, 1988]), Joel Rosenberg (*King and Kin: Political Allegory in the Hebrew Bible* [Bloomington: Indiana University Press, 1986]), Jonathan Magonet (*A Rabbi's Bible* [London: SCM Press, 1991]), Ellen van Wolde, David Jobling (*The Sense of Biblical Narrative, 2* [Sheffield: JSOT, 1986]), Mieke Bal (*Lethal Love: Feminist Literary Readings of Biblical Love Stories* [Bloomington: Indiana University Press, 1987]), and Danna Nolan Fewell and David M. Gunn, *Gender, Power, and Promise: The Subject of the Bible's First Story* [Nashville: Abingdon Press, 1993]).

may be at the moment of separation, the human beings travel bearing a full responsibility for their life and their actions, for their choices and ultimately for their death. And, in terms of biblical faith, they have also the ultimate freedom to choose or not to choose God, and that in the end is what the adventure begun with Abraham is all about.[18]

Leaving Eden is the first step toward "filling the earth" and learning to live with "ultimate freedom." As subsequent episodes show, human freedom has both constructive and dangerous consequences, and neither God nor human beings have quite figured out how to deal with its dual potential. On the one hand, birth reports and genealogies point to people freely choosing to fill the earth by engendering families and lineages. Some build cities, domesticate cattle, fashion tools, and invent music. On the other hand, some initiatives to fill the earth either get canceled out by violence, as in the case of Cain's murder of Abel, or are forever haunted by the threat of violence: Cain wanders abroad in Genesis 4, filling the earth with his descendants, but venturing out in fear ("I shall be a fugitive and a wanderer on the earth, and anyone who meets me may kill me," Gen. 4:14). Cain's descendant Lamech escalates God's own authorized vengeance ("I have killed a man for wounding me, a young man for striking me. If Cain is avenged sevenfold, truly Lamech seventy-sevenfold!" Gen. 4:23b–24; cf. 4:15). Moreover, the desire of "the sons of the gods" for "the daughters of men" instigates a wholesale, though much understated, violation in Genesis 6. By the time of the flood, the earth is filled and subdued as God had instructed, but it is filled and subdued with violence (both human and divine), and God, determining that the slate must be wiped (almost) clean, ironically responds to human violence with massive violence of his own.

In each of these stories God continues to play the role of an uncertain parent who oscillates between exercising a laissez-faire parenting strategy (as in the case of Cain and Abel and the "sons of the gods") and behaving as an overzealous disciplinarian (as in the stories of Eden and the flood). Both divine strategies result in an excess rather than a constraint of violence. After the flood God attempts, through the institution of the *lex talionis* (Gen. 9:5–6) and through the divine promise symbolized by the rainbow (Gen. 9:8–17) to ensure that neither human nor divine violence will ever reach such proportions again. The plan to fill the earth must begin again through the lineage of Noah: "And you," says God to Noah and his family, "be fruitful and multiply, abound on the earth and multiply in it" (Gen. 9:7). The table of nations in Genesis 10 indicates that Noah's family is up to the task of filling the earth. Unfortunately, the post-deluge generation decides to stay together. They are, in fact, afraid of being scattered over the face of the earth, and they proceed to build a city and tower for the sake of identity and security. In this line of interpretation, God's

---

[18]Magonet, *A Rabbi's Bible,* 114–15; cf. Gunther Plaut and Nahum Sarna, *The JPS Torah Commentary: Genesis* (Philadelphia: Jewish Publication Society, 1989).

response to their building project is not a punishment, but a reorientation, a gentle nudge (and for some interpreters, a more appropriate parental response to the childlike distraction) to continue the divine plan to fill the earth.[19] Abraham then becomes part of this dispersion, his wandering to the land of promise enabled by God's intervention at Babel.

A Double-fac(ad)ed Tower

Each of these readings capitalizes on particular spatial dimensions of the text. The first is a vertical reading. It focuses on human hubris, emphasizing the tower being built with its head in the heavens, a gesture attempting to compete with God but ultimately failing, for no matter how high they have built, God still has to "come down" to see what they are doing![20]

The second reading attends to the horizontal. The people desire to stop their migration. Like Cain, they are afraid of being scattered over the face of the earth. They want to stay in one spot, unite their labors, and create identity and security. In this reading the city is the more significant structure, the edifice that most answers the fear of being scattered abroad. Its external walls function, like language, to keep some people in and other people out. Hence, it is no coincidence that the unified language and the city walls (the barriers between insiders and outsiders) are subverted at the same moment, for it is the building of the city, not the tower, that is abandoned at the end of the story: "Thus YHWH scattered them from there over the face of all the earth; and they ceased building the city" (11:8). The tower, then, rather than being a monument, is a watchtower, guarding what is within the city walls and watching for whatever dangers may lurk without. It both protects the citizens and ensures conformity.

The reading that stresses human hubris is critical of the Babelians and sees God's response as just punishment. The reading that stresses human fear and insecurity is sympathetic toward the builders and either downplays the severity of God's reaction or critiques the response as overreaction. How can the same story effect these two very different reader responses? The text has more than one point (it is a tower with more than one turret), and its points are not necessarily compatible or mutually supportive.

Converging on Babel: The Universal and the Particular

Babel looms over the landscape of Genesis 1–11 and 12ff.,[21] a watchtower standing Janus-faced, overlooking both a "primeval" universal past and the particular future of Israel. Here at this junction the universal and the particular converge.

The story's universality is clear from its language and its setting. It is about "all the earth" and "the sons of *ha-adam.*" It is about the common

---

[19]This is the more sympathetic reading in this tradition. Some commentators speak of the Babelians' "refusal" to fill the earth as outright "rebellion" against the divine commandment.

[20]Benno Jacob, *Erste Buch der Tora: Genesis* (Berlin: Schocken, 1934); Otto Procksch, *Die Genesis: übersetzt und erklärt* (Leipzig: A. Deichert, 1913); Plaut and Sarna, *The Torah.*

[21]I'm borrowing van Wolde's metaphor, though to make a different point.

experience of human culture: to choose to live in groups for reasons of survival. It is about the common human emotion: fear of the unknown. It is about common human desires: to have an identity and a place of belonging, to create artifacts to symbolize that identity and that place, and to translate the work of imagination into visible structures that give witness to a community's presence and to its ability to make a difference in the world.[22]

This universal dimension of the story encourages our identification and elicits our sympathies for the ancient builders, in the same ways we may respond toward the other actors in Genesis 1–11. After all, do we not feel a connection with Eve as she makes the first move toward taking responsibility for her own life? Or with Cain as he struggles with the Otherness (or some might say, the arbitrariness) of God?[23] As he struggles with the call to "do well" in spite of the unfairness of life?[24] As he misses the very hard lesson about the nature of a gift, that a gift that demands or expects reciprocity is no gift at all,[25] that "if you do well, there is uplift" and that should be satisfaction enough?

And what of those washed away in the deluge? God (and the narrator) may assert all-encompassing generalities regarding the evil and violence of humanity ("the heart of humankind is only evil continually," "the earth was filled with violence," "all flesh had corrupted its way upon the earth"), but we need only peer beneath the surface of the water to find the children, the fauna, the flora, the innocent victims that are erased by the text's own rhetoric. God has responded to human violence with an overwhelming violence of his own, a violence so devastating that he, like a parent having resorted in a fit of uncontrollable rage to the physical abuse of a child, comes to regret his action and to swear that he will never respond in such a way again. Throughout Genesis 1–11 we have been led to imagine the vulnerability of the human actors. Can the God who stood by and let Cain kill Abel,[26] the God who

---

[22]On altering the world through the making of artifacts, see Elaine Scarry, *The Body in Pain: The Making and Unmaking of the World* (New York: Oxford University Press, 1985), chaps. 3, 4, and 5.

[23]See Jione Havea, "To Love Cain More than God," *Semeia*, forthcoming.

[24]Other commentators have seen God's favoring of Abel to be a divine testing of Cain. See Martin Buber, *Good and Evil* (New York: Scribner, 1953), 85ff.; Plaut and Sarna, *The Torah*, 48; Magonet, *A Rabbi's Bible*, 117–19.

[25]Cf. Derrida: "[T]he alteration of the gift into a form of calculation immediately destroys the value of the very thing that is given; it destroys it as if from the inside," *The Gift of Death* (Chicago: University of Chicago Press, 1995), 112.

[26]Cain's haunting question "Am I my brother's keeper?" implicates both himself and God. Plaut, *The Torah*, asks of this text: "If my brother's blood cries out against me, does it not cry out against You, too?" He goes on in a note:

Rabbi Shimon emphasizes this by pointing out that a slight shift in Gen. 4:10 (*'ali* instead of *'ali*) would make God, who now accuses Cain by stating, "Your brother's blood cries out *to* Me," say sorrowfully, "Your brother's blood cries out *against* Me." Rabbi Shimon, aware of the implications of his comment, says: "It is difficult to say such a thing [i.e., to read the text as it ought to be read], and the mouth cannot utter it [as it would imply the blaming of God]." He compared the God-Cain-Abel triangle to two gladiators fighting before a king. The ruler could stop the contest any minute, but he lets it proceed to the bitter, deadly end. Is he not, by his silence, involved in the killing? (47)

simply let the sons of the gods "take" the daughters of men, the God who brought about the deluge, be trusted to care about human welfare? We cannot be surprised at the human desire to stick together, to be cooperative, and even to build a tower to the heavens (as insurance against drowning in another flood).[27] Like Cain (the first city-builder), afraid to wander, needing a protective mark lest someone kill him, these people are afraid of what is "out there." It is, after all, a world that has been filled with violence once before. Thus, we have here a universal story about universal desire and universal anxiety.

On the other hand, the story's specificity is clear as well. It is about Babelians in the land of Shinar, a not-so-veiled reference to Babylon and to the building of the Babylonian Empire, a place and an event seared into Israelite memory, literature, and tradition.[28]

On the surface, Genesis 11 may tell a rather benign tale about people migrating from the east, finding a valley, and wanting to settle it by building a city and a tower. But what is the story obscuring? Between the lines of frontier exploration and cooperative construction lie traces of a different story, a story of conquest and coercion and confiscation, a story where bodies are buried between those rows of bricks.[29] Or, as it is retold in the film beloved by Hitler, Fritz Lang's classic *Metropolis,* a story where the disenfranchised workers who construct the tower are ground into dust and poured back into the city like some kind of nutritious cement.[30]

At the Top of the Tower

Traces of this reading are found in the Bible text itself. This is not the first we've heard of Babel or the land of Shinar. Through allusion, the story gestures back, pointing to a mythical trail of political reality.

> And Cush fathered Nimrod. He was the first to become a warrior in the land. He was a warrior-hunter to the face of YHWH; therefore, it is said, "Like Nimrod a warrior-hunter to the face of YHWH." And the head of his kingdom was Babel, Erech, Accad, and Calneh in the land of Shinar. From that land he went forth to Assyria (or Assyria went forth) and built Nineveh and Rehoboth-ir ("spacious city") and Calah and Resen between Nineveh and Calah; it is the great city. (Gen. 10:8–12)

---

[27]See n. 32 below.

[28]See 2 Kings 25. Daniel 1:1–2 expressly mentions Nebuchadnezzar of Babylon in connection with the land of Shinar.

[29]See the images of Babel by Etienne-Louis Boulée (1728–1799), Stanislao Lepri (1965), and Cobi Reiser (c. 1967), in which the tower is built of bodies.

[30]See the discussion of David Shapiro, "The Story of the Tower of Babel," in *Genesis: As It Is Written: Contemporary Writers on Our First Stories,* ed. David Rosenberg (San Francisco: Harper, 1996), 63–70.

The connection between violence and power has not been overlooked in rabbinic tradition:

> [Nimrod] began to rule through his power over people and he was the first to become a king, for until his time there were no wars and no king ruled. First he overpowered the people of Babel until he ruled them, then he went out to Assyria and did as he wished and grew great and built there fortified cities through his power and might, and hence it says in the next verse: and the beginning of his kingdom was Babel.[31]

The allusion to Nimrod (who, in later tradition, is explicitly credited with the building of Babel[32] and is portrayed as a mirror image of Nebuchadnezzar[33]) points to a story not of universal cooperation, but of Babylonian conquest.

The tower reaching to the heavens as a symbol of arrogance and hubris fits well with Israelite descriptions of Babylon. In the book of Daniel, images of great height are used repeatedly to depict and to critique the power and arrogance of the Babylonian Empire and the Babylonian king: the gigantic statue in Nebuchadnezzar's dream in Daniel 2, the sixty-cubit-high gold image Nebuchadnezzar erects in Daniel 3, and the great tree that nourishes and protects all living things in Nebuchadnezzar's dream in Daniel 4.

It is the great tree in Daniel 4, whose top reaches the heavens, that most vividly tells the tale of Babylonian hubris. Nebuchadnezzar's dream of the felling of the great tree comes to pass when, one day, Nebuchadnezzar stands atop his palace and congratulates himself: "Is this not great Babylon which I myself have built as a royal residence by the might of my power and for the glory of my majesty!" As in the story of Babel, Babylonian arrogance and power are symbolized by the building of Babylon (imaged in the dream as the great tree). In both cases, God's response is swift and appropriate: There is a confusing of the arrogant (Nebuchadnezzar's mind is transformed to that

---

[31]Nahmonides; quoted in Magonet, *A Rabbi's Bible,* 58.

[32]Many ancient Jewish legends associate Nimrod with the building of Babel. According to the *Midrash Hagadol,* the tower of Babel was not the first of his architectural achievements: He also built a pyramidlike structure that was topped with stacked thrones. He sat in state on the uppermost one, exacting universal tribute. According to *Sepher Hayashar* and *Tanhuma Noah* (cf. also Josephus, *Jewish Antiquities* 1:113–14; and *Perqei deR. Eliezer* 24), Nimrod raised Babel in rebellion against God as vengeance for the drowning of his ancestors, believing that the tower would keep him safe should God send another flood. He also intended to attack the heavens, destroy God, and set up idols in God's place. For an overview of these and other traditions about Babel, see Robert Graves and Raphael Patai, *Hebrew Myths: The Book of Genesis* (New York: Doubleday, 1964; repr. 1989); and James L. Kugel, *The Bible As It Was* (Cambridge, Mass.: Belknap, 1997), 123–30. The Western artistic tradition is also familiar with the traditional connection of Nimrod and Babel. See, for example, Frans Frank's paintings of Babel that include Nimrod overseeing the construction.

[33]*Genesis Rabbah* (38:13) and later rabbinic tradition tell of Abraham's being persecuted by Nimrod. In these stories Nimrod plays a part remarkably similar to that of Nebuchadnezzar in the book of Daniel (e.g., he attempts to throw Abraham into a fiery furnace) and to that of Herod in Matthew 2.

of a beast) and a scattering of all who seek security under, around, and within the great structure.

Isaiah takes the pride and arrogance of the Babylonian Empire and its king one step further and depicts Babylon as saying,

> I will ascend to heaven;
> I will raise my throne above the stars of God;
> I will sit on the mount of assembly on the heights of Zaphon;
> I will ascend to the tops of the clouds,
> I will make myself like the Most High. (14:13–14, NRSV)

At the Bottom of Babel

But as we all know, kings don't build their capital cities or their royal residences by themselves. Nor do they, no matter what they claim, attain god-like power on their own. Likewise, empires are seldom built by communities of consensual goodwill. There must be massive labor forces, and such are rarely made up of volunteers. Behind the innocent claim that each "man" said to his neighbor (in a spirit of collaboration), "Come let us build ourselves a city and a tower," are masked the enslaved and conscripted workers, and the military officers and construction overseers of "Nimrod" and others like him who forced captured laborers into the building projects of the empire.[34]

From early times, readers have been able to read between these lines. Thus testifies the *Midrash Hagadol* (11:3):

> As the tower grew in height it took one year to get bricks from the base to the upper stories. Thus, bricks became more precious than human life. When a brick slipped and fell the people wept, but when a man fell and died no one paid attention.

And similarly, the *Apocalypse of Baruch* (3:5):

> They drove forth multitudes of both men and women to make bricks; among whom, a woman making bricks was not allowed to be released in the hour of childbirth, but brought forth while she was making bricks, and carried her child in her apron, and continued to make bricks.

Isaiah has a similar memory of the Babylonian "taskmaster" whose blows were unceasing and whose persecution was unrelenting (14:3–6). "You showed [your captives] no mercy; on the aged you made your yoke exceedingly heavy" (47:6). When relief from the "destroyer"[35] comes, the captives will contemplate "a land that stretches far away" and will ask themselves, "Where is the one who counted the towers?" No longer, says Isaiah, "will you see the insolent

---

[34]In fact, the next time we hear of Shinar, its king is taking Lot captive in Genesis 14. Were it not for Abraham, Lot's fate as an imperial slave would have been sealed.

[35]The term *destroyer* is used to refer to Babylon in Isaiah 21. Although Babylon is not explicitly mentioned here, the context strongly suggests Babylon to be the allusion.

people, people of an obscure speech[36] that you cannot comprehend, stammering in a language that you cannot understand" (33:17–19).

Behind the "one language and one set-of-words" of Genesis 11 is the enforced, imposed language of the conqueror. Daniel 1's story of the Babylonian capture of Daniel and his companions testifies to the linguistic ramifications of conquest. Not only are the boys' Hebrew names changed to Babylonian names, but the children are required to learn "the literature and language of the Chaldeans" (1:4). Their captors attempt to erase their Israelite identities and to construct new identities for them as servants of the Babylonian throne.[37] Of course, Daniel and his friends have it easy compared to the countless captives forced to join the work corvées, and it is perhaps stories like those in Daniel that have led historians to conclude that the Babylonian exile was not such a bad experience after all. But if we were to combine the narrated experiences of Daniel and his friends, being stripped of their homes, their families, their names, and their language, with memories of forced labor in Isaiah, we might start to imagine the nature of the exilic injury. Multiply that injury a millionfold and we might begin to understand Primo Levi's description of life in the death camps:

> [F]or the first time we became aware that our language lacks words to express this offence, the demolition of a man. In a moment, with almost prophetic intuition, the reality was revealed to us: we had reached the bottom. It is not possible to sink lower than this; no human condition is more miserable than this, nor could it conceivably be so. Nothing belongs to us any more; they have taken away our clothes, our shoes, even our hair; if we speak, they will not listen to us, and if they listen, they will not understand. They will even take away our name: and if we want to keep it, we will have to find ourselves the strength to do so, to manage somehow so that behind the name something of us, of us as we were, still remains.[38]

In Isaiah (47:8, 10) Babylon is charged with saying "I am, and there is no one besides me." Is it such a claim of "oneness," of absolute unity and distinctiveness to which Genesis 11 alludes? Despite the many nations and languages recognized in Genesis 10, we might imagine a people migrating from the east looking for *Lebensraum,* a people thinking they were the only ones who mattered, a people insisting that all the land (that is, their land) was of one language (that is, their language) and one set of words. Is it this restricted worldview, with its accompanying ruthlessness and arrogance, that God moves to stop? The TANAKH's translation might suggest so: "And the LORD said, 'If,

---

[36]Literally, "a people deep of lip"; cf. Genesis 11:1: "all the land was of one lip."

[37]See Danna Nolan Fewell, *Circle of Sovereignty: Plotting Politics in the Book of Daniel* (Nashville: Abingdon Press, 1991), 13–22. The irony, in Daniel however, is that the narrator continues to call the young men by their Hebrew names and tells their stories in Hebrew and Aramaic (not "Chaldean").

[38]Levi, *Survival in Auschwitz,* 26–27.

as one people with one language for all, this is how they have begun to act, then nothing that they may propose to do will be out of their reach'" (11:6). Even, we might add, grinding bodies into cement to secure the foundation of Babel.

The Teetering Tower: Faltering at the Fault Line

When one considers those on both the top and bottom of Babel, the scattering in Genesis 11 becomes ambivalent: It is a punishment for the taskmasters and yet an emancipation for the enslaved and conscripted workers.[39] Without the scattering we have no Abraham setting forth for the promised land. Without the scattering we have no captives (Ezra, Nehemiah, and company) returning to Judea after the Babylonian Empire (= city/tower) has "fallen." For postexilic Israel, the Babel story becomes a reversal of sorts: Nebuchadnezzar of Babylon destroyed the house of God and the city of Jerusalem and scattered its people. Now Israel tells a story in which God thwarts the building (a temple-tower?) of the Babylonians and scatters the people.[40] Without the scattering there is no hope for Israel's future. It is no wonder that the hoped-for and the remembered destruction of Babylon takes on eschatological proportions (see Isa. 13):[41] Only through the destruction of Babylon can new histories begin.

But this is precisely why the tower-story teeters between the particular and the universal, between the critical and the sympathetic: The Judean exiles, brickmakers and bricklayers (both real and metaphorical) for the Babylonian Empire, come home celebrating the fall of Babylon and their own liberative scattering. They come home, the survivors of the Babylonian deluge (Isa. 43:2; 54:9), remembering that the earth is filled with violence and that God's response to violence often leaves massive collateral damage. They come home, nearly having lost their own name and knowing that if they want to reclaim it, they will have to find for themselves the strength to do so. They come home— to do what? To build their own city walls and their own temple. A city and

---

[39]Cf. Zechariah 2:6–7: "Up, up! Flee from the land of the north, says the LORD; for I have spread you abroad like the four winds of heaven, says the LORD. Up! Escape to Zion, you that live with daughter Babylon."

[40]The conversation between Isaiah 14 and Genesis 11 may indicate the spirit of poetic triumphalism:

"Come, let us build ourselves a city. . ." say the Babelians.
Says Isaiah of the Babylonians (14:21): *"Let them never rise to possess the earth or cover the face of the world with cities."*
"Let us make for ourselves a name…" say the Babelians.
Says Isaiah (14:20): *"Let the descendants of evil-doers nevermore be named!"*
"…lest we be scattered all over the face of the world" say the Babelians.
Says Isaiah (14:22): *"I will rise up against them, says the LORD of hosts and will cut off from Babylon name and remnant, offspring and posterity, says the LORD."*

[41]See also the artistic images (e.g., the engravings of Cornelius Anthonisz and the school of Maerten van Heemskerk) that show Babel being not simply abandoned, but destroyed.

tower. To (re)claim, to rebuild their identity and to keep from being scattered (again) across the face of the earth. [42]

And though God (Isa. 54:7–12) assures the "storm-tossed" Zion that he will rebuild her walls, in reality, it is not God's sweat or God's labor that will rebuild the walls of Jerusalem. It will be up to the returning Israelites themselves to translate the unspeakable pain of exile into the work of remaking their world. What we discover is that the building of walls is a matter of delicate balancing—between inside and outside, between pain and imagination. We're told that the people gather as "one man" in Jerusalem (Ezra 3:1), but the asserted unity of the postexilic community, like that of the builders of Babel, obscures the divisions and tensions that exist. They offer burned offerings where the temple once stood "because they were in fear of the peoples of the land" (Ezra 3:3). When the people of the land (termed "adversaries" by Ezra) offer to help rebuild the temple, the returnees respond in disdain: "It is not for you and us to build a house for our God, for we alone will build to YHWH God of Israel" (4:3). The building proceeds, but only in fits and starts, with the "sons of the exile" setting themselves over against the other inhabitants of the area. The walls of the city (Neh. 2–4) fare no better, with insiders and outsiders, the "house of Judah" and their "foes," squared off. Even the house of Judah itself is divided, with the wealthy taking advantage of their poorer kinfolk (Neh. 5:1–13). The walls of the city proceed at a great price, with the children of the poor being sold into slavery, their daughters being assaulted, and their lands and properties being confiscated (cf. Isa. 58:4–7). And once the city walls are built and the house of God secure, another scattering takes place. The "foreign" wives and the mixed children of the "sons of the exile" are sent away (Ezra 9–10; cf. Neh. 13:23–30). Where they go and how they are able to take care of themselves, we're never told.

With this, we've marched full circle around this city and this tower, artifacts so desperately needed to remake the world of postexilic Israel, artifacts to give Israel a place and a name. Worthy artifacts without a doubt. But as we circumnavigate these walls, we continue to step over bodies, the bodies of the strangers, the common laborers, the homeless women and children, the indentured children, the assaulted young women, the poor and dispossessed, none of whom can call these walls their home. They remain at the bottom of Babel, paying the price for those who want to see Babel built, for those who want to make Babel their home, their place of security, their source of identity.

---

[42]They come home to alter their world through the making of artifacts designed not to benefit their captors (cf. Levi's description of the Carbide Tower), but to benefit themselves. On the separation of work from the benefit of the product of work, see Scarry, *The Body in Pain,* 169–72. Cf. also Isaiah's promise (65:21–22) concerning the returning exiles:

They shall build houses and dwell in them,
They shall plant vineyards and enjoy their fruit.
They shall not build for others to dwell in,
Or plant for others to enjoy.

The view at the top of Babel offers no consolation either. If we scale the heights, we may get a glimpse of God coming down to take a look, but he's not likely to tell us whether his intentions are to punish or to protect, to guide or to control, to be a liberator or merely a spectator.[43]

Babel is indeed a confusing site. For every brick laid in fear of violence, there is another laid in exploitation. For every desire for security, there is a desire to control what is other and alien. For every brick laid in collaboration, there is another enforcing conformity. For every creative and self-transcendent impulse, there is an arrogant and insolent one. And for every corporate name that's made, myriad individual names are erased. Such is the tower and city of Babel. It is a watchtower built out of anxiety; it is an artifact testifying to human imagination and ingenuity; it is a monument to human pride and ambition; it is a monolith signifying the extent of human cruelty; and it is more. Bricks and bodies, mortar and mortality, it bears the load of complicated human experience, a load heavy and unstable and sometimes excessive and insufferable.

In the end, of course, the Babel of Genesis is built not of bricks but of words. We gather in its shadow, contemplating its shape and meanings, peering between its lines, beyond its facade, to discern the secrets of its construction, all the while sensing its power to shape us in unexpected ways. The text becomes our living space,[44] our school,[45] where we are invited to reflect on the various reasons why people might be compelled to construct such walls and towers and why God's response to human behavior is so frighteningly unpredictable. It is a text that resists tidy theological and ethical interpretation, where "making" (building, creating) shows itself to be "the most morally resonant of acts"[46]—and the most ambiguous. It is a text thick with construction dust and ash and smoke and mixed messages, where the undefinable connection between good and evil becomes the very mortar that holds it together. It is a text that requires closer attention to the desperate human desires to have a home, to have security, to have identity, and to be remembered for having made a difference in the landscape of human history. It also demands a more intense awareness of those who have been stripped of the hope of any of these things, who have been coerced into building other

---

[43]For an image of God as spectator during the Holocaust, see Elie Wiesel, *The Town Beyond the Wall,* trans. Stephen Becker (New York: Avon, 1964).

[44]Emmanuel Levinas ("Revelation in the Jewish Tradition," in *The Levinas Reader,* ed. Seán Hand, [Oxford: Blackwell, 1989], 190–210) speaks of the Bible as providing *espace vital* where, through reading, "we come to inhabit a place" (192). "The expression *'espace vital'...*evokes the 'nourishing terrain' of the book to which the land, in the geographical sense of the term, refers in Judaism, and so draws out its spiritual meaning" (210, n. 2). What was for the Third Reich the justification for expansion and ultimately genocide *(Lebensraum),* Levinas turns into an ironic metaphor for more intense reading and living.

[45]Levinas ("Simone Weil against the Bible" in *Difficult Freedom: Essays on Judaism,* trans. Seán Hand [Baltimore: Johns Hopkins, 1990], 133–41) describes Torah as "not a doctrine based on kindness" but "a school of kindness" (138) and of the world of the Bible being "a world not of figures, but of faces...entirely here and related to us" (140).

[46]Scarry, *The Body in Pain,* 222.

people's Babels, and who have often lost their lives in the process. Babel scatters us in multiple directions. We go as we are bid to do, straying into the margins and off the page, in our hands the bricks we may be reluctant to put down, in our ears the sounds of different voices speaking other languages, each testifying to some other dimension of Babel that we can only imagine, and in our eyes a landscape where towers and fragments of towers continue to loom in grave need of our closer scrutiny and where we ourselves must make difficult choices about what and how we will build.

Leviticus and Nausea

Jon L. Berquist

In the middle of a sentence, the book of Leviticus begins "...and the LORD called Moses..." (Lev. 1:1), signaling a discussion of priestly practice and resultant legal codes in ancient Israel. Such has been the consensus of modern scholarship, which has focused on the myriad laws or instructions that this legal corpus contains. Yet the book itself states its purpose in terms of the land: "You shall keep all my statutes and all my ordinances, and observe them, so that the land to which I bring you to settle in may not vomit you out" (20:22). If this concern with avoiding vomiting becomes the focus of the interpreter's attention, then the book becomes an antidote to nausea. The land itself is queasy at the thought of all the people whom it is about to swallow. The oft-mentioned milk and honey are absent; they are not enough to quiet the land's stomach, and it becomes imperative that the people live as righteous persons to avoid upsetting the land and causing it to vomit. Only the closely monitored life can reduce the land's nausea so that the people are not vomited.

Seen from this angle, the book of Leviticus centers on the land and its nausea. If this is the center, then the book itself orbits around it, never approaching the subject of vomit any more closely than it does in 20:22. Instead, the circle around this center is the subject of masculinity. The avoidance of the land's vomiting requires a great medicine, a remedy or *pharmakon* (Derrida's term for remedy and/or poison) that will take queasiness away from the land. This *pharmakon* is the male priestly system. Following this cue, many scholars have worked to systematize the priestly legislation, to find the structures underlying the laws, and to decode the legal code so as to reduce it to basic, foundational principles. Yet such a scholarly path obscures the practice of the law, because the priesthood deals often in meals and other foodstuffs: If YHWH and priests eat right, the land will not vomit. Leviticus constructs the relationships between priests, YHWH, and land such that the land and all stomachs are settled.[1]

---

[1]Francis Landy, "Leviticus, Deconstruction, and the Body," *Journal of Hebrew Scriptures* 2/5 (1999): 3.1, argues that this view of an unnauseated era is always and apparently counterfactual: "The book is reft with intimations of failure. From the death of Nadab and Abihu to the threat or prediction that the land will vomit you out to the culminating apocalypse, there is no doubt that the world of Leviticus will not happen."

In this sense, Leviticus reads like a culinary code, a description of how God can be fed in ways that are most pleasing. As with any gourmet meal, the presentation of the food is everything. In ancient Israel (and in most swanky restaurants today), the wait-staff must be all male, properly attired, obsequiously subservient, and rigidly compliant to the proper conduct.

But the law is more than a culinary code. The law of Leviticus is a life lived by those who obey YHWH and who work with YHWH's priests. Richard Nelson rightly cautions that "it is wrong to caricature Israelite priests as uncaring and robotic cultic bureaucrats as is sometimes done."[2] If priests are not robots, it is because they are real people—real men. The priesthood, defined by the purity of its male members, becomes the power to tame the stomach of the land. Not only are the law and priesthood an antidote or *pharmakon,* they are the *supplément,* a Derridean term for the addition or substitute that displaces. It is priestly righteousness that, in the end, may defeat the land's retching. As with any meal, much of the enjoyment is in the presentation, and this means that the right persons must be involved. Thus, the book of Leviticus devotes itself to locating the right priests and to prescribing their activities within the bounds of all propriety.

The Gender of Priesthood

Israel is usually described as a gender-stratified society, and with good reason. The assignment of roles throughout the society and the valuation of those roles involve great attention to gender, and as a whole they construct a society with a significant consciousness about gender and a desire to make distinctions and hierarchies based upon gender. In many cases roles are paired, especially when there is a more obvious biological component. Thus, the Ten Commandments urge Israelites to honor both father and mother (Ex. 20:12) for the same reasons of long life in the land that figure so prominently in Leviticus, although Exodus does not consider the land as nauseous.

However, Israelite society has many leadership roles that concentrate attention on the male. Almost all the familiar roles are assumed to be roles especially for men: king, priest, sage, prophet, judge. Yet the Hebrew Bible often notes where there are exceptions. There are queens (a paired role, although it is not a pairing of equals in most cases), and at times these queens can exercise great influence, such as Jezebel does. Of course, Jezebel is an evil queen who matches an evil king (1 Kings 16–21, especially 21:25–26); strong women in leadership roles similar to men's roles are not always valued positively. Other roles are perhaps more positively inclined toward women. When Deborah is described as a judge, she is depicted as one of the best examples of the role (Judg. 4–5). Isaiah's wife is a prophet(ess), and the prophet(ess) Huldah is portrayed very positively, as one of those involved in Josiah's reform (2 Kings 22:14–20). Although most of the sages are men, there

---

[2]Richard D. Nelson, *Raising Up a Faithful Priest: Community and Priesthood in Biblical Theology* (Louisville: Westminster/John Knox Press, 1993), 87.

are wise women as well, and some of them are highly effective in advising powerful persons, even the king (2 Sam. 14). Thus, in Israel very few social roles are strictly limited to men, with the exception of those that are paired. Although Israelite society found women's significant roles to be fewer and undervalued women's performance of roles in the majority of cases (if the Hebrew Bible is considered a representative record), every role that was usually male was not always male. The maleness of the role was not ontological, and it could not be assumed as definitional or essential. Instead, the maleness of the role's fulfillment was performed in specific instances, and in some recorded instances and stories, women performed the diverse roles of monarch, sage, prophet, and judge.

In this context, the maleness of the priesthood is all the more striking. In a culture of role diversity and gender assignment through performance, and in a text that constructs gender socially, the priesthood is defined as essentially male. The rhetorical efforts invested in the construction of a male-only priesthood are vast. Leviticus is not at all content to assume that priests are male, for in ancient Israel that assumption would only be probabilistic, not definitive. Thus, the text begins an obsession with maleness in its attempts to construct the society's only nonpaired, gender-determined role.

Determining Gender

If the priesthood is the only gender-determined role in Israel, the manner of determination is also unique. A society unused to such rigid sex-stereotyping, yet invested in a single instance of determination, constructs this role with close attention to the gender issues involved. Since maleness is an absolute prerequisite to the status and privileges of the priesthood, it must be not only determined but also protected, for without an unambiguous maleness, there can be no priests.

The determination of gender requires the gaze, that is, the observation by those qualified to pronounce the child as male. The genitalia must be observed, inspected, and evaluated, so that the priest-to-be is unambiguously declared to be male by those who can determine the priesthood. A priest must not only be male, and be seen to be male, but must have genitalia that are unambiguously male. Thus, those with crushed testicles are prohibited from the priesthood (21:17–20). Their alternate maleness makes them insufficiently male to be priests, for the priesthood requires the purity of maleness. A penis alone may qualify a man to be male, but without testicles, the maleness is in question, incomplete, inadequate for priesthood. The categories constructed by male priests allow for no mixing of absolutes; there is either male or not-male, priest or not-priest, and in-between states are relegated to the status of not-priest.

Priesthood thus begins with nakedness. Yet the vulnerability of nudity presents a different threat to the priest. Were the genitalia to be widely visible, others might question, and therefore the male parts must remain in the family, as it were. Priests are sons of priests; fathers inspect their own sons' privates in order to keep the gaze within the family of priests. No non-priest may see the genitals of a priest, lest their valuation be different. The gaze, while necessary to the determination of the priest, must be restricted, forbidden to anyone but those already within the priesthood. Thus, the priest cannot have sexual partners that come from without. Foreign women cannot be the sexual partners of a priest; the standards for the adequacy of male genitals might differ in some other culture, and there can be no parallax, no mixing of gazes. Likewise, divorced women—who presumably had seen the genitalia of the former husband—cannot be allowed to see the priests' genitals (21:14–15), for their gaze would be informed by non-priestly standards. The priest's nakedness forms the originating moment of the possibility of the priesthood, but it threatens thereafter; the gaze of the other must be avoided.

Such a priestly gaze is part of the task of the priesthood. Priests inspect the bodies of others, to observe the progress of disease or other problems of skin and body (chaps. 13, 15). Yet the priestly gaze is always outwardly directed; the gaze must never be directed at a priest, for it is in that moment of the gaze that the boy becomes the priest-to-be, when the gender is determined through inspection. From then on, the priestly gaze penetrates others, but the invisibility of the priest himself may never be violated. Michel Foucault writes similarly of the panopticon, the technologies by which persons and institutions become unseen seers who observe the world and its people, regulating them through their all-seeing invisibility. Priests live in an all-male world, yet their maleness is unseen and unsullied. The law requires that their masculinity be invisible (18:7). Thus, their gender is the same as that attributed to God—an unseen male perfection. The perfection of the priestly genitalia (21:17) is part of this mystique, as is the requirement that there be no unwanted discharges (22:4). They are perfect, because they are invisibly inviolable.

The Family and the Priesthood

The gaze of the priest looks outward, but it is the inward gaze within the family that makes a priest—the father's gaze that judges the son complete and thus genetically and genitally fit for priesthood. In this way, fathers make their sons into priests. The priesthood is genetic, inherited, and familial. This is in contrast to the typical career paths of ancient Israel. The Hebrew Bible's portrayal of occupations shows relatively few that are passed from father to son. In Genesis' early chapters, the narrative of dispersion shows how each subsequent generation develops new careers. Despite the existence of a few clans identified with similar vocations, occupational transmission within families is rare. When the narratives explicitly mention that sons follow in their fathers' footsteps, the connotations are usually negative. Aaron and Eli are two prime examples; their sons attempt to be priests, but fail at their tasks, and so God must take action to kill them (Lev. 10:1–2; 1 Sam. 2:12–17, 31–34; 3:11–14; 4:10–11). Perhaps their lives would have been spared had they taken the more usual path of career divergence.

Despite the negative examples of these two prominent priestly families, the book of Leviticus is insistent that priesthood is a family affair, at least for the males of the family. To be male in the priestly family is to be a priest; the two categories are coextensive. Yet the book of Leviticus also provides detailed instructions about how to go about the various tasks that priests must do with skill. Birth is enough to attain the role, but not enough to perform the role of priest—and the stories of the sons of Aaron and Eli make clear that role inheritance without role performance is lethal. Thus, the family of birth transforms the son into a candidate for the priesthood through its gaze, and then, through its instruction and upbringing, the family of priests trains the priest-to-be in order to produce a priest. Clearly, the other choice is death; there is no way to be male in this family except to become a priest, and those who fail at priesthood die. Priestly function and priestly ontology must match perfectly. Phylogeny must recapitulate ontogeny, or else death must result.

The pressures that this places upon the family are enormous. Whereas normal Israelite society would have involved interchange between families, priestly families must keep to themselves. There are no possible mentors outside the family; only the men within the family have the specialized knowledge that enables them to train the next generation of priests. Although ancient Israel would have typically structured a working relationship between the social institutions of the family and vocational training, for priests these two separate social groups were collapsed into one. The father is the teacher; the teacher is the father. No separation is allowed; no interaction with other social institutions is possible for the priest. If father disapproves or if father teaches wrongly, it is not just inheritance or role performance that suffers; death is the consequence. There is no outside court of appeal and there are no other relevant social structures. The entire world collapses into the family that procreates the priest, determines the priest, educates the priest, selects the right mate for the priest, and will ordain the priest. The authority for all these social activities resides in the father. There is no other. The father is judge of a priest's competence, and failure is death.[3]

The meal is the symbol of this social collapse. When the family eats, it is a meal for all the males of the family, for all of them are holy (6:18, 29). The meal they eat is a family meal and a priestly meal; it is familiar/secular and professional/sacred all at once, for there can be no difference between these for the priestly family. Food sets them apart from the rest of the people, for no one but their family eats of this meal. Likewise, the priestly garments are a separation (chap. 8). The entire family dresses alike, and no other family of

---

[3]The deathliness of priestly roles also resonates with the founding of the Levites in Exodus 32:25–29. After Aaron has constructed the golden calf for the people's worship, the people run wild, and so Moses rallies the Levites, who declare themselves to be on the Lord's side. Moses instructs them to kill brothers, friends, and neighbors (and sons, in v. 29); when the Levites do this, Moses proclaims that in this way they have ordained themselves into God's service and have thus brought blessing on themselves. Death, separation, ordination, and blessing are closely and complexly interlinked.

Israel wears clothes that resemble theirs. In these very basic elements of life, the priestly family sets itself apart and demonstrates that it is separate from the rest of the people. This separation is holiness; the Hebrew *qadosh* can be translated as "separate" or as "holy." Their priestly status of holiness is exactly what makes them different from everyone else, separate from every other institution in Israel, unlike their neighbors and more distant kin of the twelve tribes. Like a black hole, where distinctions are broken by the strength of gravity so that everything falls into one dense location, the family of priests is the institution around which all priestly life revolves and into which every priest is inevitably, irrevocably drawn–and is thus ever separate from all else.

Similarly, a priest's future is predicated upon the performance of his sons. When Aaron's sons sin, they are killed; when the remaining sons also sin, these are things that Aaron considers to have befallen himself (10:19). In these ways, the behavior of the son reflects upon the father. A failed priest endangers his own father, and every priest is dependent upon his son's adherence to the law, lest God step in with death (10:1–13).[4] In the case of Eli, death even spreads from his sons to himself; he dies in shock when he hears the news of his sons' demise (1 Sam. 4:18). A priest, then, is circumscribed in the role through the father's determination of gender, through the father's instruction in the ways of maleness and priesthood, through the ability to father sons who can be priests, and through the sons' adequate performance of the inherited and learned roles of the priesthood. If either father or son fails, the priest fails, and life itself is always at stake.

Priesthood lives on the edge of its demise, dependent on right actions and the genital gaze of father and son, at risk of the impurities of mother and daughter, caught in between the generations before and after that endanger its very survival. If any of the relatives sin, holiness dissipates from the priestly family and death may result. The priestly family is the source of identity, roles, and life itself as priest, and yet it constantly threatens death.

Priesthood beyond Family

The priesthood's relationship to the rest of the people is also always fraught with possible disaster, but in the opposite way. Priests must avoid sin to survive, but priests require the sin of the people to prevent starvation. Priests eat the sin offerings that the people bring to the altar (chaps. 4–7). This creates another relationship that determines priestly survival; if the people do not sin, the priests do not eat. In this sense, priesthood carries a complicity in the sin of the people. Yet the priests are charged with the instruction of the people in the ways of God, so that they can avoid sin. If the priests succeed, they do so only at the expense of their own livelihood and their own lives. Priestly failure means that their lives are at risk from God; priestly success means that their lives are at risk from starvation. Adherence to law is the antidote/*pharmakon* to the land's nausea, but at the price of priestly starvation.

---

[4]A daughter's actions can also cause a priest's holiness to dissipate, if the daughter enters into prostitution (21:9).

The relationship between the priests and the wider political community becomes clearer outside the book of Leviticus. Within the Pentateuch, priestly authority (which is, in most cases, coextensive with Aaron's authority) is circumscribed by the overpowering figure of Moses. When Aaron or others in his priestly family sin, Moses intercedes with God (Ex. 32:30–34; Lev. 10). The political already begins to overshadow the priestly. The law comes to the people through the priests, but it is the law that Moses receives from God (Ex. 32:15). This law, not priestly codes themselves, is the overarching determinant of divine desire. The book of Deuteronomy places Moses in an even more influential location, as he becomes the main preacher and chief liturgist for the people in their acceptance of relationship with God (esp. Deut. 27–30). This does not abrogate priestly responsibility, for the priests continue their life-and-death investment in the people's adherence to the law. The identity of Moses' replacement, Joshua, provides a further clue to the limitations placed upon the priestly role, for Joshua is a military commander (Deut. 31), and suddenly the key role in the covenant community is military, not even political, let alone legal or religious.

In the Persian period, the book of Zechariah offers a prophetic image of the second temple and its basic organization. In these visions, the priests are symbolized by a chief priest, now named Joshua, who is shabbily attired but suitably cleaned up for service, whereas the religious community itself finds its basis in the new temple to be constructed by Zerubbabel, the political leader whose very name means "seed of Babylon" (Zech. 3–4). The Persian Empire appoints the leaders to the temple, and the local imperial governor sets the stage for religious life. The explicitly Persian period visions of Zechariah that assert the later order of society reflect no change at all from the Pentateuchal images. The Empire constrains the priesthood, and yet holds the priesthood responsible for local life and for the kind of life before God that does not require forcible suppression or the invasion of distant armies as God's own punishment for the sins of the people.[5] The law promulgated by a later Persian appointee, Ezra, was to be proclaimed by the decree of the emperor (Ezra 7:25–27). These connections between the political/imperial powers and the local priesthood and their instruction of the law of God cannot be ignored; they constrain the priesthood because they set the conditions under which the proclamation of the law transpires. The priests speak forth a law as charged to do by the Empire and its political/military authority. The priests occupy a social space between Empire and colony, between political leaders and the people.[6]

---

[5]Consider also Ezekiel's idea of the prophet as watcher or sentinel, who is responsible for warning an obdurate people (Ezek. 3:12–21).

[6]However, the priesthood is not the only body to do this task of mediation. From the imperial standpoint, at least in many parts of the Persian Empire, the key to this mediation of interests is the eunuch, who is imperial mediator, but who is not a priest. In fact, the law of Leviticus explicitly forbids the eunuch's taking the priestly role, even though Isaiah 56:4–5 valorizes eunuchs who obey the law of God. The eunuch has the word (of the king). Without testicles, the eunuch perfectly testifies to the emperor.

The separation that is holiness places the priests inside this complex relationship, caught between generations and between the people and God. To be a priest is to be trapped, along with the other men inside one's family, between three power relations: God-(hu)man, Empire-colony, and father-son. The priest enforces the power of the former over the latter in each case, holding each relationship in place.

Priesthood and Overdetermination

In this context, the priests occupy a social space that is overdetermined. It is subject to multiple directions of power, and it is set in its place along the lines between these three dimensions. A priest is always between father and son, always between God and people, and always between Empire and colony. The priest is never any of those things, in and of itself. Instead, the priest exists in a liminal space, a buffer zone between spheres of social power, a dividing line between ontological categories. Priesthood is deployed in these nonspaces between—or more precisely, in the overlapping nonspace between these three dichotomies that structure Israelite existence. The priest is in an intersection, occupying the interstices in an impossible middle.

The priesthood is fraught with the ambiguities of multiple allegiances, of positions between, and of ontological impossibilities. Priests are possessed by conflicting powers and competing interests, partaking of the various realities represented by each of these social spheres. The role of mediator comes from living in a space that is neither/nor: neither Empire nor colony, neither God nor people, neither father nor son. In this empty space that is overdeterminedly between, priests become mediators, connecting categories that can have no connection.

Because priests are overdetermined, they are held in place by the lines of force that connect and keep apart each of these three pairs of social spheres. They cannot move, or else they would no longer be in any position to hold these multiple tensions at once. As a social role, they are static, immovable, rigid. In this sense, the priesthood is a linchpin, an element that connects all the rest of society together, and one that even keeps God in place within the overall system. The priesthood's phallic immobility holds together people and God, at the same time operating for the continued existence of all generations, and also keeping the Empire-colony relationship static. This ability of the priests to hold fast is exactly what settles the stomach of all the active parties. The nausea of the land eases as everything stops spinning in the social whirl that always was Israel. The land does not vomit, as the priests in their holy spaces keep perfectly still.

Transmission and Mediation

Over time, the priests hold so still that they disappear. At first, they only lose their names. The named priest Aaron gives way to the unnamed sons of Aaron (after the named sons commit sins and face the consequences of their queasy actions). Although some priests gain names in other biblical narratives and in the metanarrative of "history," the sons of Aaron are the nameless priests. Having been seen naked in order to become priests, they become invisible; no one can see them again. Even if the people look at them, the people do not see them as people; they only see priests, nameless, formless, and faceless. The function subsumes the individuals. The priest always disappears into the sign of the father, which is the law.

In this sense, priests not only transmit the law; priests are the law or, at the very least, embody the law. Priests speak forth the words of instruction and thus create social order among those who hear and obey. The words of priestly law calm the stomach of the land, curing the threat of nausea. In this, the priests function much as God functions in Genesis 1, where God's speech creates the world. Priestly speech creates and constitutes the social world. God's speech brings forth dry land from the sea; priestly speech keeps the land dry, without vomit. Law is the word that creates.

In Leviticus, this creative word of law that resolves nausea is a particularly male word, inserted into the world that surrounds it. In the terms of Jacques Lacan, it is the word of the father, who rules the household and enforces social order.[7] Lacan terms this the phallus—the word and the law inserted.[8] Leviticus revolves around this word and obsesses about the male genitals of those who speak the word. Without the priestly word, the land spews forth vomit; without male genitals, there is no priestly word. The book centers on law/word and genitals, or logos and phallus, in an obsession of phallogocentrism. Through this phallus, the word enters the people.

Yet the maleness of the text breeds within a horrific misogyny, for the women must be absent, blinded, and silent in order for the male-only priesthood to exist. Through its male exclusivity and its all-male priesthood, Leviticus reads like a primer on male bonding; it creates a community of the penetrating gaze that is always pointing outward, never allowing others to see what happens in the holy and private places. What will be the effects of this exclusivistic, hierarchical world of only men, in which women are second-class citizens if present at all, never subjects and rarely even objects? Can readers hold their stomachs? Will the priestly remedy for nausea trigger another reflexive purging? Is this book a remedy for nausea, or a poison that has caused societies to vomit out women as incompatible with the pure law of God?

But in the end, Leviticus is not about male bonding, and the reader's vision is always directed away from the obsessive voyeurism about the priestly community. Instead, the book directs the reader's eyes to the mouth of the land, to observe this almost-but-never retching soil. The remedy for such nausea is the priestly immobility, for they hold together three interpenetrating spheres of relationship: father/son, God/people, and Empire/colony. The priest is a

---

[7]Jacques Lacan, *Écrits: A Selection,* trans. Alan Sheridan (New York: W. W. Norton, 1977), 61, 66, 143.

[8]Ibid., 199–200, 310–11.

linchpin, a skewer that lances through society to pin these spheres together in their one intersection, the priests themselves, in the body, in the flesh, in the law. Once inserted into this precarious society, the priests cannot move. They are static, unchanging. One cannot even look at the priests, lest the very act of observation throw them vertiginously off-balance, in some pre-Heisenbergian uncertainty. As long as the word is guarded and performed, the priests maintain their precarious position and the land does not vomit.

The result of the good priesthood, therefore, is strength, safety, food, and righteousness; a world in which all is connected and all is in its place. Priesthood is to live as testimony to the father, the phallus, the word. To be a good father is to let the son know the father's father. The phallus/law is thus the tool of transmission; it extends to connect all. To touch the law/scroll is to touch God; to know the law is to have God's own essence in one's mouth and to share it with the people. To see the son become priest is to know that what began in one's testicles has been raised up and sent out to maintain the immobile place of the priesthood. In law, son, and scroll is the chance for priests to touch their strength.

Men, Women, and Readers

Although Leviticus' concern is the land's queasiness, readers in the early twenty-first century may well become more dyspeptic at the sight of this all-male enclave that claims to hold together all society (and the very ground on which they stand) through their acts of legal/phallic transmission. The phallogocentrism of Leviticus may effect its own nausea. Yet the text plays with its own phallogocentrism. While the prose is certainly turgid and the regulations firmly rigid, it does not itself obey all the strictures of phallogocentric writing. Such a male-focused literature is often linear and ego-obsessed, yet Leviticus reads like some literature that the work of Hélène Cixous, Luce Irigaray, and others have termed *écriture féminine.*[9] The book is nonlinear, and it supports not a single male ego (despite Moses' repeated entries into the text) but instead a multigenerational community of equals. Although the text remains phallically obsessed, pushing women almost entirely out of the book's purview, there always remain traces of what it is not. Scholars have often commented on the number of women in Hebrew Bible narratives who are nameless, often saying that this is a feature of a misogynistic text that effaces women through removing their very name and identity. But Leviticus supports a group in which each man loses his identity and becomes nameless within the group. Just as women in the Hebrew Bible so often carry no name but their father's, such is the case for these nameless sons of Aaron. Life goes on from generation to generation in bodies that are not in the text; ego is constantly deferred.

---

[9] This *écriture féminine* is writing (with) women's bodies, which are virtually absent from Leviticus. Written on bodies not texts, it is the absent *supplément* to the book of Leviticus.

In Leviticus, the law is not held up inside the priesthood, but instead shoots forth into all the people. The law is published, spread forth across pages for everyone to see. Law is no longer private; the obsessive inward/invisible focus of phallogocentrism gives way to a spectacle so all can see. The priesthood's essence is taken forth and stripped bare for the public to observe, with little mystery left. The text in this sense is voyeuristic, turning the panopticon's gaze upon the previously invisible (and still nameless) priests to observe their every move dispassionately. Whereas the society depicted in Leviticus could not see the priests, but the priests could see everyone, now the readers can observe the priesthood and peer into priests' private lives, but the readers remain invisible, inviolate, beyond the realm of the text's touch. The nameless priests are actors in a textual peep show, like characters on the stage in an all-male review.

How does this spectacle end? The actors prepare to leave the stage. For their performance, these priestly players receive a small fee and a portion of every holy meal. The book of Leviticus ends with an accounting of what is due to God (chap. 27). The panopticon turns its gaze from the actors to the readers.

The lights go up when the curtain falls; the priests are once more invisible, and we see only one another. Even the relative worth of men and women are given a price–50 shekels for a man, 30 shekels for a woman; children are proportionately less; and there is a discount for senior citizens (27:2–8).

In the end, the book stares back at the reader after all, in a bland, evaluative gaze. I conclude reading the book having been told exactly what I am worth and precisely where I fit into the world that centers on these priests. The pages rustle closed. My stomach churns.

Moses' Final Examination

The Book of Deuteronomy

Donald C. Polaski

The book of Deuteronomy consists mainly of a set of speeches, supposedly given by Moses to the Israelites as they await entry into the promised land. Moses, it seems, aims to talk his hearers (or readers) into obeying certain commands. This implies a stable power relationship in the book: YHWH, through his close associate Moses, holds power over the people of Israel. Moses' authority is itself highly developed, as Robert Polzin indicates:

> Moses is portrayed in Deuteronomy as the pre-eminent interpreter of God's words. The story describes only one instance of divine speech that was heard by the people of Israel, the decalogue of 5:6–21....What is immediately obvious here is the absolutely authoritarian, or at least authoritative, nature of Moses' interpretive function.[1]

Dennis Olson also points to this power dynamic in his description of Deuteronomy as a "program of catechesis"; the words of Moses teach each new generation the content and meaning of its tradition.[2]

This stable power relationship within Deuteronomy is mirrored by scholars' understanding of the book's political function in ancient Israelite society. In 1805, M. L. de Wette proposed that a form of Deuteronomy was identical to the book discovered in the temple during the reign of Josiah, a proposal that has been widely accepted. The book was used by Josiah as the basis for social and cultic reforms that strengthened Judean national existence at the expense of the fading Assyrian Empire. The power of Deuteronomy derived from its promulgation by the monarch. This set of assumptions, regularly found in scholarship on the Hebrew Bible, makes its way into standard introductions:

---

[1]Robert Polzin, *Moses and the Deuteronomist* (Bloomington: Indiana University Press, 1980), 9.
[2]Dennis Olson, *Deuteronomy and the Death of Moses: A Theological Reading,* Overtures to Biblical Theology (Minneapolis: Fortress Press, 1994), 11.

The publication of this book [Deuteronomy] under state sponsorship during Josiah's reign was the first serious step toward the creation of an official canon of sacred literature that would be binding upon the whole people in matters of faith and conduct.[3]

Other scholars understand the "power" behind Deuteronomy somewhat differently. Gerhard von Rad suggests that Deuteronomy had its origin with "country Levites" and the "people of the land," important political players in Judah.[4] The promulgation of Deuteronomy represented a victory for these specific political groups and was an exercise of their influence. Frank Crüsemann, in contrast, claims that Deuteronomy was an assertion of power by the people: "The sovereignty of the people underlying the law compels us to speak of something like a democracy."[5] Despite these differences, it is important to realize that they all place the nation at the center of concern. The book derives its authority from the nation-state.[6] Those "in power" made laws to which the people were made subject.

Michel Foucault vigorously contests such notions of power. Foucault does not develop a systematic theory concerning power; rather, Foucault looks carefully at a society (usually that of postmedieval Western Europe) and, in a sense, describes the relations of power that he sees operating. This kind of analysis produces a complex notion of power grounded in particular historical conditions. Foucault's work is, therefore, not simply to be transferred to ancient Israel. Nevertheless, Foucault's analysis of power invites us to think about power and to make power the focus of our reading.

Three characteristics of Foucault's analysis of power will be of importance in our reading of Deuteronomy. First, Foucault refuses to understand power as a substance that only some possess, that some hold over those who are "powerless." And although the state may be a "terminal form" that power may take, power is not primarily institutional:

> Power is not an institution, and not a structure, neither is it a certain strength we are endowed with; it is the name that one attributes to a complex strategical situation in a particular society.[7]

[3]Bernhard Anderson, *Understanding the Old Testament* (Englewood Cliffs, N.J.: Prentice-Hall, 1957), 309.

[4]Gerhard von Rad, "The Provenance of Deuteronomy," in *Studies in Deuteronomy,* trans. D. Stalker, Studies in Biblical Theology 9 (London: SCM Press, 1953), 60–69.

[5]Frank Crüsemann, *The Torah: Theology and Social History of Old Testament Law,* trans. Allan Mahnke (Minneapolis: Fortress Press, 1996), 247.

[6]The formation of the nation-states of Western Europe has had a deep and lasting effect on the reading of Deuteronomy and its supposed historical context. It is probably no accident that De Wette's views took hold as various German monarchies, especially Prussia, struggled to reform themselves to face the threat of a nationalistic and unified France under Napoleon. But it is the nation-state itself, not just the monarchical principle, that can drive interpretation. Witness, for example, S. Dean McBride, Jr.'s, claim ("Polity of the Covenant People: The Book of Deuteronomy," *Interpretation* 41 [1987]: 243) that Deuteronomy represents a "social charter" that serves as "the archtype for modern Western constitutionalism."

[7]Michel Foucault, *The History of Sexuality: Volume 1, An Introduction,* trans. R. Hurley (New York: Vintage, 1990), 93.

In that "complex strategical situation," power exists in the asymmetrical relations between subjects. As such, power is not "held," but constantly negotiated, constantly flowing between and among subjects. Power thus has no point of origin:

> [Power] is the moving substrate of force relations which, by virtue of their inequality, constantly engender states of power, but the latter are always local and unstable. The omnipresence of power: not because it has the privilege of consolidating everything under its invincible unity, but because it is produced from one moment to the next, at every point, or rather in every relation from one point to another. Power is everywhere, not because it embraces everything, but because it comes from everywhere.[8]

Second, and building on this point, power is not to be understood as legal, what Foucault calls "juridico-discursive" power or "power-as-law." This idea of "power-as-law" developed with the monarchies of Western Europe, which "made their mechanisms of power work in the form of law."[9] Western democracies have inherited this representation of power. But it does not fully describe the operation of power in these societies; indeed, it is an image Foucault finds misleading and unhelpful.[10]

The importance of this move is obvious for this reading, as Deuteronomy has been understood as a law promulgated under the authority of a king. In a sense, Deuteronomy, of all texts, may be one of the most imprisoned in the "juridico-discursive" understanding of power. Foucault leads us to look for power behind and before its assumption of a particular "terminal form": law. In order to understand power relations in Deuteronomy, we have to move behind its classification as law. Indeed, we have to attempt to understand how power relations in Deuteronomy form "a chain or a system" that leads it to be encoded as law.[11]

Third, for Foucault the question of power is never far from the question of the Subject. Specific power relations have produced the modern individual, the modern Subject. So to raise the question of power relations in Deuteronomy is to raise simultaneously the question of how Deuteronomy creates a certain Subject. Again, we cannot derive from Foucault a "theory" that we can then apply to ancient Israel to address the creation of the Subject in that place and time. Yet Foucault's approach may be instructive for such an undertaking.

Foucault sees three "modes of objectification" operative in the production of the modern individual. First, "dividing practices" either divide a self within or separate it from others. Second, scientific classification, among other operations, makes the subject the object of systematic knowledge. Third, there are a variety of techniques of power that may be called "subjectification." While the first two modes may be seen as operating on the individual from

---

[8]Ibid.
[9]Ibid., 87.
[10]Ibid., 90.
[11]Ibid., 92.

the outside in relations of domination (in essence, you are told who you are), in this last mode, the Subject is itself active. The Subject discovers who it is through active self-formation, a process of self-understanding mediated, usually, by an external authority figure.[12]

In *Discipline and Punish,* Foucault focuses on these techniques as expressed in the development of the prison. The prison uses certain methods of making the Subject take him-or herself as the object of knowledge. This is "discipline" in a double sense: It is a disciplinary regime as well as the development of a particular knowledge (a "discipline"). Thus, Foucault is not simply discussing penology; rather, the operations of "discipline" are destined to extend beyond the prison walls. The techniques of subjectification (along with the other two modes) are spread throughout society, appearing in the prison, the barracks, the hospital, the factory, and the school.[13]

Foucault understands the "examination" as a key instance of subjectification:

> The examination combines the techniques of an observing hierarchy and those of a normalizing judgement. It is a normalizing gaze, a surveillance that makes it possible to qualify, to classify and to punish. It establishes over individuals a visibility through which one differentiates them and judges them. That is why, in all the mechanisms of discipline, the examination is highly ritualized. In it are combined the ceremony of power and the form of the experiment, the deployment of force and the establishment of truth...The superimposition of the power relations and knowledge relations assumes in the examination all its visible brilliance.[14]

The examination creates the Subject in a field of power relations. Foucault's work invites us to think about Deuteronomy as an examination: an act of testing, an act of scrutiny. This examination is one of many techniques, then, that "created" a Subject called "Israel." Attending to the circulation of power in Deuteronomy will aid in understanding this enterprise.

Moses the Examiner

Deuteronomy appears to establish Moses as the empowered examiner of the people, Israel. The text's extensive use of direct address underlines this point. Moses speaks; the people listen. Or, to be more exact, the people are *told* to listen:

> So now, Israel, give heed to the statutes and ordinances that I am teaching you to observe, so that you may live to enter and occupy

---

[12]Paul Rabinow, "Introduction," in Michel Foucault, *The Foucault Reader,* ed. P. Rabinow (New York: Pantheon, 1984), 7–11.

[13]Michel Foucault, *Discipline and Punish: The Birth of the Prison,* trans. A. Sheridan (New York: Pantheon, 1977), 228.

[14]Ibid., 184–85.

the land that the LORD, the God of your ancestors, is giving you. (4:1, NRSV)[15]

The people's ability to listen is correlated to their continued life. To refuse to listen to Moses is to cease to exist.

This disequilibrium in power relations is also manifest in Moses' almost solitary existence as a named character in the book.[16] Only Moses, YHWH, and the people speak.[17] Moses and the people are thus different; Moses has a name. In addition, Moses stands as a speaker for the other major named character, YHWH, because the people are incapable of hearing from YHWH directly:

> When you heard the voice out of the darkness, while the mountain was burning with fire, you approached me, all the heads of your tribes and your elders; and you said, "Look, the LORD our God has shown us his glory and greatness, and we have heard his voice out of the fire. Today we have seen that God may speak to someone and the person may still live. So now why should we die? For this great fire will consume us; if we hear the voice of the LORD our God any longer, we shall die." (5:23–25, NRSV)

The result is to establish the utter difference between Moses and the people. The people, incapacitated by fear, realize that to hear YHWH directly is to court death. It falls to Moses to risk death and meet with YHWH.[18] Yet Moses does so without apparent fear or regret and receives assurances directly from YHWH:

> Go say to them [Israel], "Return to your tents." But you, stand here by me, and I will tell you all the commandments, the statutes and the ordinances, that you shall teach them, so that they may do them in the land that I am giving them to possess. (5:30–31, NRSV)

This text also exposes the importance of Moses for YHWH's own status. In order to communicate with the people without endangering them, YHWH needs Moses' participation. Indeed, it is often unclear in Deuteronomy whether YHWH or Moses is speaking. This lack of clarity serves to unite YHWH and Moses over against the undifferentiated mass of Israel. As examiner, Moses' power is YHWH's power.

Moses' power is developed in a most spectacular fashion in the book's final chapter. We are informed that at the time of his death, Moses' sight was still keen and "his vigor had not abated" (34:7). Although the term translated

---

[15]See also 5:1; 6:4; 9:1; 20:3; 27:9.

[16]Most other named characters are mentioned in historical summaries. Only Joshua enjoys a recurring role, appearing in chaps. 1, 3, 31, 32, and 34.

[17]In 27:1 and 27:9, Moses addresses Israel with the elders. There are also various laws, spoken by Moses, that include speech, for example, 21:7–8.

[18]Olson (*Deuteronomy and the Death of Moses,* 47) claims that Moses' role as mediator "carries with it the price of premature death."

"vigor" here is otherwise unattested, cognate words indicate that there may be sexual overtones.[19] This would not be unexpected, as male sexual activity is positively correlated, then and now, with a man's power (e.g., David in 1 Kings 1:1–4; Bob Dole's public service advertisements). Moses' eyesight and virility have remained constant, unaffected by the passage of time.[20]

The commissioning of Joshua that follows presents an intriguing set of relationships:

> Joshua son of Nun was full of the spirit of wisdom, because Moses had laid his hands on him; and the Israelites obeyed him, doing as the LORD had commanded Moses. (34:9, NRSV)

Joshua's wisdom depends on his prior relationship with Moses, not YHWH.[21] In addition, Joshua's authority over Israel also depends to an extent on this relationship. Israel's obedience also depends on YHWH's command, but here it is styled explicitly as a command *through Moses*. In both cases, Moses plays an essential role in the development of Joshua's own authority.

But it is Moses' relationship to YHWH that is most telling regarding Moses' power. First, Moses is described as a unique prophet:

> Never since has there arisen a prophet in Israel like Moses, whom the LORD knew face to face. (34:10, NRSV)

The claim here not only bolsters Moses' unique authority, but also explicitly contradicts an earlier claim regarding prophecy, a claim made directly by YHWH:

> The LORD your God will raise up for you a prophet like me from among your own people; you shall heed such a prophet. This is what you requested of the LORD your God at Horeb on the day of the assembly when you said: "If I hear the voice of the LORD my God any more, or ever again see this great fire, I will die." Then the LORD replied to me: "They are right in what they have said. I will raise up for them a prophet like you from among their own people; I will put my words in the mouth of the prophet, who shall speak to them everything that I command. Anyone who does not heed the words that the prophet shall speak in my name, I myself will hold accountable. But any prophet who speaks in the name of other gods, or who presumes to speak in my name a word that I have not commanded the prophet to speak—that prophet shall die." (18:15–20, NRSV)[22]

---

[19]See Jean-Pierre Sonnet, *The Book Within the Book: Writing in Deuteronomy*, Biblical Interpretation Series 14 (Leiden: Brill, 1997), 208, n. 23.

[20]It should be noted that this verse contradicts Moses' own testimony about his health in 31:2. See ibid., 128.

[21]Joshua's relationship to YHWH is featured in 31:14–15, 23.

[22]Polzin (*Moses and the Deuteronomist*, 35–36) takes the contrast here as evidence of two "Mosaic voices" in the text.

Here the people's fear of direct communication with YHWH grounds the institution of prophecy, an institution understood as an imitation of Moses. Moses and the prophets stand between YHWH and the people, protecting their very lives.[23]

The end of Deuteronomy, keen on establishing Moses' power, severs the relationship between Moses and the prophets. In the years since Moses, no prophet has measured up to his model or ever will.[24] Deuteronomy 34 redefines the standards by which a prophet is to be judged. It is no longer enough to have YHWH place words in one's mouth (18:18). Now, to be a "Mosaic prophet," one must have addressed YHWH face-to-face and lived. The quality of Moses' relationship to YHWH sets him apart.

Moses is not only an unequaled prophet; Moses' wonder-working ability threatens to displace YHWH's:

> He [Moses] was unequaled for all the signs and wonders that the LORD sent him to perform in the land of Egypt, against Pharaoh and all his servants and his entire land, and for all the mighty deeds and all the terrifying displays of power that Moses performed in the sight of all Israel. (34:11–12, NRSV)

In Deuteronomy, the events surrounding the exodus, especially the plagues, are the prime example of YHWH's power, often understood as "signs and wonders" *('ôtot ûmoftim).*[25]

> The LORD displayed before our eyes great and awesome signs and wonders against Egypt, against Pharaoh and all his household. He brought us out from there in order to bring us in, to give us the land that he promised on oath to our ancestors. (6:22–23, NRSV)

In 34:11, there is a slight movement away from YHWH as agent. YHWH sent Moses, who performed the "signs and wonders" that led to the exodus. In 34:12, even YHWH fades from the scene. Moses stands as one who performed "terrifying displays of power" *(hammorim haggadôl)* in front of all Israel. These actions are undoubtedly the same as those attributed to YHWH elsewhere in Deuteronomy:

> Or has any god ever attempted to go and take a nation for himself from the midst of another nation, by trials, by signs and wonders, by war, by a mighty hand and an outstretched arm, and by terrifying displays of power, as the LORD your God did for you in Egypt before your very eyes? (4:34, NRSV)

---

[23]Olson (*Deuteronomy and the Death of Moses,* 85) focuses more on the prophetic forfeiting of life as a result of divine contact. In this text, however, the future prophet is not communicated with in the dangerous way that so alarms the people. The "prophet like Moses" will allow indirect communication between YHWH and the people, saving their lives, but the prophet will not explicitly hear YHWH or see his fire.

[24]Joseph Blenkinsopp, *Prophecy and Canon: A Contribution to the Study of Jewish Origins* (Notre Dame: University of Notre Dame Press, 1977), 86.

[25]Also see 4:34; 7:19; 26:8; 29:3. Cf. Nehemiah 9:10; Psalm 135:9; Jeremiah 32:20–21.

The LORD brought us out of Egypt with a mighty hand and an outstretched arm, with a terrifying display of power, and with signs and wonders. (26:8, NRSV)

Deuteronomy 34:12 equates Moses with YHWH, a move that is hardly innocent regarding power relations.[26] In Deuteronomy's economy of power, Moses occupies a position "the people" cannot and will not inhabit.

Examining the Examiner

This picture of Moses is not without its own complications. These tensions will bring the stability of power relations in Deuteronomy into question. As noted above, Moses, the ideal prophet, has never been equaled (34:10). But Moses and YHWH have promised that Moses will indeed be equaled (18:15). Thus, Moses is the author of an unfulfilled prophecy. Given the standards outlined in chapter 18, this becomes problematic:

You may say to yourself, "How can we recognize a word that the LORD has not spoken?" If a prophet speaks in the name of the LORD but the thing does not take place or prove true, it is a word that the LORD has not spoken. The prophet has spoken it presumptuously; do not be frightened by it. (18:21–22, NRSV)

Is Moses a presumptuous prophet? Has YHWH spoken through Moses? If a prophet like Moses should arise, the claim in 34:12 would be weakened; Moses' unique status would vanish. Yet Moses would be vindicated as a true prophet on the basis of chapter 18. As long as such a prophet does not appear, Moses' unique status is inviolate, but his credentials as a prophet may be questioned. Beyond that, if Moses has spoken a word that YHWH has not spoken, the penalty is death (18:20).

This difficulty regarding prophecy even threatens the statements concerning Moses' performance of "signs and wonders." For, it turns out, even prophets who perform them and successfully predict the future may not be related to YHWH:

If prophets or those who divine by dreams appear among you and promise you omens or portents, and the omens or the portents declared by them take place, and they say, "Let us follow other gods" (whom you have not known) "and let us serve them," you must not heed the words of those prophets or those who divine by dreams; for the LORD your God is testing you, to know whether you indeed love the LORD your God with all your heart and soul. (13:1–3, NRSV)

Moses' status as prophet of YHWH is slippery. Moses is not simply a powerful figure who commands Israel. Moses' power itself is unstable.

---

[26]Blenkinsopp (*Prophecy and Canon*, 87) identifies this passage, especially its negation of the promise of a "prophet like Moses" as evidence of the "tension between theocracy and eschatology."

This understanding of Moses' power comes to clearest expression in the texts surrounding Moses' death. Despite the emphasis the text places on the asymmetry between Moses and the people, they cannot escape an identical fate: they die. The extreme picture of Moses' power in chapter 34 occurs only after Moses' death, an attempt, perhaps, to reinstate the difference between Moses and the people. Still, Moses' powerful role makes his rejection by YHWH, symbolized in the ban on his entry into Canaan, shocking:

> At that time, too, I entreated the LORD, saying: "O Lord GOD, you have only begun to show your servant your greatness and your might; what god in heaven or on earth can perform deeds and mighty acts like yours! Let me cross over to see the good land beyond the Jordan, that good hill country and the Lebanon." But the LORD was angry with me on your account and would not heed me. The LORD said to me, "Enough from you! Never speak to me of this matter again!" (3:23–26, NRSV)

Moses blames the people for his unfortunate circumstance.[27] Their actions have angered YHWH, who takes action against Moses. The very people at whom YHWH is angry are themselves not punished. Rather, they inherit the land. Moses uses the irony here to speak of the necessity of obeying a jealous deity:

> The LORD was angry with me because of you, and he vowed that I should not cross the Jordan and that I should not enter the good land that the LORD your God is giving for your possession. For I am going to die in this land without crossing over the Jordan, but you are going to cross over to take possession of that good land. So be careful not to forget the covenant that the LORD your God made with you, and not to make for yourselves an idol in the form of anything that the LORD your God has forbidden you. For the LORD your God is a devouring fire, a jealous God. (4:21–24, NRSV)[28]

But while YHWH has made a covenant with the people, the covenant does not seem, finally, to bind YHWH to punish only the guilty and bless only the obedient. Both Moses and the people are linked to a God who seems to hold all the cards.[29]

But Moses' death does not simply readjust our picture of power in Deuteronomy by demoting Moses. Moses dies outside the land and not of his own doing. The *people* are the agents that set the course of events in motion.

---

[27]Another reason for Moses' exclusion, Moses' own misbehavior, is offered in 32:51.

[28]Perhaps YHWH is "jealous" of anyone who threatens his leadership of the people. Olson (*Deuteronomy and the Death of Moses*, 37), suggests that Moses' death is "a vicarious act of atonement for the sake of the people." For further development of this view, see Patrick D. Miller, Jr., "'Moses My Servant': The Deuteronomic Portrait of Moses," *Interpretation* 41 (1987): 245–55.

[29]In fact, YHWH's capital sentence on Moses is in violation of 24:16: "Only for their own crimes may persons be put to death."

The people do not passively receive discipline from an "empowered" Moses or YHWH. Here they play a role in discipline, via YHWH, on their leader! Power does not flow from YHWH, through Moses, to the people. It circulates.

Moses Lives On

Moses' eventual absence means that the voice that animates Deuteronomy is doomed, almost from the start (1:37). Polzin claims that the voice of the narrator survives Moses' death and hence gains authority, an authority used in the Deuteronomistic history.[30] Such a point of view, however, may obscure the workings of power within Deuteronomy by insinuating that Moses' death ends or diminishes Moses' role in the play of power relations that creates Israel.[31] In my view, this death is no real death; it is simply a transition point in our understanding of the negotiation of power.

The play of power continues in the so-called "law of the king":

> When you have come into the land that the LORD your God is giving you, and have taken possession of it and settled in it, and you say, "I will set a king over me, like all the nations that are around me," you may indeed set over you a king whom the LORD your God will choose…When he has taken the throne of his kingdom, he shall have a copy of this law written for him in the presence of the levitical priests. It shall remain with him and he shall read in it all the days of his life, so that he may learn to fear the LORD his God, diligently observing all the words of this law and these statutes, neither exalting himself above other members of the community nor turning aside from the commandment, either to the right or to the left, so that he and his descendants may reign long over his kingdom in Israel. (17:14–15a, 18–20, NRSV)

This law is often seen as an idealistic attempt to limit royal authority.[32] While this may be the case, I am most interested in the ways power is negotiated within the book of Deuteronomy, especially involving the figure of Moses. Moses is present in this text in two ways. First, he narrates it. In other words, Moses' voice is active here. And in keeping with other passages in the book, Moses intimates here his own death: Only his audience will come into the land. So Moses' voice both dominates the passage and admits to its (supposed) eventual silencing.

But Moses' presence in the text has a second aspect. Moses speaks here *about* his own voice–it will apparently be written down (cf. 31:9, 24–26). In

---

[30]Polzin, *Moses and the Deuteronomist,* 72.

[31]Following Polzin, however, I would certainly agree that the play of power relations that results in the subject "Israel" continues in the Deuteronomistic history. That is, however, an undertaking much outside the scope of this project.

[32]E.g., Gerhard von Rad, *Deuteronomy: A Commentary,* Old Testament Library (London: SCM Press, 1966), 118–220; Peter C. Craigie, *The Book of Deuteronomy,* New International Commentary on the Old Testament (Grand Rapids: Eerdmans, 1976), 253; Patrick D. Miller, *Deuteronomy,* Interpretation Bible Commentary (Louisville: John Knox Press, 1990), 147–48.

addition to being written, the replication of this copy of Moses' voice is the only duty incumbent upon the king. The king, whose reign will clearly be after Moses has left the scene, will in a sense become Moses. He will read Moses' words, internalizing them, becoming the possessor of the law. While the priests may supervise the scroll, they read it only once every seven years (31:9–13). The king, who reads the scroll daily, will become Moses' most intimate acquaintance.

Yet this intimacy has its limits. Access to the words of Moses should not lead to the king's "exalting himself" (17:20). The king will discover that, unlike Moses, he is a "member of the community." The king's identification with Moses points to Moses' incomparability, and Moses' own words encourage this self-examination. The king simply directs copying, and this is all he can direct. Aside from this, his own voice is unproductive.

Moses has entered the land as a book.[33] In the "law of the king" Moses speaks with an echo that will last as long as the dynasty. And even that dynasty's collapse will prove the validity of the law. The subject, Israel, will not be produced by subjugation to a certain monarch. Moses' voice, now text, will hold pride of place in that enterprise.

The Subject of Moses' Book—Creating Israel

We have seen that the people stand in a complex power relation with Moses and YHWH. With the textualization of Moses, other dimensions of the power relation emerge. The book becomes the instrument through which the people are invited to become a people, a process mediated by Moses. It is Moses' final examination. And as Foucault has indicated, at an examination we might expect to see the blending of power relations and knowledge relations.[34]

In Deuteronomy, knowledge at first appears to be a matter of oral transmission. The "commandments," "statutes," and "ordinances" are delivered orally by YHWH to Moses, and thence to the people (6:1). The household becomes an essential locus of this instruction:

> Keep these words that I [Moses] am commanding you today in your heart. Recite them to your children and talk about them when you are at home and when you are away, when you lie down and when you rise. Bind them as a sign on your hand, fix them as an emblem on your forehead, and write them on the doorposts of your house and on your gates. (6:6–9, NRSV)

It is important to note here what the slippage from oral to written means. The verbal commands that will be reenacted in recitation and discussion

---

[33]Sonnet, *The Book Within the Book,* 227.

[34]There are other exercises of power in Deuteronomy that can be seen as "subjectification" for Israel that cannot be elaborated here. For example, the "ban" *(ḥerem),* mentioned in 2:34, 7:1–2, and 20:16–18, could be read as a kind of "dividing practice," especially given its role later in Joshua 7.

quickly become written documents. By the end of the passage, the written text is stationed at the boundary of the household.

A similar move may be seen in Deuteronomy's deployment of the "questioning child" trope:

> When your children ask you in time to come, "What is the meaning of the decrees and the statutes and the ordinances that the LORD our God has commanded you?" then you shall say to your children, "We were Pharaoh's slaves in Egypt, but the LORD brought us out of Egypt with a mighty hand…He brought us out from there in order to bring us in, to give us the land that he promised on oath to our ancestors. Then the LORD commanded us to observe all these statutes, to fear the LORD our God, for our lasting good, so as to keep us alive, as is now the case. If we diligently observe this entire commandment before the LORD our God, as he has commanded us, we will be in the right." (6:20–21, 23–25, NRSV)

This trope is perhaps most familiar for its use in the celebration of Passover (Ex. 12:26; cf. 13:14). In this case, a child is curious about the meaning of the observance. In Joshua, a child is certain to ask about the stones beside the Jordan that mark Israel's entry into the land (Josh. 4:6, 21). That a child would ask about the bustling preparation for a festival or a singularly impressive pile of stones seems to be a reflection of childhood curiosity. Deuteronomy takes this curiosity and focuses it on its own chief interest: ordinances and statutes. Thus, the child is expected to ask a bookish and rather unfocused question.

All three of these passages speak to Israel's identity. In Exodus, the child is to learn that YHWH treats Israel and Egypt differently. In Joshua, the child is told the stones are there "so that all the peoples of the earth may know that the hand of the LORD is mighty" (Josh. 4:24), a might displayed at the Red Sea (v. 23). Deuteronomy picks up these themes, but now yokes these essential moments in the formation of national identity to "the decrees and the statutes and the ordinances" (Deut. 6:20). The events of Passover, designed as a "sign on your hand and as a reminder on your forehead" (Ex. 13:9), have been displaced by a new "sign" and "reminder"–the written statutes of YHWH (Deut. 6:8). The book is a "technology of the nation," continuing the examination of Moses.

Oral performances such as the parent-child dialogue are thus made by Deuteronomy into oral rehearsals of a written text, that is, of Deuteronomy itself:

> This is the law that Moses set before the Israelites. These are the decrees and the statutes and ordinances that Moses spoke to the Israelites when they had come out of Egypt. (Deut. 4:44–45, NRSV)[35]

---

[35]On the important structuring role of this and other similar texts in Deuteronomy, see Olson, *Deuteronomy and the Death of Moses,* 14–17.

The spoken words are part and parcel of this law, which, it is evident, is a written document. The king will learn "these statutes" from a copy of "this law" (17:19). The people, on pain of curses, are to observe "all the words of this law that are written in this book" (28:58). All this anticipates Moses' actual writing of the scroll of the law (31:9).

Thus, it is finally revealed that the text the king will have copied (and that parents will recite to their children) is on reserve at the temple, having been placed there at Moses' request:

> When Moses had finished writing down in a book the words of this law to the very end, Moses commanded the Levites who carried the ark of the covenant of the LORD, saying, "Take this book of the law and put it beside the ark of the covenant of the LORD your God; let it remain there as a witness against you. (31:24–26, NRSV)

It is to remain there, to be removed (one assumes) for copying or for public reading (31:9–13). The text is thus kept at some remove from the people (except the king and the priests). It serves simply as a witness.

This seems at first glance a terribly ineffective way to produce a subject. What could a text hidden so much of the time accomplish? But Foucault reminds us that hidden power is often highly effective.[36] Despite its being hidden, the scroll's existence is an invitation for the people to take themselves as an object of knowledge, a community that can be known, and thus can know itself. Moses demonstrates this function in his claim that the scroll will be a witness against the people. Immediately after this claim, Moses asserts his knowledge of the people, defining them:

> For I know well how rebellious and stubborn you are. If you already have been so rebellious toward the LORD while I am still alive among you, how much more after my death! (31:27, NRSV)

The text will continue Moses' existence into an era in which Israel will learn more and more about itself, will become itself.

Despite its being hidden, Moses' text is well-nigh inescapable:

> Surely, this commandment that I am commanding you today is not too hard for you, nor is it too far away. It is not in heaven, that you should say, "Who will go up to heaven for us, and get it for us so that we may hear it and observe it?" Neither is it beyond the sea, that you should say, "Who will cross to the other side of the sea for us, and get it for us so that we may hear it and observe it?" No, the word is very near to you; it is in your mouth and in your heart for you to observe. (30:11–14, NRSV)

---

[36]In his discussion of the examination, Foucault comments: "Traditionally, power was what was seen, what was shown and what was manifested and, paradoxically, found the principle of its force in the movement by which it deployed that force…Disciplinary power, on the other hand, is exercised through its invisibility; at the same time it imposes on those whom it subjects a principle of compulsory visibility" (*Discipline and Punish,* 187).

The distant text is not distant after all. It is hidden, not in a distant place, but inside Israel itself. In order to find the hidden text, Israel must look into its own mouths and hearts.[37] Deuteronomy makes Israel a candidate for self-knowledge, a Subject.

So far, we have seen Deuteronomy's implications for power relations by looking only at the way power is deployed within the text. But, with the claim that this text has a social effect, namely the construction of Israel, we leave the world of the text and confront Deuteronomy's place within Israelite culture. While this is a place a Foucauldian reading perhaps should begin, not end, an analysis of the wider power relations that Deuteronomy inscribes and that are inscribed on it must wait.[38]

One point, however, should be made. While Moses' grave remains unknown (34:6), Moses' text finds a final resting place at the sanctuary. But the book, though supposedly hidden away there, is itself the book that we are reading. Deuteronomy poses as a hidden book, beyond inspection, yet its very claim to be hidden only comes into play when the book itself is opened. In other words, the reader of Deuteronomy is not only on the plains of Moab but also inside the central sanctuary. While the presence of Deuteronomy's actual readers in either place is doubtful, the fiction here may be a clue to power relations. Here a text, not relying on a monarch for authority, is placed within an institution that needed to justify its own existence in the early postexilic period. To ask which was powerful first is not the proper question; rather, we may seek to describe how these figures dance.

---

[37]This should come as no surprise given the list of public curses for secret transgressions in 27:15–26.

[38]While Foucault usually deals with discourse in relation to other social formations, he assuredly does not reduce discourse to a mere reflection of social formations. Foucault's approach here informs the reading practice known as "New Historicism." In addition, Foucault attempts to understand discourse without explicit reference to social realia in both *The Archaeology of Knowledge,* trans. A. M. Sheridan Smith (New York: Pantheon, 1972) and *The Order of Things: An Archaeology of the Human Sciences* (New York: Pantheon, 1971).

Dialogues of Life and Monologues of Death

Jephthah and Jephthah's Daughter
in Judges 10:6—12:7

Dennis T. Olson

The single adequate form for verbally expressing authentic human
life is the open-ended dialogue...To live means to participate in
dialogue...[to enter] into the dialogic fabric of human life, into
the world symposium.

> –Mikhail Bakhtin[1]

The book of Judges is dialogically rich and complex. Irony abounds.[2] Indeterminacy precludes closure in reading. Is the real judge in Judges 4 the prophet Deborah, the general Barak, or the assassin Jael? Characters shimmer with dissonant identities. The doubly named judge Gideon/Jerubbaal is both timid and bold, aniconic and idolatrous, repulsed and lured by the trappings of kingship (chaps. 6–9). Samson is a judge who does not lead, a Nazirite who breaks all Nazirite vows, a lover of Philistines who kills them. Judges is a tale of power and leadership deconstructing in a downward spiral from initial success (Othniel, Ehud, Deborah/Barak–Judg. 3–5) through a transitional period of decline (Gideon–Judg. 6–9) to a collapse of the judges' effectiveness (Jephthah and Samson–Judg. 10–16) and an eventual and horrific disintegration of Israel's religious (Judg. 17–18) and political (Judg. 19–21) fabric as a society.[3] A telling refrain brackets the final section of Judges: "In

---

[1]Mikhail Bakhtin, "Toward a Reworking of the Dostoevsky Book," Appendix 2 in *Problems of Dostoevsky's Poetics,* ed. and trans. Caryl Emerson (Minneapolis: University of Minnesota Press, 1984), 293.

[2]See Lillian R. Klein, *The Triumph of Irony in the Book of Judges* (Sheffield: Almond, 1989).

[3]Lawson Stone, "From Tribal Confederation to Monarchic State: The Editorial Perspective of the Book of Judges" (Ph.D. Diss., Yale University; Ann Arbor: University Microfilms, 1987); Dennis Olson, "The Book of Judges–Introduction, Commentary and Reflection," in *The New Interpreter's Bible,* vol. 2, ed. Leander Keck (Nashville: Abingdon Press, 1998), 723–888; J. Cheryl Exum, "The Centre Cannot Hold: Thematic and Textual Instabilities in Judges," *CBQ* 52 (1990): 410–31.

those days there was no king in Israel; all the people did what was right in their own eyes" (Judge 17:6; 21:25).[4] The remarkable density of women characters who function as barometers of Israel's health as a society invites explorations of the dialogical interplay of gender and power. In the face of Israel's repeated apostasy, the book dances theologically in Bakhtin style between God's unconditional assurances ("I will never break my covenant with you"–2:1) and God's exasperated warnings ("I will deliver you no more"–10:13).

This essay will examine one narrative in Judges that is particularly thick with dialogues of human and divine discourse: the narrative of the judge named Jephthah and his unnamed daughter in Judges 10:6–12:7. Five scenes form the structural backbone to the Jephthah cycle, and a spoken dialogue of words stands at the center of each scene. The scenes include: (1) Israel and God (10:6–16), (2) the elders of Gilead and Jephthah (10:17–11:11), (3) Jephthah and the Ammonite king (11:12–28), (4) Jephthah and his daughter (11:29–38), and (5) Jephthah and the Ephraimites (12:1–7).[5] The dialogues in each scene explore the varied effects of words under diverse conditions of dialogical openness and persuasive freedom, on one hand, and monologic constriction and violent force on the other. The name *Jephthah* means in Hebrew "he opens," and Jephthah opens his mouth in numerous dialogues, some opening to life and peace and others opening to death and violence. Jephthah is an able negotiator, using his rhetorical skills to become the leader of his people and to offer peace to his Ammonite adversary. On the other hand, the tragic climax of the Jephthah story is when Jephthah opens his mouth to speak the terrible vow concerning the sacrifice of his daughter, a vow he believes he cannot take back: "For I have opened my mouth to the LORD, and I cannot take back my vow" (11:35). In the final scene, Jephthah commands fellow Israelites from the tribe of Ephraim to speak a single word with a different dialect ("sibboleth" instead of "shibboleth"). Because they speak this one word differently, 42,000 of the Ephraimites die at the hands of Jephthah and his army. Words spoken under the freedom of dialogical openness have the potential to lead to life. Words spoken under the monologic conditions of force and violence lead to death.

Scene 1—Israel and God: 10:6–16

The Jephthah cycle opens in 10:6–16 with the usual introductory description of Israel again doing "what was evil in the sight of the LORD" (10:6). However, the nature of the evil involving the worship of other gods has worsened. In the previous era of Gideon, Israel had worshiped only Canaanite or Amorite gods (6:10, 25; 8:33). In this era of Jephthah, the Israelites extend their religious devotion to a virtual supermarket of several different foreign gods from Canaan, Aram, Sidon, Moab, Ammon, and Philistia (10:6).

---

[4]All scripture quotations in this chapter are from the *New Revised Standard Version Bible.*

[5]Barry Webb, The Book of the Judges: An Integrated Reading, Journal for the Study of the Old Testament Supplement Series 46 (Sheffield: JSOT, 1987), 41–78.

As punishment for their increasing disloyalty, the Lord allows the foreign nations of Philistia and Ammon to oppress Israel for eighteen years. As in the other judge episodes, the Israelites "cried to the LORD" for help (10:10; see 3:9, 15; 4:3; 6:7). But this time the Israelites add something unique to their typical cry for aid. They speak words of repentance and remorse for their sinful ways: "We have sinned against you" (10:10). Israel had never before confessed its sin in this way in the preceding judge stories. However, the repeated backsliding of the people has accelerated to such a point that God receives these words of repentance as a shallow ploy of manipulation rather than heartfelt contrition. God had saved the Israelites from seven different oppressors in the past. Yet each time, the Israelites rejected the Lord and returned to worship the gods of those same oppressing nations (compare 10:6 and 10:11–12). Thus, God comes to a startling conclusion: "Therefore I will deliver you no more" (10:13). God urges Israel to "go and cry" for help from these other foreign gods that Israel had repeatedly worshiped. "Let them deliver you" (10:14).

The Israelites are persistent, however, and beg God with a second word of repentance (10:15). Moreover, the Israelites bolster their words with action: They "put away" their alien gods and worship the God of Israel. The next line is crucial, but its meaning is debated. God "could no longer bear to see Israel suffer" (10:16). Many commentators assume that Israel's actions and words convinced God of Israel's genuine and deep remorse. This profound repentance, they argue, is what causes God to alter the earlier pronouncement of never again delivering Israel. Many commentators conclude that the same dynamic is at work here as with the Ninevites who repented after hearing Jonah's words of doom and thus spared their city from destruction (Jon. 3:10; see Jer. 18:7–8).[6]

However, the Lord's reaction in 10:16 is more ambiguous and indeterminate than such an interpretation allows. The verb translated as "to bear" often carries with it connotations of frustration, loss of patience, anger, and exasperation (Num. 21:4–5; Zech. 11:8–9). It is the verb used when Samson becomes so exasperated with Delilah's constant nagging that he reveals the secret of his strength in Judges 16:16. Thus, one might well read God's response in 10:16 not as God's happy agreement to deliver Israel because of its genuine and sustained repentance. Rather, God knows that this repentance will again be temporary and shallow, but the Lord in total exasperation cannot "bear to see Israel suffer." It is Israel's *suffering*, not Israel's words of deep repentance, that motivates any potential change in God's plans.[7] We assume that God will somehow reluctantly intervene. However, the text does not say that the Lord

---

[6]See Robert G. Boling, *Judges,* Anchor Bible 6A (Garden City, N.Y.: Doubleday, 1975), 193; J. Alberto Soggin, *Judges,* Old Testament Library (Philadelphia: Westminster Press, 1981), 203.

[7]Robert Polzin, *Moses and the Deuteronomist: A Literary Study of the Deuteronomic History* (New York: Seabury, 1980), 177; Webb, *The Book of the Judges,* 45–48.

immediately raises up a deliverer as in the earlier judge stories. The reader is left to wonder how God is involved in the next series of events and whether those events will lead to Israel's deliverance from its enemies. As we shall see, this ambiguity about God's role in the judgeship of Jephthah is the first of a number of indeterminate moments in the story of Jephthah the judge.

Scene 2—The Elders of Gilead and Jephthah: 10:17—11:11

The next episode opens with the Ammonite army getting ready to fight Israel. Meanwhile, the Israelites in the Transjordan region of Gilead are frantically scrambling to find a military leader who is willing to fight the Ammonites. They offer a reward to the one who steps forward: "He shall be head over all the inhabitants of Gilead" (10:18). The narrator interrupts the flow of the story and introduces us to a "mighty warrior" named Jephthah. Jephthah is an Israelite from Gilead, but he has some deficits according to Israel's social code: He is "the son of a prostitute," an outcast from his family, and a leader of outlaws who raid villages in the foreign "land of Tob" for a living (11:1–3). Jephthah's character reminds the reader of the ill-fated Abimelech who was the despised son of a concubine (8:31), in conflict with his other brothers (9:5), and the leader of outlaws (9:4). These associations with the negative figure of Abimelech do not bode well for Jephthah's future, but in the end he (unlike Abimelech) will be called one who "judged Israel six years" (12:7).

In 11:4, the narrator returns us to the story about the Ammonites' making war on the Israelite people of Gilead. Although the Gileadites had earlier rejected Jephthah, the elders of Gilead beg Jephthah in their distress to return home and save his people from the Ammonite oppressors. Just as Israel had earlier rejected God and then returned to call on God for help, so the people of Gilead return to call on Jephthah for help. Jephthah asks a legitimate question: "Are you not the very ones who rejected me?" But the Gileadites insist and offer Jephthah the position of leader "over all the inhabitants of Gilead" if he conquers the Ammonites. Jephthah then accepts the offer to fight the Ammonites with a condition that links his mission with an acknowledgment of divine freedom to choose for or against Jephthah: if "the LORD gives them over to me" (11:9). This is Jephthah's first vow involving God; his second vow will be more problematic (11:29–40). The elders of Gilead then pledge that "the LORD will be witness between us," and the deal is struck "before the LORD at Mizpah" (11:10–11). This sudden cluster of references to God suggests to the reader that Jephthah may indeed be the Lord's chosen agent to deliver Israel in spite of his questionable character. The reader's interest is piqued and focused on this ambiguous character who is both a "mighty warrior" and the "son of a prostitute," both pious adherent to God and shrewd negotiator for his own interests. In this case, Jephthah's dialogical efforts have resulted in rebuilding relationships in an atmosphere of mutual benefit and free persuasion.

Scene 3—The Ammonite King and Jephthah: 11:12–28

Jephthah has been elevated by the elders of Gilead from a rogue leader of bandits to the more honored role of a military commander of Gilead's army. Before leading the army into battle, however, Jephthah steps into another role as statesman and diplomat in an attempt to broker a peaceful resolution of the conflict with Ammon. Jephthah demonstrates his verbal abilities in presenting persuasive arguments about conflicting claims to the land of Gilead. In a lengthy defense of his position Jephthah appeals to details of Israel's history and traditions, to Israel's experience with Moab, and to the relationship of Jephthah's God to the god Chemosh. Unfortunately, the Ammonite king in the end remains unpersuaded, and military conflict becomes the only option. Thus, Jephthah throws down the gauntlet by inviting the Lord to be the judge of this dispute and "decide today for the Israelites or the Ammonites" (v. 27). Jephthah takes on the role of a prosecuting attorney in a lawsuit against Ammon with the Lord sitting as judge in the divine court. The statement is in effect a declaration of war as the Lord's decision will be determined by whoever wins the military battle.

By the end of this scene, the arena for human and divine discourse has shifted in a subtle, seemingly insignificant, but decisive way. We have moved from the arena of divine freedom to save Israel in spite of its constant rebellion. We are no longer in the atmosphere of Jephthah freely negotiating with the elders of Gilead to their mutual benefit. We are no longer witnessing two leaders—Jephthah and the Ammonite king—coming together as reasonable human subjects seeking a mutually agreeable and freely accepted resolution to a conflict. We have moved into the courtroom, a context of legal jurisdiction, enforced judgments, and monologic constriction. Violence and force become the means of deciding who is right and who is wrong.

Scene 4—Jephthah and His Daughter: 11:29–40

When the negotiations with the Ammonite king are concluded, "the spirit of the LORD came upon Jephthah" (v. 29). This is the first explicit indication in the story that God has indeed chosen Jephthah to deliver Israel from the Ammonites. Everything up to this point has involved human initiative: the Gilead elders negotiating with Jephthah to be their leader and Jephthah negotiating on his own initiative with the Ammonite king. God's name has been invoked along the way at several points, but no overt statement has indicated God's actual involvement with Jephthah. But now the spirit of God has come upon Jephthah the judge as the spirit had come upon previous judges. The divine spirit was a positive element in Othniel's defeat of the enemy king of Aram (3:10). The spirit of God had relatively little positive effect on Gideon, who remained timid and fearful even after receiving the spirit (6:34). In the case of Abimelech, God sent an evil spirit that caused not unity and strength but conflict and discord among the Israelites. Thus, when we read that Jephthah received the spirit of God, we are poised to wonder whether this will have a positive or negative effect. Part of the effect of the spirit is an ability to unite and call forth volunteers from among the tribes of Israel. Jephthah accomplishes this rallying of troops with some success as he passes "through Gilead and Manasseh." This is not a large call-up of many Israelite tribes, but involves only a small localized area in the territory outside of Canaan and east of the Jordan River. The judges seem less and less able to muster substantial coalitions of multiple tribes as the reader moves through the individual judge stories from Othniel to Ehud to Deborah/Barak and Gideon. Indeed, the next and final judge after Jephthah, Samson, will lead no Israelites in battle. Samson will fight all his battles against the Philistines alone as an individual. This increasing inability to unify Israel's tribes is part of the social disintegration of the nation as we move further along in the era of the judges.

Once we have been assured that the spirit of God has come upon Jephthah, we are prepared by the previous judge stories to assume that the battle and victory for Israel will follow immediately. However, that assumption is disrupted by an ambiguous pledge or vow made by Jephthah to God. Jephthah promises that if God gives him victory over the Ammonites, he will offer as a burnt offering either "whoever" or "whatever" first "comes out of the doors of my house to meet me" when he returns home from the battle. The Hebrew text is equivocal as to whether Jephthah intended his vow to involve the offering of a human being ("whoever") or an animal ("whatever"). Some scholars argue that Jephthah's words must intend a human sacrifice. G. F. Moore offers his own strong opinion,

> That a human victim is intended is, in fact, as plain as words can make it; the language is inapplicable to an animal, and a vow to offer the first sheep or goat that he comes across—not to mention the possibility of an unclean animal—is trivial to absurdity.[8]

Other scholars argue just as adamantly that Jephthah's vow assumed an animal in light of the structure of Iron Age houses unearthed by archaeologists in this area. Domesticated animals apparently lived along with humans inside the typical house of this period.[9] In my judgment, Jephthah's language is left intentionally ambivalent by the narrator so that the reader cannot know for sure what Jephthah's real intention was. In Bakhtin's terms, the dialogical possibilities of the text are "unfinalizable."

Another issue arises in trying to understand the significance of Jephthah's vow. What is the relationship of Jephthah's vow and the spirit of the Lord coming upon Jephthah? Phyllis Trible argues that Jephthah's vow is an act of unfaithfulness. She assumes Jephthah is aware that he has just received God's spirit. Knowing this, the spirit-filled Jephthah should trust that having God's spirit is all he needs to guarantee victory over the Ammonites. However,

---

[8]G. F. Moore, *Judges,* International Critical Commentary (New York: Scribners, 1901), 299.
[9]Boling, *Judges,* 208.

Jephthah's additional vow after receiving the spirit means that he does not yet trust God sufficiently. His vow is a calculated ploy to manipulate God as a way to ensure victory.[10] In contrast to Trible, who separates the good spirit from Jephthah's bad vow, Cheryl Exum maintains that Jephthah's vow is not made in opposition to the divine spirit. Rather, the vow is made under the influence of God's spirit. The problem is not the vow as such, argues Exum. Faithful Israelites frequently made vows to God (Gen. 28:20–22; 1 Sam. 1:9–11). The problem with Jephthah's vow was not making the vow itself but its careless wording and content. Jephthah recklessly vowed to offer as a burnt offering "whoever" or "whatever" came out of his house. According to Exum, if Jephthah would have promised to erect an altar or worship the Lord when he returned in victory, the vow would have been much less problematic.[11]

However, I would argue against Exum that the act of taking the vow in itself *in this specific context* is indeed problematic, but not for the reason Trible cites. We are not told whether Jephthah is aware of having received the divine spirit or not.[12] Therefore, we cannot join Trible in condemning Jephthah for failing to trust in a divine spirit that he may or may not have been aware he was given. Yet there is another basis on which we can condemn Jephthah. While vows may be properly offered to God in some contexts, Jephthah wrongly uses the vow *in this particular context* as a bribe or leverage to influence the divine judge in the context of a court case. Recall that Jephthah has himself set up the conflict with the Ammonites as a court battle with the Lord as judge (11:27). According to Deuteronomy's laws, any bribes or gifts to judges are strictly prohibited lest they unduly influence the judge's decision (Deut. 16:19). This prohibition is grounded in Israel's distinctive understanding of God who "is not partial and takes no bribe" (Deut. 10:17).[13] Thus, Jephthah's vow in itself violates a deeply held Israelite norm in regard to the prohibition of gifts or bribes to judges. Exum is surely correct that the wording and content of the vow are also reckless and problematic in that they open the door to all kinds of inappropriate sacrifices, including unclean animals or humans. But any vow, no matter its content, in this particular setting of a court case with God as judge is illicit and inappropriate.

Jephthah has received "the spirit of the LORD" as a gift of strength, and he has made the vow as a bribe to influence God's decision as judge in order to guarantee himself the victory. What will God's response be? We learn

---

[10]Phyllis Trible, "The Daughter of Jephthah: An Inhuman Sacrifice," in *Texts of Terror, Literary-Feminist Readings of Biblical Narratives* (Philadelphia: Fortress Press, 1984), 93–116.

[11]J. Cheryl Exum, "The Tragic Vision and Biblical Narrative: The Case of Jephthah," in *Signs and Wonders: Biblical Texts in Literary Focus,* ed. J. Cheryl Exum (Atlanta: Society of Biblical Literature, 1989), 66–67.

[12]Elsewhere in Judges, Samson is not aware of when God's spirit or presence had arrived or left: Samson "did not know that the LORD had left him" when Delilah had his hair cut and he lost his strength (16:20).

[13]Michael Goldberg, "The Story of the Moral: Gifts or Bribes in Deuteronomy?" *Interpretation* 38 (1984): 15–25.

immediately that the Lord gave the Ammonites into Jephthah's hand, and Jephthah "inflicted a massive defeat on them" (vv. 32–33). Normally such a victory would be the climax of an individual judge story, but in this case the attention of the narrator rests elsewhere. Jephthah returns home from his victory. Remembering Jephthah's open-ended vow, the reader wonders who or what will first come out of his house. The narrator reports the tragic scene: "There was his daughter coming out to meet him with timbrels and with dancing" (v. 34). Jephthah's daughter was doing what Israelite women often did, welcoming victorious soldiers home with music and dance (Ex. 15:19–21;1 Sam. 8:6–7).

But this moment of great triumph for Jephthah turns into bitter tragedy and pain. His thoughtless vow means he will have to sacrifice his daughter as a burnt offering to God. The sacrifice is all the more poignant because she is his only link to future generations: "She was his only child; he had no son or daughter except her" (v. 34). Jephthah's first words are somewhat troubling for they paint him as the victim and offer no consolation to his daughter. Jephthah accuses his daughter of bringing trouble on him as if she is somehow responsible for his reckless vow (v. 35). Jephthah appears capable of seeing the world only through his own eyes. The empathy with others necessary for authentic dialogical engagement seems missing. Jephthah's self-centered character is heightened by the contrast with his daughter. She dutifully accepts her fate for the sake of her father and Israel's security: "Do to me according to what has gone out of your mouth" (v. 36). She makes only one request–that she and her companions be allowed to "wander on the mountains" and "bewail my virginity" for a period of two months (v. 37). She does so, and then she returns to her father "who did with her according to the vow he had made." No description of the actual killing of the daughter is given beyond this. An additional note emphasizes her virginity: "She had never slept with a man" (v. 39). The scene concludes with an ongoing custom in which the daughters of Israel would go out for four days each year either "to lament" the death of Jephthah's daughter or "commemorate" her willing sacrifice (v. 40; the Hebrew is ambiguous).

In a thorough and helpful study of this text, David Marcus summarizes the fascinating history of interpretation of this tragic and troubling text, which divides into two major groups.[14] On one hand, Jewish and Christian interpreters up to the Middle Ages consistently assumed that Jephthah did indeed kill his daughter and offer her up as a burned offering to God. For example, the Aramaic Targum acknowledged that while Jephthah did sacrifice his daughter, the practice was henceforth prohibited in Israel. The Church Father Origen believed the sacrifice of Jephthah's daughter prefigured the willing sacrifices and deaths of the Christian martyrs. Jewish exegetes such as Rashi and Nachmanides appealed to the "plain sense" of the text's meaning that Jephthah did indeed kill his daughter as a sacrificial offering. On the other hand, a

---

[14]David Marcus, *Jephthah and His Vow* (Lubbock, Tex.: Texas Tech Press, 1986), 8–9.

second major group of interpreters have argued that Jephthah did *not* actually kill his daughter but rather dedicated her to a life of virginity or celibacy. The earliest example of this line of interpretation is the medieval Jewish commentator David Kimchi. He writes,

> It is quite clear that he did not kill her because the text [in verse 37] does not say "I will mourn for my life," [but only "will mourn for my virginity"]. This indicates that he did not kill her but rather that she did not know a man [remained a virgin], because the text says [verse 39] "she did not know a man."[15]

Many subsequent Jewish and Christian interpreters adopted this line of interpretation, assuming that Jephthah's daughter remained alive but celibate. Indeed, Christian scholars associated the medieval practice of nuns vowing their lives to celibate service to God with the model of Jephthah's daughter. In support of their position, these interpreters point to verse 39, which does not actually state that Jephthah killed his daughter but simply "did with her according to the vow he had made." This line of interpretation found its way into Georg Frederic Handel's oratorio entitled *Jephtha,* first performed in 1752. In Handel's retelling of the biblical story, an angel intervenes just when Jephthah is about to kill his daughter and sings these words:

> Rise, Jephtha. And ye reverend priests, withhold the slaughterous hand. No vow can disannul the law of God, nor such was its intent, when rightly scanned, yet still shall be fulfilled. Thy daughter, Jephtha, thou must dedicate to God, in pure and virgin state for ever.

This angelic interruption of the sacrifice mirrors a similar motif in Abraham's near-sacrifice of his son in Genesis 22.

Despite these alternative renderings, the dominant interpretation remains that Jephthah did indeed kill his daughter and offer her as a burnt offering. Martin Luther's comment on the text is typical: "Some affirm he did not sacrifice her, but the text is clear enough."[16] However, I find more convincing the conclusion of the careful study by David Marcus that the Jephthah story contains "ambiguities consciously devised by the narrator" to be "open to a number of interpretations" so that "the text, as it stands now, admits the possibility of either conclusion."[17] The effect of the ambivalence is to heighten suspense, to draw the reader into wrestling with the moral dilemmas and ambiguities of the story, and to increase the sense of horror at a possibility so repulsive that it is not described but left only as an imagined potentiality. This central ambiguity of the entire story—whether Jephthah killed his daughter or not—reflects the overall ambiguity of Jephthah's character that we have noted earlier. In the end, whether Jephthah's daughter was sacrificed or lived a life of celibacy, Jephthah's vow remains foolish, wrong, and unnecessary. Yet at

---

[15]Quoted in ibid., 8.
[16]Martin Luther, *Die Deutsche Bibel* (Weimar: Herman Böhlaus Nachfolger, 1939), 131.
[17]Marcus, *Jephthah and His Vow,* 52.

the same time, Jephthah received "the spirit of the Lord" and successfully delivered Israel from the Ammonite oppression. The scale of evaluation, however, is tipped more toward the negative and against Jephthah in the concluding episode as Jephthah deals treacherously with his fellow Israelites from the tribe of Ephraim (12:1–6).

Judges 12:1–7, Jephthah and the Ephraimites

The final episode in the Jephthah cycle involves Jephthah's conflict not with an external enemy but with a fellow Israelite tribe, the tribe of Ephraim. Ephraim is a northern tribe located on the western side of the Jordan River in the hill country of Canaan. Ephraim was a dominant and important northern tribe throughout much of ancient Israel's history. The book of Judges uses the tribe of Ephraim as a barometer of Israel's cohesion and social unity as a people. In the earliest and most positive phase of the judges era, the individual judges called on the tribe of Ephraim to join in the conflict against the enemy, and the tribe immediately responded (3:27; 4:5; 5:14). In the second transitional phase under the judge Gideon, the tribe of Ephraim is called into the conflict against Midian at a late stage. The Ephraimites complain bitterly to Gideon about not being invited earlier to join in the battle. Gideon soothes their hurt feelings and peacefully resolves the internal dispute with Ephraim (7:24–25; 8:1–3). In this third and most negative phase of the judges era, beginning with Jephthah, the Ephraimites are bitterly disappointed that they were not invited at all to join Jephthah's fight against the Ammonites. Although a skillful negotiator in the past, Jephthah does not deal with their complaint diplomatically. Instead, he fights against the Ephraimites and kills 42,000 of them. This internal civil war with Ephraim uncovers a growing rift within Israel itself. This intra-Israelite conflict is a sign of the dissolution of the nation of Israel that will only worsen when a full-scale civil war erupts in Judges 19–21 with devastating results.

Verse 1 opens the scene with the Ephraimites preparing for military battle and confronting Jephthah with a question. Why did Jephthah not call on the Ephraimites to join him in his fight with the Ammonites? The question is a close parallel to the Ephraimites' question to Gideon in 8:1. However, the Ephraimites' hostility is much more intense than at the time of Gideon. The Ephraimites vow to burn Jephthah's "house" down over him. The threat is somewhat hollow in that the death or lifelong virginity of Jephthah's only daughter guarantees that he has no "house" in the sense of future progeny. Jephthah responds that he had indeed called on the Ephraimites to help in fighting the Ammonites, but "you did not deliver me from their hand" (v. 2). Jephthah's claim to have invited Ephraim to join the fight is not attested anywhere in the preceding story (see 11:29). The reader is led to conclude that this is a bald-faced lie. We begin to wonder whether any of Jephthah's many words, including his confessions of faith in God, were genuine and true. The Ephraimites are not satisfied with Jephthah's answer to their complaint, and so the battle between Jephthah and his fellow Israelites from Ephraim begins.

One of the methods Jephthah employs to draw a boundary around his internal enemies is the use of language and dialect. Jephthah knows well the power of words to entrap and bring death. Jephthah's army of Gileadites secures the fords or crossing points on the Jordan River. The Jordan River is the geographical boundary between his parochial region of Gilead east of the Jordan and the rest of Israel in the land of Canaan, which lies to the west of the Jordan River. Jephthah's defeat of the invading Ephraimite army causes the Ephraimite soldiers who escaped from the battle to become the "fugitives of Ephraim," the same derisive label the Ephraimites had used for the men of Gilead (v. 5; see v. 4). When these Ephraimite fugitives tried to cross the Jordan River to leave Gideon and return home to Ephraim on the western side of the Jordan, the Gilead soldiers would stop them and force them to say the word *Shibboleth,* which means either "ear of corn" or "stream." People of Gilead east of the Jordan pronounced this word with an initial "sh" sound in their dialect. People of Ephraim from west of the Jordan pronounced the same word with an initial "s," not the "sh" sound. Thus, Jephthah's soldiers were able to detect the Ephraimites by their dialect, and they killed them as they tried to cross the river. The narrator reports that an enormous number, 42,000 Ephraimites, were killed at that time (v. 6). This scene at the fords of the Jordan River recalls an earlier judge, Ehud, who also seized the fords of the Jordan River and killed thousands there. However, Ehud fought against Israel's enemies, the Moabites, not against fellow Israelites (3:28–29). In contrast, Jephthah slaughtered his fellow countrymen, the Ephraimites, at the fords of the Jordan. Jephthah's massacre of his own people suggests a disintegration of Israel's unity from the inside, a growing threat more ominous than any outside enemy.

This gradual decline in Israel's well-being as a nation is also suggested by the fact that Jephthah's reign as a judge is the shortest of any of the judges thus far. Previous judges had won periods of forty to eighty years of peace and "rest" for Israel (3:30; 5:31; 8:28). Jephthah judged Israel for only six years. In contrast to the previous judges, the narrator does not report that Israel obtained any period of "rest" or peace in Jephthah's time. Jephthah dies a parochial "Gileadite" more than a unifying and heroic judge who left a lasting legacy for all Israel (v. 12).

Conclusion: Language, Power, and God in Judges

The book of Judges is a veritable playground for postmodern interpretive interests. Language is slippery. Meanings are multiple. Themes are dialogically opposed. Characters are fractured and ambiguous. Endings involve ambiguity, dissolution, and chaos. The Jephthah narrative in particular highlights the varied potential of language within such an atmosphere. In two instances, Jephthah uses language under conditions of freedom and persuasion. Jephthah begins as a skilled and successful user of language when he negotiates his rise to power as leader of his own people, the people of Gilead. Language can be a constructive means to build relationships and promote the mutual well-being of oneself and a wider community. But Jephthah's human skill in language has its limits, as his extensive arguments fail to persuade the Ammonites not to attack. Language as effective rhetoric requires that a complex set of conditions all be in play: the perceived integrity of the speaker, the persuasiveness of the arguments, and the openness of the listener. Truth does not "happen" unless all the elements are in place in any given context.

In two other instances, Jephthah uses language under conditions of force and control with disastrous consequences. Jephthah foolishly entraps himself in language when he feels forced to kill his own daughter through what he believes is an irrevocable and nonnegotiable vow to God. His words entangle him in a self-destructive web of his own making. Previously an avid negotiator, Jephthah now assumes a constricted monologic universe in which vows are nonnegotiable. Such a view is in line with the Deuteronomic law that demands the fulfillment of all vows freely made (Deut. 23:21–23). Yet the fulfillment of this vow, the sacrifice of his daughter, violates another of the Deuteronomic laws, which commands Israel not to engage in the abhorrent practice of other nations who "would even burn their sons and their daughters in the fire to their gods" (Deut. 12:31). Had Jephthah lived more fully into his Israelite tradition, he might have seen an opening for dialogical negotiation with God between these two monologic absolutes, a dialogue that might have led to life rather than death. In a second instance, Jephthah entraps 42,000 Ephraimites in a forced language game of "shibboleths" that leads to their deaths and furthers the disintegration of Israel's social fabric. Language is used forcibly and oppressively to define "the other," leading to death and social disintegration.

Where is God in all of this? The book of Judges provides no easy answers and sometimes only silence (21:3). As God moves and works and speaks among the forces that shape and intrude upon the life of Israel, God is indeed moved by some powerful human language and not by others. It is the cry of pain under oppression and not the plea of shallow repentance that repeatedly calls God back to Israel's defense in the book of Judges: God "could no longer bear to see Israel suffer" (10:16). For the God of Judges, it is the cry of weakness, the cry of desperation that has a particular power to bring God to remembrance of the vow God made to Israel–"I will never break my covenant with you" (2:1). Unlike Jephthah's vow, however, God's promise leads to life and a future negotiated among the complex interplay of compulsions, freedoms, and persuasions that make up the human experience of language, relationship, and community. Along the way, however, lies the charred corpse of Jephthah's daughter and next to her the mutilated body of the Levite's concubine (Judg. 19). Both they and others in Judges are victims of words spoken and actions taken in the context of force and fear in conflict with those perceived as "other." Why their cries of lament and desperation are not answered by God remains an unresolved mystery. With Israel, we lift up our voices and weep bitterly, asking, "O Lord, the God of Israel, why has it come to pass…?" (Judg. 21:3) The language of lament is at times all we have in the face of the unfinalizable and dialogical tensions that the Bible and reality place before us.

The Secret of Succession

Elijah, Elisha, Jesus, and Derrida

Hugh S. Pyper

Immediately after his encounter with God on Mount Horeb in 1 Kings 19, Elijah comes upon Elisha ploughing in the fields and throws his mantle over him. Elisha runs after Elijah to ask whether he may kiss his father and mother before following him. "Go, return; what have I done to you?" (1 Kings 19:20) is the response, an answer in the form of a question.

This is a cryptic remark, even by biblical standards, and a puzzling one. Not even the speaker and the hearer are definitively identified. The Hebrew, in typical fashion, gives us only pronouns ("he said to him"), leaving the reader to resolve their reference. The first part of the phrase is ambiguous in its own right. "Go, return" evokes echoes of the confusion apocryphally caused to hesitant foreigners leaving a Glasgow bus by the conductress' cry, "Come on, get off!" Taken literally "Go, return" is a command to remain where one is, but to remain with the new anxiety of implicit movement and the impossibility of resolving an authoritative command.

Equally enigmatic, however, is the second part of the phrase, the question "What have I done to you?" Within this text a character articulates the very question that puzzles modern readers of the preceding narrative. No explanation of the implications of Elijah's act of throwing his mantle over Elisha is offered. What *did* Elijah do to Elisha? In 1 Kings 19:6 Elijah is told to anoint Elisha as a prophet in his place, but this adds to the confusion. Does throwing one's mantle constitute anointing? There is no comparable biblical story that might help us here. Readers contemporary with the text might recognize a cultural practice, but that leaves the modern reader no better off. As it is, Elijah's question echoes the reader's ignorance rather than answering it. The text articulates its own failure to communicate.

This evokes a wider problem that has exercised the readers of these texts: Why in the middle of a mostly chronological account of the more or less unsatisfactory kings of Judah and Israel do we suddenly find a cluster of disparate legends centered on these two prophetic figures? On the analogy of the question we are pursuing, this might be rephrased: What are the stories of Elijah and Elisha "doing" in the books of Kings?

This question can itself be interpreted in more than one way. It may be taken as an inquiry into textual history. Where did these texts come from, and how did they get there? There are many learned articles on the provenance, development, and redaction of these stories, predicated on the simple observation that they are distinctive in content, style, and ideology in their present context. Yet out of this analysis, no better picture emerges than that of a student in the Deuteronomistic scribal school who has a weekend to produce a thesis on the Kings of Israel and Judah and, in desperation, cuts and pastes in a chunk of an essay on prophets and politics in the ninth century to make up the length.

What remains unanswered is a second, and just as valid, question: Why did the inclusion of this material seem appropriate or necessary? A further, seemingly obvious point is usually left unexplored as well, which may shed particular light on the one just posed. Given that one such collection seems an odd intrusion, why *two*? For that matter, why *only* two, in view of the fact that many other prophetic figures appear in the books of Kings, some not even afforded the dignity of a name? How do the two cycles and their two pro-tagonists relate?

We can perhaps glean something from Elisha's response to Elijah's actions. He regards whatever has transpired as a summons to follow Elijah. More important, however, the immediate implications are for his relation to his parents. He must now ask permission from Elijah to say farewell to them, rather than seek their consent for his following Elijah. In the phrasing of Elisha's question, an admission of a new loyalty in a new social situation is implicit. It is this fraught site of transition between Elisha as the child of his parents and Elisha as servant to Elijah that prompts Elijah's question. The repercussions of this for the understanding of relationships of filiation and affiliation in the text are, as we shall see, far-reaching.

This does not yet exhaust the range of meanings of the question, however. "What have I done to you?" can be taken as a question addressed by the text to the reader. Here, as a text articulates its readers' puzzlement over not just its meaning but its effect, we have dangled before us the kind of loose end that deconstructive readers have shown may serve to unravel the whole structure of the text if pulled gently but persistently. This would be a trivial exercise if its only result was to show that this text is text, rather akin to a child's destructive unpicking of his or her mother's knitting. So every sock can be reduced to a ball of wool. Hardly news, unless someone is trying to convince you that the sock is an indestructible and natural given in the world. Unpicking the text, however, may be one way to throw light on the question of the effect of the inclusion of this material on the reader of the books of Kings.

Robert Carroll offers a starting point when he writes, "The compilers of the books of Kings were interested in the Elijah-Elisha sagas because they gave weight to the Deuteronomistic thesis of the prophetic succession."[1] These stories are the only place in the Hebrew Bible where any suggestion of such a succession arises. Furthermore, the problem of succession underpins the issues of continuity and identity, which are central to the books of Samuel and Kings. There is a mythogenic question intrinsic to all accounts of succession. If B receives his status and powers because they are conferred on him by A, either by virtue of heredity or by some ceremony of investiture, how did A receive his powers? Unless we postulate an infinite regression into the past, sooner or later we must come to a first mover.

The Davidic monarchy is a good case in point. If kings gain their power by being descendants of David, at least in Judah, what was the basis of David's power? The answer is complex, as mythical structures are complex. Although David founds the dynasty, he is not the first king, but is adopted as Saul's successor. Succession then does not depend on physical descent. There is another figure involved as mediator of kingly power in this story, and that is Samuel, who confers kingship on both David and Saul and then rescinds it in Saul's case. Yet there is a hereditary principle at work, too, where the expectation is that the heir will be a son. In Judah, this principle is adhered to, while in the Northern Kingdom, the situation is more ambiguous. Kingship moves from house to house, yet each time there is the beginning of a new hereditary line. The issue of filiation and nonfiliation is constantly negotiated in the text.

The tales of Elijah and Elisha bridge a major discontinuity in Israel's monarchy, the transition from the house of Omri to the rule of Jehu. There is no continuity of blood between the two houses or any valid transfer of power on the level of kingship or by the priesthood. What continuity there is comes through the notion of a prophetic line. Elisha has to be shown to be the proper bearer of Elijah's power, so that the one who denounces Ahab and the one who confers legitimacy on Jehu are validly in line. In the absence of a narrative of transference between Ahab and Jehu, a narrative of continuity between Elijah and Elisha is supplied.

The ultimate legitimator of any continuity of authority in the biblical text is Yahweh. Narratologically speaking, Elijah and Elisha as spokesmen for God are sites where language signed by the name of Yahweh can enter the text. Whatever the historical function of prophets, and it is a moot point as to whether that term should be applied to Elijah or Elisha at all, being prophets is their narrative function in the text. Through them, divine speech can enter the textual world.

Yet, as was indicated above, this is only part of the question. The issue of dynastic succession may give a narratological explanation of the generation and inclusion of this anomalous material, but it does not account for either the oddities of the succession episode itself or for the dynamics behind the elaboration and juxtaposition of the two cycles. Accounting for this, I shall argue, problematizes the issue of succession and therefore continuity in the

---

[1]Robert Carroll, "The Elijah-Elisha Sagas: Some Remarks on Prophetic Succession in Ancient Israel," *Vetus Testamentum* 19 (1969): 400–15.

textual world, which in turn raises questions about the relation between the reader and the text. To unravel this, it is first necessary to look to the relationship between the two cycles.

When the Elijah and Elisha cycles are compared, both the similarities and the differences are striking. That there is a relationship is undeniable in view of the interdependence of the two cycles. Attempts to account for the provenance of their elements and the history behind their incorporation into the present text of Kings merely reveal the complexity of this relationship.[2] Both are collections of various types of narrative; both prophets engage in miraculous healing and feeding; both confront kings with divine instructions. Some incidents, most notably the restoration of life to the son of a woman with whom the prophet has extensive dealings, are similar enough to seem like variants of a common story.

Yet there are also consistent differences. In John Gray's opinion, "When we compare the Elisha saga,…we are impressed with the comparative sobriety of the Elijah cycle."[3] This is echoed by Blenkinsopp's description of Elisha as "in all respects, a more 'primitive' figure, embodying the more destructive forces that could be concentrated in that kind of personality."[4] Fokkelien van Dijk-Hemmes elaborates on this contrast when she writes "Elisha's portrait provides a stark contrast to his great predecessor Elijah. The stories about Elisha seem to be parodic offshoots of stories about Elijah. The same narrated events are recounted in a grotesque way; the narration becomes more fanciful when it concerns Elijah."[5]

The introduction of the word *parody* here is the significant one in this context.[6] Gary Saul Morson usefully offers three features that may alert a reader to the possibility that a particular text is a parody, even in the absence of its original. These three are

1. exaggeration, particularly the heightening of contrasts
2. incongruity, countergeneric elements
3. punning, perverse reading of polysemic elements[7]

---

[2]A useful summary of such discussions can be found in chapter 4 of Steven L. McKenzie's *The Trouble with Kings: The Composition of the Book of Kings in the Deuteronomistic History* (Leiden: Brill, 1991), 81–98.

[3]John Gray, *I and II Kings: A Commentary,* rev. ed. (London: SCM Press, 1970), 336.

[4]Joseph Blenkinsopp, *A History of Prophecy in Israel,* rev. ed. (Louisville: Westminster John Knox Press, 1996), 63.

[5]Fokkelien van Dijk-Hemmes, "The Great Woman of Shunem and the Man of God: A Dual Interpretation of 2 Kings 4:8–37," in *A Feminist Companion to Samuel and Kings,* ed. A. Brenner (Sheffield: Sheffield Academic Press, 1994), 228.

[6]Its implications are developed by Jopie Siebert-Hommes in a comparison of the stories of the widow of Zarephath and the Great Woman of Shunem. She reads these as parodic variants where Elisha, in contrast to his predecessor, seems to have difficulties in performing the role expected of him and has to be reminded by the woman of his duties. See Jopie Siebert-Hommes "The Widow of Zarephath and the Great Woman of Shunem: A Comparative Analysis of Two Stories," in *On Reading Prophetic Texts: Gender-Specific and Related Studies in Memory of Fokkelien van Dijk-Hemmes,* ed. B. Becking and M. Dijkstra (Leiden: Brill, 1996), 250.

[7]Adapted from Gary Saul Morson, "Parody, History and Metaparody," in *Rethinking Bakhtin: Extensions and Challenges,* ed. G. S. Morson and C. Emerson (Evanston, Ill.: Northwestern University Press, 1989), 67.

The first two are evident in the Elisha cycle. Elisha works both on a smaller, one could say more trivial, scale than Elijah and on a larger scale. On the one hand, he floats an axe head and uses flour to counteract the poisonous effect of wild cucumbers. The bizarre episode where he summons bears to maul the boys who mocked him verges on Morson's category of the countergeneric. On the other hand, he prevents a Syrian invasion and advises not one but three kings at a time. Elisha ranges further and deals more actively in the wider political life of the region, being involved in the succession of not only Israel's kings but also of Syria's. This exaggerated range of activity led Barré, for one, to see a dichotomy in the Elisha figure, contrasting the realistic description of the political figure in 2 Kings 9–11 with the magical problem solver of the earlier stories.[8] Whereas he seeks to use this clue in the historical analysis of the stories, his observation serves to confirm the reading of Elisha as Elijah "writ large," so to speak. Moreover, the dichotomy in his characterization serves as a parodic amplification of a duality already to be found in Elijah.

A detail in 2 Kings 2:9 may serve to confirm this. The standard English translations have Elisha request a "double portion" of Elijah's spirit. More literally, Elisha asks for the "mouth of two" of Elijah's spirit, an expression that occurs also in Zechariah 13:8, meaning not "double" but "two-thirds," that is, two parts out of three. More pertinently, it is the expression used for the firstborn's entitlement in Deuteronomy 21:17. The "double portion" of the firstborn is patently not twice the whole inheritance, but a share twice as big as that of the other heirs. Read literally in one sense, it can be taken to mean Elisha seeks to be "twice the man" Elijah is. In another sense of literal meaning, it shows that this doubleness is actually a weakening of the spirit. Elisha is not *twice* the man, but *two-thirds* the man Elijah is. The doubling paradoxically entails a reduction in the spirit. For our purposes we may go further and read this as an instance of parodic punning, which often involves the literalization of figurative expressions. Elisha is a redoubled but divided Elijah.

The texts of the Elisha cycle, then, contain passages that can be read as parodic rewritings of elements in the Elijah cycle. Whether or not the Elijah material preceded the Elisha material in actual composition—and indeed the opposite case has been argued—they appear in this relationship in the order of reading. The Elijah material provides a model against which the similar but very different Elisha cycle is read. This relationship is always reversible. The Elisha narratives send the reader back to discover the implicit doubleness of the figure of Elijah himself through their teasing similarities and differences. "Go; return" can be taken as a clue to the constant shuttling between these cycles that the reader is induced to undertake.

Elijah's Divisive Unity·

To identify the doubleness of Elijah as a key trope in this text may seem to cut against a common conception of Elijah as the champion of unity, of one

---

[8]L. M. Barré, *The Rhetoric of Political Persuasion* (Washington, D.C.: Catholic Biblical Association of America, 1988), 65.

God and one people of Israel. Doubleness is something Elijah explicitly disapproves of, as is clear in his challenge to the people assembled on Carmel: "How long will you go on hobbling on two sticks?" or "...limping with two different opinions?" (1 Kings 18:21).

Yet as David Jobling explores in his essay "'The Jordan a Boundary': Transjordan in Israel's Ideological Geography,"[9] the ideological drive to see Israel as unity is itself divisive. Geographical boundaries seldom coincide with cultural boundaries, a point only too painfully evident in the ethnic conflicts of the twentieth century. There is almost bound to be a mismatch between Israel as land and Israel as people. There are people living within the land who are not Israelites, and people living beyond it who are or claim to be. The problem is compounded because there may also be different concepts of the geographical limits to what counts as the land. Jobling analyzes this in the case of the Transjordanians, who are part of Israel and yet are on the wrong side of the river. The crossing of the Jordan becomes an important symbolic boundary.

Elijah is the fulcrum of this doubleness. It is he who demands of the people that they make a decision either for Baal or Yahweh. He is the one who insists on the dichotomy, dividing the people into two camps. The implication is that his audience has hitherto sought to treat the two gods as compatible, maintaining some kind of unity among their worshipers. They are the ones who are not acknowledging difference. In Elijah's rhetoric, they are compromising Israel's identity by blurring the boundaries between themselves and their neighbors.

What is intriguing then, is the amount of time that Elijah himself spends outside Israel, conceived in these symbolic rather than political terms, breaching these very boundaries. All we know of his antecedents is that they came from Transjordanian Gilead, and the first action that he takes is to flee to the Wadi Cherith, east of Jordan. He then travels to Zarephath, in Sidonia, to the home of a widow who is not a worshiper of Yahweh. He then appears somewhere in Israel and summons the people to Mount Carmel, one of the "high places" so often condemned by the prophet, and the crest of the natural boundary between the Israelite south and the kingdoms of Tyre and Sidon, even though biblical Israel's claim to land runs beyond that point. Thereafter, he flees across the Jordan in a parodic retracing of the journey of Israel through the desert to Mount Horeb.

More radically, there is an element in Elijah's stories that puts all boundaries in question. We feel for Obadiah when he takes the prophet to task for instructing him to carry the potentially duplicitous message "Elijah is here" to the king (1 Kings 18:8). That is all very well, but where is "here"? Obadiah works himself into a fine old state as he recreates what is potentially the highly comical scene, from the reader's point of view if not Obadiah's, in which he leads a baffled and furious king to the point now designated "here"

---

[9]David Jobling, "'The Jordan a Boundary':Transjordan in Israel's Ideological Geography," in *The Sense of Biblical Narrative: Structural Analyses in the Hebrew Bible,* vol. 2 (Sheffield, JSOT Press, 1986): 88–134.

only to find that the spirit has carried Elijah off "I don't know where" (1 Kings 18:9–12). In 2 Kings 2:15–18, the sons of the prophets seem to think something similar to be a perfectly possible explanation of Elijah's disappearance. Elisha apparently knows better, but in the end gives permission for a search party to be sent out to find out what he has already told them. Elijah breaks the boundaries of space and, in the ambiguity of his death and return, of time.

The Double Name

This doubleness between setting and breaking the bounds of Israel is implicit in the name "Elijah." It can be translated as "Yahweh my God."[10] Its meaning is ambiguous depending on where the stress is put: "*Yahweh* my god" or "Yahweh is *my* god." It can either be a claim of exclusive loyalty to Yahweh—whatever god anyone else might follow, I follow Yahweh—or a claim to some exclusive possession and even control over Yahweh—Yahweh is in my pocket. The conflict between these two meanings underlies the ambiguities of the stories that follow. This is clearly seen when, as a result of Elijah's triumph at Carmel, he is driven out over the Jordan into the desert again, eventually ending up at Horeb in a parodic repetition of Moses' experiences on the same mountain. Elijah complains bitterly of his aloneness. "I, even I only, am left," he laments, setting up a line of division between himself and all the rest of Israel. This would mean that the claim in his name "Yahweh is *my* God" is true de facto. If no one else is worshiping Yahweh, he truly is Elijah's sole possession. Yet that same God points out that seven thousand others are left. Elijah's flight into the solitude of the desert is to be reversed. "Go, return," says Yahweh to Elijah (1 Kings 19:15), using the very words which, as we have seen, stand between Elijah and Elisha. He is to live up to his name's confession of loyalty by returning and anointing successors.

Key ambiguities of Elijah's stories are thus inscribed in his name. To put it another way, the stories write out the significance of his name in narrative. A typically pregnant remark of Derrida's may be relevant here:

> When a proper name is inscribed right on the text, within the text, obviously it is not a signature; it is a way of making the name into a work, of making work of the name, but without this inscription of the proper name having the value of any property rights so to speak.[11]

The writing out of Elijah's name in the text of Kings serves precisely to disrupt any discourse of property rights in a God who runs beyond all human boundaries. Yahweh is not bound to Elijah, or even to Israel, and the attempt to reverse the claim of loyalty due by both to Yahweh serves to disrupt rather than preserve their identity.

---

[10]Dictionaries and commentators differ as to whether the first element of the name is to be construed as simply the construct, or whether the *yodh* is to be interpreted as the first person pronominal suffix. Both forms of the construct are to be found in the biblical material, but for the purposes of this reading, all that is necessary is that the possessive interpretation is an option. Gray, in a comment that has more implications than he develops, surmises that this name, which he translates as "My God is Yahweh," "may well have been a name assumed to give point to his mission" (Gray, *I and II Kings*, 336).

[11]Jacques Derrida, *Positions*, trans. A. Bass (London: Athlone Press, 1981), 365.

Introducing the name of Derrida into the discussion of Elijah is not arbitrary. Derrida himself makes the association clear in an essay on Joyce's *Ulysses:*

> Of course you do not believe a word of what I am saying to you at the moment. And even if it were true, and even if, yes, it is true, you would not believe me if I told you that I too am called Elijah: this name is not inscribed, no, on my official documents, but it was given me on my seventh day. Moreover, Elijah is the name of the prophet present at *all* circumcisions. He is the patron, if we can put it like this, of circumcisions.[12]

As patron of circumcisions, Elijah is patron of the cut that marks identity, the divide that leads to inclusion in the people. In the biblical story however, the only cutting he does is to sever the heads of the already cut bodies of the priests of Baal, a cut that marks exclusion from Israel.

In "Ulysses Gramophone," Derrida provides a reading of Joyce's novel that resonates with the biblical reading we are pursuing. Derrida identifies two Elijahs at work in the text of *Ulysses.* The first Elijah is the "great operator," the "head of the megaprogramotelephonic network" as Derrida puts it. This exuberant coinage is a name for the system in general. In the case of Kings, it is the system of oppositions and exclusions that shore up Israel's identity and textual coherence. The second Elijah is the deconstruction of the first, "if Elijah is the name of the unforeseeable other for whom a place must be kept."[13]

Elijah is thus the figure for the system of codes, the breaking of that system, and the inextricability of the two. "But there we are," Derrida continues, "this is a homonym; Elijah can always be one and the other at the same time; we cannot invite the one, without the risk of the other turning up. But this is a risk which must always be run."[14] John Caputo summarizes Derrida's reading of Elijah here as follows:

> Derrida here marks the difference (in highly Nietzschean terms) between a negative, reactive reappropriating self-enclosing circumcision, vs. a light-footed, affirmative, yea-saying *mohel* whose cut is made in order to affirm the other, *tout autre*–like a Dionysiac rabbi...not the self-destructive castrating cut denounced by Hegel, but the cut that breaks the bonds of the self-enclosure of the same and makes possible the in-coming of the other.[15]

One involves the other, however. It might be tempting to play with mapping this difference onto the two names at work in the text: Elijah, the self-enclosing circumcisor who creates division by seeking unity, and Elisha, the Dionysiac rabbi whose doubleness leads to a new unity that both depends on and subverts the very geographic and religious categories we have been discussing.

---

[12]Jacques Derrida, "Ulysses Gramophone: Hear Say Yes in Joyce," in *Jacques Derrida: Acts of Literature,* ed. D. Attridge, trans. T. Kendall and S. Benstock (New York: Routledge, 1992), 284–85.
[13]Ibid., 295.
[14]Ibid.
[15]John Caputo, *The Prayers and Tears of Jacques Derrida: Religion without Religion* (Bloomington, Ind.: Indiana University Press), 260.

Elisha's concern with the people of Syria is notable, but a key moment of rupture comes in the story of the healing of Naaman (2 Kings 5:8–19). Not only does he cure this emissary of the Syrian king, but the key mark of identification between Israel's God and the land is deconstructed when Elisha gives Naaman permission to take two mules' burden of earth from Israel so that he may be standing on holy ground outside its boundaries (vv. 17–19). The point of stability in the system, the land itself, its very substance as well as its boundaries, can be subverted. Elijah's unification of worship is fulfilled but then deconstructed when a loyal follower of Yahweh can be found at worship in the temple of the Syrian god Rimmon. The divided opinions on which the people were limping find some sort of unification in the healed Naaman, whose leprosy is transferred into Israel in the person of the servant Gehazi.

So far, our reading has oscillated around the tensions between unity and doubleness in the text. In the interview that functions as a preface to *Acts of Literature*,[16] Derrida deals with this very question. Asked whether literary criticism is a response that enhances the singularity of a piece of literature, his response is, predictably, both yes and no. Yes, the uniqueness of the text must be enhanced, but that uniqueness in itself is dependent on the relation of the text to the general: "Any work is singular in that it speaks singularly of both singularity and generality. Of iterability and the law of iterability."[17]

In a most suggestive paragraph, this is expanded in relation to reading:

Singularity "shared" in this way does not keep itself to its writing aspect, but also to the reading aspect and to what comes to sign, by countersigning, in reading. There is as it were a duel of singularities, and duel of writing and reading, in the course of which a countersignature comes both to confirm, repeat and respect the signature of the other, of the "original" work, and to *lead it off* elsewhere, so running the risk of *betraying* it, having to betray it in a certain way so as to respect it through the invention of another signature just as singular.[18]

Can we suggest that what is striking about the series of prophetic legenda that comprise the Elijah and Elisha cycles is the manifestation of this insight? Can we read Elisha as the countersignature of Elijah, betraying Elijah's work by "leading it off" dichotomously both out of Israel into the dealings of international politics and the gods of other people, and inwardly, into the quasifamiliar and domestic exploits of the miracle worker among the sons of the prophets? In the interplay of these mutually deconstructing texts, these two signatures, Elijah/Elisha: "My god is Yahweh"/"My god saves," open an aporia where the structures of filiation and successions are implied, subverted, and betrayed, both in the sense of being revealed and in the sense of being abandoned in being exposed.

---

[16]"'This Strange Institution Called Literature': An Interview with Jacques Derrida," in *Acts of Literature* (New York: Routledge, 1992), 33–75.

[17]Ibid., 69.

[18]Ibid.

Derrida may also provide an insight into the consideration of the nature of succession and the role of these stories in both underpinning and subverting this key problem of the books of Kings. In his essay *Sauf le nom* (postscriptum) Derrida quotes Angelus Silesius as follows:

Nothing lives without dying
God himself, if he wants to live for you, must die:
How do you think without death to inherit his own life?

He then asks, "Has anything more profound ever been written on inheritance? I understand that as a thesis on what *inherit* means (to say). Both to give the name and to receive it. Save [*Sauf,* Safe]."[19]

Death is the motor of succession—without death there is no need for the question to arise. However, Elijah and Elisha in different ways problematize death and therefore the concept of succession. In 1 Kings 19 the answer to our question "What have I done to you?" is not as simple as "I have appointed you to replace me." Far from taking over from Elijah, Elisha disappears from the text until 2 Kings 2 and the story of Elijah's translation.

It is in that chapter that the real exchange takes place, after Elijah is taken up into heaven in a whirlwind and a fiery chariot, a familiar but baffling story. Whatever happens, he leaves no trace of himself except his mantle. No grave marks his presence—or absence. However, the word *death* is absent from this chapter. Nowhere is it stated that Elijah died. In acknowledgment of this, a long tradition of exegesis, beginning in the biblical text itself, has expected Elijah's return from heaven. "Go, return": Elijah is the one figure in the Hebrew Bible who could be said to fulfill this command.

In Elisha's case, the text is explicit that he "died and they buried him" (2 Kings 13:20). Yet he too lives on textually. After his death a burial party is surprised by Moabite raiders and throws the body into Elisha's grave in order to escape. Unlike Elijah, Elisha has a grave, which we might expect would be a site of reverence and remembrance for this powerful man of God. Yet Elisha's grave is patently in debatable land, both in and out of Israel. Moabite raiders are commonplace, and there is not much evidence of resistance by the burial party. Moreover, what does the dumping of the corpse in Elisha's grave say about their respect either for Elisha or for the dead man they are carrying? Do they even know that Elisha is buried there or is his grave forgotten?

The twist, of course, is that immediately on touching Elisha's bones, the dead man "revived and stood on his feet" (2 Kings 13:21). A miracle, naturally, but we might wonder at his reaction on being revived only to face the prospect of imminent slaughter by the Moabite raiders his friends have fled. The story stops here, giving us no help in deciding whether this is an incredible escape or an incredible piece of bad timing. Elisha confers life beyond the grave, but the text is ambiguous, to say the least, about whether this is to be welcomed or not.

Both Elisha's and Elijah's stories exhibit strange features that breach the most fundamental of boundaries in the Hebrew Bible, that between life and death. Apart from the narratives of their passings, both seem to do this in the

---

[19]Derrida, *On the Name,* ed. T. Dutoit (Stanford: Stanford University Press), 82.

complementary stories of the raising of a boy to life (1 Kings 17:17–24; 2 Kings 4:18–37). Through this subversion of death they also subvert the notion of succession. Elijah overleaps Elisha to become his successor's successor in the biblical text.

Elijah's name reappears in the penultimate verse of Malachi (Mal. 4:5), where his coming is promised before the Lord's day. This becomes the penultimate verse of the Christian Old Testament. Elijah's mission as spelled out in the subsequent verse, the final verse of the Old Testament, is to turn the hearts of the fathers to their children and children to their fathers, in order to avert the Lord's curse. Fathers and children are turned to one another, or more literally "caused to return." "Go, return," we may remember. What he is to do is to repair the structures of filiation, which, as we have seen, the narratives of 1 and 2 Kings throw into question. The one who took Elisha from his parents and who sundered the succession of Ahab's house is to bring a new reconciliation between parent and child. Elijah's appearances in the New Testament texts develop and problematize this motif.

As for Elisha, his name does not reappear in the texts of the Hebrew Scriptures or in the New Testament. He has apparently little or no textual afterlife, consigned as he is to his grave in 2 Kings. The rabbinic tradition regards him as insignificant compared to Elijah. Yet precisely by virtue of his coming after Elijah, his story is taken as a basis for the gospel accounts of Jesus' life, particularly in Luke.[20] The identification of John the Baptist with the Elijah of Malachi means that Elijah's successor Elisha ("My God Saves") informs his near namesake, Yehoshua (he saves), who comes after John.[21] Luke's Jesus, in a strictly textual analysis with no trivialization implied, is at least in part a parody of Elisha. Without venturing into a whole new complex of issues, the issues of filiation and succession and their problematization are at the heart of the gospel narratives of Jesus and the multiplication of texts and readings that have arisen from these in the last two thousand years. The New Testament sees a complete revision of what the boundaries of Israel are taken to be and who is to inherit the promises of the Old Testament.

"What have I done to you?" runs the question with which we began this investigation. It remains unanswerable, but the effects of the textual disruptions we have uncovered run at least as far as the "leading off," to use Derrida's phrase, of the future of Israel into the Gentile discourse of Christianity. This

---

[20]This identification is worked out more fully by Thomas L. Brodie in his *The Crucial Bridge: The Elijah-Elisha Narrative as an Interpretive Synthesis of Genesis-Kings and a Literary Model for the Gospels* (Collegeville, Minn.: Liturgical Press, 2000). Although Brodie's thesis and techniques are very different from those in the present article, his work testifies to a similar intuition over the pivotal role of these narratives in the structuring of the biblical corpus.

[21]In the light of Derrida's characteristically terse text quoted above on the giving and receiving of the name in inheritance, we might reflect on earlier changes in names in Kings. "Elisha" ([My] God Saves) replaces "Elijah" ([My] God Yahweh). What has been dropped is the theophoric element of the name, replaced with an element that translates the word that echoes through Derrida's meditations on succession and narrative theology: "Save/*Sauf.*" To continue this line of association into the New Testament, Elisha is replaced by Yehoshua, "He saves," a name which takes up the root "save" but which in Hebrew also begins with the three letters that end Elijah's name, three of the four letters of the tetragrammaton.

discourse is predicated on a cohesion of the motifs of the deaths of Elijah and Elisha, the one taken up to heaven, and the one whose death leads to the springing to life of the abandoned corpse of another. Jesus dies, is buried, springs to life, and ascends. His corpse is reanimated by contact with itself; his human death is overcome by the contact with God that permeates his physical being.

The gospel reader, then, is faced by a powerful rereading, or "misreading" (in Harold Bloom's terms)[22] of these anomalous texts in Kings, which become not an interruption, but an irruption of a new economy of life through death, rather than life against death. The Yahweh of Kings not only breaches the boundaries of time and space textually; the peculiar power of the divine character is that the boundary between the textual world and the reader's world is breached. If Yahweh is boundless in the text, then if he exists, he exists also in the reader's world and his questions are addressed across the boundary between text and reader.

The reader is faced with a new question: "Go, return; what have I done to you?" The textual voice claims an identity with the voice of the God who has gone and returned from himself to himself, gone from the world in the ascension but with the promise of return. The reader is faced with the question of whether he or she will enter the world of the biblical narrative and become part of an Israel unbounded by time or space, or reimpose the barriers between text-world and life-world. "Return," after all, is synonymous in Hebrew with "repent." Or will the reader oscillate between the two, "going and returning" endlessly from a position where the worlds mesh and one where they remain utterly incompatible?

Postmodern readings of biblical texts serve as a powerful tool to point out the force and the unanswerability of the questions that the text in its very textuality poses to its readers about their own constructedness, their own insertion in the economies of succession and filiation. They offer no answers. They can only chart in a particular way the questions of the text that invite, but cannot require, answers from the reader. It is in answering or not answering such a challenge that the reader becomes the answer to the text's question: "What have I done to you?"

---

[22]Harold Bloom, *A Map of Misreading* (Oxford: Oxford University Press, 1975).

Divining Ruth for International Relations

Musa W. Dube

The book of Ruth is known for the deep friendship of two women, Ruth and Naomi. Ruth looks into the face of her departing mother-in-law and says:

> Entreat me not to leave you or to return from following you; for where you go I will go, and where you lodge I will lodge; your people shall be my people and your God my God; where you die I will die, and there I will be buried…And when Naomi saw that she was determined to go with her, she said no more. (1:16–18)

Church liturgy has transferred these "woman-to-woman" words into a heterosexual marriage pledge. If, however, we are faithful to the book of Ruth, the marriage is between two women. Ruth leaves her home, travels with Naomi, lodges with her, and finally she bears a child to her. Indeed, we are told that when Ruth gave birth to a son, "the women in the neighborhood gave him a name, saying, 'A son has been born to Naomi'"(4:16–17). That the latter verse is at the close of the book indicates their unbroken marriage.

This seemingly woman-centered book has received many interpretations from various women readers, who bring different methods and backgrounds to focus on the many aspects of Ruth. For example, when Musimbi Kanyoro read the book with Kenyan women they saw Ruth

> as the obedient and faithful daughter-in-law for [Kenyan] culture dictates that marriage is forever–to a family, not to an individual. Thus the death of Naomi's son did not invalidate the marriage of her daughter-in-law. Ruth was then seen as the normal good woman who does what culture expects of her and becomes blessed. Custom and tradition…also stipulate honour and respect and help for older people, be they relatives or not. That Ruth chose to stay with

Naomi was normal to [Kenyan] women as is the rising and setting of the sun.[1]

In her commentary on Ruth, A. J. Levine notes that while Ruth vows to cling to her mother-in-law forever, "Naomi never acknowledges her daughter-in-law's fidelity. Following Ruth's speech, she is silent."[2] Does this mean that Naomi does not commit herself to Ruth? If so, why? This should be clearer by the end of our reading. The diverse interpretations of Ruth by women readers are captured by Athalyah Brenner's recent volume *Ruth and Esther: A Feminist Companion to the Bible.*[3] Among these, we find a Native American reader, Laura Donaldson, focusing on Orpah, who returned to her mother's house and her gods, instead of on Ruth, who "succumbed to...hegemonic culture," and who is a "version of the Pocahontas Perplex."[4] Brenner, a Jewish reader, compares the experiences of Ruth with labor immigrants of present-day Israel and finds that Ruth's pledge to Naomi is akin to "a slave's love for his master in Exodus 21:2-6."[5] Judith McKinlay, a descendant of colonial settlers of New Zealand, focuses on Naomi's character as an assimilator,[6] while Musa W. Dube, with her background of orality from Botswana, ignores both Ruth and Naomi and focuses on reading the unpublished letters of Orpah.[7]

These readers attest that Ruth, like any other text, is a mine or a mosaic of social relations, where readers go to make their picks. We find female to male, mother-in-law to daughter-in-law, mother to son, daughter to mother, wife to husband, woman to woman, master to servant, friendship, widowhood, courtship, neighborliness, migrant labor, and international (Moab and Israel) relationships in the book of Ruth. These social relationships are a magnetic force, drawing many readers precisely because they see and relate these social relations to their own social relationships. The book, in other words, divines its readers, confirming or confronting their various social experiences and offering alternatives. In this paper, my focus is on international relationships portrayed by the book of Ruth, through examining Ruth and Naomi as two women who represent two different nations, Moab and Judah, from a divination perspective. First, I give a brief introductory exposition on the biblical text as a divination set. Second, I examine international relations portrayed in Ruth by diagnosing their health and observing the ways in which they seek life-affirming international relationships.

---

[1]Musimbi R. A. Kanyoro, "Biblical Hermeneutics: Ancient Palestine and the Contemporary World," *Review and Expositor: A Quarterly Baptist Theological Journal* 94/3 (1997): 372.

[2]Amy-Jill Levine, "Ruth," in *The Women's Bible Commentary,* ed. Carol A. Newsom and Sharon H. Ringe (Louisville: Westminster/John Knox Press, 1992), 80.

[3]Athalyah Brenner, *Ruth and Esther: A Feminist Companion to the Bible,* 2nd ser. (Sheffield: Sheffield Academic Press, 1999).

[4]Ibid., 140–41.

[5]Ibid., 159.

[6]Ibid., 151–58.

[7]Ibid., 145–50.

The Bible as a Divining Set for Social Relations

For Batswana and other Southern Africans, reading a divination set with a professional diviner-healer was, and still is, tantamount to reading an authoritative book of social life. Diviner-healers are consulted to read divining sets in order to diagnose various problems and to offer solutions to consulting (nonprofessional) readers. Divining sets, which could be composed of various objects such as carved bones, beans, beads, coins, and so forth, are not fixed or closed canons or stories. Rather, each consulting reader (henceforth CR) writes and reads her/his own story with the diviner-healer in the reading session.

More than a century and a half ago when Robert Moffat, a missionary, first read and interpreted the Bible to Batswana, their first response was to regard it as a "talking book" and a divination set.[8] Today the Bible has become one of the divining sets among Batswana African Independent Churches (AICs) faith healers.[9] Many Christian spiritual healers no longer use only the original/ traditional divining sets for their CR.[10] Instead, they also open the Bible and read its stories to diagnose the relationships of CRs, that is, to identify the causes of their problems and to seek the appropriate treatment that will heal their troubled relationships and their physical ailments as a whole. Health among Batswana, and most Southern African communities, is closely associated with social relationships. Illness is synonymous with unhealthy relationships, while health is closely associated with healthy relationships. The process of healing physical illness thus begins with attending to all the social relationships of the CR's life before a medication is offered for obvious physical ailments. One's physical body is thus regarded as part of the larger social body.

With this understanding, professional healer-readers read the Bible to diagnose the existing social relationships and experiences of CRs. They read the Bible to offer solutions for troubled relationships and to encourage the creation and maintenance of life-affirming relations in society as a major therapy for hurting bodies. Reading divining texts in Setswana beliefs is, therefore, about the right to live a whole life, to have healthy and affirmative relationships in society, as well as about the challenge to create and to maintain healthy relationships within both the family and the wider community. Central to the divination framework is the belief that people are interrelated and must stay interconnected and interdependent. Good health means healthy relationships. Ill health means disconnections or unhealthy relationships. As people, we are therefore responsible for our own health and the health of the

---

[8]While there are other forms of divination, through the Spirit or prophecy, visions, and dreams, my paper confines itself to divination that involves reading a text of some sort and in which the diviner remains composed. See Jean Comaroff and John Comaroff, *Of Revelation and Revolution: Christianity, Colonialism and Consciousness in South Africa* (Chicago: University of Chicago Press, 1991), 299.

[9]Musa W. Dube, "Divining the Text For International Relations (Matt. 15:21–28)," in *Transformative Encounters,* ed. Ingrid Rosa Kitzberger (New York and London: Routledge, forthcoming), where I give a more detailed story of the Bible as a divination set among the AICs.

[10]James Amanze, *African Christianity in Botswana* (Gweru: Mambo Press, 1998), 150.

people around us; that is, depending on the relationships we create, we can make ourselves and others ill. It is this ethical thinking that makes Southern African divination a reading of social relations of our world.

Undoubtedly, the healer-reader and the divining set itself are important to the process of reading and healing social relationships. The healer-reader is an ethical social figure who interacts with many troubled CRs. She or he sits down with each one of them to read the divining set in order to establish the source of physical ailments and to offer solutions that heal not only the consulting individual but a whole set of social relations surrounding every reader. On these grounds, a diviner-healer is a central figure in the society.

But how does a divining set expose the circumstances surrounding the relationships of each consulting reader? There are a number of factors at work, namely, the involvement of Divine powers, the set itself, the diviner, and the CR contribution. First, the diviner-healer involves Divine powers by asking them to expose all the healthy and unhealthy relationships of the CRs as s/he opens the divining set. Virtually, godly spirits are asked to come and write the story of the CR. At this stage of prayer, the CR is also involved. S/he is asked to be the first to handle, breathe on, or open the divination set in order to write his/her story on it. Sometimes, s/he is asked to pick a piece from the set that represents him/her. But such a choice is sometimes made by the diviner-healer, using the age and gender of the CR. For example, if someone is a young woman, she would be assigned a piece that symbolizes a youthful female figure.

Second, the divining set itself consists of all the central human relationships. These various relationships are also represented by a number of factors. Each piece in the set represents a particular figure, such as parent, spouse, or sibling with young, elderly, male, and female figures. The carvings also tell the story of the CR. Last and most important, the pattern formed by the pieces of the divining set and the direction they face once it's thrown open, indicate the circumstances surrounding the relationships of the CR. The pattern writes a story about one's relationships with her/his neighbors, parents, spouse, Divine powers, life, and death, indicating which relationships are healthy and which ones are unhealthy.

With the story written down by the divining set, the reading process begins. The diviner-healer walks the consulting reader through each pattern formed and the circumstances revealed by the set, asking the CR to confirm or deny if they represent what s/he knows about his/her life. If the CR is not satisfied, up to three throws of the set will be done, and the CR and the diviner-healer will read the patterns formed and the commentary they are making about the CR's life. If the CR is still not satisfied after the third reading, s/he is free to consult another diviner-healer. The CR is therefore an active and, indeed, an integral participant in the reading and writing of her/his own social story from and into the divining set. In cases where the CR cannot attend the reading, close relatives can consult on her/his behalf. After this reading, the diviner-healer will prescribe a medication for the physical pains that brought the CR to seek a reading, but more often than not, the diviner-healer usually lays responsibility on the CR. The latter is charged with the responsibility of righting the wrongs surrounding the social relationships of his/her life.

The reading of a divining set is thus not as esoteric as laypersons tend to think; neither are the diviner-healer and the divining sets possessors of exclusive knowledge; nor is hidden knowledge brought by the CR. The diviner-healer acknowledges her/his limitations of knowledge by inviting the participation of the Divine powers and the CR. The CR also acknowledges her/his own limitations by visiting the diviner-healer for a reading. Needless to say, the divination set will not write or tell any story until both readers begin to throw it open and read it. Divination is thus a process of the production of social knowledge that demands ethical commitment from all participating readers. It involves the realization that one is socially connected and has a responsibility to create and maintain healthy relationships as well as to avoid those that negate the affirmation of life. Both readers are charged with the responsibility to execute social and physical healing.

These points, I believe, capture most of the major assumptions of divination as an ethical method of reading in Southern Africa. They also expound on how the divining set functions as a social book of life. Reading a divining set is, therefore, an ethical art that entails the production of knowledge. It requires a substantial understanding of social relations and acknowledgment that one must attend to the interconnection and interdependence of all relationships. I am thus drawing on this ancient art as a method of reading that scrutinizes all human relationships and encourages the creation and maintenance of healthy relations, not as a pioneer, but by following in the steps of my regional AICs healer-readers of the Bible.

In what follows, the book of Ruth itself will be my divining set and I am a CR. I regard all other published readers of Ruth as diviner-readers. As a CR, my reading is in communication with published readers of Ruth, though my story of reading the divine set remains my own. However, not all diviner-readers are healer-readers, save those who regard their reading practices as ethical efforts to contribute toward building better interpersonal and international relations. This entails the responsibility to assess the health of all the existing social relations and to encourage the creation of good relations. As a CR, the problems that bring me to read Ruth as a divining set are as follows: (1) I seek to decolonize the production of knowledge in biblical studies that tends to largely use Western ways of conceptualization and analysis. (2) I am committed to an interdisciplinary approach in biblical studies, and I regard my paper as a study that focuses on international relations, Southern African divination systems and practices, and Ruth. (3) My focus on international relations is also largely about my social standing as a citizen of Botswana, indeed of Africa as a whole—I am increasingly aware of the impact of international relations on all aspects of our lives.

Divining Ruth for International Relations

As I throw open the pages of Ruth and peruse its stories, I read it as a divining set that consists of numerous interconnected and interdependent social relations. While it must be underlined that divination focuses on reading all social relationships of the text/divining set to interpret the state of the interconnection of the CR, I am reading the book of Ruth with a particular focus on international relationships. This does not mean that I shall not focus on other social relations, such as gender, race, class, or age, but I shall touch on these insofar as the latter are interconnected with and highlight international relations. Many of these relations have been attended to by a number of Ruth readers. As an African of Botswana CR, I am particularly conscious of international relationships and their impact on economic, political, and social lives as reflected in our historical and present times. Further, since we now live under the shadow of globalization, I am eager to understand the international relationships of the past and present from various divining sets; that is, I am asking: What international relationships emerge from Ruth? What is the state of their interconnection? Are they healthy or unhealthy? If they are good, is the model usable in our present day? If they are not good, what is the cause and what remedy is offered? Although not all these questions will be addressed directly, they nevertheless inform the contours of my divining of Ruth for international relations.

Reading Ruth and Naomi as Moab and Judah: What International Relations Emerge?

In the days when the judges ruled, there was famine in the land, and a certain man of Bethlehem in Judah went to sojourn in the country of Moab, he and his wife and his two sons. The name of the man was Elimelech and the name of his wife Naomi, and the names of his two sons were Mahlon and Chilion; they were Ephrathites from Bethlehem in Judah. They went into the country of Moab and remained there. But Elimelech, the husband of Naomi, died, and she was left with her two sons. These took Moabite wives; the name of one was Orpah and the name of the other Ruth. They lived there about ten years; and both Mahlon and Chilion died, so that the woman was bereft of her two sons and her husband. Then she started with her daughters-in-law to return from the country of Moab, for she heard in the country of Moab that the Lord had visited his people and given them food. So she set out from the place where she was, with her two daughters-in-law, and they went on the way to return to the land of Judah. (1:1–7)

Two countries, Moab and Judah, immediately surface. Judah is reportedly struck by famine, but Moab is seemingly fertile. Elimelech and Naomi and their two sons do what seems to be the reasonable thing: They leave Judah and move to Moab, where there is food, fertility, and life. But their experiences in Moab indicate that such a judgment was a gross miscalculation by Naomi and Elimelech. Soon after their settlement, Elimelech dies. Naomi is left with her two sons, who proceed to marry Moabite women, but their marriages are childless. Soon after, both sons die. The divining set tells us that Naomi "was bereft of her two sons and husband" (1:5b). In addition to Naomi we have two young widows, Ruth and Orpah. Things happen fast in Moab, and they are largely, if not solely, negative. A diviner-reader realizes that the relationship of the people of Judah to Moab is certainly unhealthy: It is characterized by infertility and death. Irony is glaring in this divining set, for while at first it seemed that Moab was the land of fertility and Judah of famine, it turns out to be the other way around. Why? Is this a statement about Moab? This should become clear as the story continues.

But just then hope rises in the skies of Naomi, for she hears "that the Lord had visited her people and given them food" (1:6). Since Moab had dealt bitterly with Naomi, it only seemed reasonable for her to return to her people and land. Naomi insists that her daughters-in-law must remain in Moab, for she cannot promise them any more husbands. Her words reflect the patriarchal setup of the time, that women's survival depended on marriage. Orpah pays heed to Naomi's words and returns, but Ruth insists on going with her mother-in-law.

The journey back to Judah and the insistence of Ruth to accompany Naomi is central to reading the international relationship of Moab and Judah. In the return of Naomi, another woman takes a journey to a foreign country. Ruth travels to Judah through marriage relations, just as Naomi traveled to Moab. Similarly, Ruth represents Moab just as Naomi represents Judah. The experiences of Ruth in Judah and of Naomi in Moab will highlight the international relationships of Moab and Judah.

Ruth the Moabite in Judah

The story of Ruth's journey to Judah is closely modeled on Naomi's journey to Moab. Although the text does not say that Moab was struck by famine, this is evident in the three deaths and the childlessness of the marriages. This famine drives them to move to Judah. Further, the good news of food in Judah precedes their journey back. Some readers may say this was not Ruth's motivation for taking the journey to Judah, rather, that she traveled because of her commitment to her mother-in law. Her reason is not so different from the reason behind Naomi's journey to Moab. Naomi's initial journey to Moab is not her own decision or initiative. Instead, the text says a certain man sojourned to the country of Moab because of famine in Judah, and Naomi, his wife, came along (1:1). Both Naomi and Ruth, therefore, travel to and live in foreign countries through marriage relationships rather than through choice.

Naomi and Ruth arrive safely in Judah. When "they came to Bethlehem the whole town was stirred…and the women said, 'Is this Naomi?' She said to them, 'Do not call me Naomi [Pleasant]; call me Mara [Bitter], for the Almighty has dealt very bitterly with me. I went away full, and the Lord has brought me back empty" (1:19–21). While the words of Naomi summarize her experiences in Moab, they also make a statement about Judah. That is, even in famine one's hands are full in Judah, while in Moab one is wrapped in famine even when it seems there is fertility/food. What are the experiences of Ruth in Judah? Will Ruth, a foreigner, eat from the fertility of the land, or is this another famine disguised in fertility such as what Naomi found in Moab? Will she get involved in another childless marriage? Will Naomi lose even what she brought with her, including Ruth? Will their experiences be pleasant or bitter? Basically, the similarities and differences of Naomi's and Ruth's relationships with Judah tell us about the international relations of Moab and Judah.

Is Judah Pleasant or Bitter to Ruth the Moabite?

In 1:22, the divining set signals Ruth's positive relationship with the land of Judah by stating that "Naomi and Ruth the Moabite…came to Jerusalem at the beginning of the barley harvest." The beginning of harvest is a season of possessing the fruits of the land. Reading further, we hear Ruth taking the initiative by asking Naomi if she could "go to the field and glean among the ears of grain" (2:2). Naomi allows her to, and Ruth happens "to come to the part of the field belonging to Boaz, who was the relative of Elimelech" (2:4). Boaz finds Ruth gleaning in his field, and he encourages her to keep her "eyes upon the field they are reaping," and if she is thirsty, he encourages her "to go and drink what the young men have drawn" and to continue gleaning in his field until the end of harvest (2:9). Ruth, thankful for his kindness, asks, "Why have I found favor in your eyes, that you should take notice of me, when I am a foreigner?" (2:10). Boaz points to Ruth's commitment to Naomi and commends her for leaving her parents, land, and people. Boaz then pronounces that Ruth will be rewarded by the Lord God of Israel under whose wings Ruth has "come to take refuge" (2:11–12). Ruth is invited not only to harvest and drink but also to eat her fill until she takes away some leftovers for Naomi. Ruth is also protected in Judah as Boaz repeatedly instructs that she should not be molested, "reproached," or "rebuked" (2:9–15). So far Ruth is not Mara in Judah, she is Pleasant.

In Ruth's pleasant experiences, the divining set indicates a notable difference between Moab and Judah. That is, in Moab the story remained mum about the riches/fruits of the country. Although the very movement of Naomi's family to Moab is associated with famine in Judah, the text says nothing about the harvests and waters of Moab. As a CR, I do not see Naomi harvesting in the fields of Moab or drinking from the waters of its land. I do not see Naomi eating its food (if she did, it must have been fairly poisonous, enough to eliminate all the members of her family!). Rather, I see Naomi losing what she brought to Moab and returning to Judah "empty." Another significant difference indicated in the divining set is the role of the Divine powers in the lands of Judah and Moab. If Moab had food and water, the divining set not only refrains from speaking explicitly about them but also does not state the sources of its fertility. In Judah, however, the Divine role is explicitly recognized as the prime mover over its people and those in the land. The return of food in Judah (1:6), the experiences of Naomi in Moab (1:19–21), and the protection of Ruth (2:12–13), for example, are associated with the Lord God of Israel.

In Moab the active role of the Divine powers is scarce or even absent. I do hear Naomi instructing her daughters-in-law to return to their mothers' houses and evoking Divine blessings upon them (1:7–9). Her words, however, highlight a number of things. First, I see the absence of the Lord God of Israel with Naomi's family in Moab. Naomi herself states that the hand of the Lord God was "against" her and "dealt bitterly" with her in Moab such that she returned to Judah "empty." Second, I realize that although Orpah returned "to her mother and her gods" (1:15), thus indicating that Divine powers existed in Moab, the divining set does not ever say or indicate that Naomi came under the refuge and blessing of the Divine powers of Moab. Third, although Orpah returns to her mother and gods, that is, back under their protection, I am not told her story: Nothing is said about how she enjoyed the harvests, the waters, and the blessings of the gods of Moab. The silence of Orpah's story, however, is not really silent, for it leaves me with Naomi's experience in Moab to interpret her life and land. In Orpah's untold story, Moab remains the land of famine as attested by death, childless marriages, and lack of godly powers at work. The portrait is a major statement about Moab that, as we shall see, also indicates its relationship with Judah.

Following the story of Ruth and Naomi as a narrative of Judah and Moab, we see the two women cultivate their space further. Ruth moves from gleaning in Boaz's fields to harvesting barley in his house, at the advice of Naomi. She finds him having eaten, having drunk, and sleeping next to a "heap of grain" (3:7). Boaz is in the midst of pleasure and plenty. Ruth sleeps at his feet (private parts), and when Boaz wakes up, she asks him to "spread his skirt over her" since he is the next of kin. Just as in the fields, Boaz pronounces more blessings on Ruth: "May you be blessed by the Lord, my daughter; you have made this last kindness greater than the first, in that you have not gone after young men" (3:10). With this move, Ruth has successfully proposed a marriage relationship to Boaz. He treats her with respect and promises to consult with other relatives of Elimelech who may be interested in marrying her. Boaz then sends Ruth home early with more barley so that she should not return to her mother-in-law "empty-handed" (3:17).

Boaz begins to negotiate his marriage to Ruth right away. He convenes a legally witnessed meeting with the closest relative who might be interested in Ruth, but Boaz does not openly discuss marriage. Rather, he negotiates about a piece of land that belonged to Elimelech and asks the man if he wishes to redeem it (4:1–6). The man agrees. Boaz then informs him that "the day you buy the field from the hand of Naomi, you are also buying Ruth the Moabite, the widow of the dead in order to restore the name of the dead to his inheritance" (6:5). It hit me unexpectedly to see Boaz making such a direct connection of the land and the woman, Ruth. The man withdraws. Perhaps he was also surprised. Boaz then openly declares responsibility for the widow of Mahlon. Those who are gathered accept Boaz's move, declaring a blessing on the marriage and saying that Ruth, like Leah, Rachel, and Tamar, should build the house of Israel, prosper, and bear children that will make Boaz outstanding. The divining set quickly confirms that a son, Obed, who becomes "the father of Jesse, the father of David" is born (4:17).

Ruth, who left Moab in order to cling to Naomi, marries Boaz. Is this betrayal? The narrative gets even more interesting, for just when we think Naomi has disappeared, when we think Ruth's pledge to her mother-in-law cannot contain the strong marriage commitment to another woman, especially since she finally marries a man, the text reasserts its earlier perspective:

> So Boaz took Ruth and she became his wife; and he went in to her, and the LORD gave her conception and she bore a son. Then the women said to Naomi, "Blessed be the Lord, who has not left you this day without next of kin; and may his name be renowned in Israel! He shall be to you a restorer of life and a nourisher of your old age; for your daughter-in-law who loves you, who is more to you than seven sons, has borne him." Then Naomi took the child and laid him in her bosom, and became his nurse. And the women of the neighborhood gave him a name, saying, "A son has been born to Naomi." (4:13–17)

This latter part of the story adds to our divination for international relations of Judah and Moab. As a CR I ask myself this question: What makes Ruth, a young woman married to a young man in Moab, childless and widowed while in Moab? She is not permanently infertile, because after she moves to Judah, she marries an older man and immediately brings forth a child. Medically, a number of good answers could be advanced, such as that Mahlon was infertile. Whatever medical explanations we may advance, they won't be different from the fact that the divining set portrays him as an impotent young man with a very short span of life. But an older and fertile man, Elimelech, also comes to a sudden end in Moab while his age mate, Boaz, remains alive in Judah, proceeds to marry the young widow of his son and to father a son who brings forth an important descendant–David. The question, however, is whether this tells us something about the international relationship of Judah and Moab. As I probe the divining set a little bit more, I am quite struck by the words of Boaz when he declares his intention to marry Ruth. He says, "Ruth the Moabite, the widow of Mahlon, I have bought for my wife, to perpetuate the name of the dead in his inheritance, that the name of the dead may not be cut off from his native land." What a striking event that Ruth is bought! Of course, it is not for her own gain, but for perpetuating Mahlon in his land, which is Judah. She is bought to serve the life of Mahlon in Judah, to "build Israel"–Mahlon is not dead! Hence, we realize that the son is born to Naomi, not to Ruth or to both of them.

The reasons given for Ruth's marriage to Boaz lead me back to the divining set and to scrutinize the relationships surrounding the marriages that occur in Moab. Evidently, marriages occur in both nations, but the difference is in their fruits. In Moab, Ruth and Orpah's marriages are childless while Naomi loses her sons and her husband. Barrenness and bitterness glare in Moab. In Judah, Ruth's marriage is immediately fruitful. A son is born, who becomes an ancestor of David's. Ruth, therefore, not only has access to the fruits of the land but is also fruitful herself. She can fittingly call herself Pleasant, Naomi. With these explanations given for Ruth's marriage to Boaz, I am in a position to glean the reasons for barrenness and death in Moab: Mahlon, Elimelech, and Chilion cannot inherit in the land of Moab, or by that land. They are cut off, for it is not their native place. In Judah they are reinstated, for it is their native land. Ruth's move to Judah, her clinging to Naomi, now appears under a different light as she becomes a piece of property bought and used for the perpetuation of Mahlon. Here I tend to agree with those diviner-readers who note that Naomi does not commit herself to Ruth's pledge, signaling that this is not a relationship of equals. It also brings me closer to diviner-readers who hold that Ruth's pledge to Naomi rings with the tones of a slave-to-master relationship rather than expressing mutual love between women or two friends. This, unfortunately, connotes the relationship of Judah to Moab.

Conclusion: What Healing Befits Our International Relations?

At first reading of the divining set, something is quite attractive in the experiences of Ruth in Judah. She arrives as a powerless foreigner with no economic power, gleaning behind the servants (2:3, 7), and a childless young widow exposed to danger (2:9, 22). Yet she is allowed to take her own initiatives in the midst of danger, to explore opportunities and to succeed (2:1–2; 3:9). Further, Ruth takes advice and guidance (3:1–5) from the natives of Judah. It is particularly gratifying to note that Ruth is lovingly protected, given respect, blessed, and allowed to retain her identity as "Ruth the Moabite" (2:6; 4:5, 10). On the whole, Judah is a land of plenty, of blessings and of success, where pleasant relationships can be built. Indeed, in Judah barley seems to be everywhere, and Ruth has access to it.

But then as a CR, I am left aghast by the experiences of Naomi in Moab. Here I am confronted by silence, irony, death, and barrenness, which, as said earlier, instructs the reader to avoid Moab or embrace it at a great price of disaster and death. This sharp contrast of lands of blessings and of curses does not speak well on the international relations of Judah and Moab. Given this sharp contrast, the story of Naomi in Moab makes the wonderful story of Ruth in Judah unusable as a model of liberating interdependence between nations, for one can only embrace the story of Ruth in Judah by subscribing to the characterization of Moab as a godforsaken land whose resources (Ruth) can be tapped for the well-being of Judah.[11] The resources of Judah (Elimelech and his two boys), however, cannot be tapped for Moab, hence their death and barrenness. It becomes clear that Ruth (Moab) is a wife to Naomi (Judah), that she is the one who leaves her lands, her people, her gods, and, finally, bears a son to Naomi. Theirs is a patriarchal marriage—which is a relationship of unequal subjects. Ruth/Moab is a wife, the subordinate one who leaves her interests to serve the interests of Naomi/Judah, her husband.[12] Not surprisingly, she bears a child to Naomi/Judah, not to herself and Naomi. Ruth is acknowledged for serving the interests of Naomi/Judah: The child or gain is not hers nor that of Moab, her land.

The divining set, therefore, indicates that the relationship of the two nations is not healthy. It is not a relationship of liberating interdependence, but of subordinates and dominators. It does not say that Moab can equally benefit from the resources of Judah (Elimelech, Mahlon, and Chilion). According to the divining set, the root of ill health emanates from Judah's refusal to recognize the Divine powers at work in Moab. Moab is regarded as a godforsaken land, a cursed land, where Israelites cannot bloom. Judah is its opposite. This ill health is responsible for the death and barrenness in the book of Ruth.

Who then suffers from the unhealthy relationship of Moab and Judah? Moabites or both nations? Undoubtedly, Moab suffers more, but the suffering affects both nations, precisely because the two nations are interconnected. Both nations need to acknowledge and develop a relationship of liberating interdependence. The latter describes a relationship where both subjects are fairly and equally treated for their own good. At the moment, Judah attempts to deny that it can, and needs to, depend on Moab, given that the latter is nothing but a land of death and disaster. The denial is a futile exercise because it is self-evident. For example, the journey of Elimelech to Moab in the wake of famine in Judah attests to the fact that even the strongest nations, even those who regard themselves as blessed lands of plenty, need the support of other nations, despite their tendencies to deny the relationships. Further, Ruth the Moabite gives birth to a son whose line begets David, an outstanding figure in the history of Israel, thus resonating with Leah, Rachel, and Tamar, other non-Israelite women who contributed significantly to Israel. This, however, is not a relationship of liberating interdependence, because Judah is unwilling to contribute equally to Moab. Judah rejects Moab's right to equally benefit from their relationship—as indicated by the deaths of three Israelite

---

[11]The art of portraying the Other negatively is an ideology of domination, which has been shown by both gender and postcolonial studies. The dominator (colonizer or patriarchy) characterizes its victims negatively in order to justify the exploitation of the latter. What one reads in Ruth compares very well with the portrait of African people and land in Joseph Conrad's *Heart of Darkness* (New York: Columbia University Press, 1999). While the land is a deadly wilderness, it still holds many profits for the colonizer.

[12]The identification of lands with women is generally recognized as carrying an ideology of domination. But it becomes more pronounced in postcolonial literature, where foreign lands or targeted colonies are often represented by a woman and the colonizer by a man, as in the tale of Pocahontas.

men and the portrayal of Moab as, Ruth, a wife who must be subordinated. To build a relationship of liberating interdependence, however, demands that their interconnection be openly encouraged—built to be fair to both—and recognized as the core of their existence and survival, for nations are not islands. Nations are never "pure" or "independent," but interdependent, interconnected, and multicultural.[13] This recognition calls for embracing the responsibility to create and maintain healthy relations as an indispensable medication in healing our world and in proclaiming life and success within and without our nations.

---

[13]See Edward Said, *Culture and Imperialism* (New York: Alfred Knopf, 1992), 336.

Is Hokmah an Israelite Goddess, and What Should We Do about It?

David Penchansky

In Proverbs, Hokmah (Lady Wisdom) emerges as a full-blown literary character. She first appears on the street corner, urging young men to listen to her (Prov. 1:20–33). She will later invite them to her house for a feast (Prov. 9:1–11).[1] In Proverbs 8 Hokmah declares herself, discloses herself, and gives her history. The poem begins with that same street invitation.[2] She speaks of her attributes, how she only says truthful and righteous things. She gives life and counsel to kings.

She presents herself as an Israelite goddess. This, of course, runs counter to the prevailing notion that the Hebrew Bible affirms that only one God exists. I suggest that contemporary interpretations of the Hokmah figure in Proverbs are dramatically skewed by monotheistic beliefs and by the modern notion that the biblical religion progresses from belief in many gods to belief in only one. This progression (it is believed) constitutes an improvement, or even a culmination in religious development.

The Presence of Hokmah

Hokmah in Mythic Time

I will focus particularly on the last third of Hokmah's self-declaration, found in Proverbs 8:22–31. Here Hokmah brings us to the cosmic realm by use of such words as *me'az*, literally "from then," meaning "that distant time," ("of long ago" in NRSV) and *'olam*, defined as "eternity," "past age" ("ages

---

[1]The "house" might be a temple, which would suggest Hokmah as a goddess with her own cult. I am grateful to my colleague Professor Corrine Patton for this insight.

[2]In direct competition with another woman also inviting young men to her house, called in Proverbs the Strange Woman or the Foreign Woman (Prov. 2:16–19; 5:3–14). For references to "the evil woman" (6:24–35; 7:6–23), and the "foolish woman" (9:13), see Claudia Camp, "Woman Wisdom as Root Metaphor: A Theological Consideration," in *The Listening Heart: Essays in Wisdom and the Psalms in Honor of Roland E. Murphy,* ed. Kenneth G. Hoglund et al. (Sheffield: Sheffield Academic Press, 1987), 71–72.

ago" in NRSV). Hokmah takes us back in time, further back than "once upon a time," all the way to the beginning, to mythic time. Mythic time, inhabited by gods and primal objects, is the time of origins. In this poem Hokmah shares the stage with *Tehom,* "the deep, the primal waters," perhaps the uncreated raw stuff of the universe. The *Tehom* looms large in this description; although created subsequent to the birth of Hokmah, *Tehom* is compared to Hokmah at every opportunity. "I was born when there was no *Tehom,*" or we could say, "I was born long before *Tehom* was created." *Tehom* might be regarded as the blank slate upon which YHWH inscribes the universe. She also precedes the mountains, the heavens, and the fountains, a veritable Jungian paradise of archetypes.

Hokmah claims priority over all these others. She says, for instance, "Before the mountains had been shaped/Before the hills…I was there" (8:25, 27). Also, she witnessed the creation of all these: "When he established the fountains of the deep…then I was beside him [YHWH]" (8:28, NRSV).

Hokmah's Origin

The poet uses three verbs to describe Hokmah's beginnings, and they seem qualitatively different from the origination verbs of the other primal objects. Hokmah is "acquired,"[3] "birthed,"[4] and "poured out."[5] YHWH produces her as mother and father. A later tradition (Sir. 24:3) suggests that she proceeds out of YHWH's mouth, as Athena emerged from Zeus' head.[6] Lang says it best:

[3]George Landes notes regarding the word *qnny,* "the meaning 'to beget, produce, create,' would seem to be earlier than the much more common 'to buy, acquire, possess'" in "Creation Tradition in Proverbs 8:22–31 and Gen. 1," in *A Light unto My Path: Old Testament Studies in Honor of Jacob M. Myers,* ed. H. N. Bream (Philadelphia: Temple University, 1974), 281. Mitchell Dahood also translates this as "begot" in "Proverbs 8:22–31. Translation and Commentary," *Catholic Biblical Quarterly* 30:4 (October 1968): 512–21. R. N. Whybray concurs, saying, "Although there is only one word that strictly means sexual birth in the passage…the other two verbs have alternative meaning that include sexual birth. *q-n-h* is used in some places to mean 'give birth,' as when Eve says she has 'gotten' a child from the Lord. And 'set up' *nasak* can mean to have been 'woven' together in the womb," *Proverbs: Based on the Revised Standard Version,* The New Century Bible Commentary (Grand Rapids: Eerdmans, 1994), 131. See also Helmer Ringgren, *Word and Wisdom: Studies in the Hypostatization of Divine Qualities and Function in the Ancient Near East* (Lund: Hakan Ohlssons Boktryckeri, 1947), 101–2.

[4]Bernhard Lang makes the observation, "She is not the product of the artisan's skill, nor has she been conquered in battle to be made part of the ordered world. Rather, she has been *born* or brought forth by birth. Wisdom says of herself, 'I was born *(holati),*'an expression used to refer to human birth *(Monotheism and the Prophetic Minority: An Essay in Biblical History and Sociology* (Sheffield: Almond Press, 1983), 63.

[5]Also from Landes (281), "the verb *nskty,* if the Masoretic pointing is correct, refers to a creation by 'outpouring,' apparently a very archaic idea in the ancient Near East, though used only here in that sense in the Old Testament." Lang agrees in *Wisdom and the Book of Proverbs: An Israelite Goddess Redefined* (New York: Pilgrim Press, 1986), 63. William Foxwell Albright suggests that the word refers "primarily to the outpouring of generative semen," in "The Goddess of Life and Wisdom," *American Journal of Semitic Languages* 36 (1920): 286.

[6]Lang observes, "Within religious history there are several gods without mothers, and Wisdom may belong to these. The Greek goddess Athena, for instance, is the daughter of Zeus, but she has no mother…Similarly, the Egyptian god Thoth…sprang from the head of Seth. Such paradoxical phenomena are labeled 'male pregnancy' and 'male birth,' ideas not entirely foreign to the Bible. One can refer to the creation myth according to which Eve was taken from within a man's, Adam's, body" (Lang, *Wisdom,* 64–65).

While the creation of the material world can be referred to in terms of craftsmanship and building activities…Wisdom's creation must be spoken of in personal terms: Wisdom was "begotten," "fashioned" (as in the womb), and eventually "born." Gods are not created as the world is created; they are begotten and born, not made. There is a qualitative difference between gods and the realm of the created.[7]

Rather than portraying Hokmah as a mother-goddess, YHWH himself becomes the birth parent: "The process of Yahweh's conception, bearing and birth of Wisdom is here depicted without reservation."[8]

Hokmah's Activity

She plays, frolics, and rejoices. The *Tehom,* by contrast, is inscribed, the mountains are shaped, and the heavens are established. The fountains abound in water. These others function as *things* for Hokmah to admire. Two verbs describe Hokmah's activity. She "plays," from the verb *sqh;* and she "delights," *sh'shu'ym.* She declares herself a "daily delight,"[9] "playing before him always." Michael Fox observes, "Wisdom does not seem to directly affect the course of events…Wisdom fills her role less by doing than by *being.*"[10] He goes on to say, "The emphasis on Wisdom's play in vv. 30–31 seems to be a deliberate refutation of the notion that wisdom had an active productive role in the work of creation."[11] She plays in the created world and delights in humanity. As Claudia Camp observes, "No oppressive order, not even Yahweh's, is secure where children play, lovers meet, and life comes forth."[12]

'Amon—The Mystery Word

Hokmah employs one key word to describe herself. The word is *'amon,* and occurs in this form only here in the Hebrew Bible.[13] This word, by its position in the poem of Proverbs 8, must be at the center of every interpretation. But *'amon* resists reduction to one plain meaning. Terrien observes, "The precise meaning of the notoriously difficult word *'amon* defies demonstration."[14] The main interpretations "require the supplying of vowels different from those of the Masoretic tradition."[15] The earliest readers of this poem did not uniformly

---

[7]Ibid., 77.

[8]Claudia Camp, *Wisdom and the Feminine in the Book of Proverbs* (Decatur, Ga.: Almond Press, 1985).

[9]It is usually translated "daily *his* delight," but "his" is not in the Hebrew and is not required by the context.

[10]Michael Fox, "Ideas of Wisdom in Proverbs 1–9," *Journal of Biblical Literature* 116:4 (1997): 629.

[11]Fox " *'Amon* Again," *Journal of Biblical Literature* 115:4 (1996): 700.

[12]Camp, "Woman Wisdom as Root Metaphor," 61.

[13]"The passage in Jeremiah 52:15, plural, but its identification is controversial and an unreliable precedent"–so Samuel Terrien, "The Play of Wisdom: Turning Point in Biblical Theology," *Horizons in Biblical Theology* 3 (1981): 135; see also Michael V. Fox, " *'Amon* Again," 699.

[14]Terrien, 135. R. B. Y. Scott agrees, stating, "From an early date there was much uncertainty about the vocalization and meaning of this important word" ("Wisdom in Creation: The *'amon* in Prov. 8:20," *Vetus Testamentum* 9 [1960]: 215.)

[15]Scott, *Proverbs and Ecclesiastes,* Anchor Bible Commentary (Garden City, N.Y.: Doubleday, 1965), 72.

translate it. The first witnesses, the Septuagint and the Wisdom of Solomon, translate it (or interpret it) as "master workman," "architect." But early on, some of the rabbis argued for "nursling, beloved child."[16] Bernhard Lang translates Proverbs 8:31, "I was beside him as an infant whom he (the Creator) has nursed."[17]

A third interpretation of this word has gained acceptance in the last few years. While using the definition "master architect," *YHWH* becomes the subject: "I was there with him, [YHWH] the Master architect."[18]

"Beloved child" better fits the context. In these verses Hokmah is born. She delights and plays. A "little child" does such things. Hokmah does not create or design the universe, and so "Master architect" would seem out of place. The very ambiguity of the term, however, maintains Hokmah's independence. Divergent portraits of Hokmah contend over this word, which allows for a fluidity of interpretation. These are only the most widely held of the theories.[19]

The Problem of Hokmah

The Problem Introduced

The writer of Proverbs 8 identifies Hokmah as an Israelite goddess. Whether she makes the universe or simply observes its creation, she remains a bone in the throat of those who insist that Israelite ideology is uniformly monotheistic. Carole Fontaine observes:

> The unanswered question of this scholarly reconstruction is the manner in which Israelite sages would have borrowed material from traditions so roundly condemned elsewhere in the canon.[20]

At first glance, Proverbs 8 is a relatively straightforward passage. As I read it, a female figure in a self-declaratory speech claims divine origin in the mythic past, playing and rejoicing before YHWH as he created the world. It appears that YHWH has created the world for his little child's entertainment, to give her delight and joy. But this poem, nine verses, has generated a nearly overwhelming amount of controversy in the history of interpretation. Why?

---

[16]This might not be a translation, but a deliberate midrashic misreading (Whybray, *Proverbs*, 134).

[17]Lang, *Wisdom*, 66.

[18]Dahood is one who has taken this position (513).

[19]Lang (*Wisdom*, 65) gives an overview of the basic interpretations of *'amon:*

1. I was at his side as an *infant.*
2. I was at his side as a *confidant.*
3. I was at his side as *master builder* (or architect).

Hartmut Gese gives an interesting spin on the translation: "When he (God) marked out the foundations of the earth,/then I was with him *on his lap*/and I was daily his delight" (*Essays on Biblical Theology* [Minneapolis: Augsburg, 1981], 31).

[20]Carole Fontaine, *Traditional Sayings in the Old Testament: A Contextual Study* (Sheffield: Almond Press, 1982), 502. Burton L. Mack quotes Hans-Friedrich Weiss to the effect that "the figure of Wisdom is a 'stranger'" in Judaism, "which really cannot be harmonized with Jewish thought" (*Wisdom and Hebrew Epic: Ben Sirah's Hymn in Praise of the Fathers* [Chicago: University of Chicago Press, 1985], 51). Perhaps though, that is because we do not fully understand the intricacies of Jewish thought.

I am struck by how frequently Hokmah appears in the ancient literature. Sirach 1:1–10; 24:1–3, the Wisdom of Solomon 7:1–9:18, and Baruch 3:9–4:4, all expand on the description of Hokmah in Proverbs 8.[21] They identify her as the embodiment of the Torah. The rabbis continue the tradition and see her as the Shekinah, the presence of God. The Christians change her gender and she becomes the Christ, through whom all things came into existence, firstborn of creation, who was before all things, before the foundation of the world, begotten, not made.[22]

Camp correctly observes that Hokmah engages in

> a virtual usurpation of Yahweh's prerogatives, e.g., as giver of life and death (8:35–36); as the source of legitimate government (8:15–16); as the one to be sought after and called (1:28); as one who loves and is to be loved (8:17); and as the giver of security (1:33) and wealth (8:15–16).[23]

As Scott puts it, "She speaks for herself and with her own authority, like a goddess."[24]

One therefore finds within the very heart of the Hebrew Bible at least this one passage that explicitly challenges the Israelite theology of "radical monotheism," which Bernhard Lang calls "Yahweh-aloneism."[25] "Yahweh-aloneism" is the belief that only one God exists, and all other gods are delusional. That certainly is a *kind* of monotheism, but there are other varieties, many of which allow for the existence of spiritual beings other than YHWH.[26] Larry Hurtado has observed:

---

[21]Scott provides a concise summary of later occurrences of the Hokmah figure: "The Wisdom of Solomon speaks of 'Wisdom, the fashioner of all things' (7:22 EV), as 'an associate in His works' (8:4), and as 'fashioner of all that exists' (7:6), Philo (*de Sacerdot 5*) says that 'the universe was fabricated' through the agency of the Logos-Wisdom; the same thought appears in John 1:3, 'through him all things came to be'; in Col. 1:15–16, 'the firstborn of all creation, for in him all things were created'; and in Heb. 1:3, 'through whom also he created the world.' The influence of Proverbs 8 on these passages, and consequently on later Christological doctrine, is evident" (Scott, *Proverbs,* 69–70).

[22]"The definition in the Nicene Creed, 'begotten not made,' may have rested in part on the birth metaphor in vss. 24–25 and the translation 'little child' for *'amon* in vs. 30," Scott, *Proverbs,* 73. See also the comments of Roland Murphy in *Proverbs,* Word Biblical Commentary (Nashville: Thomas Nelson, 1998), 281. See also Scott, "Wisdom in Creation," 215.

[23]Camp, *Proverbs,* 28.

[24]Scott, *Proverbs,* 39.

[25]Lang, *Wisdom,* 116–25.

[26]Lang quotes Koch saying, "The deity, not polymorphous but manifold, approaches man in various extensions, refractions or modes, however one may call this concept. The poet's monotheism is not monolithic. Shaddai is one of these specific refractions, one aspect of God which relates to the human individual" (Bernhard Lang, *Monotheism and the Prophetic Minority: An Essay in Biblical History and Sociology* [Sheffield: Almond Press, 1983], 51). In another book, Lang asserts, "It is evident that the notion of a 'goddess of the king,' which was part of a widespread royal ideology, was also familiar in Israel and played a part in shaping the image of wisdom in Proverbs 8. In fact, Wisdom must have been the name, or one of the names, of the Israelite kings' divine patroness" (Lang, *Wisdom,* 61). Camp suggests, "The female imagery operated in such a way as to make this a viable religious symbol in an era without a king. Far from being a peculiar or foreign element, it provided key points of linkage to both ethos and world view, creating one form of symbolic substitute for the monarch" (Camp, *Proverbs,* 282).

It is clear that ancient Jews often envisioned a host of heavenly beings, including powerful figures likened to God and closely associated with God. But does this plurality of heavenly beings indicate that Graeco-Roman Jewish religion was not monotheistic, or does it rather indicate that historical expression of monotheistic commitment may have been fully compatible with acknowledging important heavenly beings complementary in some way to, but also distinguished from, the "one God"?[27]

Raphael Patai observes:

In view of the general human, psychologically determined predisposition to believe in and worship goddesses, it would be strange if the Hebrew-Jewish religion, which flourished for centuries in a region of intensive goddess cults, had remained immune to them. Yet this precisely is the picture one gets when one views Hebrew religion through the polarizing prisms of mosaic legislation and prophetic teaching.[28]

Hokmah is such a being. But recent interpretations of Proverbs 8 flee from the multitheistic implications of this Israelite goddess. They either deny that she was a true Israelite, or they make her something other than a goddess.

Solutions to the Problem

Whybray states unequivocally, "Whatever remnants of polytheism may be detected in these chapters, there is no question that the text in its present form is monotheistic."[29] How various scholars come to this (strained!) conclusion comes next for consideration.

Some claim that she is not an Israelite, for instance, because she is a reflection of Israel's distant past when the people were pagans.[30] But there is no indication that this passage or its sensibilities are preexilic. This conclusion is reached by assuming the postexilic period to have been radically monotheistic; thus, the figure of Hokmah must be earlier. However, if one

---

[27]Larry W. Hurtado, *One God, One Lord: Early Christian Devotion and Ancient Jewish Monotheism* [Philadelphia: Fortress Press, 1988], 7. He goes on to note, "Graeco-Roman Jews seem to have been quite ready to accommodate various divine beings...Part of the problem in estimating what Jews made of heavenly beings other than God 'ontologically' is that scholars tend to employ distinctions and assumptions formed by Christian theological/philosophical tradition" (21).

[28]Raphael Patai, *The Hebrew Goddess* (New York: Ktav, 1967), 18.

[29]Whybray, *Proverbs*, 27.

[30]Although most date Proverbs 1–9 in the postexilic period, Lang takes a contrary position: "Contrary to common opinion, the first nine chapters of Proverbs are not a late, perhaps fourth-century preface that attempts to make the rest of the book sound more religious. These chapters are not only much older, but also form an independent work with a preface...and conclusion" (Lang, *Wisdom*, 4). Scott sees this poem as a remnant of an earlier time: "The vivid personification reflects the imagery of older mythological material" (Scott, *Proverbs*, 39). Judith M. Hadley dates the passage thus: "Prov. i–ix seems to defy all attempts at a precise dating. Suggestions range from the early monarchic period to the early post-exilic era, with perhaps the majority of scholars placing it in the fifth to fourth centuries BCE," ("Wisdom and the Goddess," in *Wisdom in Ancient Israel: Essays in Honour of J. A. Emerton*, ed. J. Day [Cambridge: Cambridge University Press, 1995]), 239.

questions the exclusive dominance of the Yahweh-alone party in Israel, the argument for a preexilic pagan connection becomes circular. Lang claims that the later editors did not understand the text in this older way:

A polytheistic reading of the poems on Wisdom may help us to understand their original meaning, but misses the intention of the editors who are committed monotheists.[31]

He believes that a later monotheistic writer has demythologized the polytheistic references. He privileges the later reading as more characteristically Israelite.

Others say Hokmah is not Israelite because she is foreign, coming from (it has been suggested) Sumer, Egypt, Canaan, Babylon, or Greece.[32] Certainly there is foreign influence in Hokmah. She shares pedigree and holds much in common with many other female divine figures. However, there is no reason to contend that genuine Israelite figures must be hermetically separate from commonly held notions of the Divine. I contend rather that Hokmah inhabits a universe in which YHWH, the Israelite chief god, reigns supreme. She is Israelite by any measure, *unless* one imposes Yahweh-aloneism as the chief standard of Israelite identity.

Finally, some claim that she is not a true Israelite because only the common people believed in her. She was not part of the "official" monotheistic religion. However, the distinction between the "official" religion of the leaders and the "popular" religion of the uneducated masses must be questioned. Is not this argument a collaboration with the Yahweh-aloneists to silence rival Israelite voices? Berlinerblau suggests:

An elitist literati may *intentionally misrepresent* the religious beliefs of all other groups. Thus, the particular ideology of the literati may have been so "interest-bound" with the hegemonic perpetuation of monotheistic Yahwist, that their views on the religion of other classes and groups will inevitably be pejorative and misleading.[33]

Whereas some state that Hokmah was not Israelite, others assert that she is Israelite but not a goddess. Among those who accept Hokmah's Israelite pedigree but deny her divinity, I isolate two positions. She is frequently called a hypostatization, an embodiment of one of the attributes of God.[34] Hokmah's distinctiveness and separateness from YHWH make this position difficult to justify from the text of Proverbs 8. She is beside him, with him, bringing him

---

[31]Lang, *Prophecy,* 53.

[32]See John S. Kloppenborg, "Isis and Sophia in the Book of Wisdom," *Harvard Theological Review* 75:1 (1982): 61. Camp observes, "In rather unabashed fashion, Wisdom takes over imagery associated with Ma'at, Astarte-Ishtar, Anat and royal goddesses, sharing some of these features with the strange woman" (in "Woman Wisdom as Root Metaphor," 61).

[33]Jacques Berlinerblau, "The 'Popular Religion' Paradigm in Old Testament Research: A Sociological Critique," *Journal for the Study of the Old Testament* 60 (1993): 13–14.

[34]Ringgren was the first to describe Hokmah as hypostasis. Hadley notes: "The term is apparently taken over from Christology, where it is used in an attempt to provide some degree of individuality while still maintaining a monotheistic theology" (235).

delight. Hypostasis does exist in the Hebrew Bible in places where an attribute of YHWH is linguistically separated from YHWH and given a quasi-independent existence. For example, "goodness and mercy" in Psalm 23, some depictions of justice *(mishpat)* and righteousness *(tsedekah)* are attributes of God, but are described with a kind of separateness. Regarding Hokmah, Roland Murphy adds:

> There is no journey in the Bible comparable to this, just as there is no personification comparable to that of wisdom. Justice and peace may kiss (Ps. 85:11 [10]), and alcohol may be a rowdy (Prov. 20:1), but only wisdom is given a voice that resembles the Lord's (Prov. 8:35, "whoever finds me finds life").[35]

The presence of hypostasis in the Bible does not mean that Hokmah in Proverbs 8 *is* hypostasis, nor does the presence of hypostasis in the Hebrew Scriptures necessarily determine that the Hebrew Bible is Yahweh-aloneist. There can be a universe populated by many gods, and still the mythologies, stories, and poems about a particular god may contain hypostatic descriptions.[36]

For others Hokmah is a mere figure of speech, not a mythological figure. Carole Fontaine describes this position:

> Woman Wisdom and Woman Stranger become "mere" literary devices whose symbolic meaning becomes relatively insignificant...Woman Wisdom is seen as the embodiment of the sages' teaching or the voice of the world order addressing men.[37]

But she lives so vividly in the literature that I don't see her as a "mere" anything. All these interpreters agree on one thing, that postexilic Israel could not contain a full-blown Israelite goddess. And the radical monotheism they impose on the postexilic period resembles exactly the theology of the interpreters themselves. I concur with those scholars who suggest otherwise.

---

[35]Roland Murphy, "The Personification of Wisdom," in *Wisdom in Ancient Israel: Essays in Honour of J. A. Emerton,* ed. John Day et al. (Cambridge: Cambridge University Press, 1995), 222–23.

[36]Among those who identify Hokmah as hypostasis, there is some disagreement as to whether Hokmah was created as a hypostasis from an attribute of YHWH, or rather "was an originally independent divine figure which only 'secondarily attached' to the deity" (Camp, *Proverbs,* 212).

[37]Fontaine, "The Personification of Wisdom," in *Harper's Bible Commentary* (San Francisco: Harper Collins, 1988), 503. Ultimately, Lang takes this position. He says, "Should one place our poems, therefore, in the supposedly safe, orthodox religious climate of the late postexilic period, in which anything polytheistic and pagan had long since ceased to be appealing to the Jewish mind? In a period therefore, in which the poet could start to 'play' with ancient mythology because it had lost its *religious* power over the mind while keeping its *aesthetic* fascination?" (Lang, *Wisdom,* 115).

The Promise of Hokmah[38]

Claudia Camp, in the article "Woman Wisdom as Root Metaphor," leaves a cryptic note: "I want to thank Carole Fontaine for encouraging me to look for the Goddess behind woman wisdom."[39] She further suggests in the same article that Hokmah might serve as a model for those in a Jewish or Christian context who want to explore goddess worship.

Roland Murphy appears to accept the presence of an Israelite goddess, and seems to have no difficulty with the concept. He says that she "seems to be divine...She is a surrogate of YHWH. [She is] the 'feminine' in God... [And later, he says], Proverbs 1–9 attributes to this incomparable figure a divine status."[40]

This figure, by means of her own relationship to YHWH as a daughter to a beloved father, enhances the eminence of YHWH. And such worship is consistent with most understandings of the first commandment, "You shall have no other gods before me." Hokmah is decidedly not "before" YHWH in terms of priority or hierarchy. Hokmah is never described as a mother. She gives birth to no one. She is a daughter and a teacher.[41]

When an interpreter describes YHWH as the only God in the Hebrew Bible, that interpreter has shifted the meaning of the word *god.* The definition shifts from the more consistent one of "supernatural being with powers, who dwells in mythic time," to "the one being without beginning or end, who has all power." By shifting the definition in this way, the radical monotheists have assumed that which they were setting out to prove. By assuming that in order for a being to be god, that god must be absolutely by her/himself in the category of deity, the argument lapses into circularity.

There are many beings in the Hebrew Bible and in other ancient Near Eastern literature who are supernatural, have dramatic powers, and dwell in mythic time. In the ancient Near Eastern literature, and even in the Hebrew Bible, these beings are called "gods" (in Hebrew, *'elohim*). They are called other things as well, but "gods" is the common designation. The only reason they are stripped of this title by subsequent interpreters is that the interpreters begin by assuming that there can be only one god. They assume this because this is what they believe personally. They assume and read the Hebrew Bible

---

[38]Carol A. Newsom suggests that Hokmah provides a *negative* model of women, employed to serve the patriarchal institutions of Israel in "Woman and the Discourse of Patriarchal Wisdom: A Study of Proverbs 1–9," in *Gender and Difference in Ancient Israel,* ed. Peggy L. Day (Minneapolis: Fortress Press, 1989), 157. Camp takes a contrary position. She says, "Although, once again, a valid critique could be made regarding the co-optation of the goddess in service of the male deity, the fact remains that the Goddess is there within Woman Wisdom if we want her" (Camp, "Woman Wisdom as Root Metaphor," 61).

[39]Camp, "Woman Wisdom as Root Metaphor," 61.

[40]Murphy, *Proverbs,* 280.

[41]Therefore, Christianity is a religion that has a supreme god, and that supreme god has a son who is also god, who is in some way still the single god, angels, demons, and ascended saints who dispense favors in response to prayer and devotion. If there is a religion that allows for this and is still called monotheism, clearly we have to either consider what the definitions of monotheism are or question whether traditional Christianity has ever been monotheistic.

in this way not for exegetical reasons, but for ideological reasons. Although there is nothing inherently wrong in their doing that, I have two objections to it. First, the biblical text itself (Prov. 8) does not support the claim of monotheism, and yet the claim is made as though on the basis of exegesis. Second, when one reads the Bible through radically monotheistic eyes, one loses a good deal of the richness of the ancient Israelite mythological world. One is forced to ignore certain literary figures and make circuitous routes through this seemingly difficult text—a text that is difficult only because of the presumptive theological assertions.

With the exception of Camp, critics are virtually unanimous in their assertion that between monotheism and polytheism, monotheism is the superior ideology, that the movement of Israel was from polytheism to monotheism through a series of stages, and therefore Hokmah must be somehow marginalized.

They all assume some modification of an evolutionary/developmental model.[42] This model assumes three things:

- that the movement of Israel was a linear movement from polytheism to monotheism
- that this movement constitutes an improvement, either because it is more right in some absolute sense, or because it is functional, evidence of a more sophisticated and philosophically reflective society
- that the radical monotheistic ideal is more characteristically Israelite

Even Norman Gottwald, a politically sensitive biblical critic, believes that the ideal, revolutionary society of tribal Israel worshiped only one god, distinguishing them from their Canaanite overlords, who worshiped many gods. Gottwald equates admirable, revolutionary, egalitarian fervor with radical monotheism, and oppressive tributary societies with polytheism. Although Gottwald dramatically rewrites the narrative of the initial Israelite settlement, he still accepts the direction of movement in the Israelite experience from polytheism to radical monotheism, and he regards Yahweh-aloneism as pristine and noble (as do most others). Lang notes regarding Gottwald, "I am afraid that this eloquently conjured 'monotheistic experiment' is a modern idealization of Israel's origins, the romantic idea of an ancient peasant revolt, wishful thinking rather than a plausible reconstruction of historical events!"[43] I find it astounding that there is such near-universal agreement regarding this point, although there is little or no evidence in the Hebrew Bible that supports it.

We must consider, however, another picture of how this developed. It appears that both radical monotheism and degrees of polytheism coexisted

---

[42]James Barr correctly observes that most opposition to the evolutionary model in discussions of biblical theology is more apparent than real. Some notion of evolutionary development is present in virtually all academic discussions of Israelite belief. *(The Concept of Biblical Theology* [Minneapolis: Fortress Press, 1999], 85–99).

[43]Lang, *Prophecy,* 18; see Norman Gottwald, *The Tribes of Yahweh* (New York: Orbis Books, 1979), 18–22, 32–44.

throughout the entirety of Israelite history, at least up until the first century. Those aspects of Israel that did not conform to the standards of radical monotheism were in fact sources of the most creative energies in Israel. The figure of Hokmah is a good example of this.

I suggest that traditional biblical concepts of monotheism be taken from the standard formulations of the first commandment and the first lines of the Nicene Creed. Neither of them requires the kind of interpretation that the radical monotheists suggest, and in fact, "You shall have no other God before me" positively suggests interpretations other than the radical monotheism.

It doesn't matter what point of view one takes regarding this issue, whether polytheism moves to monotheism in a direct line or whether the change took place suddenly at the beginning, gradually, or only late in their history. In every instance it is movement in the same direction, and in all cases the value of the movement is from bad to good. I contend that there is no evidence from within the Hebrew Scriptures to suggest such a movement. Rather, people held to the same range of theologies throughout most of the Israelite history.

Our conception of Hokmah, our interpretation of Proverbs 8, must allow for the presence of Israelites who had a range of beliefs regarding YHWH in relationship with other gods. There were those who regarded YHWH as first in a pantheon of gods, those who regarded YHWH as the only legitimate god for the Israelites, and the Yahweh-aloneists. The Yahweh-aloneists were a minority party through most of their history, but they were the group that appeared to be in control during the Persian period, during the formation of the canon.

Hokmah inhabits a world in which loyalty to YHWH did not preclude the delight of a goddess of Wisdom. Different theologies coexisted, side by side. They contended against each other, sometimes violently, but they didn't ever succeed in making the culture homogeneous. Divergent views existed throughout Israel's history. There are passages in the Bible not written by the Yahweh-aloneists and not sympathetic to their beliefs. The entire mythology of Hokmah would likely not come from the hand of a Yahweh-aloneist, because it would give too much credence to gods other than YHWH. There are those who say that the symbols of feminine divine figures had slipped so far below the horizon of the postexilic Israelite that their trappings could be used with impunity.

Conclusion

If we clear out the claims against Hokmah, we are left with a divine, supernatural figure whose chief activity is characterized as play. Camp observes, "Play is a fundamentally liminal, deconstructive activity. For Wisdom, it takes place at the heart of the interaction between God and humans, and, thus, at the heart of the theological endeavor."[44]

---

[44]Camp, "Woman Wisdom as Root Metaphor," 61.

She tells us why Hokmah is so important, and why Hokmah needs to be within our horizon, contributing to the idea of divinity. I want a God who plays, not just a God who works, a God who looks more like Mae West than Walter Cronkite. Hokmah, who entices students with seductive language, is still taking lovers.

Nocturnal Egression

Exploring Some Margins of the Song of Songs

Fiona C. Black

This essay represents a conversation of dissonant voices or intertexts, wherein, availing myself of a few postmodern freedoms, I try to come to terms with a disturbing incident in the Song of Songs. That incident is the stripping and beating of the Song's protagonist by the watchmen during her search for her lover (5:6–7). The conversation has its beginnings in an earlier, coauthored paper on Edward Burne-Jones's stained-glass version of the Song.[1] I want to take up a few of the issues that that paper raised and address a way of reading the Song that Burne-Jones's windows prompt.

In the course of exploring the windows in relation to the biblical book, Cheryl Exum and I observed the artist's efforts to make a story of a text that often resists cohesive readings. Additionally, we wondered about the role of various "negative" aspects of the Song in terms of its perceived idealized presentation of love. We wrote:

> What would happen to the place of honour held by the biblical Song of Songs if, rather than suppressing these recalcitrant details, we foregrounded them?…When we look at Burne-Jones's Song of Songs in stained glass, we see…a challenge to biblical interpretation to reassess its comfortable assumptions about the biblical book and to re-examine what it has been reluctant to see.[2]

That possibility has never faded from my mind, especially now that I have a visual image to put to–indeed, from which I cannot dissociate–one of the text's more disturbing details. In the context of the windows, the frame

---

[1] Fiona C. Black and J. Cheryl Exum, "Semiotics in Stained Glass: Edward Burne-Jones's Song of Songs," in *Biblical Studies/Cultural Studies: The Third Sheffield Colloquium,* ed. J. Cheryl Exum and Stephen D. Moore, Gender, Culture, Theory 7, Journal for the Study of the Old Testament Supplement Series 266 (Sheffield: Sheffield Academic Press, 1998), 315–42.

[2] Ibid., 342.

that depicts that scene is striking for its inclusion in Burne-Jones's story and for its central location (from the viewer's perspective) and violent content (see fig. 1). In the biblical Song, the scene is buried a little better, but nevertheless comes as a shock, a perplexing and disturbing component of what seems otherwise to be a delightful, if sometimes unstraightforward, presentation of the lovers' escapades.

The postmodern turn allows for a few freedoms within the current climate of biblical scholarship that facilitate my investigation of Song 5:6–7. Like other contributors to this volume, I will refrain from trying to "define" postmodernism (arguably an inappropriate endeavor), but will instead note several important postmodern ideas that will be useful here. These are a resistance to coherence (or an emphasis on counter-coherence or difference); a recognition of marginal voices; an acknowledgment or encouragement of plurivocality in readers and their texts; and a promotion of intertextuality. The idea, thus, will not be to settle the meaning of my chosen text, or even to make it cohere with the rest of the book, as biblical critics have attempted to do in the past.[3] Rather, instead of allowing the scene to fade into the background, where it lies waiting to shock unsuspecting readers, I wish to foreground it.

Why foreground this text? Why undertake a counter-coherent reading of the Song? I do so not to remove the scene's shock factor, but to explore its potential to disrupt. This means seeing the beating as more than simply a

---

[3]The scene is usually passed over or feebly excused in an effort to justify interpreters' ideals about the book as an idyllic love poem. Such moves only serve to highlight the problem.

"negative moment" in the lives of the lovers, a risk of the trials of love, but as a key to new interpretive avenues. These avenues have relevance for two ongoing issues in Song scholarship. The first is how to read the book. Truly, the investigation of counter-coherence in the Song of Songs might seem a bit paradoxical, since, in many ways, it is already an incoherent and incohesive text, with its shifting speakers, wild and mutating imagery, and rapid scene changes. It is not nonsensical, but it does seem to play a game with readers' novelistic desires and voyeuristic interests. Consequently, efforts have been made in the past to settle the poetic structure of the book or to find an interpretive key to its ordering.[4] What happens to the Song, however, if that interpretive urge is resisted, and that which unsettles is brought to the fore? The second issue for Song scholarship is the acclamation of the female protagonist as the center of the story by feminist critics. Indeed, she seems to be a well-developed subject: Here her voice predominates, and, unlike her counterparts in the Hebrew Bible, she appears to enjoy a personal and sexual freedom that is unparalleled.[5] It seems too good to be true. If the beating may be taken as a challenge to the woman's autonomy, what is the significance of the scene, beyond its most literal implication that a woman is impeded, and violently so, in her search for her lover?

There is enough in what I have adumbrated to embark on a counter-coherent reading. I want, however, to add to it by inviting other texts into the discussion. One is an early reading in *Song of Songs Rabbah* that helps explore the issues I have mentioned in unique ways by including other biblical texts

---

[4]See my article on interpretation of the Song and readerly desire, "What Is My Beloved? On Erotic Reading and the Song of Songs," in *The Labour of Reading: Desire, Alienation and Biblical Interpretation,* ed. Fiona C. Black, Roland Boer, and Erin Runions, Semeia Studies (Atlanta: Scholars Press, 1999), 35–52.

[5]See, for example, Athalya Brenner, *The Song of Songs,* Old Testament Guides (Sheffield: JSOT Press, 1989), 90; Brenner, "On Feminist Criticism of the Song of Songs," in *A Feminist Companion to the Song of Songs,* ed. Athalya Brenner (Sheffield: JSOT Press, 1993), 28–29; Fokkelien van Dijk-Hemmes, "The Imagination of Power and the Power of Imagination: An Intertextual Analysis of Two Biblical Love Songs: The Song of Songs and Hosea 2," in *A Feminist Companion,* 169–70; Marcia Falk, "The Song of Songs," in *Harper's Bible Commentary,* ed. James L. Mays (San Francisco: Harper and Row, 1988), 528; Carol Meyers, "Gender Imagery in the Song of Songs," in *A Feminist Companion,* 208, 211; Ilana Pardes (with some reservations), *Countertraditions in the Bible: A Feminist Approach* (Cambridge: Harvard University Press, 1992), 118–19, 128; Phyllis Trible, *God and the Rhetoric of Sexuality* (London: SCM Press, 1978), 161; Renita Weems, "Song of Songs," in *The Women's Bible Commentary,* ed. Carol A. Newsom and Sharon Ringe (London: SPCK/Louisville: Westminster/John Knox Press, 1992), 160. For two dissenting feminist voices, see J. Cheryl Exum, "Developing Strategies of Feminist Criticism and Developing Strategies for Commenting the Song of Songs," in *Auguries: The Jubilee Volume of the Sheffield Department of Biblical Studies,* ed. David J. A. Clines and Stephen D. Moore, Journal for the Study of the Old Testament Supplement Series 269 (Sheffield: Sheffield Academic Press, 1998), 206–49; and Daphne Merkin, "The Woman in the Balcony: On Rereading the Song of Songs," in *Out of the Garden: Women Writers on the Bible,* ed. Christina Büchmann and Celina Spiegel (New York: Fawcett Columbine, 1994), 238–51, 342.

(e.g., Ex. 32).[6] And, centuries later, the linguistic and psychoanalytical theorist Julia Kristeva also dabbled in the Song of Songs.[7] Some of the issues I raise in this paper will additionally benefit from her insights and from her broader work on the abject.[8]

Margins and Centers

My discussion is ultimately concerned with margins and centers, about what does and does not belong, about what must be removed or rebutted because it threatens order. For Kristeva, the abject fills such a role in the symbolic order, hovering between subject and object. Whatever threatens that order, be it food, bodily effluvia, refuse, or death, these items "*show* [*us*] what [*we*] permanently thrust aside in order to live…Abject. It is something rejected from which one does not part, from which one does not protect oneself as from an object."[9] Although it typically involves the body and its boundaries, the abject is additionally important to the maintenance of the social order. It is "what disturbs identity, system, order. What does not respect borders, positions, rules. The in-between, the ambiguous, the composite." These must be thrust aside so that order can be maintained. The "one by whom the abject exists is thus a *deject* who places (himself), *separates* (himself), situates (himself), and therefore *strays* instead of getting his bearings, desiring, belonging, or refusing."[10]

Kristeva observes that the abject accompanies all religious structurings in the form of taboo. She traces it through the Levitical prohibitions concerning food and bodily behaviors, locating a special connection with the maternal body there, and then into the Christian scriptures, where it is internalized and becomes sin.[11] And in the Song? Whereas the implications of the abject for the book are far-reaching, it is possible only to dabble here with our chosen text of 5:6–7. The Song teeters on the margins. It sets up a specialized space, a second garden of Eden–prebanishment–where biblical readers encounter what appear to be unique subject matter, poetic style, and gender politics.[12]

---

[6]Jacob Neusner, *Song of Songs Rabbah: An Analytical Translation,* 2 vols.; Brown Judaic Studies 197–98 (Atlanta: Scholars Press, 1989).

[7]Julia Kristeva, "A Holy Madness: She and He," in *Tales of Love,* trans. Leon Roudiez (New York: Columbia University Press, 1987), 83–100.

[8]Kristeva, *Powers of Horror: An Essay on Abjection,* trans. Leon Roudiez (New York: Columbia University Press, 1982). Timothy Beal's excellent and influential article on the ambivalence of Yahweh as examined using Kristeva's work on intertextuality and the abject should be mentioned here: "The System and the Speaking Subject in the Hebrew Bible: Reading for Divine Abjection," *Biblical Interpretation* 2 (1994): 171–89.

[9]Kristeva, *Powers of Horror,* 3–4. Original italics.

[10]Ibid., 8.

[11]Ibid., 17, chaps. 4 and 5. See Beal's critique of Kristeva's work on the abject in Leviticus and her failure to problematize the symbolic order sufficiently ("The System," 176). The implications of Kristeva's work on the abject for the Song of Songs are many, and it is with regret that I cannot pursue them in detail here. My Ph.D. thesis, "The Grotesque Body in the Song of Songs," University of Sheffield, 1999, interacts with the abject more fully.

[12]For the Song's connection to the Genesis text, see Francis Landy, "The Song of Songs and the Garden of Eden," *Journal of Biblical Literature* 98 (1979): 513–28; and Trible, *God and the Rhetoric of Sexuality.*

Perched on the margins, the Song signals its own special status; it alerts us to important content. But that content will be highly unexpected and marginal itself, for within that world a very recognizable (and familiar) system of expected moral and sexual conduct exists. Through it, the Song's protagonist unwittingly journeys and speaks of love, and from it, she must ultimately be ejected by the keepers of that order because she threatens its undoing.

The Song and the Margins

The Song has an uneasy fit in the Hebrew Bible in that its subject matter and style are quite out of the ordinary. This is not to say that the subject of love (even human love) is not treated in the biblical text or that there are not beautiful and imagery-laden poetic texts to be found elsewhere. Nowhere else, however, do we find such a concentration of rich poetic material, and nowhere else is there a sustained and explicit treatment of human erotic desires and behaviors. It is not surprising that the book is reputed to have had a difficult passage into the canon.[13]

In Kristeva's estimation, the Song as amatory discourse is extraordinary in other ways, too. As with other representations, biblical love is expressed chiefly through metaphorical discourse. Metaphor allows for a certain fluidity of meaning that is entirely appropriate to the conveyance of the uncertainties of love. Indeed, the amatory figure of speech "as condensation and displacement of semantic features points to an uncertainty, not concerning the *object* of love...but an uncertainty concerning the bond."[14] Kristeva explains:

> It is the very enunciatory pact, in its amatory particularity and on account of the intensity of affect required on the part of two lovers (who are the two speakers), that disturbs the normal, univocal exchange of information...In order to become, for the other, more evocative of the experience that is germane to the loving subject—for such is the objective of amorous dialogue—each bit of information is loaded with semantic polyvalence and thus becomes undecidable connotation.[15]

Several features undergird the Song's amatory technique for Kristeva: the elusiveness of the lover; the aleatory order of the verse and the book's apparent "compositional disorder"; the condensation of the "message" of the book into minimal portions that give a universal meaning; and dialogue, rhythm, repetition, and alliteration, all rigorously ordered.[16] These features

---

[13]See Marvin H. Pope's review of the process of canonization in *Song of Songs: A New Translation with Introduction and Commentary,* Anchor Bible 7c (Garden City, N.Y.: Doubleday, 1977).

[14]Kristeva, "Holy Madness," 92. Original italics.

[15]Ibid., 91.

[16]Ibid., 89–92.

create a text that is full of tension and jouissance, that is unreadable and yet universally understood, decidedly unique in the history of love.[17]

Already on the "margins" of discourse, the Song compounds its marginality by featuring a protagonist who is an oddity. The woman's role certainly appears to be uniquely liberating in comparison with that of other biblical women. Feminist critics rightly point out the predominance of the woman's speech, her pursuit of her own desires and wishes, and her ostensible sanction by society to do so.[18] Kristeva even finds her to be the "first woman to be sovereign before her loved one," liberated by virtue of being a loving and speaking subject. Through her amorous speech, she is empowered to create herself an equal to her lover's sovereignty.[19] Speech is really the key here. To all intents and purposes, the Song's protagonist talks herself into a unique space within the biblical corpus.

But within that speech are two peculiar dreamlike asides, searching scenes (Song 3:1–5; 5:2–8).[20] To whom are they spoken? Are they a recounting of the woman's desires and their repercussions to her lover, who appears then in the third person? Or to the daughters of Jerusalem, to whom she appeals at the end of each narration (3:5; 5:8)? What is their significance for this reputed "central" position the woman boasts in the Song? Are they simply two tales among many of search and discovery, that represent, with their alternate endings, the full range of the lovers' experiences? Or might they be, perhaps, the de-centering–the abjecting–of the woman?

The Searching Scenes

The two searching scenes are concentrated narrative moments roughly in the center of the Song's poetic kaleidoscope. We do not usually speak of narrative with respect to the Song, which is a series of short poems related by

---

[17]Kristeva's insights on the Song in this respect are astute. I find as I continue her chapter, however, that I cannot support her ultimate claims about the nation's imagined relation to God as that of a loving woman to a husband (95–98). She neglects to observe the insidiousness of that other side of the marital metaphor, which is evident in the so-called porno-prophetic texts of Isaiah, Jeremiah, Ezekiel, and Hosea. Kristeva's view of the biblical god is, as Beal has pointed out, univocal (Beal, "The System," 174), as is her view of biblical love: it is joyful and affirming ("Holy Madness," 100).

[18]See n. 5, above. The sanction is not universal, as we shall see in 5:7. The woman is also aware of other societal restrictions (1:6; 8:1).

[19]Kristeva, "Holy Madness," 99–100. Note that Kristeva is not arguing for any kind of female supremacy for the woman, as some feminist biblical critics have, or even a liberation in the manner in which feminist biblical scholarship has seen it (freedom from the constraints of patriarchy). Rather, the woman is liberated and made sovereign by the combination of her speaking and loving. Kristeva is referring to the appearance of the woman as a subject in a modern sense: "Limpid, intense, divided, quick, upright, suffering, hoping, the wife–a woman–is the first common individual who, on account of her love, becomes the first Subject in the modern sense of the term. Divided. Sick and yet sovereign" (100). Such a statement jibes with Kristeva's evaluations of love as an empowering re-creating force, especially in the psychoanalytic process. It also plays on her analysis of the Jewish God and monotheism.

[20]The sequences in Song of Songs 3:1–5 and 5:2–8 are usually referred to as the dream scenes, since it is generally assumed that the woman is dreaming in both texts, even though she does not explicity say she is.

an elastic repertoire of images.[21] Some poems describe the lovers' bodies; others situate them in various contexts (the hills, the king's chambers, etc.); still others express the longings of the couple for each other and their meetings or missed encounters. It is provocative that in the midst of this pastiche of images and scenes, two similar moments–similar to each other but distinct from the material around them–interrupt the Song's poetic rhythm.[22] In these scenes the Song manages to retain its characteristic level of activity, intense and insistent, but at the same time accomplishes a staticity, a "perfectly achieved tableau."[23] This dreamlike, slowed time requires pause and special attention to what transpires.

Song of Songs 5:6–7 functions as a repetition or retelling of the earlier search in 3:2–4. There, the protagonist is dreaming or thinking about her lover and gets up in order to search for him in the city. She encounters watchmen whom she consults as to his whereabouts. Then, as she herself says, scarcely had she passed them when she comes across her lover and is reunited (3:4). In the repeated sequence, the woman seeks her lover as before, but is unable to find him because he has disappeared before she can answer the door. She encounters the same watchmen as before, but has no time to ask them for help. Instead, inexplicably, she is stripped of her veil or mantle and beaten. And she does not find her lover. The scene ends with a plea to the daughters of Jerusalem (who seem to have appeared out of nowhere, as in 3:5), that if they see the missing man, they tell him that she is weak with love. In this scene, being weak or sick with love takes on an ironic meaning, quite distinct from any usual sanguinity to be found in the sighs of pining lovers. Indeed, שׁחוֹלת אהבה אני (5:8) might be a rather unfunny pun in translation, for it is because of her journey for love that she is "weakened" by the watchmen. What might such a weakening mean? Let us take a closer look.

Safely tucked in bed, the woman has been disturbed by her lover, who knocks at her door. What follows could be a stock episode in any love story, a narrowly missed meeting. Underlying this one, though, is a veiled account of another kind of encounter, a sexual one, where "hand," "hole," "door," "myrrh," and "open" connote the lovers' genitals and body fluids, intromission, and withdrawal.[24] The point is not, I think, to decide at what level one wants

---

[21]Speculation on the number of poems in the Song has been abundant. See M. Timothea Elliott, *The Literary Unity of the Canticle,* Europäische Hochschulschriften 371 (Frankfurt-am-Main: Verlag Peter Lang, 1989) for a recent and comprehensive review.

[22]This is not a metrical observation, but a stylistic one.

[23]Francis Landy, *Paradoxes of Paradise: Identity and Difference in the Song of Songs* (Sheffield: Almond Press, 1983), 45–47.

[24]It is important, I think, not to be definitive about what the openings are (i.e., whether or not they are anatomical), and in what manner penetration occurs. I prefer to leave the Song doing what it does best, affecting readers by being suggestive. Opinions vary: proponents of coitus here include Pope, *Song of Songs,* 519; opponents include Roland Murphy, *The Song of Songs: A Commentary on the Book of Canticles or the Song of Songs,* Hermeneia (Minneapolis: Fortress Press, 1990), 171, and Michael D. Goulder, *The Song of Fourteen Songs,* Journal for the Study of the Old Testament Supplement Series 36 (Sheffield: JSOT Press, 1986), 41.

to hear the Song speak, but to notice the book's ambiguity over whether the lovers meet here at all, and in what capacity. Moreover, the signs of meeting all have marked implications for the woman's place at the center of the Song.

The narrative details from the point of disturbance to the beginning of her search have in common the vital significance of bordering the body. There is the obvious physical bordering of the house, which keeps the woman separate from her lover, and the door that the lover attempts to penetrate and is later opened (too late) by the woman. On a more euphemistic level, there is the bordering of the body with its "door" and "opening" and the (attempted?) merging of the hands/penis with that body and with fluid. Finally, there is the undressing and dressing of the woman, even the opposition of clean and soiled feet. These last prompt an important question for the woman, the significance of which will later become evident to readers: "I have taken off my cloak, how can I put it on again? I have washed my feet, how can I soil them?" This is to say, "I am border/contained, how can I uncontain myself?"

After her failed encounter, the woman finds herself confronted by the watchmen, the ultimate keepers of the borders and the "guardians of public morality."[25] In the earlier scene in 3:1–5, her movement matched theirs: She rose and left the confines of her house; she went around the city, looking; the watchmen went around the city (also looking); they found her; she passed them by; she found her lover. All is dynamic, and all ends in success with the sequestering of the lovers in the safety of another house. In the second scene, however, that first search, which is emphasized, almost exaggerated, with its repetition of seeking and finding, becomes truncated, horribly abbreviated. As far as we know, the woman goes out in search of her lover, but there is no description of the journey, no acknowledgment of her dressing herself and going outside. We only know that she "opens" to her lover (a door?), and that she seeks, but does not find.

The opacity of the scene with its truncating of the search is significant. It seems that the second scene responds to the success of the first. In 5:7, the watchmen find her, as before, but her questioning of them is prevented. (Correspondingly, her call to her lover is unanswered.) Whereas they had no opportunity to answer her in 3:5, here she does not ask. But their "answer" to her looking comes nonetheless, and it is violent and unexpected. The woman is quite specific as to her ensuing treatment. She is found (מצא), beaten (נכה), wounded (פצע), and stripped of her clothing (נשא רדיד את).[26] Most readers will repudiate the thought of any sexual violence here. In fact, it is quite

---

[25]Landy, *Paradoxes of Paradise*, 146.

[26]רדיד is used only once elsewhere in the Hebrew Bible (Isa. 3:23) to denote one of the garments (veil?) of the daughters of Zion, which will be stripped from them by Yahweh, as he lays bare their naked parts in punishment for their profligacy.

common that the violence of the scene is resisted, or somehow excused.[27] The "finding" and stripping, beating and "wounding" of a woman at night by a group of men is extremely suggestive of rape, however, and this is a possibility that should not be excluded for this scene.[28]

Unsurprisingly, the thematics of her earlier, failed encounter in 5:2–6a, are repeated and augmented here in her encounter with the watchmen. In the Burne-Jones piece, the confrontation takes place right at the walls, near a gate. Because of foreshortening, the woman's head actually fills the opening in the gate, making her threat to exceed her allowed boundaries vivid and imminent. Beating and wounding are also border crossings, corporeal ones; rape, if it occurred, the more so.[29] Stripping, too, is a violation of boundaries, in a more obvious way perhaps than the beating, for the results might be more physically evident. It is not important to engage in a debate as to the nature of this garment (רְדִיד) in comparison with the one she has removed herself (כֻּתֹּנֶת) and whether she is completely, quasi-, or not at all naked. The key is the symbolic un-bordering of the woman and the agent of that

---

[27]Roland Murphy suggests that "perhaps her failure to discover the man at once (as in 3:4) is enough to account for this graphic detail of physical beating" (*The Song of Songs,* 171). Pope ignores the problem altogether, save to observe that it is reminiscent of the goddess Ishtar/Inanna's descent to the underworld, during which time she is stripped of various garments (*Song of Songs,* 527). John Snaith says only that the violence is "quite unsuitable for the police" (*The Song of Songs,* New Century Bible Commentary [Grand Rapids: Eerdmans, 1993], 76). Brenner reassures, "Love brings pain as well as joy, but this pain does not have far-reaching physical and social consequences. Even though the woman is beaten, she is not sexually molested for her immodesty" (*Song of Songs,* 83). D. Garrett suggests that the beating represents anxiety over the loss of the woman's virginity—that it is metaphorically her virginity that assails her (*The New American Commentary: An Exegetical and Theological Exposition of Holy Scripture. Proverbs, Ecclesiastes, Song of Songs* [Nashville: Broadman Press, 1993], 409, 412), and Pardes, similarly, says it is anxiety over her impending exposure (*Countertraditions,* 137). Michael Goulder seems to justify the beating, observing that it, even in the form of whipping to the point of drawing blood, was useful in maintaining order in the harem, for "wild women circulating in the place shrieking" would be quite unacceptable. In his perception, she is stripped (of her only piece of clothing, her nightgown) and then beaten by the eunuch/watchmen (*Song of Fourteen Songs,* 42). Landy skirts the issue somewhat in a discussion of shame, where he notes the relation of the moral disapprobation of the lovers with the repressed desire of the watchmen. The parallel passage of 3:1–4, where the watchmen do not answer the woman, suggests to Landy a certain "ambivalence towards licentiousness," and there it might "be inferred that patrols were not always disapproving, and might even assist lovers (*Paradoxes of Paradise,* 225). The stripping in 5:7 suggests the woman's shamelessness and her shaming by the watchmen, revealing "society's latent fears and desires" (226). Landy's contrast of the two scenes highlights our problem: Why approve in one search, and violently disapprove in the next?

[28]Goulder's argument that her wounds could not have been serious by virtue of "what follows" (i.e., sexual intercourse—citing Song 6:11) is tenuous, and applies the narrative movement of this scene to the rest of the Song, which seems a dubious enterprise (*Song of Fourteen Songs,* 42).

[29]In Burne-Jones's window, a thick band of iron separates the top and bottom halves of the picture, cutting the woman off at the waist and the man at the knee. In the bottom half of the frame, the woman's body is disarrayed and her right leg is drawn back. The man's leg is decidedly phallic and intrudes between her legs. Yet the top half disturbs what the bottom half implies. Though he grasps her roughly with one hand, he cannot abuse her because of the lantern he holds in the other clenched fist (see Black and Exum, "Semiotics in Stained Glass," 338–39).

unbordering. The first removal is undertaken in the confines of her house and by her own hands, with these now-ironic questions, Should she dirty her feet? Should she dress herself (and leave the house)? No, she should not. The second removal occurs in the streets. Together with her beating, the watchmen's stripping her limits her literally in her journey by stopping and shaming her, and delimits her figuratively, by identifying and breaking through the borders that contain her.[30] If she will not contain herself, they will.

The watchmen's act is, moreover, transgressive. As keepers of order and preventers of violence, they use disorder and violence to repress the actions of the woman. Their treatment of her is unexpected and inappropriate both to the amorous designs of the Song and to the "right" sexual relation that the protagonist seeks with her lover. The woman's acts, however, are also transgressive, and this appears to be the reason for her treatment. In return for leaving her house (the "proper" environ for women in the patriarchal order),[31] she is "reminded" by the keepers of patriarchy just where she should be at night. In return for her sexual license, she is reminded to stay covered, and she is reminded, painfully, to guard the boundaries of her own body and its desires. She is pushed from the center of the Song as a speaking, loving subject. The symbolic borderings and un-borderings that dominate this scene and its failures of proper or appropriate communication are signs of her precarious position with respect to the center and her eventual abjection from it. No wonder that, almost dumbstruck, she must ask the daughters of Jerusalem to pass on her message to her lover.

A Woman in Love and a Golden Calf

Years earlier, on the slopes of Mount Horeb, quite another transgression took place. In the *Song of Songs Rabbah,* Song 5:7 is explicated with the story of the golden calf in Exodus 32. On first reflection, the story seems a rather odd comparison to make, but it is useful here in that it continues the thematics of the beating scene and elaborates on the place of the abject in preserving the biblical social order.

The connection between the two stories is made through the watchmen. They are identified as those who "went from gate to gate" and "slew every man his brother" (Ex. 32:27). In the Exodus story, the slaying by the Levites is carried out at the behest of Moses, who punishes the people on behalf of Yahweh because of their idolatry. When he sees what they have done, Moses is angry and breaks the tablets, and he takes the calf and grinds it to dust. He mixes it with water and makes the people drink it.[32] The people are called to

---

[30]Landy contrasts the stripping that shames with the veil that possibly allures (*Paradoxes of Paradise,* 254), so that the latter becomes a cause of the former.

[31]For example, Carol Meyers locates a specialized and ultimately powerful place for women in the domestic scene in ancient Israel (*Discovering Eve: Ancient Israelite Women in Context* [Oxford: Oxford University Press, 1988], 139–88, especially 160).

[32]Compare Deuteronomy 9:21, where Moses merely throws the dust into the stream that runs down the mountain.

order, and they must also order themselves as those who will serve Yahweh (Levi) and those who will not. These keepers of the law are then called to take a sword and go from gate to gate—from border point to border point—killing whoever lies in between who does not belong.[33]

Like the woman in the Song, the people must be ejected from the order that they contravene, in their case by the ultimate abject, death, and not merely by its signs (beating, rape). As a people (as Israel), they must not be annihilated, however, for that would mean the decimation of the entire order. In the same manner, the woman is not killed, only violently made to occupy her "proper" place. Interestingly, like the watchmen's, Moses' behavior is also transgressive of the order he seeks to defend. In his anger, he breaks the very signs of the law that have been created to show the people how to order themselves. He makes the people drink the sign of their violation, arguably enforcing a kind of extreme covetousness, where what is desired and worshiped is ingested, becoming a part of those who desire it. Finally, he requires the killing of the apostates (presumably he was aware of the sixth commandment), who are referred to not as lawbreakers, but as the brothers, neighbors, and sons (the intimates—the inner circle) of the faithful. This after he has originally pleaded for the peoples' lives (Ex. 32:10–14). But no matter. All is in the service of preserving order and preventing chaos that would take a number of forms: breaking of the law; anger of Yahweh; destruction (prevention of creation) of a people; ridicule of the enemy.

We are not such a far cry from the protagonist in the Song of Songs after all. The story of the golden calf relays the importance of system and identity for the people and the measures that are taken to preserve them.[34] In the Song, the terms of system and identity are translated to the level of the sexual and moral conduct of the people. The abject, however, hovers over both and is the means whereby order is maintained.

Ending in the Middle

We left the woman in the Song in the middle of the book—the middle but not the center. Through the Song's unique searching scenes, the protagonist is violently thrown (ab-jetted) from her central place as speaking, loving subject because she disturbs system and order. She does not respect borders, positions, rules. In Kristeva's terms, she is like the criminal with a conscience, the killer who claims he is a savior.[35] She is, correspondingly, the woman who loves and who dares to pursue that love in a manner most unbefitting a biblical woman.

---

[33]The watchmen are also referred to as the watchmen of the walls, meaning the walls of the Torah (Neusner, *Song of Songs Rabbah,* vol. 2, 106).

[34]That the identity and preservation of the subject (Israel) is crucial to this reading should not be underestimated. This theme is also brought to bear in another intertext in the midrashic discussion of Song of Songs 5:7, Ezra 5–8. Sadly, there is not space to discuss this part of the midrashic reading here.

[35]Kristeva, *Powers of Horror,* 4.

Is this an ending? In a concluding step, I caught myself being tempted to find a way to reestablish the woman's position, or somehow recover the loss from my own "negative" ending by appealing to the rest of the book or to the necessity and vitality of the abject for the preservation of order (what is abject must always be present, so that it may be abjected). Unsurprisingly, that kind of ending did not sit well either, especially since it must be through violence that the woman maintains her important role in the social order. At what price autonomy? I began this paper by intending a counter-coherent reading, and therefore its end surely should remain as resistant to resolution and cohesion as its beginning. The beating scene must leave us unsettled, then, as a constant challenge to the temptations of cohesive reading for the Song of Songs and to its celebrated gynocentrism. Our protagonist's love and "sovereignty," as Kristeva would have it, is bittersweet indeed.

Isaiah 5—6

Called and Sent

Peter D. Miscall

An important aspect of the postmodern turn is the awareness that an interpretation, using whatever method, is one among many other possible interpretations. One consequence is the need to weave into the study a discussion of its methodological assumptions, the type of evidence cited and argued, its goals and limits, and such. This collection of essays and the accompanying volume of methodological essays answers this need. They present the impact of postmodernism on biblical studies in both theory and practice; in the postmodern realm, "theory and practice" is still a useful distinction even though theory or method cannot be rigorously separated from practice or exegesis. Much postmodern discourse is characterized by the use of the virgule of "both/and" and not that of "either/or."

Postmodern study explores and celebrates new ways to read the biblical text. The readings may focus on the translation and presentation of a short passage or on the debates between historical, feminist, and psychoanalytical analyses. The different interpretations may confirm or dispute others, or they may go their own way and engage others only tangentially. Critics present and debate interpretations and all the accompanying methods and theories to enrich our understanding of the Bible, its world, our world, and ourselves.

This essay is a modest undertaking that does not address issues such as sociological and theological implications. Feminist, ideology-critical, and other studies deal with the latter in a variety of ways. My mode of reading could impact them in different ways, but I am not making any claims to support or question any other such studies.

I briefly introduce my approach, plunge into the analysis, and close by reflecting on the implications for interpreting Isaiah and for biblical interpretation in general. This is a close reading of a selected portion of Isaiah's text using literary, not historical-critical, categories. Thus, I do not address the debates about dating the book and sections within it and, specifically, about whether or not Isaiah 6 reflects an actual experience of Isaiah ben Amoz. Reading Isaiah as one coherent work does have implications for the historical use of the book, but these will be left for another time.

I am interested in how interpretive strategies limit and control or loosen and open our reading. Even specific grammatical and syntactical decisions are not entirely free of our larger theories. Reading and interpretation are both the process and the product of the complex interaction of the reader and the text. Neither text nor reader dominate. The latter are the interpretive poles of exegesis and eisegesis. Reading combines the two in a way that cannot be reduced to a formula such as 50-50 or 60-40. It is both/and, reader/text. If we focus on the text, it is still "we" who are making choices to include certain textual aspects at the expense of others. If we focus on the reader, we are still reading one particular text. It does make a difference whether we read Hamlet or Isaiah.

This essay's focus is Isaiah 5–6 as an integral part of the book. I employ literary categories such as voice, imagery, themes, and word patterns. A shift in interpretive terms produces different perspectives on, and readings of, Isaiah. A literary interpretation of Isaiah as one work, rather than the standard view of three Isaiahs with varying redactional levels, may seem radical enough without the additional step of saying that such a reading reveals both the limits of method and how the text always exceeds interpretations.

Many of the contemporary authors and works discussed in the accompanying volume, and at points in this volume, have influenced my ways of reading. They are too numerous to acknowledge in a brief essay, but one work does stand out. Roland Barthes' *S/Z* remains near my desk because of the number of times I have read it in the last twenty-five years and because Barthes expresses much of what I say in a more powerful, poetic fashion than I or others.

Isaiah is a grand vision covering all creation and time, from the first creation to the new heavens and earth. The vision depicts God's ways with the world and the world's ways with God. Within this large expanse, Isaiah (shorthand for the book and its author[s]) focuses on the periods of the late eighth and the sixth centuries B.C.E. and on the fate of Israel and its neighbors, near and far. These peoples appear as personifications in the vision, for example, the people Israel, the woman Zion–Jerusalem, Assyria, and Lady Babylon. The all-inclusive reach of the vision is matched formally by the poet's use of a wide variety of vocabulary, imagery, themes, and literary styles. To put it simply, Isaiah attempts to say as much as possible in as many ways as possible.

In the book we both hear (speeches; audition) and see (scenes; vision). This lends the book a dramatic aspect so that we can ask who speaks, to whom, and about what? A narrator, or dramatist, opens the book announcing whose vision this is—"The vision of Isaiah ben Amoz that he envisioned"– what it is about—"Judah and Jerusalem"—and when it was received—"in the days of Uzziah, Jotham, Ahaz and Hezekiah, kings of Judah." This named character, Isaiah, from the eighth century B.C.E. reappears in the introductions in 2:1 and 13:1 and in the stories in chapters 7, 20, and 37–39. We may assume that he is the speaker of much of the vision, but, with the exception of the above passages, the dramatist never names him as the speaker. In the stories in 7, 20, and 37–39, this Isaiah delivers pronouncements specific to a given situation, but 1:1, 2:1, and 13:1 are so general that critics debate the extent of what they introduce. For example, does 1:1 introduce just chapter 1, chapters 1–5, 1–12, or the whole book?

I relate the infrequency of the use of the name Isaiah to the book's concern with prophet and prophecy in general. What is a prophet? What does a prophet say and do? Why? To what effect? A prophet is characterized first by discourse and not by personal identity. Isaiah ben Amoz is an individual exemplar for the vision, but not the only or even the main prophet within it. By discourse, I intend both oral speech as exemplified throughout the book, and writing as exemplified by the book itself. A prophet is orator and poet, and the book's main speaker is poet and prophet. Isaiah's vision is about prophets and prophetic speech and is itself a prophetic work, a grand poem.

To return to the opening, the prophet calls on heavens and earth to listen. Such general speech, which is for all to hear, is characteristic of the vision and is interwoven with addresses to named characters, such as Israel, Zion, Assyria, and Lady Babylon. This is a corollary of identifying the prophet first by discourse, since the specific addressee of a given speech is often not as important as the speech itself. The poet quotes YHWH:

> Hear, O heavens! and give ear, O earth! For YHWH speaks:
> "Children I rear and bring up, but they rebel against me.
> The ox knows its owner, and the donkey the crib of its master;
> Israel does not know, my people do not understand.
> Woe! Sinful nation; iniquitous people;
> > offspring who do evil; children who act corruptly!
> They forsake the Lord; they despise the Holy One of Israel; they turn
> > back. (1:2–4)

I have deliberately omitted closing quotation marks because it is not clear when YHWH stops speaking and the prophet starts. YHWH may stop after "do not understand," after "who act corruptly" or at other points until the close of verse 8 since others say "we" in verse 9. In verse 10, the poet explicitly quotes YHWH, "our God." Some translations, ones such as JPS and NIV, place closing marks after verse 3; others, such as NRSV and REB, use no quotation marks. JPS, NIV, and NRSV break chapter 1 into separate sections by printing extra spaces between the chosen sections, for example, NRSV marks off verses 4, 5–6, and 7–9.

The overlap of divine and prophetic speech is central to the vision. God and prophet stand in a reciprocal relationship. Without a human prophet to speak or write it, the divine word would go unspoken, unheard; without a divine word to proclaim, a human prophet would be only an orator or a poet, not a prophet of YHWH. Thus, it is often impossible to demarcate the lines between divine and prophetic discourse.

The overlap is in evidence in the Song of the Vineyard. "Let me sing for my beloved/a song of my lover about his vineyard" (5:1; JPS). The prophet introduces the song and is interrupted in verses 3–6 by the beloved, by YHWH, who denounces the vineyard and announces its destruction. The poet concludes the poem by clarifying the point in verse 7. On the other hand, YHWH could speak the introduction using third person to cloak himself. He drops the impersonal tone and speaks directly in verses 3–5. Verse 7 is then the poet's or YHWH's comment.

The ambiguity of speaker in Isaiah is matched by a plurality of addressees. Israel is my example. The prophet opens the book calling the entire world to listen, and 1:2–4 continues the open-ended discourse. Within this section, Israel is referred to as both masculine plural—"children"—and singular—"my people." The alternation between singular and plural continues throughout the vision and produces a multiple portrayal of Israel as a character. He can appear as a singular individual ("my people" 3:12; 5:13) or as a group. The group can be a unit (in 1:5–7 and 5:3–5, "you" is masculine plural) or variously divided between rulers and people as in 1:10 and 3:13–15 or the different versions of the righteous versus the wicked as in 1:19–20 and 3:10–11.

The poet introduces Zion-Jerusalem as a character in 1:8. Her sad state is lamented in 1:21; she is addressed in verses 22–23, and her crimes are listed. There is a distinction between her princes and the widow and orphan. Jerusalem appears only as the city (5:3; 5:14) in the passage that we are reading and not as the woman character.

The Vineyard Song contains images and themes of a vineyard (see 1:29–30; 3:13–15), careful preparatory work, and the subsequent work of destruction. (The emphasis on "work" is signaled by the repetition of the Hebrew root עשׂה in vv. 5:2, 4–6.)[1] The major dual theme is justice and righteousness and their lack, injustice, which is marked by bloodshed and oppression of the poor. This dual theme pervades the vision of Isaiah.

The ambiguity of speaker, the variety of addressee, and the themes and imagery continue in the series of six woes (הוֹי) in 5:8–23. The dual theme of justice/injustice is central. The first woe condemns landgrabs. Ironically, the owners are left alone, and only dearth results from the greed; the poet continues the play on the verb עשׂה, to do and yield, in verse 10. The depiction of desolation here and in 5:5–6 anticipates that in 6:11–13; the parallel is signaled by the repetition of "without inhabitant" (אֵין יוֹשֵׁב: 5:9; 6:11) and "in the midst of the land" (בקרב הארץ: 5:8; 6:12).[2] The proclamation is YHWH's speech to the prophet: "In my ears YHWH of hosts (spoke/swore)."[3] This continues the theme of hearing that opened the book.

---

[1]See Rémi Lack, *La symbolique du livre d'Isaie* (Rome: Biblical Institute Press, 1973), 40.

[2]I note the use of בער "to burn or devour," in 5:5 and 6:13 and of the root שׁמם, "to be desolate, waste," in 5:9 and 6:11.

[3]"Ears" recalls the imperative "give ear" in 1:2 and 10. There is no verb for speaking or swearing in the MT; LXX provides "for he was heard." I agree with Watts that some such verb is implied but that MT does not have to be emended (John D. W. Watts, *Isaiah 1-33,* Word Biblical Commentary 24 (Waco, Tex.: Word Books, 1985), 57–59.

The woes are addressed to a plural group who are the leaders and/or the people in general. The emphasis is on the corruption and exploitation, not on the identity of those perpetrating it. These people, who pursue only their own interests, totally disregard the work (roots פֹּעַל and עָשָׂה) of YHWH. This work includes both the divine demands for justice and the proclamations of disaster that follow the violent injustice. The disregard stresses the theme of vision, sight: They neither look, נָבַט, nor see, רָאָה.

In verses 13–17 the poet shifts from denunciation to a vision of the devastating effects on the people and on all humanity. NRSV and NJB capture the immediacy of the vision by using the present and perfect tenses rather than the more frequent future. "My people"–YHWH and/or the prophet are the speaker(s)–is a singular group that suffers from hunger and thirst. Sheol feels no such pangs as she opens her maw to consume nobility and *hoi polloi.*[4] The humiliation of humanity matches the descent; the elevation of YHWH, in turn, counters the lowering. The brief vision closes with a pastoral scene of flocks grazing among the ruins.[5] The scene is bivalent: the devastation of ruins with only flocks left (see 17:1–3 and 27:10–11) and the calm security of flocks feeding (see 14:30 and 30:23–26). The vision in 5:13–17 is bound by contrasting movement and by the theme of hunger, gluttony, and quiet feeding. It is a harsh reminder of what YHWH's work can be.

The four woes in 5:18–23 denounce the perverted people "who say to evil, Good, and to good, Evil" (v. 20). They are wise in their own estimation, but not in that of prophet or deity. They want the work and the plan[6] of the Holy One of Israel to hasten to fulfillment so that they may see and know it. Sight and knowledge are definitively denied them in 6:9: "See, see, but don't know!" Ironically, they use the verbs *to hasten* and *to speed* that form the ominous name Maher-shalal-hash-baz in 8:1–4.

The end of the final woe, "Those who declare the guilty innocent and remove the innocence of the innocent from them" (v. 23), is a summary of the text to this point. All, in a variety of ways, have blocked or ignored the justice that YHWH demands, that exalts and sanctifies him. It is now fire, not humans, Sheol, or flocks, that eats. The poet employs plant imagery to emphasize the totality of the desolation. Grass goes down and dust goes up; root and blossom are destroyed. I use present tense to capture the immediacy of the passage; even though it traverses past, present, and future, the statement focuses on now. The people have rejected, do reject, and will continue to reject YHWH's teaching. This is a vignette within Isaiah's grand vision.

Therefore, as a tongue of fire devours stubble, and as dry grass sinks
down in the flame, So their root is a stench, and their blossom goes

---

[4]The possessive pronoun, *her,* attached to the three nouns in 14b, can refer to Jerusalem as in NRSV and REB or to the fact that the doomed people now belong to Sheol, who has opened "her" throat and mouth in 14a.

[5]The syntax and text of 17b are difficult and may reflect some textual corruption, but the scene is clear.

[6]The verbal root יָעַץ, which underlies "plan," is frequent in Isaiah in nominal and verbal patterns. It is the basis of the name "Wonderful Counselor" in 9:6 (see 28:29).

up like dust; For they reject *the* teaching of YHWH of hosts, and the speech of the Holy One of Israel they despise. (v. 24)

The Hebrew verb system is characterized more by the aspect than by the tense of its forms. This gives translators of Hebrew poetry leeway in what tense(s) to employ. The opening quotation of YHWH in 1:2, using a *qatal* in Hebrew, is "for the Lord has spoken" in NRSV and "for the Lord speaks" in NAB. The latter expresses the fact of YHWH's speech, not a particular time. NJB stresses immediacy with its "for Yahweh is speaking." Isaiah 2:2–4 is generally translated using the future tense; the passage presents "what will happen." But we can translate with a present tense to capture the vividness, the presentness.

> This will be in the latter times:
> The mountain of the house of the Lord is established
> As tallest of the mountains, as the highest of the hills,
> And all the nations flow to it, many peoples come and say,
> "Let us go up to the mountain of the Lord..."
> They beat their swords into plowshares and their spears
> into pruning hooks;
> Nation does not lift a sword against nation,
> and they no longer learn war.

This is not a claim that such changes in tense produce the best translation, but that they provide another perspective on the text. No two languages neatly match in terms of vocabulary, syntax, tense, and such, and translation is always a matter of choice and compromise; some aspects of the original are reflected in the translation at the expense of others. Translating אִמְרַת 5:24 as "speech," or "discourse," rather than the usual "word," emphasizes the length, in both time and space, of YHWH's address. It parallels the expansive "Torah." "Word" connotes a single, focused entity.

Verse 25 intensifies verse 24 and similarly punctuates the entire vision. Translations vary in their treatment of the verse and its relation to its context. NIV and REB have no break between verses 24 and 25, while JPS and NRSV do. JPS prints verses 25–29 as one passage. NRSV presents verse 25 separate from its context, while REB prints verses 24–25 as one passage and 26–30 as another. In NIV, 22–25b is a passage and the refrain in 25c is separate from verses 22–25b and 26–30. BHS prints 25–30 as a section separate from the preceding, while the older BHK has no break between verses 24 and 25. Although the latter two are not translations, they do represent an interpretation of the Hebrew text as preserved in ancient manuscripts; interpretation reveals itself in the arrangement of the passage in verse form and in the use or nonuse of spaces and indentations.

The translations differ in the tenses they use, varying between past–"he stretched out his hand" (NRSV)–perfect–"he has stretched out his hand" (REB) –and present–"he raises his hand" (NAB). JPS and NRSV present a past action of wrath with present effects–"his hand is stretched out still." NIV and others have a present action and effects. "The Lord's anger burns…his hand is raised."

NIV and NJB translate verses 26–29 in the present–"he lifts up a banner for the distant nations"[7]–while most others use a future–"he will raise a signal for a nation far away" (NRSV). In NRSV, for example, this produces a narrative quality for verses 25–26: YHWH was angry, but his hand is still extended, and he will soon raise a signal. Consistent use of the present yields a vision comprising a group of scenes without application to a specific time. YHWH is enraged; his hand is extended, and he (or it, the hand) is raising a signal. Present tense, in this instance, denotes omnitemporality rather than delimitation to one time.

The omnitemporal quality is marked in the Hebrew by the use of a variety of verb forms: *weqatal,* participle (active and passive), *yiqtol, qatal,* and *weyiqtol.* This apparently free alternation of verb forms is characteristic of Hebrew poetry and is much more a matter of the type of action, the relation of the verbs within the passage, and the demands of poetic form than a simple matter of tense.[8]

The superhuman force is a divine instrument that YHWH signals and whistles for. It takes form in Isaiah as the Assyrian and Babylonian armies, the cosmic host of chapter 13, and Cyrus. Not one of these manifestations, particularly the human armies, is purely human; the divine power, whether destructive or restorative, lies immediately behind the armies. I see no reason to interpret the force at the close of chapter 5 as only Assyria.

Translations vary in their rendering of the final verse of chapter 5. Most connect it with the preceding; NJB has only a comma separating it. JPS separates it from the preceding with an empty space.[9] Most employ a future tense even if they rendered verses 26–29 with a present; the phrase "in that day" signals a shift in point of view to a future time. NJB continues the present tense from verses 26–29. I use tricola for the first part, not the usual bicola. "It" reflects the masculine singular forms and the fact that the force is a tool of YHWH,

> The hooves of its horses seem[10] like flint
> and its wheels like a whirlwind,
> its roaring like a lion.

---

[7]NRSV, NJB, and others change the Hebrew to "a nation far away" on the basis of the parallel in Jeremiah 5:15. Regardless of the number in the opening phrase, the poet describes the approach of one force. The verbs and pronouns are masculine singular even though most translations use a third masculine plural.

[8]See my discussion in *Isaiah 34–35: A Nightmare/A Dream* (Sheffield: Sheffield Academic Press, 1999), 28–32 and 37–39.

[9]NAB is the most radical. It prints 30a in brackets and omits 30b without note. Apparently it connects the passage with 8:20–21 which, in turn, is printed with 14–25. See Hans Wildberger, *Isaiah 1–12: A Commentary,* trans. T. H. Trapp (Minneapolis: Fortress Press, 1991), 188–278, for a detailed presentation of a rearrangement of parts of Isaiah 5–6 and 9–10.

[10]The verb, חשׁב, and the related noun, מחשׁבה, are significant terms in Isaiah. They refer to confusing appearance and reality (2:22; 29:16; 40:15–17; 53:3–4), to transformation (29:17; 32:15), and to the gulf between human and divine ways (55:7–9; 59:7; 65:2).

It roars like young lions;
it growls and seizes prey;
it carries off and there is no one to rescue.
It growls over it on that day like the growling of Sea.[11] And he[12] looks
[נבט] to the land[13] and there is:[14] darkness, distress,[15] and light
darkening in clouds. In the year king Uzziah died, I saw [ראה] the lord
[אדני] sitting on a throne, high and lofty, and the skirts of his robe fill
the temple. Seraphim are standing above him, each with six wings:
with two they cover their faces, with two they cover their feet and with
two they fly. One calls to another:
Holy, Holy, Holy, YHWH of Hosts!
His glory fills the entire earth! (5:28b–6:3)

The transition in scenes is marked by the shift from "that day" to the
notice of Uzziah's death and from the indefinite "he/it" to the definite "I" of
the prophet. The prophet puts himself on the scene with the previous mention
of "my ears" (5:9). The scenes are bound by the repetition of the verbs to
look, נבט, and to see, ראה, from 5:12. One sees only gloom; the prophet sees
the lord and creatures, seraphim, whose name plays upon fire. The gloom
carries over in the notice of the king's death, in the prophet's sense of guilt,
and in the closing announcement of devastation. If we take YHWH as the
subject of "looks," we have the contrast of the deity looking into darkness
with the prophet, amidst that gloom, looking up and seeing YHWH on his
throne.[16] The smoke surrounding the prophet symbolizes the gloom.

Neither scene has a specific setting. The temple and the house (6:1, 4)
refer to both earthly and celestial dwellings. YHWH dwells on high and with
the humble (57:15; 66:1–2). Both scenes continue the consistent mix of sight
and hearing. We, the readers, see the army and hear its roar; we and the
prophet see king YHWH and hear proclamations and questions. The prophet's
message is a total denial of the people's ability to understand (heart), hear
(ears), or see (eyes). The point is hammered home by the repetition of nouns
and verbs in 6:9–10. Finally, the call of the invincible force is matched by the
call of the prophet; doom is the goal of both. The prophet brings the message,
and YHWH its execution.

---

[11]I capitalize *Sea* to highlight the allusion to the Canaanite myth when the sea deity Yamm
threatens to swallow the god Baal; see 5:14; 23:4; 25:7; 27:1; 51:9–10; and 63:11 for other allusions. The mythic allusion fits with the superhuman nature of the advancing force.

[12]The antecedent is unclear. It can be the force ("it") or YHWH; the NRSV employs an
impersonal "if one looks."

[13]ארץ is "the land," "the country" (NJB), and "below" (JPS).

[14]"There is" reflects the deictic particle that occurs with the opening description of the on-
rushing force: "Look! hastily, swiftly they come!" (5:26).

[15]צר distress, is a homophone for צר, flint, in verse 28. I only note some of Isaiah's work
and play with words including homophones, similar roots, consonants in different arrangements,
rhyme, assonance, and such. This is another textual area that contributes to the richness and
diversity of Isaiah's vision.

[16]See 18:3–6 for an interesting parallel scene of seeing and hearing.

The poet repeats the declaration of divine elevation and holiness from 5:16. A similar combination is found in 57:15; the phrase "high and lofty" (רם ונשא) is in both passages. The cleansing of the prophet and the removal of his sin allude to the refining of Jerusalem and the removal of her impurities (1:25) and to the many similar acts throughout the vision. Isaiah 1:25 and 6:6–7 both employ the root סור, "to depart" and "remove," and feature a delightful play with the words צרף, "to burn" or "refine," שרפים, "seraphim," and רצפה, "burning coal."

If this were a longer reading of Isaiah, we would continue the development of word and root play and the discussion of the passage's place in its context in Isaiah. The latter would assess the impact of the parallel and contrasting texts that occur throughout Isaiah, parallels based on terminology, structure, themes, and imagery. As in this brief analysis, this would produce alternative readings, highlight choices that a translator/interpreter would make, and produce a richer reading of Isaiah, but it would not produce or support only one way to read the vision.

In treating Isaiah as one work, I read with my presuppositions and literary categories to see what kinds of readings are produced. This is not an attempt to prove these presuppositions and categories as the only proper way to interpret the vision. I posit a certain type of coherency when I approach Isaiah as a grand poem. "Certain type of coherency" commits me to a different way of reading Isaiah than would "unity" or a "unified whole." This literary approach itself is one among an innumerable group of literary modes of reading.

Even though my analysis is limited to a select text and to a small number of issues, themes, and images, I am still able to display the richness, complexity, and ambiguity of the Isaianic text. The latter are both "there" in the text and yet a product of my reading that is open to ambiguity and polysemy (again the telltale "both/and"). I locate them in a textual space concerned with issues such as the aspect and tense of the verbs, the speaker including the use of quotation marks, and the division of the text into reading sections. Examples from contemporary translations of Isaiah display some of the possibilities open to a translator/interpreter in each issue. Translation includes not just the words used but also the way they are presented on the page, including all manner of spacing, punctuation, and the presence (or not) of chapters and verses.

I refer to "textual space" and not a "textual level" because, in biblical studies, the latter too often implies a hierarchy in which issues such as textual variants and problems, the verbal system, the division of the text, and such are thought of as basic and primary like the "lower criticism" of old. Interpretation is "higher" and based on the prior textual work. "Prior work" itself implies a temporal hierarchy. Textual work is done first, and only then is the text interpreted. The assumption is that such textual study and translation are free, or at least relatively free, of the problems that beset interpretation. The latter include questions of philosophy, theology, history, literary form, and such.

Yet even these specific issues of text criticism, verb aspect and tense, punctuation, and poetic structure involve variety and ambiguity. How one resolves each to produce a given translation/interpretation encompasses one's assumptions about the larger text and one's categories for reading/interpretation. Reading, interpretation, and translation are all different aspects of the same process that comprises both text and reader. I use the virgule to reflect this mutuality. For example, if one assumes, as I do, that the overlap of divine and prophetic speech is an integral part of the vision, then distinguishing the speaker, YHWH or the prophet, and placing quotation marks are not the issues that they will be for someone who assumes the necessity of clearly demarcating the speakers and speeches.

Finally, I present an unbroken text that parallels the advancing force with the prophet's vision of YHWH. I do not treat the latter, chapter 6, as a separate section or a distinct genre, and therefore do not enter into the debate as to whether this is a "call narrative" or only a "commissioning." And I maintain the anonymity. The poet says "I," not "I, Isaiah."

Genre is a type or category of literary work. It is a name that serves as a guide, which varies in rigor, to reading a given piece. To term Isaiah a vision written in poetry leads to readings quite different from those produced by seeing Isaiah as a loosely redacted collection of material of widely varying age. In biblical studies, genre is most frequently used to refer to material much shorter than an entire book. Critics discuss judgment and salvation oracles, woe oracles, lawsuits, and such and not the genre of Isaiah or Jeremiah. For them, genre serves to break a work into independent units whose independence and integrity have to be maintained in any interpretation. Isaiah 6 has to be read as Isaiah's call or commissioning. Genre, in this limited focus, divides a work into manageable units, and, all too often, biblical studies stay at this level. Division into smaller segments historically precedes genre analysis since it already exists in the partitioning of the biblical text into chapters and verses; division into sections for regular reading in synagogue or church preceded this. Breaking a text into manageable sections is a practical necessity in reading and interpretation; I have focused on Isaiah 5–6, not 4–7. But to present one division as the only one is not a necessary step; division, at this point, goes from being helpful and descriptive to being controlling and prescriptive. Isaiah 5–6, 4:2–7:17, or 6:1–8:11 can each be read as continuous texts just as well as two or more textual units, and the "units" can vary in length and content.[17]

I close with a few reflections on the power and control inherent in the interpretive enterprise; they are evident in my terms *manageable, controlling,* and *prescriptive.* As open and as plural as it may try to be, any reading, any interpretation, attempts a certain control of the text and thereby of the audience receiving that reading. A significant number of contemporary biblical studies, whether termed postmodern or not, explore the many ways that institutions

---

[17]See Roland Barthes, *S/Z,* trans. R. Miller (New York: Hill and Wang, 1974), especially 10–16.

directly and indirectly influence the production of biblical interpretations and translations. The institutions include those with religious, academic, and national interests; the interests are seldom clearly distinguished in a given institution, such as a church or university. The studies comprise a wide range of approaches, such as feminist, sociological, ethnological, historical, and linguistic.

When pursued with these interests, the type of close reading employed in this essay can aid in revealing the presence and effects of control in textual areas often spoken of as outside of such influence. Such "basic" matters as how we understand Hebrew poetry and how we translate a text from Isaiah and present it on a page are guided and affected by forces and goals that we, as individual readers, are usually not aware of. I, like any writer/reader, must await the reactions of other readers to learn more fully what I have done and not done in this essay.

An Ending That Does Not End

The Book of Jeremiah

Walter Brueggemann

The book of Jeremiah is occasionally judged by critical scholarship to be "unreadable," that it lacks coherence and is so marked by disjunction that it cannot be seen whole.[1] What is meant, of course, is that it cannot be read sensibly according to our Western habits of coherent literature that make a single, sustained affirmation.[2] The book of Jeremiah is indeed unreadable, unless one can allow for the plurality of voices that are shrill, disjunctive, and in conflict with one another, for that is what is given us in the book.[3]

I

The book of Jeremiah is "unreadable," it seems clear enough, because it is a commentary on, a reflection about, and an engagement with an "unreadable" lived experience. Without facing all the complexities and uncertainties of critical history, it is clear that something decisive happened in and to Jerusalem with the Babylonian assault, culminating in the destruction and deportation of 587 B.C.E.[4] The community of deportees, along with other

---

[1]See Louis Stulman, *Order Amid Chaos: Jeremiah as Symbolic Tapestry,* The Biblical Seminar 57 (Sheffield: Sheffield Academic Press, 1998), 26–27 and passim.

[2]A case is readily made that in their canonical form the prophetic books have been ordered according to the themes of judgment and hope; see Brevard S. Childs, "Jeremiah," in *Introduction to the Old Testament as Scripture* (Philadelphia: Fortress Press, 1979), 345–54, and Ronald Clements, "Patterns in the Prophetic Literature," in *Canon and Authority,* ed. George W. Coats and Burke O. Long (Philadelphia: Fortress Press, 1977), 42–55. While helpful, such an approach of necessity must ignore many of the nuances that here concern us.

[3]In addition to Stulman, *Order Amid Chaos,* see especially Christopher R. Seitz, *Theology in Conflict: Reactions to the Exile in the Book of Jeremiah,* Beihefte zur ZAW 176 (Berlin: Walter de Gruyter, 1989).

[4]Critical judgments on the nature of the crisis of 587 cover a broad range and spectrum, from the maximal view of D. L. Smith-Christopher, "Reassessing the Historical and Sociological Impact of the Babylonian Exile (597/587–539 BCE)", in *Exile: Old Testament, Jewish, and Christian Conceptions,* ed. James M. Scott (Leiden: Brill, 1997), 7–36, to the skepticism of H. M. Barstad, *The Myth of the Empty Land: A Study in the History and Archaeology of Judah During the 'Exilic' Period* (Oslo: Scandinavian University Press, 1996). For a review of the problem from a skeptical perspective, see *Leading Captivity Captive: 'The Exile' as History and Ideology,* ed. Lester L. Grabbe, JSOT Sup 278 (Sheffield: Sheffield Academic Press, 1998).

communities of displaced and/or bewildered Jews, had a long time to reflect on that strange event that we may, for convenience, peg at 587. That reflection, however, was not clear, singular, or coherent, for it was marked by a host of uncertainties that precluded a "readable" commentary.

The obliqueness of the event is in part political. Jerusalem before 587 and several interpretive communities after 587 were filled with disputatious opinion that in some large part served vested interests. The questions of what went wrong and whom to blame are preliminaries to the seizure of initiative and the assertion of legitimacy for the future (as in Jer. 24).[5] That is, every reflection is in some measure a positioning for the future.

Along with such political bewilderment and posturing, moreover, these lived events evoked serious and imaginative theological reflection. Characteristically, Israelite interpreters proceeded with the assumption that YHWH is a key and decisive player in these events, and therefore "prophetic" discernment–voices that claim to speak on behalf of YHWH–are in play. The role and purpose of YHWH in these events, however, are not obvious. For that reason, bewilderment and dispute are the order of the day, theologically as well as politically. It is a theological debate or quarrel about a historical experience, the meaning of which is unclear, that lies behind the "unreadability" of the book of Jeremiah.

The interplay of competing interpretations is in part a function of long-standing competing traditions–Mosaic, Davidic, and Zionist among others. Beyond that, the interplay of competing interpretations arises because it is clear in some quarters that none of the old traditions are adequate for this moment, and something new, different, and venturesome must be said here in a wholly new circumstance. Underneath that, moreover, we may imagine that the practice of such lived interpretation is done by discerning people who themselves are *not sure* what they are witnessing and living through, and therefore *not sure* what is to be said.

II

The theme for reflection seems to be given in the events themselves. It is an *end*–what happened in 587 is an end of the royal line, the end of a certain kind of temple practice, the end of a certain social cohesion and coherence. Beyond that, not much is certain, and it depends on how deeply the communities want to go about the end.[6] Is it the end of the community of Jerusalem as a viable cult operation? a viable political entity? Is it the end of faith? Is it the end of YHWH's attentiveness and fidelity? Or is there more yet, and if so, on what basis?

---

[5]On the question of blame, see Stulman, *Order Amid Chaos,* 120–36. Stulman shows how the object of blame varies from text to text.

[6]The case of Hananiah in chapter 28 indicates that some did not go deeply at all into the crisis. Hananiah, moreover, is to be understood not simply as "false," but as a practitioner of Zionist ideology that assumed Jerusalem's long-term guarantee against disaster.

It requires no great imagination to see that different interpreters and different commentators rooted in different interpretive traditions, situated in different circumstances, and given different personal inclinations with different social status at stake will judge the matter differently. Thus, capacity to hold together such differences in comment and reflection without reconciling them or without privileging any of them, is definitional for "unreadability" and surely qualifies as "postmodern." Indeed, one can make the claim that 587 ended a certain form of Jerusalem's "modernity" that operated with a single set of claims that ensured certainty and privilege.[7] "Unreadability" may reflect twentieth-century contemporary interpreters, well-schooled in modernity and accustomed to reading texts "modernly," standing in the face of a "postmodern" text as bewildered as were the framers of that text.

III

It is not necessary to specify the many poignant ways in which the poetic vision of the book of Jeremiah anticipates and imagines the end in material conventionally judged "early and genuine."[8] The imaginative entry into the *finality* of life with YHWH is enacted in rich and daring symbolization such as, for example, that of a broken marriage that culminates in "abandonment" (3:1–4:4) and terminal illness (8:18–22; 30:12–15).[9] That material, familiar to us and explicated most sensitively by Abraham Heschel, offers the most powerful and elemental truth of suffering that "the end" produces, which can only be voiced in poetry.[10]

Of that "ending," I wish to specify only some uses of the verb *kalah* that anticipate a complete termination:

You have struck them, but they felt no anguish;
You have consumed *(klh)* them,
but they refused to take correction. (5:3)[11]

I will scatter them…

---

[7]It is, of course, an anachronism to use the term *modern* in this way. The notion of a "Solomonic Enlightenment," moreover, has been largely dismissed by current scholars. Given both of these realities, it is still nonetheless clear that the Solomonic enterprise did indeed shift the basic assumptions of society; the embrace of those new assumptions symbolized by Solomon's temple is exactly what is placed in jeopardy by the events around 587.

[8]I intend to beg all questions of historicity concerning the person of the prophet and what he may have uttered. See Walter Brueggemann, "The Book of Jeremiah: Portrait of the Prophet," in *Interpreting the Prophets,* ed. James Luther Mays and Paul J. Achtemeier (Philadelphia: Fortress Press, 1987), 113–29.

[9]James Muilenburg, "The Terminology of Adversity in Jeremiah," in *Translating & Understanding the Old Testament: Essays in Honor of Herbert Gordon May,* ed. Harry Thomas Frank and William L. Reed (Nashville: Abingdon Press, 1970), 42–63, has explored the use of images and metaphors in the judgment motif in Jeremiah. More recently my colleague Kathleen O'Connor has gone more poignantly into some of these metaphors. See "The Broken Family Mended: Jeremiah 31," (forthcoming) and "Unfaithful Passions: Coding Women Coding Men in Jer. 2:1–4:2," the latter with Pete Diamond, *Biblical Interpretation* 4 (1996), 288–310.

[10]Abraham Heschel, *The Prophets* (New York: Harper & Row, 1962), chaps. 16–17 and passim.

[11]All scripture quotations in this chapter are from the NRSV unless otherwise noted.

and I will send the sword after them, until I have consumed *(klh)* them.
(9:15; Eng. v. 16)
They shall perish *(klh)* by the sword and by famine, and their dead
bodies shall become food. (16:4)

In these three cases, the verb *klh* bespeaks a decisive ending. In 5:3, the
statement is on the lips of the poet, in 9:15 and 16:4 it is a divine oracle in
prose.

These three uses are matched by a negative use of *'aḥar* in 5:31:

What shall you do when the end *('aḥarth)* comes?

In 10:25, moreover, the verb *klh* is used, only here the end is at the
hands of the nations and not the direct work of YHWH:

They have devoured *('kl)* Jacob;
they have devoured *('kl)* him
and consumed *(klh)* him,
and have laid waste *(mm)* his habitation.[12]

That much is commonplace. The statements fit our usual assumption about
prophetic judgment in general and Jeremiah in particular. It strikes us as
conventionally appropriate for what might be said, either in anticipation of
587 or in reflection on it by the prophetic materials that are "early and genuine."

IV

What interests us, however, is that this rather straightforward conclusion
about the loss of 587 is held with great unease in the tradition, unease that
contributes precisely to the "unreadability" of the text. I will comment in
particular on three texts that are situated in what is commonly regarded as
"early and authentic" poetry from the prophet.

In a context of savage anticipation of the undoing of creation (4:23–26)
and a conclusion that asserts YHWH's resolve not to relent or turn back from
a determination to destroy (v. 28), comes 4:27:

For thus says the LORD: The whole land shall be a desolation; yet I
will not make a full end *(klh)*.

The verse is clearly at deep odds with those around it and contradicts the
characteristic announcement of the end. Indeed the two parts of the prose
verse itself are at odds, for the first phrase ends with "a desolation." There
have been, of course, various strategies to "comment" on the last line in ways
that contribute to "readability." Perhaps the verse is a prose insert, as the
NRSV seems to suggest. Or the negative *lo'* can be converted to *lah* ("to her").
Or with William Holladay, one may revocalize to "and none of it."[13] Obviously,

---

[12]There is likely a play on the two terms "devour" *('kl)* and "consume" *(klh)*.

[13]William L. Holladay, *Jeremiah 1: A Commentary on the Book of the Prophet Jeremiah Chapters
1–25,* Hermeneia (Philadelphia: Fortress Press, 1986), 166–67.

all these efforts are to find a way out of a statement that is unambiguous but does not "fit" the main claim of the lines around it.

The same "problem" is evident in 5:10. The small textual unit of 5:10–13 has the characteristic elements of a speech of judgment. The indictment is that Israel and Judah have "been utterly faithless" and "have spoken falsely." The sentence is "destroy" and "strip." The lines conclude with a statement of deep resolve to destroy, not unlike the final line of 4:28.

In the midst of that speech of judgment, and just after the verb "destroy" *(sht)* comes our verb:

But do not make a full end *(klh).* (v. 10)

Again the verse is problematic for a single reading. Here the preferred strategy simply deletes the negative in order to "correct" the "inconcinnity" and bring the line into conformity with the context.[14]

Our third text, 5:18, is again situated in a context of massive, relentless destruction. Verse 17, speaking of the "enduring nation" that will destroy, is dominated by the verb "devour" *('kl).*

They shall eat up *('kl)* your harvest and your food;
they shall eat up *('kl)* your sons and your daughters;
they shall eat up *('kl)* your flocks and your herds;
they shall eat up *('kl)* your vines and your fig trees.

The verse culminates with a different verb for "destroy" *(yrš).* Verse 19 is commonly judged to be in prose, but clearly refers to the wholesale destruction, again with marks of a speech of judgment:

Indictment:
    You have forsaken me and served foreign gods in your land.

Sentence:
    You shall serve strangers in a land that is not yours.[15]

The justification for destruction in Jerusalem (v. 17) and deportation (v. 19) is unambiguous. Then, in the midst of this clarity about the end, comes verse 18:

But even in those days, says the LORD, I will not make a full end *(klh)* of you.

The prose character of the verse plus the introductory phrase likely marks this verse as an "intrusion."[16]

---

[14]Holladay, *Jeremiah 1,* 183, following Wilhelm Rudolph, *Jeremia,* 3d ed., Handbuch zum Alten Testament 1/12 (Tübingen: Mohr [Siebeck], 1968). Holladay notes that because of the "inconcinnity," LXX adopts a different maneuver for the text.

[15]Patrick D. Miller, Jr., *Sin and Judgment in the Prophets: A Stylistic and Theological Analysis* (Chico, Calif.: Scholars Press, 1982), 67, lists this text among those in prophetic utterances in which the anticipated judgment matches in detail the affront.

[16]Again notice the play on *klh* and *'kl,* the latter occurring four times in the preceding verse.

In all three texts, 4:27, 5:10, and 5:18, explanations can readily be given about why this utterance ("not an end") does not belong where it is or does not mean what it says. Studied and conventional critical strategies easily dispose of the texts that "do not fit." The several critical maneuvers are examples of the standard ways in which criticism serves to make the text "readable."

It is worth observing, of course, that these critical "corrections" are not required or mandated by the text itself, but are judged to be necessary by the critical commentator, he or she having decided beforehand what the text must say (or cannot say). The critical commentator characteristically has decided beforehand that the text must speak with one voice that is the dominant voice, so a lesser, challenging, conflicting, competing voice in the very same text is untenable and must either be silenced or made to conform. Note well, I do not say that such a reader has decided *substantively* ahead of time what must be said, that is, that this is an ending; rather, such a reader has decided "modernly" ahead of time that there can be only one voice and that here this one, characteristic voice is the voice of an end. Thus, the dominant voice, by critical maneuver, is given complete hegemony in the text. The substantive outcome that is likely incidental to such a maneuver is an unqualified, unmitigated assertion of an end, no voice to the contrary. Thus, the text three times says:

I will not make a full end (4:27),

Do not make a full end (5:10),

I will not make a full end of you (5:18).

The text undoubtedly says that three times. But it must not and cannot say that, and so when we finish, it does not! By now the text has become "readable."

Our work here, however, is to consider "postmodernly" rejection of such readability that refuses the text's own terms. In this context, I take our "postmodern" responsibility to be to refuse such a flattened, hegemonic reading and to pay heed to the lesser voice that seems odd in this conversation. That is, our work is to see what this strange, disruptive utterance might intend, rather than to silence or distort it. In these three cases, we must wonder why the final form of the text would say "not a full end" in such a way as to speak against the "end speech" of the dominant strain.

The lived outcomes of 587 were never clear. The "meaning" of the "end" was not given in the "facts" themselves, but awaited interpretive utterance.[17]

---

[17]The facts did not speak for themselves, but awaited construal. The problematic character of the "facts" is evident in the work I have cited in note 4. Indeed, the much talk there of "ideology" is an argument that the "facts" have been wrongly construed, thus insisting upon yet a different construal that is taken to be as more congruent with "what happened." Indeed Robert Carroll, "Exile! What Exile? Deportation and the Discourses of Diaspora," in *Leading Captivity Captive: "The Exile" as History and Ideology,* ed. Lester L. Grabbe, Journal for the Study of the Old Testament Supplement Series 278 (Sheffield: Sheffield Academic Press, 1998), 64 n. 8, comments on "this obsession" with the "Bible as history." The appeal to "facts" against theological interpretation, of course, is itself also an ideological enterprise, only slightly different in texture.

No one knew what happened in 587 until what happened was "said," until it was given some construal. It did not take great imagination to see an end in the events, even though what was *seen* was *said* imaginatively in the poetic traditions of the prophets (2 Kings 21:12). The remaining issue, after the utterance of an end, is whether such an utterance has fully exhausted what has happened. These three modest statements that I have cited assert a conviction that there is more in the event that remains to be said. It is easiest to conclude, as critical scholarship has characteristically done, that these are "later" judgments, reflecting a subsequent experience of the community that had in fact not ended, that found new signs and measures of YHWH's fidelity. That is what is meant by the dismissive and conventional label "gloss."

It occurs to me, however, that already closer to the event itself, not necessarily "late" and without waiting generations for new data in new context, some might have made this disquieting utterance/counter-construal. Perhaps "not a full end" is simply an emotional refusal or inability to see what is there; such a thought, moreover, permits the counter-thought that perhaps the conviction of an end, so fully stated in the Jeremiah tradition, was an ideological effort to see more than was there, because it was not an end. That is, we cannot simply assume that the "speech of end" is correct while the contrary speech is not. Perhaps "not a full end" is wishful thinking, such a deep cherishing of what was that its end was unthinkable and therefore, finally, unspeakable. Or perhaps "not a full end" is a doggedly determined theological affirmation that while the political, economic apparatus had ended, YHWH is no quitter and that YHWH's faithful passion is not coterminous with visible arrangements. Or perhaps it is not resistance or wishful thinking or determined faith, but simply a vacillation before unclear evidence, vacillation designed precisely to keep things open against the dominant judgment, not because the end could not be faced, but because it is not known yet what might constitute compelling evidence of an end. In this alternate opinion, "not a full end" is to be taken as deliberately dialectal and dialogical with "a full end," not wanting to nullify the other opinion, but wanting to keep open that for which not enough is known to give certain closure.[18]

It is entirely possible to probe what might have been intended in these statements as I have done—or at least to report how they strike this reader—without attributing too much authorial intention to the options.[19] I judge that the major responsibility of this discussion in any case is not to consider primarily the text but to consider our interpretive habits. Our critical habits are mostly intolerant of minority views and counter-convictions. Our habit is to give no privilege to mystery, bewilderment, or unresolve, precisely so that there can

---

[18]See Walter Brueggemann, "Shattered Transcendence? Exile and Restoration," in *Biblical Theology: Problems and Perspectives; In Honor of J. Christiaan Beker,* ed. Steven J. Kraftchick et al. (Nashville: Abingdon Press, 1995), 169–82.

[19]A postmodern approach is not greatly interested in authorial intent but is more likely to proceed from "the final form of the text."

be a single reading, either a single reading to be taken up by a believer or a single reading to provide a "grain" against which an academic skeptic can read.[20] What these three utterances recognize, however, is that lived reality is not so single, neat, or obvious as to permit a single, unchallenged construal. Such a text as these invites living with unresolve that may, in this case, be a God-given, God-enacted unresolve.[21] It could be, if we engage a second naivete that is genuinely naive, that the God who enacted 587 did not know, could not see, had not yet decided if this is an end—too soon to say, because this God is capable of twists and turns that defy our usual readability.[22]

V

It turns out that these three utterances did indeed speak the truth, for the identifiable community of Israel as YHWH's people did not end, and indeed "Jerusalem" did not end. This truth-telling may be understood as the belated conviction of another generation that subsequently produced emerging Judaism. This belated conviction could be expressed as William McKane's "rolling corpus," so that what was decisive and resolved eventuated otherwise against the "early" judgment.[23] But even if that is the case, the three statements turn out to be telling the truth and protesting against the single-minded harshness of the "speech of end." That this is not an end can be understood *historically* as Judaism emerges. That it is not an end can be understood *literarily* as the scroll "unrolls." That it is not an end can be understood *theologically* in terms of the One who plucks up and tears down being the same One who plants and builds, the One who will not be fully contained in or caught completely in the "speech of end."

Given the openness that our three utterances maintain against closure, we may consider several extrapolations from "not an end." Among these is, most importantly, 30:11:

> For I am with you, says the LORD, to save you;
> I will *make an end* of all the nations
> among which I scattered you,
> but of you I will *not make an end,*
> I will chastise you in just measure,
> and I will by no means leave you unpunished.

---

[20]As a case in point, see the comments of Timothy Beal, "The System and the Speaking Subject in the Hebrew Bible: Reading for Divine Abjection," *Biblical Interpretation* 2 (1994): 171–89, concerning the way in which Julia Kristeva has given a single reading in order to read against that single reading. Beal shows that the initial judgment of a single reading in the Micah text is itself a distortion of the text.

[21]That is, according to my judgment, the problem is not simply a problem with a text that is not single, but with the God witnessed to in the text as unresolved, that is, not single in intent.

[22]On "second naivete," see Mark I. Wallace, *The Second Naivete: Barth, Ricoeur, and the New Yale Theology,* Studies in American Biblical Hermeneutics 6 (Macon: Mercer University Press, 1990). For an example of such a reading, see Walter Brueggemann, "The 'Uncared For' Now Cared For (Jeremiah 30:12–17): A Methodological Consideration," in *Old Testament Theology: Essays on Structure, Theme, and Text* (Minneapolis: Fortress Press, 1992), 296–307.

[23]William McKane, *A Critical and Exegetical Commentary on Jeremiah I,* International Critical Commentary (Edinburgh: T. & T. Clark, 1986), l–lxxxiii.

Now this utterance is in "The Book of Comfort," where such a statement is no longer objectionable, as it has been judged to be in the three earlier cases. The dominant verb is "save" *(ys')* and no longer "destroy." That dominant verb permits the statement "not a full end," though the chastisement and punishment can now be kept on schedule. What interests us is that the negative statement—"not a full end" (not "corrected" here by any critical scholar)—is matched by a positive use of the same verb: "I will make an end *(klh)* of all the nations." The poetic tradition is indeed capable of saying this directly when that is what is intended, without any correcting assistance from criticism. Now that great claim can be said directly, unambiguously, "an end to all the nations," surely meaning Babylon and all its allies and functionaries. Indeed, such an end is required if Israel is to have "not an end," for it is the end of Babylon that makes "not an end" a reality for Jerusalem.

This same rhetoric that apparently applies to Babylon in 30:11 is twice used, in very different contexts and genres, with reference to Egypt. In the Oracles Against the Nations, it is particularly with reference to Egypt that our phrasing is used in the context of a salvation oracle for Israel:

> As for you, have no fear, my servant Jacob,
> says the LORD,
> for I am with you.
> I will make an end *(klh)* of all the nations
> among which I have banished you,
> but I will not make an end *(klh)* of you!
> I will chastise you in just measure,
> and I will by no means leave you unpunished. (46:28)

Even though this verse is in the long chapter concerning Egypt, the assertion here is a positive one concerning Jacob/Israel. There is to be *no fear* because there is *no end* of Jacob/Israel. The verse closely parallels 30:11. The "not an end" is again matched, as in 30:11, with an "end" for the threatening superpower that challenges the will and authority of Yahweh. There is to be an ending, but not for Jacob/Israel!

In slightly different rhetoric, the polemic against Egypt occurs at the end of the final prose denunciation of Egypt, or more specifically "all you Judeans who live in the land of Egypt":

> I am going to watch over them for harm and not for good; all the people of Judah who are in the land of Egypt shall perish *(klh)* by the sword and by famine, until not one is left. (44:27)

Now there is to be a Jewish ending, and it is not here corrected or modified by criticism, as in the three earlier cases I have cited. This final polemic would seem to be on the lips either of Jews who remained in Jerusalem or, more likely, Jews who were in Babylon and became the dominant voice of emerging Judaism. In either case, there is no dissenting voice here to suggest that the end pronounced over Egyptian Jews is "not an end." Except that we should notice that this is a Jerusalem or Babylonian text.

Perhaps in a text of Egyptian Jews (that we do not have), there might have been a whimsical, hopeful utterance, "not an end." Or if not such a text or even such an utterance, perhaps an unheard prayer or an unrecorded affirmation or an unuttered wish. We have seen how criticism may belatedly silence such yearning or determination. Perhaps there were other devices for silencing to make sure that this Jewish community in Egypt heard only an imposed finality. After 30:11, which may pertain to *Babylon* and after 46:28 on *Egypt* and 44:27 on *Jews in Egypt,* we may also note finality voiced toward Babylon that is the ground of Jeremianic hope expressed as *Realpolitik.* Babylon must end for there to be "not an end" in Jerusalem:

> You who live by mighty waters,
> rich in treasures,
> your end *(qets)* has come,
> the thread of your life is cut. (51:13)

VI

In the end [*sic*], the issue is not only canon-making or even competition between interpretive communities, but concerns the force of newness that goes under the name of YHWH. Finally, the tension in the text is theological, even if that theological tension inevitably comes in historical and/or literary expression. "In the end," the book of Jeremiah honors these silenced utterances and affirms that 587 was indeed "not an end." Now, with a different term, there is indeed an "afterward" for this community-not-ended:

> In the latter *('aharth)* days you will understand it clearly. (23:20)

> For surely I know the plans I have for you, says the LORD, plans for your welfare and not for harm, to give you a future *('aharth)* with hope. (29:11)

> In the latter *('aharth)* days you will understand this. (30:24)

> There is hope for your future *('aharth),* says the LORD, your children shall come back to their own country. (31:17)

This is not an afterward that the community can describe. It is an afterward not in hand, not yet given. It is not-yet-lived history. It is, rather, passionate poetic conviction that requires utterance that moves past history and past uttered verdicts of closure, to say much more than is known, to imagine more than can be seen.

In many places, the book of Jeremiah has "a sense of an ending."[24] The final form of the book is, however, unsure and restless with such a sense. Its sense of an ending is a historical judgment, but a historical judgment that floats in an ocean of freighted theological conviction. In the end, this restlessness

---

[24]The phrase, of course, is from Frank Kermode, *The Sense of an Ending: Studies in the Theory of Fiction* (Oxford: Oxford University Press, 1968).

refuses an ending, refuses to let observed data dictate the edges of faith. For that reason, apparently without a clear sense of an ending, no clear ending for the book of Jeremiah could be managed. There are, to be sure, efforts at such an ending, and they are not to be taken lightly; but they are, each one, provisional.[25]

1. The best-known ending, most obvious, is in the Hebrew text that persists in English translation in 52:31–34; it concerns the ongoing exile of King Jehoiachin, ongoing for thirty-seven years. But the discussion of Gerhard von Rad, Martin Noth, and Hans Walter Wolff evidences that this "ending" is not clear.[26] Indeed, perhaps this ending is designed exactly to reflect the conversation of "end/not an end" that we have seen in our three texts, that is appropriate to this construal of reality with YHWH—not closed, but not known.

2. If for the moment we can take chapter 52 as an addendum borrowed from 2 Kings 25, we may consider 51:59–64 as an ending; clearly verse 64b has the cadence of a literary and intentional ending. Babylon is "sunk." That sinking creates space and possibility for Jerusalem. There is indeed an ending, but it is for the empire and not in Jerusalem. The ending is rather in Babylon, where Nebuchadnezzar had imagined that his domination would never end (see Isa. 47:10).

3. If we continue to bracket chapter 52 and, in addition, allow for the movement of the Oracles of the Nations (chaps. 46–51) to chapter 25 along with LXX, then 45:5 becomes the ending.[27] Jeremiah 45:1–5 is an oracle that confirms a massive ending of "the whole land":

> Thus says the LORD: I am going to break down what I have built, and pluck up what I have planted—that is, the whole land. And you, do you seek great things for yourself? Do not seek them; for I am going to bring disaster upon all flesh, says the LORD. (45:4–5a)

There is, however, a qualifier for Baruch:

> But I will give you your life as a prize of war in every place to which you may go. (45:5b)

---

[25]On alternative endings, see the nice phrase concerning chapters 45 and 52 by Stulman, *Order Amid Chaos,* 69–71: "Endings with Embryonic Beginnings."

[26]See Gerhard von Rad, *Old Testament Theology I* (San Francisco: Harper & Row, 1962) 84, 343; Martin Noth, *The Deuteronomic History,* Journal for the Study of the Old Testament Supplement Series 15 (Sheffield: JSOT Press 1981), 12, 74, 98; and Hans Walter Wolff, "The Kerygma of the Deuteronomic Historical Work," in *The Vitality of Old Testament Traditions,* ed. Walter Brueggemann and Hans Walter Wolff, 2d ed. (Atlanta: John Knox Press, 1982), 86, 100. See also more recently the intertextual approach of Jan Jaynes Granowski, "Jehoiachin at the King's Table: A Reading of the Ending of the Second Book of Kings," in *Reading Between Texts:Intertextuality and the Hebrew Bible,* ed. Danna Nolan Fewell, Literary Currents in Biblical Interpretation (Louisville: Westminster/John Knox Press, 1992), 173–88.

[27]On the shape of the Greek text of Jeremiah, see J. Gerald Janzen, *Studies in the Text of Jeremiah,* Harvard Semitic Monographs 6 (Cambridge: Harvard University Press, 1973).

Baruch here is many things. He is the aide of the prophet who has been taken to Egypt (43:6). But he is also a cipher for the continuing faithful community of Jews who stayed close to the truth of Jeremiah, perhaps to the entire construal of the tradition of Deuteronomy. Baruch is also point man for scribalism that here becomes Torah teacher who assured new forms of faithfulness and well-being to Judaism.[28] He is all these; to him (them) is uttered an exception of well-being–not a final end.[29]

There are many endings to the book of Jeremiah. But there is no ending. Because there is "not a full end." All of this, the lack of an ending, will "be understood in latter days," days perhaps not unlike our own (23:20; 30:24). For now the "latter days" may be postmodern, when we refuse any reduction that makes matters simple and manageable. It occurred to me that the modernist passion for a single voice may be a mark of modernist despair that expects nothing. It is in the tensive conversations of disputed interpretation that newness comes. Thus, "single reading" may be not only an intellectual commitment. It may also be a theological commitment to closure that expects nothing and will receive nothing. The modest counter-voice of 4:27; 5:10; 5:18 refuses such closure. We do well to listen again, without silencing or distorting a faint alternative to ending.

---

[28]See James Muilenburg, "Baruch the Scribe," in *Proclamation and Presence: Old Testament Essays in Honour of Gwynne Henton Davies,* ed. John I. Durham and J. R. Porter (London: SCM Press, 1970), 215–38; J. Andrew Dearman, "My Servants the Scribes: Composition and Context in Jeremiah 36," *Journal of Biblical Literature* 109 (199): 403–21; and more broadly, Philip R. Davies, *Scribes and Schools: The Canonization of the Hebrew Scriptures* (Louisville: Westminster John Knox Press, 1998).

[29]Seitz, *Theology in Conflict,* 280 and passim, suggests that Baruch, along with Ebed-Melek, are "singled out as exceptions to the respective judgments." That is, they are exempted from the general condemnation and as such open a way to the future, because not all are to be destroyed.

An Abusive God?

Identity and Power/Gender and Violence in Ezekiel 23

Mary E. Shields

The text of Ezekiel is occasioned by an identity crisis, more specifically, a *divine* identity crisis. Written by a prophet who had presumably been exiled to Babylon in 598 B.C.E., the text deals with the problems associated with political defeat in the ancient Near Eastern world. The primary problem is divine: How can a deity whose country is defeated, whose people are exiled, still be divine? How can such a deity continue to have power? What kind of relationship can such a deity have with the people whose primary texts have guaranteed them that YHWH has chosen them and their capital city, Jerusalem; whose texts have indicated YHWH would always keep them, their temple, and their city safe?

Ezekiel 23 addresses this identity crisis in a roundabout way, in the guise of an extended metaphor. The metaphor posits Samaria and Jerusalem as two sisters, Oholah and Oholibah, who become YHWH's wives[1] yet do not fulfill proper wifely or motherly duties. Focusing on sexuality, the text discusses the sisters' "whorings" (זנות) with foreigners/foreign countries. These whorings are portrayed in such a fashion as to elicit condemnation from a male audience.[2] The descriptions of the two sisters' actions are also formulated so as to set them over against YHWH. Using conventions associated with gender and sexuality, this text seeks to address YHWH's identity crisis in order to re-establish YHWH's power and authority. In the end, YHWH does (re?)establish control over the people, thereby shoring up his own identity as proper male head of household, which in turn proves his sovereignty as the deity.

The power of using sexual imagery is that the conventions governing gender and sexuality are almost always taken as a "given" in any culture, or,

---

[1]Note that Leviticus 18:18 prohibits a man to marry two sisters.

[2]The primary audience of this text would have been those with social standing in the culture, that is, men.

129

in other words, "the way things ought to be." Judith Butler, however, has argued that "sexuality itself is an historically specific organization of power, discourses, bodies and affectivity."[3] Thus, sexuality is "an artificial concept which effectively extends and disguises the power relations responsible for its genesis." In this paper I will investigate the strategies, power lines, and identities that emerge and converge in the descriptions of gender, sexuality, and violence in Ezekiel 23. I argue that if we pay attention to the various ways in which both the women's and God's identities are constructed in the chapter and look for the power relations responsible for these depictions, we will see that the very conventions of sexuality used to shore up divine identity actually become problematic in their application, providing the way to deconstruct sexuality and the deity as they are depicted in the text. Through a detailed analysis of Ezekiel 23, I aim to reveal the fractures in divine and other identities that open up possibilities for transformation. It is my hope that this analysis will provide a starting point from which such transformation can begin.

It is most interesting that the Targums of Ezekiel have expunged the sexual imagery of Ezekiel 23.[4] It is therefore strange that modern commentators have not seen any problems with the language. In fact, in varying degrees, most scholars support the use of the marriage metaphor. Hengstenberg[5] and Block[6] are the only scholars I read who actively affirm the rhetoric of the chapter. Block's justification of the imagery is surprising given the recent date of his commentary. Other male scholars may be roughly divided into two camps with regard to imagery used in this chapter. The first group is composed largely of compliant readers who accept the gender characterization with little or no discussion, while the other group addresses the characterization directly in some way. Fohrer,[7] Allen,[8] Zimmerli,[9] Greenberg,[10] Bertholet,[11] Carley,[12]

[3]Judith Butler, *Gender Trouble: Feminism and the Subversion of Identity* (New York: Routledge, 1990), 92.

[4]See *The Targum of Ezekiel: Translated with a Critical Introduction, Apparatus and Notes,* trans. Samson H. Levey, Aramaic Bible 13 (Wilmington, Del.: Michael Glazier, 1987); and *Targum Jonathan to the Prophets,* trans. Pinkhos Churgin (New York and Baltimore: KTAV, 1983). Indeed, the excision of the marriage metaphor occurs in the Targums to the other prophets as well.

[5]E. W. Hengstenberg, *The Prophecies of the Prophet Ezekiel,* trans. A. G. Murphy and J. G. Murphy (Edinburgh: T & T Clark, 1869), esp. 195.

[6]Daniel I. Block, *The Book of Ezekiel Chapters 1–24,* New International Commentary on the Old Testament (Grand Rapids: Eerdmans, 1997), 734. Block defends Ezekiel's rhetoric by stressing his aim, which was "to shock his audience, not to titillate them with pornographic images" (734). Yet his continual attention to the more explicit aspects of the passage belies his comments.

[7]Georg Fohrer, *Ezechiel,* Handbuch zum Alten Testament 13 (Tübingen: JCB Mohr [Paul Siebeck], 1955).

[8]Leslie C. Allen, *Ezekiel 20–48,* Word Biblical Commentary 29 (Dallas: Word Books, 1990).

[9]Walther Zimmerli, *Ezekiel 1,* Hermeneia (Philadelphia: Fortress Press, 1979).

[10]Moshe Greenberg, *Ezekiel 21–37,* Anchor Bible (New York: Doubleday, 1997). His discussion is noteworthy in that he appends a section to his commentary on chapter 23, attacking all feminist criticism by misrepresenting what feminists are trying to do, including calling them "judgmental" and accusing them of "promoting a new reality" that "necessarily clashes with Scripture" (491).

[11]Alfred Bertholet, *Das Buch Hesekiel,* Kurzer Hand-Commentar zum Alten Testament 12 (Freiburg: JCB Mohr [Paul Siebeck], 1897).

[12]Keith W. Carley, *The Book of the Prophet Ezekiel,* Cambridge Bible Commentary (Cambridge: Cambridge University Press, 1974).

and Eichrodt[13] fall into the first camp, with the last three commentators stressing the political nature of the text over the metaphor/allegory in which it is embedded. Ellison[14] also downplays the imagery. The second group of scholars tends either to rationalize or rehabilitate the story in Ezekiel 23. Craigie,[15] Hals,[16] and Clements[17] are representative of this group. For these commentators, the message evidently justifies the means. Among recent (male) commentators, Blenkinsopp is the only one to address and deplore the language head-on. He writes:

> We cannot and should not ignore the antifeminism [*sic*] in the prophetic literature…The ambiguity, suspicion and fear caused by female allure, and even more by the biological processes connected with birth and menstruation…may help to explain but do nothing to render these attitudes less distasteful to the enlightened reader. In reading the story, all we can do is concentrate on the point of the allegory, which is Israel's history of infidelity and failure.[18]

Accordingly, he skips over the pornographic and explicit language in his analysis. Unlike the other scholars mentioned, he is not a compliant reader; he neither implicitly or explicitly accepts the gender conventions assumed in the portrayal of the women, nor justifies the use of the imagery itself. In these latter two respects he is refreshingly close to recent feminist discussions of this text.

Three feminist approaches deserve mention here, because they directly address the language and, at times, the conventions behind it. Galambush's 1991 doctoral dissertation is the first overtly feminist publication on this text.[19] Her focus is on the metaphorization of Jerusalem in the book of Ezekiel, including its ancient Near Eastern background, its situation relative to the other prophetic texts using the marriage metaphor, and the political allegorization of the imagery in Ezekiel 16 and 23. Her insightful close reading of Ezekiel 23 has many points of contact with mine; some of these will be noted in the course of my own analysis. Weems's book on the marriage metaphor in the prophets is the second.[20] Her discussion of the conventions with which the prophets play in their depiction of Israel/Jerusalem as YHWH's wife is similar to my own in my doctoral dissertation on Jeremiah.[21] This

---

[13]Walther Eichrodt, *Ezekiel: A Commentary,* trans. Coslett Quin, Old Testament Library (Philadelphia: Westminster Press, 1970).

[14]H. L. Ellison, *Ezekiel: The Man and His Message* (Grand Rapids: Eerdmans, 1956).

[15]Peter C. Craigie, *Ezekiel,* The Daily Bible Study Series (Philadelphia: Westminster Press, 1983), 172, 174.

[16]Ronald M. Hals, *Ezekiel,* Forms of the Old Testament Literature 19 (Grand Rapids: Eerdmans, 1989), 168, 169.

[17]Ronald E. Clements, *Ezekiel,* Westminster Bible Companion (Louisville: Westminster John Knox Press, 1996), 106, 108.

[18]Joseph Blenkinsopp, *Ezekiel,* Interpretation (Louisville: John Knox Press, 1990), 99.

[19]Julie Galambush, *Jerusalem in the Book of Ezekiel: The City as Yahweh's Wife,* Society of Biblical Literature Dissertation Series 130 (Atlanta: Scholars Press, 1992).

[20]Renita J. Weems, *Battered Love: Marriage, Sex, and Violence in the Hebrew Prophets,* Overtures in Biblical Theology (Minneapolis: Augsburg Fortress, 1995).

[21]Mary E. Shields, *Circumcising the Prostitute: The Rhetorics of Intertextuality, Metaphor, and Gender in Jeremiah 3.1–4.4* (Ann Arbor: University of Michigan, 1996).

description forms a fine background to my reading of Ezekiel 23.[22] The final author to be mentioned here is Fokkelien van Dijk-Hemmes.[23] My reading has much in common with hers (although we arrived at these independently). I will highlight some of these commonalities below; where we differ is in the depth of my analysis and my focus on the character of God. Indeed, Van Dijk-Hemmes and the other scholars, both feminist and traditional, privilege God in their readings to varying degrees. It is in addressing YHWH's agency as a character in Ezekiel 23 that my article contributes the most to scholarship.

Before beginning my analysis of Ezekiel 23, a very general outline of the chapter may be helpful for orienting the reader:

Introduction	v.v. 1–4
Oholah	v.v. 5–10
Description of her "whoring"	vv. 5–8
Consequences of her "whoring"	vv. 9–10
Oholibah	vv. 11–35
Introduction	v. 11
Description of her "whoring"	vv. 12–21
First consequences of her "whoring"	vv. 22–30
Second consequences of her "whoring"	vv. 31–35
Oholah and Oholibah's Judgment	vv. 36–49

In the introduction to the chapter (vv. 1–4), the narrator, who is YHWH in this text, creates identities for Jerusalem and Samaria. Following the usual prophetic introductory formula (v. 1), YHWH addresses the prophet: "Mortal[24] there were once two sisters, daughters of one mother." The duplicate description emphasizes their gender twice. It is unusual in the ancient Israelite gender economy that they are not identified in relationship to a man. By not having a father, they belong to no one (and therefore perhaps don't have a male's protection?). Verse 2 continues the emphasis on gender, this time stressing the sisters' sexuality and sexual activity: "They whored (זנה) in Egypt; they whored (זנה) in their youth. There their breasts were fondled, and there their virgin nipples were pressed." Various forms of the root זנה appear twenty times in the space of this chapter; the narrator appears quite literally to be

---

[22]Weems's discussion of the assumed audience and the shared assumptions between the prophet and his audience is especially helpful in this regard. See esp. 35–67. For example, she writes, "The portrait of Jerusalem the adulterous wife shifted sympathy away from the city and in the direction of the husband/God as the one who has been victimized and betrayed" (45). I will develop this point in a somewhat different manner in my discussion of the masking of YHWH's agency below.

[23]Athalya Brenner and Fokkelien van Dijk-Hemmes, "The Metaphorization of Woman in Prophetic Speech: An Analysis of Ezekiel 23," in *On Gendering Texts: Female and Male Voices in the Hebrew Bible,* Biblical Interpretation Series 1, ed. Athalya Brenner and Fokkelien van Dijk-Hemmes (Leiden: Brill, 1993), 167–76. Reprinted in A. Brenner, ed., *A Feminist Companion to the Latter Prophets,* The Feminist Companion to the Bible 8 (Sheffield: Sheffield Academic Press, 1995), 244–55. An earlier version is in *Vetus Testamentum* 43/2 (1993): 162–70.

[24]Lit. בֶּן אָדָם, son of humanity.

obsessed with whoring. The focus on breasts as visible markers of sexuality is also repeated in the text (vv. 8, 21, and 34); in the first two repetitions, they are also associated with Egypt.

Verse 4 introduces us to the final identifying markers of these sisters. First, we are given their names: Oholah is the elder sister, and Oholibah the younger. Then, surprisingly, given the first identification as those who "whored in their youth," YHWH says, "They became mine, and they bore sons and daughters." In the space of two and a half verses, five gendered identifications are given to the female characters of the chapter, all of them having to do with prescribed gender roles and sexuality: sister, daughter, whore, wife, and mother. Moreover, the gender roles assigned to them do not agree. Within the legal economy of ancient Israel, one who was a good daughter, wife, or mother could not act in a sexually promiscuous manner; hence, the sisters' sexual positions are ambivalent from the outset. Their identifications also mar a primary female binary opposition (wife or daughter versus whore). Already, a multiplicity of identities conflict with one another, making the women suspect.

A final identification is made in the latter half of verse 4: Oholah is identified as Samaria, while Oholibah represents Jerusalem. This identification as political entities (the capital cities of Israel and Judah respectively) further multiplies and troubles the sisters' identities. We are no longer reading about two women, but rather we see that sexual codes are being applied to two cities. Thus, the narrator is using gender and sexuality to construct Oholah and Oholibah merely as types to fit his[25] narrative purpose. Moreover, by applying these codes, the narrator makes a very powerful rhetorical move, especially in light of the identity crisis occasioned by the loss of one country (Israel, represented by Samaria in this text), and the threatened loss of another (Judah, represented by Jerusalem here).[26] Samaria and Jerusalem are fractures in the divinely ordained order. These capital cities are also ambiguously identified (there is no paternal marker for the daughters–politically they could be said to *belong* to Babylon at this point in time). By using the language and conventions of gender, including marriage, to describe the two cities, and by YHWH claiming them as his own, the text sets up the reader to place the blame for their defeat on the cities rather than YHWH himself. The application of gender codes disguises how YHWH scapegoats the cities, which is a form of blaming the victim.

Van Dijk-Hemmes calls into question the identification that is primary for the remainder of the passage: whore. She writes, "the activities of the two sisters–activities which are signified by *znh,* 'play the harlot'–are specified in...verse 3 not as action but as receptivity. 'They' were acted upon."[27] She

---

[25]The narrator, YHWH, takes on a masculine identity, husband, in this text, hence the masculine pronoun used throughout this paper.

[26]With the date of the text falling between 598 and 586 B.C.E., Jerusalem has already been lost in the sense of being conquered. Although the leaders of Judah will revolt once more, they will not gain freedom from Babylon's domination.

[27]Van Dijk-Hemmes, *The Metaphorization of Women,* 172.

accurately calls such description a "misnaming of female experience."[28] According to Van Dijk-Hemmes, the actions of Egypt could more adequately be described in the following manner: "They were sexually molested in Egypt, in their youth they were sexually abused."[29] She goes on to argue that calling such activity *znh* betrays a lack of logic. To put it another way, Israel's slavery in Egypt is being depicted as caused by Israel. Moreover, "the imagery of women is indispensable for conveying a message which is a contradiction in terms: the people are guilty of their own past enslaving inasmuch as women are, by definition, guilty of their own sexual misfortunes."[30] Phyllis Bird, however, has shown that the term *znh* actually portrays any sexual activity outside of marriage.[31] Thus, *znh* is an accurate use of the term in this context. Nevertheless, Van Dijk-Hemmes' comments regarding blaming the victim are also accurate and, further, support my point. The misnaming of women's experience is the strategy that allows YHWH to disguise his scapegoating of the cities. In essence, YHWH blames the women for what Egypt, Assyria, and Babylon did, much like those who say that the Holocaust was caused by the Jews. While most of us are horrified by the latter statement, this move in Ezekiel 23 is successful, as can be proven by just a glance at the commentaries on Ezekiel 23 that accept uncritically this reading of Israel's history.[32] As I will argue below, it is the privileging of YHWH that allows such a reading to stand.

The use of gender and sexuality to construct the identities of Oholah and Oholibah is rhetorically powerful in three other ways as well. First, the agent in and subject of these verses is YHWH. He sets up their identities; he constructs a sexual and marital history for the sisters. The constructs themselves reflect the power structures of sexuality in ancient Israel: A woman belonged to her man ("they became mine," v. 4) and fulfilled the role of carrying on the male line ("they bore sons and daughters," v. 4). In this sense, the sisters themselves are merely constructs of cultural conventions governing women. Second, since sexuality and gender are most often seen as a "given" in society, as "natural," through identifying the cities as women, the narrator invokes cultural standards that are unlikely to be questioned. In making the cities women, the narrator sets up a binary opposition, male versus female, that will be in operation throughout the chapter. Such an opposition sets up the sisters as the Other, the not-men, who are defined only by their relationships to men; the sisters are objectified through their identifications as women, whores, wives, mothers. The preoccupation of YHWH with the visual markers of the

---

[28] Van Dijk-Hemmes, *The Metaphorization of Women,* 172–73, following T. Drorah Setel's definition of the misnaming of female experience as one of the features of pornographic texts. See "Prophets and Pornography: Female Sexual Imagery in Hosea," in *Feminist Interpretation of the Bible,* ed. Letty M. Russell (Philadelphia: Westminster Press, 1985), 86–95, as well as van Dijk-Hemmes' discussion, 170–72.

[29] Ibid., 173.

[30] Ibid., 173.

[31] Phyllis A. Bird, *Missing Persons and Mistaken Identities: Women and Gender in Ancient Israel,* Overtures to Biblical Theology (Minneapolis: Fortress Press, 1997).

[32] See those commentaries mentioned above.

sisters' sexuality, their breasts (שָׁדַיִם and/or דַּדֵּי, vv. 3, 8, 21, and 34) further objectifies them and distances them from YHWH.[33] Finally, the very structure of the chapter objectifies the women: The reader can only view them through the speech and eyes of YHWH. Granted no speech, they have no identities apart from those constructed for them by YHWH. Thus, they are never constituted as separate subjects.

Yet the identity of YHWH is also already problematized here. Unlike Jeremiah, who portrayed the wilderness period as "the good old days" when Israel was faithful to YHWH (cf. Jer. 2:2), Ezekiel describes no initial faithful period; he portrays the people as unfaithful from the very beginning (cf. Ezek. 20:5–8, where the people are depicted as never having abandoned their worship of Egyptian idols). With such a negative identification, the actions and motives of YHWH (who is the "I" of the piece) are called into question. If YHWH knew they whored, why would YHWH marry them? With virginity prized in this culture (see the law codes of Leviticus and Deuteronomy) both for property and inheritance purposes, marrying someone who has had sex with another man causes problems: If children are born, who is the father? To whom do the women and the children really belong? Whose line will be carried on through these children?[34] YHWH is taking a chance by marrying women who had already whored in (with?) Egypt. His absolute control is already in question. Moreover, the misnaming of the women's experience noted above reveals a deceptive move on the part of YHWH, one that seduces the audience "into viewing women or girls as responsible for and even guilty of their own violation."[35] If one is looking carefully at the way in which these metaphorical women are depicted, the character of YHWH is already called into question by the very terms used to describe their first sexual encounter. Yet this character problem is disguised by the rhetoric itself. Gender rhetoric is used to set the reader up to blame the women, who, according to conventional standards, should be grateful that YHWH took them at all. The reader is expected to see the sisters' subsequent "whoring" as even worse than their original "unfaithfulness."

The remainder of the chapter is divided into three sections, the first discussing Oholah (vv. 5–10), the second discussing Oholibah largely in (negative) relation to her sister (vv. 11–35), and the third describing both sisters' activities in cultic terms (vv. 36–49). Each of the sections shares a similar

---

[33]Both the structure of the passage framed entirely as the speech of YHWH and the preoccupation with and objectification of the female body are similar to Ezekiel 16, which is a sister passage to Ezekiel 23. See my recent article "Multiple Exposures: Body Rhetoric and Gender Characterization in Ezekiel 16," *Journal of Feminist Studies in Religion* 14 (1998): 5–18, for many similarities between Ezekiel 16 and this passage. Indeed, my reading of both is also similar. While I focused exclusively on gender and body rhetoric in that reading, in this paper I am looking more closely at issues of identity.

[34]This text has some resonances with Hosea 2, where YHWH commands Hosea to marry a prostitute. Unlike that text, however, which gives reasons for YHWH's dictate, Ezekiel 23 does not seem to answer many of the questions posed here.

[35]Van Dijk-Hemmes, *The Metaphorization of Women,* 173. Note that though the next logical step of her argument would be to look at YHWH's agency, she stops short of that move.

structure, beginning with a description of the sister's actions followed by YHWH's response, which is always a punishment of some kind. Focusing on sexuality, the text discusses the sisters'/cities' "whorings" (זנה) with foreigners/ foreign countries: Egypt in verses 3, 8, 19–21, and 27; Assyria in verses 5, 7, 9, and 12; and Chaldea and/or the Babylonians in verses 14–17. Their whorings are condemned, and their lovers are used to utter judgments (vv. 10, 24) and to deliver punishment (vv. 9–10, 22–27, 28–31, 32–34, and 45–47). In keeping with the political subtext, their punishment is continually described in terms of war: The sister being discussed is either killed (v. 10), mutilated (v. 25), or mutilates herself (v. 34); her sons and daughters are "taken" (vv. 10, 25) or "killed by the sword" (v. 47); all who remain will be killed by the sword (v. 25); whatever is left will be devoured by fire (v. 25; in v. 47, their houses will be burned).[36]

The punishment is also sexual in nature: Verse 10 declares that Oholah's lovers will "expose her nakedness;" verse 26, addressed to Oholibah, says, "They will strip off your garments and they will take the objects of your beauty." Verse 29, also speaking to Oholibah, says, "they will leave you naked and bare, and the nakedness of your whorings will be exposed." The language of these verses is clearly rape language (identical language is used in Ezek. 16:39 to describe gang rape). Rape is the "normal" result of war.[37] In this context of sexual promiscuity, it is a punishment in kind. The sexual nature of the punishment is all the more disturbing given its initiation by YHWH (it is carried out by the women's lovers).[38]

Even though the text focuses on sex and sexuality and uses sexual means to punish at times (exposure and gang rape), the use of war imagery in the punishment scenes indicates a preoccupation with political associations and identifications. In addition, the text invokes cultic associations, as indicated by the multiple use of the term גלל (idol) strewn throughout the text (vv. 7, 30, 37, 39, and 49), and by the extended description of the sisters' cultic "abominations" (v. 36) in verses 38–42. In fact, even their names, Oholah ("she who has her tent") and Oholibah ("my [YHWH's] tent is in her"), invoke cultic associations with the tent of meeting where YHWH was present in the

---

[36]Julie Galambush presents an excellent discussion of the ways in which the sexual history of the two sisters can be read as a discussion of their political alliances with other nations in *Jerusalem in the Book of Ezekiel*, 111–15. The political events she recounts form the political/histori- cal subtext to the portrayal of Samaria and Jerusalem in sexual terms.

[37]Cf. the story of Dinah, Genesis 34, as well as Judges 21. See also Claudia V. Camp and Carole R. Fontaine, eds., *Women, War and Metaphor: Language and Society in the Study of the Hebrew Bible, Semeia* 61 (Atlanta: Scholars Press, 1993). Also, the articles in *Semeia* 61 by Susan Niditch (39–57) and Susan Brooks Thistlethwaite (59–75) are especially instructive of the ways in which rape in war reinforces male domination.

[38]Harold Washington argues that ancient Israel was a rape culture, in which rape is institu- tionalized in such a way as to reaffirm men's control over women ("'Such a thing is not done in Israel'; Rape and the Cultural Construction of Gender in the Hebrew Bible," a paper presented at the 1997 Central States Society of Biblical Literature). In Ezekiel 23, rape serves the function of buttressing YHWH's ultimate control over Oholah and Oholibah.

time of the wilderness.[39] These political and cultic associations illustrate that the text is dealing with a multiplicity of identities: political and religious identities are treated under the guise of sexual identity. With regard to these levels of identity, the sisters represent one half of the sexual binary opposition, with their lovers and YHWH representing the other half. In addition to the opposition between female figures and YHWH, the male figures (lovers/ nations) are portrayed as competitors with YHWH for the sisters' affections. This competition and the power struggle it represents will problematize the characterization of YHWH throughout the chapter.

To see how these issues play themselves out in the rhetoric of the text itself, I will deal with each section in detail. The first section deals with Oholah (Samaria), and begins with YHWH's statement: "Oholah whored (lit.) under me" (v. 5), that is, while under his authority, or while she belonged to him. The phrase shows that her actions were beyond the proper boundaries, but the actions themselves also indicate that YHWH's authority and control are less than complete. Her lovers are identified as the Assyrians, thus continuing the mingling of sexual and political identities.

The next phrase, "she lusted after her lovers," is the first of seven times lust (עגב)[40] is attributed to the female characters in this passage, the others being verses 7, 9, 11, 12, 16, and 20. In this section of Ezekiel 23, it is used three times, twice referring to Oholah's lust for the Assyrians (vv. 5, 9), and once referring to her lust for idols (v. 7). The identification here (also where Oholibah's lovers are identified) moves beyond the metaphorical world into international politics and religious worship. These "lovers" represent threats to YHWH's power and divinity as well, though the rhetoric masks that aspect of the text. Moreover, YHWH, by stressing lust three times in the section, focuses on the unrestrained sexuality of Oholah, emphasizing her actions, which are completely outside the bounds of convention. This focus in turn is a fixing of responsibility; YHWH is at pains to show that the sisters desire to be unfaithful.

In the description in verse 6 of Oholah's lovers, the visual focus is highlighted in the allusion to color, attractiveness, and rank: "those dressed in violet [the color of royalty], governors, and prefects, all of them handsome young men, riders on horseback." The men whom she chose as lovers are not the dregs, but rather the wealthy and powerful, the best of their society; that all of whom she chose were the "choicest of the Assyrians" is stressed in verse 7.

---

[39]See Eichrodt, *Ezekiel*, 328. Galambush also argues that in both Ezekiel 16 and 23, "a metaphorical connection is drawn between the women's 'tents' and their sexual organs" (*Jerusalem in the book of Ezekiel*, 111, n. 58). In the same footnote, she connects the "tents" of Oholah and Oholibah with the description of Jerusalem as YHWH's sanctuary in Ezekiel 16:10–14. This connection makes sense, especially in light of YHWH's accusation in 23:38–39 that the sisters defiled his sanctuary. By defiling themselves (vv. 7, 13), they also are defiling his sanctuary.

[40]The active verb comes from a root that, in Arabic, can mean to admire or to be beloved (F. Brown, S. R. Driver, and C. A. Briggs, *A Hebrew and English Lexicon of the Old Testament* [Oxford: Oxford University Press, 1962], 721.) It is confined to this chapter within the entire Hebrew Bible. The only context where a verbal form is used outside of Ezekiel is Jeremiah 4:30, where the present participle is a substantive referring to Jerusalem's lovers.

Verse 7 also gives the first formal indictment of her actions: "With all after whom she lusted, and with all their idols she defiled herself/was defiled." The *Niphal* verb form (נטמאה) could be translated either reflexively or passively. In this case, retaining the ambiguity serves the passage well. It is clear later on that Oholibah's lovers defile her (v. 17), but these are actions that would also defile oneself (cf. v. 47, where the sentence for whoring is meted out to the sisters). Since *she* is the one punished,[41] the reflexive connotation should be read together with the passive.

Verse 8 has Oholah returning to the Egyptians, referring once again to Egypt's activities with her in her youth. Although the verse begins by saying that what follows are "her whorings," some blame does seem to be set on the Egyptians since they are the subject of the verbs: "They lay with her in her youth, they pressed her virgin nipples, and they poured out their (masculine plural) whorings on her." This is one of the few passages in the Hebrew Bible using the root זנה to refer to male sexual activity. The NRSV, interestingly, translates this root as "playing the whore" when referring to the sisters, but when the root is used to refer to the male characters, it is translated as "lust" (the NRSV reads, "They poured out their lust upon her"). This translation obscures the fact that both actions are described in the same terms, terms that, moreover, have connotations of transgressed boundaries. Hence, the NRSV highlights the woman's actions while clouding those of the men, further complicating the gender and sexual politics present in the text. Block takes this idea a step further, actually turning the text around to make the women the doers. He writes, "The sisters' conduct leaves nothing to the imagination: they offered their breasts and nipples to the men of Egypt."[42] This statement is plainly unsupported by the text; the action is unquestionably that of Egypt. In fact, I agree with Van Dijk-Hemmes that the phrase used, *škb 't*, should be translated as "lay upon/raped" based on its use in Genesis 34:2 and 2 Samuel 13:14. Her translation of verse 8 is:

> Her harlotry from (her days in) Egypt she did not abandon
> For they lay upon/raped her in her youth
> And these men pressed the teats of her maidenhood
> And they poured out their harlotry upon her.[43]

As she says, the words here, far from portraying the actions of Oholah, really describe "violence which is acted upon" her.[44] Van Dijk-Hemmes' argument, however, misses the point of the verse through her focus on the

---

[41]Her lovers, rather than being punished too, are actually co-opted into being the agents of YHWH's anger and revenge.

[42]Block, *Ezekiel 1–24*, 734.

[43]Van Dijk-Hemmes, *The Metaphorization of Women*, 174.

[44]Ibid.

audience.[45] The true point of this verse is a reversal in culpability: In political terms, the slavery of Egypt is being blamed on Israel's unfaithfulness. Thus, the gender construction of the passage continues to disguise YHWH's scapegoating of these women.

Verses 9 and 10 contain YHWH's response to Oholah's actions. Beginning with לכן (therefore), the term used throughout the prophets to introduce the punishment following an accusation, first-person speech returns: "Therefore, I will give you into the hand (power) of your lovers, into the hand of the Assyrians after whom you lusted." Verse 10 describes the punishment itself which includes exposure of her nakedness, taking her sons and daughters, and killing her with the sword. Clearly, YHWH is behind the punishment, claiming responsibility for giving her into the hands of her lovers, but YHWH is just as obviously out of sight. He has the lovers do his work for him, and the violence associated with the punishment is horrific (though it will get worse). This punishment goes beyond a legal response to Oholah's actions; it is *revenge*.

As this analysis has already shown, identity is never fixed or stable in this text. The text continually slips in and out of the metaphorical world, aligning sexuality, politics, and the historical realm through transparent references to political alliances and idol worship. Problematically, the text also slips out of the metaphoric relationship into the reality of cultural attitudes regarding gender in its discussion of male-female relations: In verse 10 Oholah is to become a byword to "the women" (cf. v. 48, which will be discussed below). In this statement, sexual and textual politics converge, with the site of male authority becoming the female body.

Having killed off Oholah, the narrative turns to Oholibah her sister. Oholah's/Samaria's story is dealt with in short shrift (six verses as opposed to the twenty-four verses allotted to Oholibah); she is primarily a foil for Oholibah. Politically, Samaria was never central to the biblical story; it was always portrayed as the *other* city, which resulted when the people rebelled and split off in the time of Rehoboam. Samaria is also portrayed throughout the books of Kings as a place where YHWH is not worshiped properly.[46] Jerusalem, on the other hand, *is* central; it is portrayed in the royal (Davidic) theology as the place where God chose to dwell, and in which God put God's house. Therefore, God *must* be worshiped properly there or the identity of God comes into question in terms of potency, sovereignty, and authority. As we shall see, these issues come into play in the length of text devoted to Oholibah (Jerusalem), in the negative comparison with her sister, in the very language used to describe Jerusalem's and her lovers' behavior and appearance, and

---

[45]She writes, "The audience, which has already been required to perceive the metaphorical maiden's sexual abuse as harlotry, is now seduced into viewing this abuse as something Oholah had enjoyed so much that she could not do without it" (*The Metaphorization of Women*, 174). While this may indeed be the result of the rhetoric (cf. Block, *Ezekiel 1–24*, 738, who calls Oholah's behavior "sexual addiction"), the point of the verse lies elsewhere.

[46]See, for example, the famous story of Elijah and the prophets of Baal in 1 Kings 17–19, where the queen and many of the people are actually worshipers of Baal.

in the increased violence and multiplicity of judgments and punishments against her.

This section begins with identifications and is focused on the visual. A series of three points of view are described by YHWH in verses 11–14, each introduced with the verb רָאָה, "to see." Verse 11 reads, "And Oholibah saw her sister and her lust and became more corrupt; her whorings were greater than those of her sister." Thus, the first identification in this section sets Oholibah over against Oholah, declaring Oholibah worse than her sister. The point here is to show Oholibah to be more guilty that Oholah. The idea is that adultery is bad enough, but to see an example of the terrible consequences of adultery and still follow the same path is much worse.

Verse 12 details the men after whom she lusted (עגב) in the same terms used in verse 6 to describe Oholah's lovers. Just as Oholah lusted after the Assyrians, so does Oholibah. Similarly, the focus is again on rank and appearances: "governors, prefects, commanders, clothed to perfection, mounted horsemen, handsome young men, all of them."

Verse 13 reintroduces YHWH's viewpoint, once more comparing the sisters: "And I saw that she had defiled herself/been defiled [another use of the *Niphal* of טמא]; the way of one was for both of them." In other words, they acted alike. Verse 14, however, shows the differences: "She increased her whorings by seeing men engraved on the wall, images of Chaldeans engraved in red ocher." The same form of the verb is used to introduce this phrase as in verse 11, preserving the parallels between the views. Thus, verse 11 begins with "and she saw," verse 13 begins with "and I saw," and this phrase in verse 14 begins again with "and she saw." The structure of these verses indicates that perspective is important to this text. What is obscured by the language, however, is that all the references to "seeing" are in fact one outlook—that of YHWH, who is the omniscient narrator. We only know what "she saw" from YHWH's point of view. Is his view accurate? The text is constructed in such a way as to deflect us from that question. As I will argue below, once one gives any sort of autonomy to the female characters (after all, they *chose* to have sex with other men, and their sexuality was obviously out of the control of their husbands), this perspective becomes important in uncovering the fractures in YHWH's identity.

The text of verse 14 is also excessive: Oholibah's lust is incited not just by men whom she knows/sees, but by mere images. Verse 15 continues with a visual description of these men: "girded with belts on their loins, and flowing[47] turbans on their heads." Similar to previous descriptions, the narrator next focuses on their rank: "All of them had the appearance of officers,"[48] after

---

[47]The Hebrew here is difficult. The term translated with the NRSV as "flowing," סרוחי טבולים, comes from a root meaning to dip or be moistened. Brown, *Hebrew and English Lexicon*, 371, posits a second Ethiopian root, meaning to wind about or wrap up, suggesting "overhanging" or "pendant" turbans.

[48]The Hebrew literally reads "third ones." Brown, *Hebrew and English Lexicon* suggests that these might have referred to "the third man (in chariots)" (1026). It is interesting that a new term is introduced relating to rank in the description of the lovers. Such rank and power are competitive with YHWH's power.

which he identifies their nationality: "the likeness of Babylonians, Chaldea the land of their birth." Presumably there was something about their looks that indicated their country of origin. One more time, sexual and political identities converge.

The focus on appearance becomes clear in verse 16: "When she saw them, she lusted after them[49] and sent messengers to them, to Chaldea." Verse 17a reads, "And the Babylonians came to her, to the bed of love,[50] and they defiled her with their whorings."[51] The second half of the verse describes the effect on Oholibah: "And she was defiled by them and she became alienated from them."[52] Verse 18 continues the description, making a female character the subject of the verb גלה, "to expose," for the only time in this piece: "And she exposed her whorings and her nakedness." The verse also describes YHWH's reaction: "And I became alienated from her," a phrase parallel in construction to that describing Oholibah's response to her lovers.

Verses 19–21 switch the object of Oholibah's desires to Egypt, a transparent reference to her switch of political alliances. Here YHWH frames her actions as increasing or multiplying (ותרבה) her whorings. This increase comes about through her "remembering the days of her youth when she whored in/with the land of Egypt." Verse 20 continues with an explicit description of her lust:[53] "Their member was that of he-asses, and their emission that of stallions." The focus on size and quantity in the description of the markers of the Egyptians' sexuality indicates potency from a masculine point of view. Here, the fact that a masculine construction of sexuality is being overlaid on the female character(s) is most visible in the piece.[54] Verse 21 completes the description of Oholibah's whorings, for the first time addressing her directly: "And you sought the lewdness of your youth when the Egyptians fondled your nipples because of[55] your virgin breasts." YHWH's visual preoccupation

---

[49]Lit. "She lusted after them, to the appearance of her eyes."

[50]The Hebrew word for love here is דדים, a word play with דדים, the breasts mentioned in verses 3, 8, and 21. Thus, the image of her breasts is brought to mind in the description of the couch. Indeed, if the phrase, למשכב דדם, is repointed slightly (למשכב דדים), the first word could refer to the act of lying with someone sexually (Brown, *Hebrew and English Lexicon,* 1012), and the second term could refer to the visual markers of Oholibah's sexuality (breasts). The appearance of the Hebrew allows (especially for native readers of Hebrew) the latter connotations to be "seen."

[51]Note that the NRSV once again obscures the term זנה in its reference to male actions; it reads, "And they defiled her with their lust."

[52]The Hebrew phrase ותקע נפשה מהם literally says, "and her being became alienated from them." In this context the phrase refers to her political action of switching alliances.

[53]The Hebrew object פלגשיהם is difficult here. It literally means concubines, but in this case BDB suggests a connection with the state of being a concubine (concubinage). Taken with the rest of the verse, the sense seems to be that she wanted to become a concubine because of the Egyptian's potency.

[54]Van Dijk-Hemmes has a similar reading to my own, putting it this way: "The depiction of Oholibah's desire in terms of the size of (animal-like) male members seems not just an example of mere misnaming of female experience, but an actual distortion of it. Instead of reflecting female desire, this depiction betrays male obsession" (*The Metaphorization of Women,* 175).

[55]Lit. למען. The Hebrew text may be corrupt here. The parallel construction in verse 3 uses the verb מעך, and the Syriac and Vulgate translations use this verb. However, the Hebrew does make sense as it stands.

with Oholibah's body, as well as his competition with Egypt, is apparent in the accusation.

Verses 22–27 contain YHWH's first response to Oholibah. This time, however, YHWH addresses Oholibah directly and begins with the prophetic introduction: "Therefore, Oholibah, thus says YHWH." The punishment and judgments are strongly reminiscent of Oholah's: YHWH gathers her lovers against her. However, this time the identities of the lovers whom YHWH gathers begin with the Babylonians (remaining true to history, in which the Babylonians are the ones to conquer Jerusalem). YHWH describes the Babylonians in the same terms used in verses 6 and 12, focusing on their rank, power, and handsomeness (v. 23). Then, breaking the frame of the metaphor, verse 24 describes all the weaponry the "lovers" will bring against them. Once more, political and sexual identities converge; war is the prescribed vehicle of vengeance. The description of weaponry is followed by the declaration, "I will give the judgment to them, and they shall judge you according to their ordinances."

Verse 25a contains the first *overt* description of YHWH's emotions: "I will direct my jealousy against you, and they will deal with you in rage." The following verses contain the actual punishment, which is even more horrific than that which befell Oholah. Verse 25b reads, "They will cut off your nose and your ears; your posterity will fall by the sword; they will take your sons and daughters; and what remains will be devoured by fire." Shalom Paul has argued effectively that there is a close analogue in Middle Assyrian Law to the prescribed judgment of cutting off the nose and ears.[56] According to Paul, cutting off the nose is one of the options given in MAL A:15 to a husband whose wife has committed adultery.[57] Therefore, this punishment is an example of being judged "according to their ordinances" (v. 24). In Middle Assyrian Law, however, the man with whom the adulterous wife is caught is also supposed to be made a eunuch.[58] Significantly, in Ezekiel 23 there is no analogous punishment for those with whom Oholibah committed adultery; she is the only one who is punished. Here is one of the places the metaphor breaks down, but it does so in such a way as to inscribe all the punishment on the woman's body.

Yet the punishment is still not complete; in verse 26 YHWH turns to further means of humiliation: "They will strip off your garments and they will take the objects of your beauty."[59] As in Oholah's judgment, YHWH is strangely absent from the violent actions here. Rather than punishing her himself, YHWH has her lovers do the sentencing (judging) and punishing for

---

[56]Shalom Paul, "Biblical Analogues to Middle Assyrian Law," in *Religion and Law: Biblical-Judaic and Islamic Perspectives,* ed. Edwin B. Firmage, Bernard G. Weiss, and John W. Welch (Winona Lake: Eisenbrauns, 1990), 333–50; see esp. 342–46.

[57]Ibid., 345. See also his discussion of MAL A:4, 344–45.

[58]Ibid.

[59]The NRSV translates the latter phrase as "jewels." I think, given the context and the similarities with Ezekiel 16:39, that the "objects of beauty" may be sexual in nature.

him. At the same time, however, he is claiming for himself the ultimate authority ("I will bring," v. 22; "I will give the judgment to them," v. 24; "I will direct my jealousy against you," v. 25; "I will put an end to your lewdness from the land of Egypt," v. 27). Furthermore, he tries to extend his authority even over her thoughts and desires by telling her, "You will not long for them (lit. 'lift up your eyes to them'); you will no longer remember them" (v. 27). Here, as before, Egypt is seen as the primary competitor for Oholibah's affections.

Yet, as if the dams have broken with his statement of jealousy and rage, one response is not enough. A new introductory formula appears in verse 28 introducing YHWH's second response to Oholibah's actions: "Thus says the Lord YHWH, Look! I am about to give you into the hand (power) of those whom you hate; into the hand of those from whom you became alienated." This new introduction is followed by a sexual punishment for sexual actions in verse 29: "They will deal with you in hate: they will take all your property and leave you naked and bare, and the nakedness of your whorings will be exposed."

Verse 30 clarifies who bears responsibility for the sexual violence: "Both your lewdness and your whorings will do these things to you because of your whoring after nations; because you defiled yourself [*Niphal* of טמא] with their idols." Placing the blame for sexual abuse on the victim is a classic tactic of abusers. The use of sexual *violence*, which is intended to terrorize, dominate, and subdue, is "justified" by the actual or supposed instances of insubordination. Given the distancing effect of having the lovers carry out YHWH's revenge, YHWH's agency in the retribution is masked, perhaps also cloaking the excessiveness of the actions themselves.

Verse 31 ends this subsection in the same manner as the narration regarding Oholibah began, using a comparison with her sister: "You followed [lit. 'walked in'] the path of your sister, and I will place her cup into your hand." The punishment of verses 28–30 is apparently still not enough for YHWH, because the introduction of the "cup of your sister" provides the occasion for yet another description of retaliation. Verse 32 contains yet another introductory "Thus says YHWH." This time a short poetic piece follows, discussing the cup ("of your sister, Samaria," v. 33) that YHWH will make Oholibah drink. The cup is described as "deep and wide" (v. 32) and "a cup of devastation and waste" (v. 33). The results for her will be to make her a laughingstock and a derision (v. 32) and to make her full of drunkenness and grief (v. 33). The most disturbing aspect of this subsection, however, is verse 34, where YHWH says to Oholibah: "You will drink it and drain it and you will chew on its potsherds. You will tear out your breasts. For I have spoken, oracle of YHWH." With the cause/effect scenario, the cup oracle is sexualized: She will disfigure the very attributes that were the focus of Egypt's sexual attentions.[60] By having Oholibah mutilate

---

[60]Cf. Greenberg, *Ezekiel 21–37*, 484. For a different reading of the sexualization, see Block, who yet again attributes actions to Oholibah that in the text are attributed to a lover: "She who had shamelessly craved the fondling of her breasts by her lovers will tear them off in her inexpressible grief" (*Ezekiel 1–24*, 756).

herself, YHWH's agency is again cloaked, and sexual punishment for a sexual crime is again inflicted. The *self*-infliction of the punishment accentuates *her* responsibility for her previous actions. It is also clear, just as it was in verse 20, that this is a masculine fantasy of punishment and violence. The end result is unequivocal in verse 35, which opens with the last "therefore" clause of the chapter: "Therefore, because you have forgotten me and cast me behind your back, now bear your wickedness and your whorings." In this case she literally bears or carries those consequences ex-scribed from her own body.

Even this statement of punishment is not enough, however. The final section of the chapter, verses 36–49, addresses both sisters, bringing the prophet into the frame for the first time. Although Oholah had been written out of the text through being killed in verse 10, her trace reappeared in verses 32–24 in the guise of the cup. Here she is actually reinscribed in the story: "And YHWH said to me, 'Mortal, will you judge Oholah and Oholibah? Then tell them their abominations" (v. 36).

Verses 36–48 focus on the sisters' cultic "abominations," describing idol worship (vv. 37, 39, and 49) through the metaphor of committing adultery.[61] The specific cultic abominations of which they are accused include: child sacrifice ("They offered their sons, whom they had born to me, to be devoured" [v. 37], also described as "slaughtering their sons to idols" [v. 39]); defiling YHWH's sanctuary (vv. 38 and 39); and polluting YHWH's sabbaths (v. 38). The Hebrew word בניהן ("their sons") can in some instances refer to children of both genders. However, in every other reference to children in Ezekiel 23, sons and daughters occur together (v. 4, 10, 25, 47). Therefore, the phrase, "they offered their sons," in verses 37 and 39 refers specifically to sacrifice of sons. In a sexual economy where women represent mere objects of exchange, it is the male line that is important. Significantly, taking YHWH's sons and giving them to foreign gods problematizes YHWH's line. Again, power and politics converge in a gender-specific construction.

In verses 40–42 the sisters are also pictured as sending a messenger (cf. v. 16) to "men coming from afar" for whom they bathed, painted their eyes, and decked themselves with ornaments (v. 40). In a scene reminiscent of the description of Oholibah's whoring with the Babylonians, the sisters sat on a bed (cf. v. 17) with a table spread before it on which was *YHWH's* incense and *YHWH's* oil (v. 41). The focus on cultic objects (incense and oil) in verse 41 continues the description of the idol worship. Verse 42 describes a partylike scene with drunkards placing bracelets on the sisters' hands and beautiful crowns on their heads.

YHWH's response to these abominations is set out in verse 43: "And I thought, to complete the adulteries, now she [Oholibah] is whoring (with) her

---

[61]The Hebrew term is נאף. It appears here for the first time in this passage, and is the term that will be used most frequently in this section. I will translate it "commit adultery" to differentiate it from זנה, translated as "to whore" throughout.

[Oholah's] whorings–she also."[62] Verse 44 continues: "And they will enter her[63] like one enters a prostitute; thus they came (in)to Oholah and Oholibah, women of lewdness." In verse 45, YHWH has others, as before, utter the judgment. This time it is "righteous men" who will judge them legally, by using "the judgment for committing adultery and the judgment for shedding of blood" (v. 45).

Verse 46 opens with the last introductory formula of the chapter: "For thus says YHWH," followed by YHWH's call for the punishment to begin. As he predicted earlier, YHWH has others do the punishing for him, this time bringing up an assembly (קָהָל) against the sisters (v. 46), which will stone them, kill their sons and daughters with the sword, and burn their houses with fire (v. 47).[64] Although a legal sentence has been pronounced in verse 45, the actual punishment is both legal (stoning) and political (war), hence linking once again the political and the sexual in his description.

Verse 48 contains the hoped-for results of the punishment: "And I will put an end to lewdness from the land, and all the women will be chastened[65] and will not commit lewdness as you have done." The move from the metaphorical realm into the realm of historical male-female relations is troublesome. Rather than Oholah and Oholibah being mere figures for the historical relationship between YHWH and Israel, they are now anti-role models for women who read or hear the text.[66]

The referents of verse 49 are ambiguous, making the statement in verse 48 even more troublesome: "And they [masculine plural] will set their [feminine plural] lewdness upon them [feminine plural], and they [feminine plural] will bear the sins of their [feminine plural] idols." Who is the male "they" at the beginning of verse 49? Do the two feminine plural objects refer to the two sisters having their lewdness set upon themselves? Or, given the chastening of the women in verse 48, are the women to bear the sisters' lewdness and sins? Either way it is clear that there is no possible redemption for the women in this passage–their sexuality and sexual actions will always be inscribed. Indeed, they will always be identified solely with those actions. Thus, the conclusion of this text reinscribes sexual and social gender constructions

---

[62]Unfortunately the text is so corrupt that it makes no sense as it stands. Zimmerli refuses to translate it (*Ezekiel 1*, 479). The best suggestion I have seen to date is that of Galambush, *Jerusalem in the Book of Ezekiel*, 73, 77), who repoints the לְבַבְל as a *Piel* form of בלל, which means "to complete." This translation follows hers.

[63]Following the LXX (the MT is singular: וַיָּבֹא). In addition to several versions, according to J. Lust, this reading is also attested in the Qumran fragments ("Ezekiel in Manuscripts in Qumran," in *Ezekiel and His Book: Textual and Literary Criticism and Their Interpretation*, ed. J. Lust [Leuven: Leuven University Press, 1986], 98–99). The verb itself can mean to come into or enter. My translation plays with the highly sexualized context.

[64]In the case of Oholah, this punishment is literally overkill! She was already killed in verse 10! One also wonders how many sons and daughters the women could have had since they have been taken twice (vv. 10, 26), and the sons have been offered and slaughtered in verses 37 and 39. We have slipped out of metaphor into political and historical reality with these words.

[65]The Hebrew verb here actually means to be disciplined, chastened, or chastised. Interestingly, the NRSV actually tones this down, translating, "so that all women may take warning."

[66]Note that the primary audience is male. Yet by stepping out of the frame and creating a warning addressed to women, the text can be seen to have women as a secondary audience.

developed throughout the chapter. The message for women is clear: Sexual politics allow women only the positive roles of wife and mother; stepping beyond those roles sexually will result in the terrifying violence, anger, and vengeance that this text exhibits. If a woman is not subordinate in some way, the biblical text itself in the form of Ezekiel 23 gives the warrant for a very violent response. Moreover, that response is conveyed in the voice of God (the "I" of the passage). Here is not only biblical, but *divine* justification for domestic violence.

This chapter relies on a construction of gender where the women are merely objects, where they never take on subject status. As we have seen, the narrator (YHWH) has been at pains to portray these women in objectifying terms that completely sexualize them: They are identified entirely by their whoring and by the visual markers of their sexuality. The convergences and multiplicities of gender and identity, however, carry the seeds of this text's deconstruction. This construction of male/female relationships only works when men have complete control over and can define women's sexuality. However, this very passage reveals that such control is elusive. Even God doesn't have it. In the attempt to shore up his control, indeed his very identity, God's control is continually subverted in the text. Put simply, this construction of gender does not work.

In other words, YHWH tries to have it both ways in this chapter. While the women are portrayed in objectifying terms, and the violence heaped upon them is intended to relegate them entirely to the object position, their actions as described by YHWH reveal that the women are *not* solely objects. One aspect of gender construction obscured by the narrative is the agency of the women themselves. They are not merely reducible to one side of the binary ordering principles of this text (e.g., subject/object, inside/outside, wife or mother/whore, etc.). Their identities are multiple: wives and mothers, yet whores; worshipers of YHWH, yet worshipers of idols. They are also identified as political entities (Samaria and Jerusalem), those who worship idols, those who are to serve as a warning or chastisement to women. Oholah is "a byword among women" (v. 10); Oholibah is one who "remembers" her former lover, Egypt (v. 19). Both seek sexual fulfillment.

Moreover, the sisters are not reducible to the object side of the subject/ object binary opposition. Their actions indicate that they have not allowed themselves solely to be objects. They have acted outside the bounds allotted to them, thus taking on subject status. After marrying these women, YHWH discovered that he still did not have control over their sexuality; they not only found new lovers but went back to their former lover, Egypt. Oholah was supposed to serve as the cautionary example to Oholibah, but even this backfires; Oholibah is worse than her sister (v. 11). The only final control YHWH can have is to kill them, but, as we have seen, the one woman who is killed (exscribed) from this text, Oholah (v. 10), is reinscribed at the end (vv. 36–49). Paradoxically, YHWH needs these women to shore up his identity; he needs them to be objects to his subject. He is dependent on them and their actions to make his status as God secure again. And it is that very need and dependence that is not met through this text. Even further, it is that dependence, together with his concern for identity, that provides the seeds for deconstructing both male sexuality as it is portrayed in this text and the character of God. That deconstruction, I argue, is necessary if this text is to have any trans-formative possibilities.

In writing about gender constructions and their connections with identity, Judith Butler suggests that any construction of identity goes beyond the construction itself: There are consequences to constructing it in such a way.

> Paradoxically, the reconceptualization of an identity has an *effect;* that is, as *produced* and *generated,* it opens up possibilities of "agency" that are insidiously foreclosed by positions that take identity categories as foundational and fixed. Construction is not opposed to agency; it is the necessary scene of agency, the very terms in which agency is articulated and becomes culturally intelligible.[67]

The task, then, is to look for agency in the text and explore how agency produces effects beyond the construction of identity itself. The agency of the sisters has already been discussed above. Rather than being confined solely to their positions as wives and mothers, they are defined through their whoring. Yet the whoring itself indicates agency. Hence, agency is problematic in terms of the female characters in the text. I propose that the same is true of the primary male character, YHWH.

YHWH's agency in this construction is both foregrounded and masked. It is foregrounded in the fact that the text is entirely a first-person speech delivered by YHWH. The "I" language claims for that "I" full subjecthood, and claims for its pronouncements universal significance. YHWH's agency is also foregrounded in the numerous interpolations of the introductory formula, "Thus says the Lord, YHWH."[68] His agency, finally, is foregrounded in the power language of the text. For example, his first such statement, "I will give [Oholah] into the hand of her lovers," indicates that YHWH even claims ultimate control over the lovers; he *gives* her into their power or control. Implicitly, YHWH has the power to keep her out of their control. Similar cases appear in verse 22: "I will bring [your lovers] against you"; in verse 24: "I will give judgment to them"; and in verse 28: "I am about to give you into the hand of those whom you hate." Further indication of that self-assertion of power and control comes in verse 27, in which YHWH declares he is in charge of the result of the violent punishment described just previously: "I will put an end to your lewdness" (cf. v. 48 for a similar construction). Finally, the divine agency of God is asserted in the last phrase of the chapter, "And you [masculine plural] shall know that I am YHWH." YHWH claims ultimate

---

[67]Judith Butler, *Gender Trouble: Feminism and the Subversion of Identity* (London and New York: Routledge, 1990), 147.

[68]Lit. hwhy ynda rma hk. The ynda (Lord), though appearing throughout the book of Ezekiel, is usually deleted as a secondary addition. However, in the book it *functions* to highlight YHWH's power/authority: YHWH is the *'Adonai, the* Lord, the one with all power and control. Thus, use of the word reinforces the identity (re)construction being attempted in Ezekiel.

control over events, consequences, and punishments. God is almost portrayed as the puppet master pulling the strings.

This claim to full control is complicated, however, by the fact that in the ancient Near Eastern worldview, a defeated people's God is *not* in control, *not* all-powerful. Thus, the gender construction of YHWH and the lovers versus Oholah and Oholibah masks the political reality of Jerusalem's (YHWH's) defeat by other nations. Foregrounding control within the gender construction of the chapter *effects* this obfuscation. On the political level alone, this construction of identity does not work. I will argue below that reformulating YHWH's identity in terms of gender also does not work.

While YHWH's agency is foregrounded in certain ways, in other more disturbing ways, YHWH's agency is masked in Ezekiel 23. By keeping the focus solely on the sisters and their actions, YHWH can remain hidden. Their actions and their bodies become the focal points; they are the ones on whom sexual, political, and social identities become inscribed. While the sisters' bodies are repeatedly exposed through description, sexual activity, and punishment, his body is nowhere evident.[69] He also hides behind others to do his dirty work for him in this text. It is he who brings her lovers against her; it is he who gives them the responsibility of proclaiming judgment (vv. 10, 24). Even when he is no longer discussing the foreign powers as lovers, he gives the responsibility of judgment to other men: first to the prophet (v. 36), and then to "righteous men" (v. 45). While he gives each sister into the hands of her lovers, it is those lovers who carry out the actions in each case (vv. 9–10, 24–26, 29). Indeed YHWH's emotions remain largely hidden except in one case where he acknowledges that he is placing his jealousy against them (v. 25). Even in that case, however, his statement of jealousy is followed immediately by projecting rage on her lovers and detailing the mutilation, and so forth, that the *lovers* will carry out because of that rage. Although this construction makes the lovers his instruments, they nevertheless are mere representations of his own actions and emotions. If he is ultimately in control, he is also ultimately responsible for terrifying acts of violence and revenge. To the extent that divine agency is veiled, divine responsibility is also shrouded.

If one looks further at the agency of YHWH, one finds cracks in YHWH's identity and control. Looking at the *sexual* economy of the text, YHWH's identity and control begin to unravel. If YHWH *were* in such control, how could the women act as they did? The very fact that they "whore," and not just with one man/nation but several, and the fact that they choose the "choicest," most "handsome young men," men of rank, suggests that the divine agency is not as powerful as claimed.

The multiple descriptions of the lovers suggest even more: Within the sexual economy described in the text, YHWH's identity as the ultimate male also has fractures. Although YHWH is attempting to assert power and control

---

[69]Even though he claims (at least some of) their children as his own in verse 37, the Hebrew grammar hides his agency. The text reads, "even their children, whom they bore for me."

(even over emotions and thoughts, v. 27), the very description of the sisters' lovers indicates just how out of control he is. The description also indicates how precarious his identity is. Not only can he not control his wives' sexuality, but his description of the lovers reveals the *lovers'* power: They are young and handsome, officers, men of rank (e.g., successful and powerful). His description of the Egyptians indicates that they are potent as well (v. 20).[70] The latter description may indicate a sense of lack in this area, particularly since it seems out of place, even gratuitous in the context. Together with the fact that the lovers are described not just once but three times in terms of their looks, rank and prestige, this description suggests at the very least some ambivalence about his own sexual/political identity. In other words, the envy in YHWH's descriptions of the men suggests a sexual identity crisis of his own.

As noted above, Jerusalem is the grounding of YHWH's identity. In a very real way, YHWH is dependent on Jerusalem as the center and focal point of his power. Without Jerusalem, YHWH has no visible power; hence the motivation of the chapter, and indeed, of the book: "that you may know that I am YHWH" (v. 49). The loss of Jerusalem means loss of divine status for YHWH. Therefore, YHWH needs to reinscribe himself as the ultimate subject. Describing his relationship to Jerusalem in terms of male/female relationships that use cultural conventions of gender in which the woman is merely the object of exchange between men (she goes from belonging to her father to belonging to her husband) allows for such a reinscription–at least on the surface. By asserting his power and control over Jerusalem, YHWH says to everyone, "I am indeed YHWH." Thus, the narrator is trying to reconceptualize YHWH's identity through the vehicle of this gender construction. But there is something wrong here. God, the unknowable, the unrepresentable, is nonetheless represented in this text. YHWH is actually the antireflection of the sisters. As a reflection, however, he is completely vulnerable and dependent on them. Without them, he doesn't exist as a deity, hence their reinscription at the end. Yet the text itself reinscribes the threat they present as well, leaving YHWH's identity and power never completely shored up, never completely unified. Thus, the horrific violence in the text doesn't work in the end either. Although Oholah and Oholibah are killed, raped, mutilated, and otherwise punished, they live on as warnings (*object* lessons) to other women not to take on the position of subject; they also live on as testaments to YHWH's power and identity. Unfortunately for YHWH, they also live on as threats to that power and identity, for the text illustrates both in its construction and its rhetoric that such power and identity are never fixed or stable. As a result, the violence used as the vehicle of reinstating power and control is also open to deconstruction.

Such a construction of God is in need of deconstruction because it is dangerous; it has vast potential for misuse and abuse. The discussion above has already shown how this construction is harmful to women, but I would

---

[70]It is interesting that it is the Egyptians' male organs that are also described in Ezekiel 16:26. The Egyptians are clearly the "sticking point" with YHWH in Ezekiel.

argue that it is harmful to men as well. As I have argued elsewhere,[71] the power of this imagery is that it is addressed to men who are imaged as whores. Men reading this text are under pressure not to identify themselves as women but rather as men. More specifically, the pressure is to identify with *YHWH* as the exemplar of male identity and behavior. The problems with that pressure should be obvious. Robert P. Carroll supports my point: "The YHWH of these narratives [Ezek. 16 and 23] is a tyrant and a bully–an abusive husband of a kind utterly unacceptable to modern readers. This YHWH is a monster, guilty of bouts of pornographic violence."[72] He says further, "The anchoring of such images of violent action in the activities of YHWH only strengthens the ideology of violence informing the text. For a violent god breeds violent men–or, better still, violent men produce violent images of gods."[73] That this is portrayed as the literal word of God (i.e., in God's voice) makes it even more horrifying.

This study has revealed how both the female and the male sexual identities are fractured in Ezekiel 23. Sexuality, gender, and identity prove to be slippery, unstable constructions, even as they are presumed to be fixed. The fractures in each of these configurations allow for new, hopefully transformative possibilities. The very problems that these categories pose by not being fixable or stable allow us to step back and question the constructions themselves. As Judith Butler indicated in the quote at the beginning of this piece, sexuality is not really a "given," or "natural." It is itself a political construct that "extends and disguises the power relations responsible for its genesis."[74] Once the fissures in the sexual identities of all the characters in the text are exposed, the entire text begins to unravel. It is in that unraveling, I suggest, that transformative possibilities can be opened.

If we begin to question the very frameworks that construct male/female, subject/object, loved one/hated one, and so on, a path is opened to reconfigure our understanding of those structures and the identities they construct. Here the discourses that take us beyond binary oppositions to try to formulate identity in new ways may be helpful. As identity is revealed to be a product of unexpressed power dynamics, what can happen if the underlying dynamics are changed? Can we move beyond a divine figure who is identified in such

---

[71] In my 1996 dissertation, *Circumcising the Prostitute: The Rhetorics of Intertextuality, Gender and Metaphor in Jeremiah 3:1–4:4*, which is currently being revised for publication in the Journal for the Study of the Old Testament Supplement Series, and in "Multiple Exposures," 5–18.

[72] Robert P. Carroll, "Whorusalamin: A Tale of Three Cities as Three Sisters," in *On Reading Prophetic Texts: Gender-Specific and Related Studies in Memory of Fokkelien van Dijk-Hemmes,* ed. Bob Becking and Meindert Dijkstra (Leiden: Brill, 1996), 77.

[73] Ibid., 76. It must also be noted, however, that these are two of the few points where Carroll and I agree. He consistently argues against feminist interpretations of passages containing the marriage metaphor for God and Israel. While this is not the place for a sustained critique of this facet of Carroll's work, suffice it to say that he fails to see that the rhetoric itself is a product of the conventions of gender and sexuality with which the text works, rather than, in his terms, an overlaying of "an a priori and determining feminist ideology" on the text (Robert P. Carroll, "Desire Under the Terebinths: On Pornographic Representation in the Prophets–A Response," in *A Feminist Companion to the Latter Prophets.*

[74] Butler, *Gender Trouble,* 92.

violent, horrific ways? Can we move beyond the subject/object split to find ways in which both men and women can be subjects without denying subjecthood to the other? If these constructions do not work, we need to find others that do. That is the next task to be undertaken. [75]

---

[75]Earlier versions of this article were presented at the 1998 Annual Meeting of the Society of Biblical Literature in Orlando, and the 1999 Central States Regional Meeting in St. Louis, where I received the regional scholar award for it.

Called to Do Justice?

A Bhabhian Reading of Micah 5 and 6:1–8

Erin Runions

When I began work on Micah 5 and 6:1–8, I had great hopes of finding the well-known verse "He has shown you, oh human, what is good, and what Yahweh seeks from you: to do justice, and to love faithfulness and to walk wisely with your God" (Mic. 6:8), to orient readers' subjectivity toward justice. This was largely because one of the things that I have been concerned with in my work is whether textual systems can affect readers as subjects, and by this I mean as speaking, acting agents who are always-already shaped and positioned by language and ideology.[1] I have wondered whether texts like Lacan's Other (language) and Althusser's policeman (ideology) can hail or "interpellate" readers, whose response through a process of identification forms or reforms their subjectivity, or in other words, their possibilities for agency.[2] Following on this, I (rather idealistically) hoped to find this passage in Micah calling readers to identify with subject positions and identities poised to do justice at every turn. But upon close reading of the text, I realized that the call for justice here is complicated by ambiguities both within the text and without. On the textual level, the identity constructed for the nation Israel seems to shift between positions of resistance and domination, between the downtrodden

---

[1]For a good overview of the discussions on subjectivity and ideology, see Paul Smith, *Discerning the Subject,* Theory and History of Literature 55 (Minneapolis: University of Minnesota Press, 1988).

[2]"The interpellation of subjects into ideology" is Althusser's conception of the way ideology functions to shape people's subjectivity. Althusser suggests that individuals recognize, or rather, misrecognize, themselves in ideological discourses. Althusser uses the analogy of a policeman hailing someone with a "Hey you," whereupon the person recognizes herself as "you" and turns around, as if guilty. Thus, a person addressed and interpellated by ideology recognizes herself, and behaves accordingly; see Louis Althusser, "Ideology and Ideological State Apparatuses (Notes Toward an Investigation)," in *Essays on Ideology* (London: Verso, 1984), 1–60.

For a discussion of interpellation with relation to a Lacanian view of language, see Slavoj Žižek,, *The Sublime Object of Ideology,* Phronesis (London: Verso, 1989).

153

and the aggressor, thus framing the call for justice in a somewhat ambivalent fashion. This complication is intensified at the extratextual level by my own conflicted identity as a white North American reader wanting to be committed to justice. By what process do I identify with the text; how do these complications affect my identification with the text; and does this affect my subjectivity in any way?

In this paper, I would like to explore the relationship between textual identities and readerly identifications with such identities as they affect the call to justice in this passage. To this end, I will look at the ambivalent and contradictory marks of the identity Micah constructs for the nation Israel in Micah 5–6:8, the subsequent impact of the reading process on the text thus marked, and the possible effects of this process on readers' subjectivity. The theoretical stimulation for this reading is the work of postcolonial theorist Homi K. Bhabha on the ambivalent construction of national identity. Bhabha's thinking on the kinds of discourses used in articulating national identities illuminates the ambivalences within the discourses on nation in Micah and enables me to consider how such ambivalence continues through the reading process, the effect of this on readerly identifications, and ultimately the implications of ambivalence for the call to justice in Micah 6:8.

I limit my discussion to Micah 5–6:8 not because these texts form some kind of autonomous or well-defined unit, but because together they reveal a wide range of textually inscribed subject positions, both grammatically and metaphorically. Because I am interested in the relationship between identity, subjectivity, and justice, I have chosen, somewhat arbitrarily, to end with the previously mentioned call for justice of Micah 6:8. Ending at 6:8 is not, however, a particularly contentious move, since it is usually understood as the conclusion to the pericope.

Ambiguous Textual Identities

Micah is an excellent text for an investigation into conflicting textual and readerly identities and identifications, as it has long been observed for its constant and unsignalled shifts in speaker and addressee. Micah 5 and 6 contain a good sampling of the kinds of textual shifts in identity that are prevalent throughout the book. The first three verses of chapter 5 contain an address to "*you, oh Bethlehem of Ephrathah*" by "*me,*" an unidentified speaker describing a future ruler who is coming forth from *you* (Bethlehem) to *me* who rules in the name of Yahweh. Verses 5–6 (4–5, Heb.) of chapter 5 then shift to an inclusive address using "*we*" and "*our,*" still unidentified, describing how *we* will resist Assyria's colonization. Verses 7–9 (6–8, Heb.) shift again, now to a third-person description of the *remnant of Jacob,* which is presumably a remnant as a result of oppression, yet which acts here as an oppressive force among the nations, as a lion, tearing and destroying whatever it passes. But in verse 9 (8, Heb.) the third person shifts abruptly back to the second person, stating that "*You* will raise your hand against your foes, and all your enemies will be cut off." Here *you* seems to take the place of the third-person, devouring lion-remnant of Jacob, though this connection is not explicitly stated. But then, verses

10–15 (9–14, Heb.) follow with a first-person oracle of Yahweh in which *I* threaten *you* with violence. *I* threaten to cut off *your* horses and chariots, your idols, so that you will no longer bow to the work of your hands. *You* are no longer the conquering lion-like remnant, but are now the target of destruction. The chapter ends with a generalized flourish of angry aggression against nations who do not listen.

Chapter 6 continues this series of disjunctions. The chapter begins with *you* as a plural (a form not seen in chap. 5), by virtue of a masculine plural imperative, calling *you* to listen to Yahweh. Then in 6:1b, the imperative form changes, and *you*, seemingly addressed by Yahweh's speech, becomes singular again, called to rise up and dispute to the mountains. But then in verse 2 *you* are the (masculine plural) mountains called to listen to Yahweh's dispute. Then *I* begin speaking in verses 3–5, as Yahweh giving voice to my complaint against *you* (masculine singular), who are now identified as *my* people. In these lines, *I* ask how I have wearied *you*, and by way of vindicating myself *I* remind *you* that *I* brought *you* out of Egypt, out of the house of slavery. *I* also refer *you* to the tradition, asking you to remember the words of Balaam in response to Balak. This call to remembrance includes the phrase "from Shittim to Gilgal," which, as scholars point out, marks the movement of the people of Israel from the wilderness across the Jordan into the promised land and recalls the conquest tradition.[3] Then rather abruptly in verses 6–8, *I* no longer seem to speak in the voice of Yahweh. Rather, *I* am found asking what kind of sacrifices would please Yahweh. This section of text ends, by way of answer to *you* (masculine singular)—no longer my people, but modified by the vocative "oh man," (hereafter translated as "human")—as you are told to do justice, to love faithfulness, and to walk wisely[4] with your God.

Who then is called to do justice in this passage? For argument's sake, I will consider the overall addressee in these passages to be the nation of Israel as many commentators take it to be.[5] However, because of the indistinct use of the pronouns *I* and *you* and because of their fluctuation with respect to the position of aggressor, or aggressed, it is not clear what kind of identity is being formed nor who is included in this identity, and certainly not what stance this identity takes with respect to the call to justice.

Homi Bhabha and Ambivalent Identities

The ambiguity of the identities in Micah 5–6 brings to mind a theme elaborated by Homi Bhabha throughout his work on nations and identities:

---

[3]Hans Walter Wolff, *Micah: A Commentary,* trans. Gary Stansell (Minneapolis: Augsburg, 1990), 176; Delbert R. Hillers, *Micah: A Commentary on the Book of the Prophet Micah,* Hermeneia (Philadelphia: Fortress Press, 1984), 78.

[4]The Hebrew word usually translated as "humbly" ("walk humbly") only occurs here and in Proverbs 11:2, where it is connected with "wisdom." Wolff, *Micah,* 182, points out that it also occurs in Sirach 16:25; 32:3; 34:22; 42:8, with the meaning "well considered," "prudent," or "circumspect." I have used "wisely" to connote all of the above meanings.

[5]For examples, see Wolff, *Micah,* 176; Hillers, *Micah,* 78; James Luther Mays, *Micah: A Commentary,* Old Testament Library (Philadelphia: Westminster Press, 1976), 141.

that of the "ambivalence that haunts the idea of the nation."[6] In spite of the fact that Bhabha is concerned with modern nations, his theory is relevant to the biblical text not only because he deals specifically with language, text, and the process by which national identity is written but also because of the kind of critique he makes of modernity's construction of "the nation." Throughout his work, but particularly in his contributions to the book *Nation and Narration,*[7] Bhabha critiques modernity's universal ideal of the nation as a homogeneous, sovereign, autonomous political entity[8] by looking at the articulations of cultural difference within nations and the ambivalences that this creates. He suggests that narratives of nationhood are continually disrupted and destabilized by the different everyday cultural locations from which these narratives are spoken (what Bhabha calls the "enunciatory present").

For Bhabha, ambivalence is caused by a tension between what he calls the pedagogical and performative cultural discourses that constitute national identity.[9] Pedagogical discourse constructs a people as a historical or patriotic object, "giving the discourse an authority that is based on the…historical origin or event."[10] The performative process, on the other hand, is that "repetitious, recursive strategy"[11] in which individual people, not necessarily unified in their beliefs or by their willingness to be represented by the national identity, take part in producing national culture through day-to-day activities and through their interaction with, or enunciation of, the national story or identity. Ambivalence is a result of the movement between the pedagogical and the performative. The "pedagogical object," that is, the self-contained national identity, is intersected by the open-endedness of its being told, its enunciation by a community that is far from unified. As Bhabha puts it, in performance "the…Nation *It/Self,* alienated from its eternal self-generation, becomes a liminal form of social representation, a space that is *internally* marked by cultural difference and the heterogeneous histories of contending peoples."[12] Put very simply, the pedagogical object cannot hope to be representative of all the people within the culture, so when individuals interact with it, or enunciate it, the static "national identity" breaks open and becomes less dominant and less definitive.

Bhabha focuses his attention on the performative production of the national narrative, because it is here that he finds possibilities for "imagining the possibility of other contending and liberating forms of cultural identification,"[13] forms of cultural identification that break away from notions

---

[6]Homi K. Bhabha, "Introduction: Narrating the Nation," in *Nation and Narration,* ed. Homi K. Bhabha (London and New York: Routledge, 1990), 1.

[7]Ibid., and Bhabha, "DissemiNation: Time, Narrative and the Margins of the Modern Nation," in *Nation and Narration,* 291–322.

[8]Bhabha, *Nation and Narration,* 293.

[9]Ibid., 299.

[10]Ibid., 297.

[11]Ibid.

[12]Ibid., 299.

[13]Ibid., 311.

of cultural supremacy that justify discrimination. This he calls liminal identification, or I might say identification with the margins and the internal difference within the margins.[14] He discusses performativity in a number of ways, but I would like to highlight only two of these ways here, albeit in a simplified fashion, as informative for this passage in Micah. The first is performativity as a repetition of the pedagogical object (the national icon, the historical "origin") in a way that changes it. Bhabha distinguishes between the "continuist, accumulative temporality of the pedagogical, and the repetitious, recursive strategy of the performative."[15] He uses Derrida's notion of the supplement to explain this "recursive strategy," speaking of a doubling of the pedagogical object through daily repetition that, like double entendre, at the same time *adds to* and *substitutes for* meaning (of the pedagogical object). Thus, the performance of the national narrative both adds to the (pedagogical) national tradition (accumulating historical expressions of it) and substitutes for it, interrupting the tradition, articulating it differently, and allowing for new kinds of identifications with it. Bhabha is emphatic that this does not mean that the meanings of the national sign/icon/object are simply plural, but rather that the supplement or repetition of the sign changes its mode of articulation.[16]

Another related way that Bhabha describes the performative production of national narrative is as the split in language between the subject of the statement and the subject who speaks/reads/identifies with it.[17] The subject written into a statement and the people (in the time of its writing and over the years) reading, speaking, or identifying with that subject position (in Bhabha's terms "enunciating" it), inhabit two very different, perhaps even incommensurable, cultural and discursive environments. Thus, for Bhabha, an image of a nation set forth in language—some kind of national icon (pedagogical object)—may set out to validate a certain kind of authority or elevated self-conception; however, the fact that it is repeated differently every time it is enunciated makes it difficult for it to be established as definite and final. The very split in language between the statement and the enunciation of that statement "deprives it [the cultural icon] of the certainty and stability for centre or closure."[18] The constant sliding from the subject position of the statement

---

[14]See also, Bhabha, *The Location of Culture* (London: Routledge, 1994), 182–85.

[15]Bhabha, *Nation and Narration,* 291.

[16]Ibid., 305–6, 311.

[17]Bhabha builds this argument in "DissemiNation," using Claude Lefort's discussion of the split in language in the construction of ideology. Elsewhere he speaks of the common semiotic account of the split between *énoncé* and *énonciation;* see Bhabha, *The Location of Culture,* 36. For a range of different views on this split, see Emile Benveniste, *Problems in General Linguistics,* trans. Mary Elizabeth Meek (Coral Gables, Fla.: University of Miami Press, 1971), 218; Jacques Lacan, *Écrits: A Selection,* trans. Alan Sheridan (New York: W. W. Norton, 1977), 298–300; Lacan, *The Four Fundamental Concepts of Psycho-analysis,* ed. Jacques-Alain Miller, trans. Alan Sheridan (New York: W. W. Norton, 1981), 138–42. For a helpful overview see Kaja Silverman, *The Subject of Semiotics* (New York: Oxford University Press, 1983), 45–53.

[18]Bhabha, *Nation and Narration,* 298.

to the subject position of enunciation does not allow the national icon to establish itself as definitive or authoritative.

Reading Ambivalent Identities

I return now to Micah 5:1–6:8, modifying Bhabha to my purposes somewhat, to look at the ways in which the pedagogical (the cumulative force of the signs of the text) is disrupted by the performative (repetition and enunciation of signs). If the images in the passage are read all together for their overall impact, they establish a national image (or pedagogical object),[19] which is connected to Yahweh in some way, and which is figured as an oppressed remnant that will triumph in the future. This seems to be the effect of the accumulation of images: the ruler coming from the insignificantly small Bethlehem to rule in the name of Yahweh (5:2; 5:1, Heb.), the remnant of Jacob, who is like dew from Yahweh, yet eventually becomes a fierce lion (5:7–8; 6–7, Heb.), and the call to "my people" to remember how "I" (Yahweh) brought you from exodus to conquest (6:3–4). This is further portrayed by the rulers raised up to combat the invading Assyrians in 5:5–6 (4–5 Heb.), though no mention is made here of Yahweh. Together these images seem to evoke an enslaved people on the verge of liberation.

The most consistent sign related to this image of oppressed remnant turned victorious throughout the passage is the masculine singular *you.* This pronoun, more than any other sign, seems to represent the pedagogical object. There is the small insignificant *you,* Bethlehem in 5:2 (5:1, Heb.), which also seems to stay present in 5:3–4 (2–3, Heb.) by virtue of the continued description of ruler originating from *you.* There is the *you* who cuts off your enemies in 5:9 (5:8, Heb.) and who, by virtue of similar behavior, seems to be linked to the third person, devouring, ravaging remnant of Jacob just prior in 5:8 (5:7, Heb.). And there is the *you,* my people, rescued in the exodus, turned colonizer in 6:3–4. *You* are the oppressed remnant turned victorious. *You,* I might say, is the short form for the pedagogical object.

However, the repetition and/or enunciation of the masculine singular second-person pronoun is not static, nor identical, in this passage, and when these differences are attended to, the kind of performative rearticulation and disruption of the pedagogical object described by Bhabha comes into view. I would like to observe how this happens by looking at three instances of the repetition and "sliding" of the sign *you* (masculine singular). These are: the annihilated *you* in 5:10–15 (9–14, Heb.), the *you* my people in 6:4–5, and finally the call to *you,* oh human, in 6:8. I would also like to explore what might happen to readers' identifications with these signs in the process.

Two issues mentioned earlier become pertinent here: first, the reader's interpellation into and identification with the text, and second, the split between

---

[19]For a different kind of discussion of repetition in the establishment of Israelite identity, see Roland Boer, "Green Ants and Gibeonites: B. Wongar, Joshua 9 and Some Problems," *Semeia* 75 (1996): 129–52.

the subject of the statement and the subject enunciating it. Briefly then, because the second-person form is an address to which the usual response is as a speaking, acting subject, *I*, it can be argued that through its use, the text opens up grammatical subject positions, which call or "hail" readers. Further, because second-person forms are "empty" (i.e., the referent is not fixed) readers can easily take up or respond to them as *I*.[20] Readers can then be urged to make certain kinds of identifications according to how that empty subject position is modified. For instance, if I respond as a reader to a *you* in the text, which is subsequently modified by some nominal subject, for example "my people," the text places me structurally in a position of identification with "my people."[21] But such identifications are always only partial, because of the split in language between the subject of the statement and the subject of enunciation. The reader can never "be" the subject (*you, Bethlehem, my people, oh human)* of the statement. Inserted into the position of *you,* the reader is bound to some extent by the structures of the text, but this *you* is always dissected by the reader's own subject position.

Both issues (the way the text interpellates readers and the split between the subject of the statement and the subject of enunciation) bear on the kinds of identifications that readers make in reading. Although the reader (subject of enunciation) may momentarily be positioned as the subject of the statement by the text, presumably she has an identity and subjectivity external to the text that stays consistent, at least for the duration of a reading of the text. The *I* with which the reader responds to the *you* of the text is continuous, even where the text seems disjointed, and this compels, or at least allows, the reader to make connections between discrete instances of the *you* in the text that perhaps would not be made if the image was described in the third person.

Rearticulating the Nation

All this being said, what might be the effect, on both textual and readerly levels, of the three slightly different repetitions of the sign *you* mentioned above on the image of the oppressed remnant turned victorious (pedagogical object)? The first of these instances (5:10–15; 5:9–14, Heb.) serves to illustrate

---

[20]I am obviously influenced here by Althusser's moment of interpellation, but I am also drawing on the work of Emile Benveniste for whom *I* and *you* create a moment in discourse in which the speaker can posit herself as subject. These pronouns are reversible in nature; the use of one automatically invokes the other: "the one whom 'I' defines by 'you' thinks of himself as 'I' and can be inverted into 'I'" (*Problems in General Linguistics,* 199). Film theory has also drawn Althusser and Benveniste together to suggest the interpellation of the viewer into the filmic text; see Kaja Silverman, *The Subject of Semiotics,* 43–53; 194–236; Colin MacCabe, "Theory and Film: Principles of Realism and Pleasure," *Screen* 17/3 (1976): 7–29; MacCabe, "The Discursive and the Ideological in Film: Notes on the Conditions of Political Intervention," *Screen* 19/4 (1979): 29–42.

[21]The positioning of the reader in this way is similar to the way that a number of film theorists have spoken of shot/reverse shot sequences in film. With a camera shot the viewer becomes aware of what, or whom, is not visible and is therefore placed in the position of this absent person. Then with the reverse shot, this absence is filled in by the image of what is missing. An identification is forced with the reverse shot, and in this way the subject fills in the absence. See *Screen* 18/4, 1978.

the kind of slide that occurs in the repetition of the sign *you* in the reading process. In 5:10–15 (9–14, Heb.), *you,* just previously cutting off your enemies (v. 9; v. 8, Heb.)–with no warning (or marker of subject change)–are suddenly told that you yourself will be cut off: your horses and chariots cut off (v. 10; v. 9, Heb.), your cities and fortresses devastated (v. 11; v. 10, Heb.), and your cultural practices plucked away. You will no longer bow down to the works of your hands (vv. 12–14; vv. 11–13, Heb.). These things are predicted by the first-person speaker in an oracle of Yahweh. One moment *you* are an active and aggressive subject affiliated with Yahweh, the next *you* are a quite different subject, one whose activities are harshly curtailed by Yahweh. The resistant fighter in 5:8–9 (5:7–8, Heb.) is now set to be destroyed.

Although this shift could be explained in a number of (text-historical) ways, what is interesting for my purposes is that when it is enunciated in the reading process, a connection can be made by the reader between the disjointed *you*'s of 5:8–9 and 5:10–15 (5:7–8 and 5:9–14, Heb.). The reader, interpellated into the text by the subject of the statement, *you,* responds as the subject of enunciation, *I.* But as a subject with some continuity, the *I* of enunciation holds the two disjointed subjects of the statements together: *I* once lifting my hand against my enemies am now being destroyed by Yahweh. This identification–substitution I might even say–made between the *you* of 5:8–9 (7–8, Heb.) and the *you* of 10–15 (9–14, Heb.) rearticulates the pedagogical object (oppressed remnant turned victorious) as merely the oppressed remnant, giving a face to the oppression and obliterating any chance of victory.

Conflicting Subject Positions

Leaving this jarring disjuncture in chapter 5 aside for a moment, I turn to the second slightly different iteration of the sign *you* in this passage. In particular, I would like to consider the masculine singular imperative (understanding the imperative as a second-person form) in 6:4–5 to remember the exodus and the story of Balak and Balaam in Numbers 22–24.[22] This imperative brings in an intertext that dissects the pedagogical object considerably. In Numbers 22–24, Balak requests Balaam to "curse this people that came out of Egypt, because they are *too powerful for me,* so that I can drive them out" (Num. 22:5–6). In other words, Balak's plea is a plea of resistance by one certain to be overtaken by Israel's colonizing force. Balaam answers Balak in full colonial rhetoric, predicting conquest (see Num. 23:24; 24:8–9, 17–18). This insertion into the Mican text calls *you,* my people, to take on an identity that seems to drop the "oppressed" part of the oppressed remnant turned victorious.

Further, this intertext also repeats the images of the exodus (6:4) and of the lion (5:8–9; 5:7–8, Heb.), used in the construction of the pedagogical figure of the oppressed remnant turned victorious. In his second and third oracles,

---

[22]I am not making any claims here about whether or not the author of the text was referring specifically to Numbers as we have it written.

Israel is predicted as a lioness that will devour her foes and break their bones (Num. 23:24; 24:9), repeating the image of the trampling lion in Micah 5:8 (5:7, Heb.) The exodus theme appears again (23:22 and 24:8) in both these oracles just prior to the devouring trampling lion (23:24; 24:9). The repetition of these signs in the intertext articulates the pedagogical object differently, connoting an aggressive and colonizing force instead of a force resistant to colonization. This process of repetition, it would seem, rather than allowing liberatory forms of cultural identification to emerge, as Bhabha suggests, reinforces an ethic of domination and colonization.

Yet the recursive strategy does not stop here. In a strange reversal, this rearticulation of the pedagogical object, while constructing the remnant of Jacob as a colonizing force, at the same time constructs an image of Balak and the Moabites in a position similar to the pedagogical object I have been discussing—as a people resisting colonization. Moab, however, is not portrayed as having a fate of future victory, but one of destruction. Balaam prophesies, "Let me inform you [masculine singular] what this people will do to your people in days to come...A scepter comes forth from Israel, it smashes the brow of Moab" (Num. 24:14, 17, trans. Milgrom). Here then another substitution is made: *you,* Barak/Moab, the nation resisting colonization (to be defeated) repeats, but differently, *you,* Israel, the nation resisting colonization (to be victorious). Going one step further, this supplementation of the Mican text recalls 5:9–14, in which *you* are suddenly destroyed. The reader, identifying with the *you* in the text, is positioned to make the identification—what Bhabha might call a liminal identification— between *you* as "my people" and *you* as the oppressed enemy, Barak/Moab.

But I would make another move to argue that the recursive sliding of the signs in the text and the negotiation between text and reader in this way questions the authority of the text. This liminal identification (Israel to be destroyed, like Moab to be destroyed) challenges the veracity of Balaam's prophecy as it is used in Micah. Balaam prophesies that Moab will be destroyed, but at the end of his oracles, Barak goes on his way, not particularly nonplused it seems (Num. 24:25), and in reality Moab is never fully wiped out. In fact, in Numbers 25 the Israelites are involved with Moabite women, and this is attributed in the tradition to the scheming of Balaam (see Num. 31:16), after he finishes giving his oracles[23]—a detail that not only blurs the distinction between Israelite and Moabite, but also further puts into doubt the authority of Balaam. With the pedagogical source text thus challenged, Micah's ability to predict the destruction of Israel, presumably as punishment, is also put into question. The text's authority is put into question by the circulation of its own signs.

---

[23]For a thorough discussion of the Balaam tradition, see Jacob Milgrom, *Numbers,* Jewish Publication Society Torah Commentary (Philadelphia and New York: Jewish Publication Society, 1990), 467–80.

Justice?

Finally, I arrive at the last repetition of the sign *you* in Micah 5–6:8: *you, human,* called to justice. This, because it follows a question in the first person– by a questioner who is concerned with what rituals will please Yahweh–seems to be an answer addressed to an individual. Thus, it seems that the call to justice here is a call to the individual member of the nation. However, because the second-person masculine pronoun has been used throughout the passage, the reader (subject of enunciation) can make the identification between individual and nation. The reader is thus interpellated both as individual and as nation, bringing into view a tension between individual will and national formation. What kind of justice can be done by a *you* who has been formed at once as the colonized and the colonizer, as the destroyer and the destroyed?

Rather than answer this (rhetorical) question, I would like to instead look at how this might resonate with the reader's own ambivalence with respect to justice. Not only does the reader enunciate the text, opening it up into an ambivalent space, but the text, in a sense, also enunciates the reader. Just as the reader's subject position(s) can open up the text, so also the text's subject positions could shed light on the reader's identity. Let me personalize this operation. I am called in this text to do justice. But I am interpellated at once as an individual caring about what will please the divinity, and as an identity that exhibits a conflicted stance toward justice, an identity that is struggling with its history as a slave turned colonizer, yet which is also engaged in resisting colonization and at the same time threatened with destruction. But this is not a position with which I am unfamiliar; in fact, I recognize myself in it. My own subjectivity is marked, like the text, with inconsistencies vis à vis justice. The systemic oppression that I have faced as a woman has pushed me to be engaged in a wider range of resistances to colonizing forces that threaten dissolution, whether that be patriarchy or transnational corporations. I have no assurance of "victory" in these acts of resistance. Yet as white, North American, and of a privileged class, I am also guilty of propagating many forms of oppression. Indeed, by virtue of being North American, I am still the colonizer. When I am called to do justice, do I know what that is? Would I even be capable of doing it? Is there a way out of this web of conflicts?

I would argue that this web is precisely the ambivalence of which Bhabha speaks. This ambivalence could operate as a mire of hopelessness and a generator of apathy. But Bhabha wants to see it as the site of hybridity[24]–an important concept in his work–which surpasses the idea of cultural diversity and captures the necessity of negotiating cultural difference.[25] Bhabha emphasizes "the importance of the hybrid moment, of political change. Here the transformational value of change lies in the rearticulation, or translation, of elements that are *neither the One...nor the Other...but something else besides,*

---

[24]Bhabha, *The Location of Culture,* 85–92, 102–22.
[25]Ibid., 38, 58.

which contests the terms and territories of both."[26] New possibilities for political change, and I read this as change for justice, emerge when liminal identifications are made and differences are negotiated and mobilized in new forms of struggle.

This kind of approach is similar to that of others writing on identity formation and politics,[27] who also want to see conflicting and conflicted subject positions as a model for a kind of coalition politics in the struggle for justice– a form of solidarity in which people, recognizing themselves as both oppressed and oppressor, engage in a process of critical reflection and action.[28] For over a decade Ernesto Laclau and Chantal Mouffe have been talking about the possibilities for radical democracy through the recognition of a "subject constructed at the point of intersection of subject positions."[29] This has been taken forward by others, such as Judith Butler, who argues against a kind of essentialist coalition politics that makes unity a prerequisite for action. She puts it well when she says: "Perhaps a coalition needs to acknowledge its contradictions and take action with those contradictions intact. Perhaps also part of what dialogic understanding entails is the acceptance of divergence, breakage, splinter, and fragmentation as part of the often tortuous process of democratization."[30] Likewise, in a recent collection on identity formation, editors Smadar Lavie and Ted Swedenburg build on the work of Bhabha to suggest, "The fragmentation of identity articulat[es] minority constituencies across disjunctive and differential social positions [so that] political subjectivity as a multi-dimensional, conflictual form of identification [could be] mobilized and able to build coalitions."[31] Thinking through these kinds of suggestions about coalition-building in my discussion above, I might suggest that the rearticulation of identities brings diverse subject positions into view and allows for liminal identifications that are transformative and urge new working relationships.

Conclusion: The Text Again

So perhaps there is method in the text's madness after all. Perhaps the very ambiguity of the textual shifts in identity is part of a rhetoric that has the effect of shaking readers and listeners out of what Bhabha would call the "essentialism or logocentrism of a received political tradition," and into a "*negotiation* of contradictory and antagonistic instances that open up hybrid

---

[26]Ibid., 128.

[27]Judith Butler, *Gender Trouble: Feminism and the Subversion of Identity* (London and New York: Routledge, 1990); Ernesto Laclau and Chantal Mouffe, *Hegemony and Socialist Strategy* (London: Verso, 1985); Smadar Lavie and Ted Swedenburg, "Introduction," in *Displacement, Diaspora, and Geographies of Identity* (Durham and London: Duke University Press, 1996), 28–40; Anna Kruzynski, "Alliances in Social Movements," unpublished paper.

[28]Kruzynski, "Alliances," 18–26.

[29]Laclau and Mouffe, *Hegemony,* 12.

[30]Butler, *Gender Trouble,* 14–15.

[31]Lavie and Swedenburg, "Introduction," 16.

sites and objectives of struggle."[32] This negotiation makes me aware of my own position and of the discourses that form other positions and political ends, as well as pushes me into new forms of action. This, I might suggest, is where the text affects my subjectivity. Not only does it present to me a full textual view of my own contradictions, but it allows me, urges me, to make a (liminal) identification with one who is oppressed like me, but who is politically, radically, and conflictually different from me. It shows me the face of oppression and then shows me as the cause of similar oppression. Further reflection on this identification persuades me to seriously consider coalition politics as a way of mobilizing to fight for justice.

So to return to my initial question, "Called to Do Justice?" I am torn, but not really, between the possibility that, on one hand, the text's conflicted call to justice is simply invalid and, on the other, that through the enunciation of this conflict, the reader is called, enunciated, to recognize the contradictory positions she holds with respect to justice, and is pushed toward new hybrid sites and new objectives of struggle.

---

[32]Bhabha, *The Location of Culture,* 25.

How to Read a Tainted Text

The Wicked Husbandmen in a Post-Holocaust Context

Tania Oldenhage

In the early 1990s, I participated in a Protestant church service in Germany and was asked to read the gospel. The prescribed text for that Sunday was the parable of the Wicked Husbandmen. I was familiar with this story but utterly unprepared to hear myself reading it aloud. My role as a speaker, standing next to the altar and facing the congregation, trapped me in a catastrophic plot of increasing violence—abuse, insult, murder, destruction. After my final sentence, I sat down with a vague but intense feeling of discomfort, a feeling that still haunts me as I write.

I begin with this recollection in order to make as concrete as possible the abstract phrase in the title of this essay. The church service I attended was a "post-Holocaust context" insofar as my audience and I shared memories of the German past. I spoke the parable of the Wicked Husbandmen to a public whose cultural identity was bound up with the atrocities of National Socialism. What I find striking about this context, moreover, is the fact that the parable was read without comment. After I sat down, the service continued as though I had not spoken a word. Since the parable was not framed by any explicit interpretive discourse, its meaning was highly ambiguous. I cannot tell how the violent story was heard by the people in the church nor am I exactly sure how I read it. But I have been interested in commentaries on the Wicked Husbandmen ever since, and the question that gives my interest its vigor is this: What kind of interpretation, what kind of critical remark or hermeneutic gesture, would I have wished to interrupt the church service? What kind of symptom was my feeling of unease, and what kind of intervention did it call for?

The Problem of Anti-Judaism

Biblical critics have given a name for the thing that is wrong with the story: anti-Judaism, an age-old interpretive pattern that treats the story as an

165

allegory for the troublesome relations between God, the Jews, and the church.[1] The persistent violence of the tenants, according to this reading, represents the evil ways in which the Jews have treated God's prophets and, finally, God's Son, Jesus Christ. "They took him, flung him out of the vineyard, and killed him" (Mt. 21:39). The owner's reprisal refers to God's rejection of the Jews. "He will bring those bad men to a bad end" (Mt. 21:41). And the story's final twist, the handing-over of the vineyard to other tenants, stands for God's election of the Gentile church. In Matthew's interpretation: "The kingdom of God will be taken away from you, and given to a nation that yields the proper fruit" (Mt. 21:43). Read in this vein, the drama around the vineyard is rendered into a tale of Christian supersessionism.

In his essay "A Fresh Analysis of the Parable of the Wicked Husbandmen in the Light of Jewish-Catholic Dialogue," Aaron Milavec describes vividly this anti-Jewish reading pattern:[2]

> For hundreds of years this parable has been read in churches, and the ordained pastors have routinely explained to their congregations that Jesus used this parable to expose the murderous extremes to which the Jews were capable in their resistance to God and their pursuit of selfish interests. According to the terms of the parable, the Jews had finally gone too far. Murdering "the Son," Jesus Christ, was the last straw. God's patience was strained to the breaking point. As a result, God abandoned Israel—the Jews were to receive no more prophets—and God decided to give his inheritance to the Gentile Church. In such terms, the parable of the wicked husbandmen has carried a long legacy of anti-Judaism within the Christian tradition. (p. 81)

Milavec shows that this anti-Jewish pattern of interpretation has been transported from the patristic period up to our own time, "the post-Holocaust Era." He says that after "the existential shock occasioned by the Holocaust" (p. 84), anti-Judaism has been avoided to a certain degree. However, "the theological framework which engendered this devaluation of Judaism continues to operate under the untouchable rubric of being the objective content of what the wicked husbandmen originally meant for the inspired writers and their contemporaries" (p. 84). At the heart of this theological framework, Milavec detects the identification of the owner's son with Jesus Christ and the implicit idea that the parable is about the killing of Jesus by the Jews. Milavec concludes: "If the tacit content of the parable of the wicked husbandmen is to

---

[1]Rosemary Radford Ruether cites the parable of the Wicked Husbandmen as an example of the anti-Jewish flip side of the early christology. See her pioneering work *Faith and Fratricide: The Theological Roots of Anti-Semitism* (New York: Seabury Press, 1979), 92.

[2]The essay is published in Clemens Thoma and Michael Wyschogrod, eds., *Parable and Story in Judaism and Christianity* (New York: Paulist Press, 1989). This volume is the result of co-operative efforts by Jewish and Christian scholars to deal with the many relationships between their respective literary traditions.

associate the punishment of Israel with the death of Jesus, then, in and of itself, the parable is anti-Jewish" (p. 84).

When the text is read and heard today, without commentary, as it was read in the church service I mentioned above, these anti-Jewish resonances are at play. For Milavec, as for many others who find themselves in "a post-Holocaust Era," these resonances are also deeply disturbing. During the last two decades an increasing number of Christian scholars have acknowledged that the anti-Judaism associated with the New Testament has been a factor in the history of the Holocaust.[3] For these scholars, the parable of the Wicked Husbandmen, with its fierce anti-Jewish undertones, has turned into a tainted text, a jarring cultural object. Reading it without serious reservations has become one of those numerous "no longer possibles" that characterize our post-Holocaust culture.[4]

Dismissing the text, casting it out from the cultural reservoir as has been done with other "tainted material," is not really a viable option. The parable will remain canonical. It will also continue to be a living piece of the Christian tradition as long as it is included in the lectionary. All the more pressing is the question of appropriate reading strategies. How can we read this story after the Holocaust? Milavec's "fresh analysis of the parable" offers a powerful proposal that I would like to outline here.

Milavec's central strategy is to distinguish between the parable's anti-Jewish reception history and its original meaning as intended by the gospel writer Mark. His aim is to show that, originally, the parable of the Wicked Husbandmen was a "*true Jewish* story—the *true Jewish* account of how God does indeed act in history" (p. 99). To make this case, Milavec recovers the Jewish horizon of understanding at the time of Mark. He says that by rewriting the parable for his gospel, Mark evokes a theme familiar to his audience: Persistently, God keeps sending his prophets even though Israel, again and again, treats them badly. However, the punishment of the tenants does not represent the punishment of Israel as a whole. In contrast to the famous vineyard parable in Isaiah 5:1ff., which ends with the destruction of the vineyard, Mark has the tenants destroyed, not the vineyard. At stake is not the fate of Israel but that of its leaders, who persistently misuse their authoritative power. Therefore, God will take this power away from them and entrust it to others. Milavec surmises that Mark deliberately does not give an exact clue as to who these "others" will be. What can be said, however, is that "the others" in Mark's understanding are definitely not the Christian church, but a Jewish group, "not an alternative to Judaism but an alternative within Judaism" (pp. 106f.).

---

[3]While there is by no means a straightforward causal link between Christian anti-Judaism and the Nazi genocide, traditional anti-Jewish stereotypes played into Nazi rhetoric and politics. For a strong argument, see Raul Hilberg, "Precedents," in *The Destruction of the European Jews* (New York: Holmes & Meier, 1985), 5–24.

[4]See Eric Santner, *Tainted Objects. Mourning, Memory, and Film in Postmodern Germany* (Ithaca, N.Y.: Cornell University Press, 1990), 8f.

Milavec concludes, "The legacy of anti-Judaism attached to the parable of the wicked husbandmen from the patristic period down to our present day cannot be judged as part of the original inspiration guiding Mark in the creation of his Gospel" (p. 109). Instead, the parable's message, as Mark wanted it to be understood, was "decidedly favorable to Judaism": It holds on to the idea that the Jews are God's chosen people; it suggests that Israel will not be destroyed, and that "the others" who replace the wicked husbandmen will be a group within, not outside of, Judaism. If the tenants cannot be defined as "the Jews" as opposed to "the Christians," a Christian audience can no longer simply identify with "the others." Instead, contemporary leaders of the church may find in the Wicked Husbandmen a mirror image and are asked to remain cautious and self-critical vis-à-vis their own leadership. I quote from Milavec's final paragraph:

> In the end, consequently, critical inquiry carefully scrapes away the anti-Jewish image that had been carefully painted over the basic outline of the parable of the wicked husbandmen. Another image, older and fresher, appears. This image is not that of Christian superiority and Jewish guilt for the death of Jesus, which has for so long been displayed in the Church. Rather, this new image has the potential for unsettling the onlooker by tearing away those religious assurances which shield one from the terrible judgment of the living God. (pp. 110–11)

I would like to raise some questions about this proposal. According to Milavec's vision, the parable of the Wicked Husbandmen, originally pro-Jewish, was falsified—"painted over"—by an anti-Jewish image. And a "critical inquiry" such as his own has the power to "carefully scrape" such an image "away." These sentences promise a solution to the problem of anti-Judaism, a full recuperation of the parable with its afflicted reception history. Mark's original intent, once restored by the hands of the historical critic, operates in Milavec's vision as a redemptive source capable of rectifying misinterpretation, of undoing Christian notions of superiority, and of getting rid of anti-Jewish bias and stereotyping.

I think that these hopes are justified on some level. In the various contexts of Christian teaching, Milavec's work on Mark 12:1–12 might help readers to unlearn deeply sedimented anti-Jewish reading habits and to look at the parable with new eyes, in a "fresh" way. Specifically, Milavec's effort to read the parable as a "*true Jewish* story" might engage many readers in an important process of rethinking Jewish-Christian relations. One may want to imagine a time when future generations encounter this story uninfluenced by what Milavec considers its false anti-Jewish image, generations of Christians who naturally relate the story to the first-century Jewish horizon of understanding that Milavec (together with many other scholars today) has tried to recover.

But I also think that read in our own time, in a "post-Holocaust Era," as Milavec calls it, the parable of the Wicked Husbandmen raises difficulties that cannot be reduced to the problem of anti-Judaism. Milavec's central concern is not the Holocaust but an anti-Jewish interpretive pattern that, in its essence, is the same whether we find it in the second or the twentieth century. Milavec's evocation of the events of the Holocaust might indicate the reasons that he wished to offer "a fresh analysis" of Mark 12, but the analysis itself moves strictly within the parameters of historical criticism. Milavec's aim is to recover an "original" meaning of the parable; he is focused not on the twentieth century but on ancient times. His turn to Mark's intent bypasses, I think, urgent questions of remembrance that still haunt us more than fifty years after the events.

What made me so uncomfortable during that church service in Germany were the parable's anti-Jewish undertones and something else. The story reminded me of the Holocaust not only because of its association with Christian supersessionism but also because of some traits inherent in the story that no recovery of an "original meaning" can do away with. Milavec's "fresh analysis," or a comment informed by this analysis, would have interrupted the service in important ways. But it would not have been able to deal with the ways in which the Wicked Husbandmen parable evokes the Holocaust itself.

Holocaust Resonances

I wish to offer a second reading of the parable, one that opens up the historical-critical focus on the parable's original setting and traces the Holocaust resonances of the story. Helpful in this endeavor is Paul Ricoeur's essay "Biblical Hermeneutics," which was published in 1975 and became an influential contribution to the literary approach to the Bible. Ricoeur does not refer to the events of the Holocaust nor does he discuss the parable of the Wicked Husbandmen in any detail. But, as I want to show, his hermeneutic theory is able to powerfully illuminate the difficulties of a post-Holocaust reading of a text such as our parable. For Ricoeur, a parable is not to be subjected to the rule of its original context; its meaning does not equal the "original inspiration" of an author, as Milavec assumes. Against Milavec, Ricoeur would argue that the story of the Wicked Husbandmen has gained autonomy from its author and its first audience by being read and communicated–actualized, as Ricoeur says–in ever new situations.[5] The process of decontextualization in regard to the parable's original setting, Ricoeur writes, is followed by recontextualizations, and these "new contexts of discourse and of life" (p. 71) should be considered in the act of interpretation.

---

[5]Paul Ricouer, "Biblical Hermeneutics," in *Interpretation Theory: Discourse and the Surplus of Meaning* (Fort Worth, Tex.: Texas Christian University Press, 1976). Responsible for this autonomy, according to Ricoeur, is the form or literary genre of parables, which "secures the survival of the meaning after the disappearance of its *Sitz im Leben* and in that way starts the process of 'decontextualization' which opens the message to fresh reinterpretations according to new contexts of discourse and of life" (71). Milavec responds to this kind of argument in the last footnote of his essay: "The contemporary Church, having abandoned its teaching of contempt, is now once again in a favorable situation for rediscovering some lost meanings and even for pioneering new understandings which harmonize with the recently recovered sense that there exists a common heritage which unites Christians and Jews" (Milavec, "A Fresh Analysis," 117). However, this remark is marginal and has no integral part in Milavec's work.

On the basis of these hermeneutic assumptions, I will try to interpret the parable of the Wicked Husbandmen, taking my cues from Ricoeur's essay. This means above all that I treat the parable as a metaphorical narrative endowed with the power to lead its recipients to a new vision of life beyond the well-known views of things. A metaphor redescribes reality, and, if I follow Ricoeur, so does the parable of the Wicked Husbandmen.[6]

The challenge for me as the interpreter lies in determining the metaphorical tension that characterizes the parable and gives rise to this remarkable process of redescription. The tension is clear in metaphors: It lies between two terms that, according to their lexical usage, are incompatible (e.g., this book is a dungeon), but whose irritating combination provokes the reader to make sense of it. The tension of parables is less obvious. What exactly is it that causes an audience to move from the story to something outside it, that makes me aware of the fact that the parable is not just an autonomous world in itself, but that it says something about human reality? In fact, Ricoeur himself is ambiguous about this question and suggests more than one possibility.[7] To continue with my task I will orient myself to the following suggestion.

The parables, Ricoeur observes, are often characterized by strange traits that disturb their apparent realism. The everyday life setting of the parables is frequently interrupted by exaggerations, surprising developments, and improbabilities. Ricoeur calls this trait the "extravagance" of the parables of Jesus. And it may be this "extravagance"– "the presence of the extraordinary within the ordinary" (p. 99)–that irritates the ideal listener in such a way that she searches for a meaning outside the narrative. Thus, I need to determine the kind of extravagance that characterizes my parable. To do so Ricoeur would ask me to take a close look at the dramatic structure of the narrative, by which he means "the challenge which the *plot* displays for the main characters, and…the answers of these characters to the *crisis* situation" (p. 97).

---

[6]I focus on Matthew's version of the story because I want to counteract the historical-critical search for the most authentic text. I am interested in the parable as it is transmitted and translated today. My reading also stands in stark contrast with the one proposed by John Dominic Crossan in *Parables: The Challenge of the Historical Jesus* (New York: Harper & Row, 1973), 96. By focusing on the parable's short version in the gospel of Thomas, Crossan reads the tenants' behavior not as evil but as smart action. His focus on Thomas bypasses the story's intense brutality, which my reading tries to highlight.

[7]Does the tension lie between two versions of reality grafted in the narrative itself–a realistic story and an improbable story suggested by the improbable traits in the parable? Or is the tension one between the narrative's surprising take on things and our normal way of seeing? Ricoeur also suggests that the tension lies within the contextual background of the parables. He affirms this possibility in his essay "The Bible and the Imagination," in *Figuring the Sacred: Religion, Narrative and Imagination,* trans. David Pellauer, ed. Mark I. Wallace (Minneapolis: Fortress Press, 1995), 144–66. On the basis of two parables– "The Wicked Husbandmen" and "The Sower"– he discusses the intertextuality through which these stories refer to each other as well as to other parts of the gospel. As Ricoeur himself acknowledges in his 1975 essay, the metaphorical tension remains ambiguous. In fact, scholars (Wolfgang Harnisch, Hans Weder, Herrmann-Josef Maurer) who appropriated Ricoeur's work have focused on the metaphorical tension *within* the narrative. I am following this line of thought because I am interested in the parable as an isolated gospel reading.

The main characters of the parable of the Wicked Husbandmen are the owner of the vineyard, the tenants, and the collectors, including both the slaves and the owner's son. As the plot develops, three interactions among these people occur: the contractual agreement between the owner and the tenants, the tenants' recurrent rejection of the collectors, and finally the owner's destruction of the tenants. The first interaction sets up the situation and opens up a variety of possibilities. Will the tenants conform to the agreement made with the landowner or will they break the contract?

The second interaction answers this question in a startling way. Not only do the tenants refuse to deliver the owner's share, not only do they break the contract, they also violate basic human relations by beating and even killing the collectors who are repeatedly sent to them. This second interaction is a process of increasing brutality that has as its climax the owner's decision to send his son and the subsequent deliberate murder of the son by the tenants. At this point the plot has led to a crisis situation that, again, opens up various possibilities. Will the tenants' violence persist? Will it lead to their final victory over the owner or will the owner repay the tenants for their outrageous crimes? The tension of this crisis situation is enforced and prolonged by the question: "When the owner of the vineyard comes, how do you think he will deal with those tenants?"

The third interaction is narrated in the future tense: "He will bring those bad men to a bad end." With this sentence, the crisis is already resolved: The tenants do not triumph, but lose their lives. The handing-over of the vineyard to "other tenants" is an epilogue that has no further influence on the basic structure of the plot. To summarize, the dramatic structure of the parable leads from a peaceful business deal to an outburst of violence and finally to an equally violent revenge.

Again, this analysis is necessary, because it "provides an appropriate basis for the *metaphorical* process", as Ricoeur says (p. 97). I should now be able to determine the element of extravagance that compels the reader to take "the narrative as referring to some similar structure of human experience outside the narrative" (p. 98). Ricoeur himself detects this element in the behavior of the owner, who puts his own son at the mercy of the murderous tenants. He writes: "Consider the extravagance of the landlord in the 'Parable of the Wicked Husbandmen,' who after having sent his servants, sends his son. What Palestinian property owner living abroad would be foolish enough to act like this landlord?" (p. 115).

At this point, I would venture to disagree with Ricoeur. His definition of the parable's extravagance, it seems to me, does not really result from an analysis of the story's plot.[8] My own analysis points to the strange discrepancy between the possibilities opened up by the first interaction and the actual way

---

[8]It seems to me that Ricoeur is guided by a typical Christian prejudice. Doesn't Ricoeur's suggestion result precisely from the son-Jesus identification that Aaron Milavec critically discusses?

in which the plot develops. The tenants' reaction to the owner's rightful demands is far beyond normal behavior. The tenants do not just refuse to act according to the terms of a lease, they refuse to respect basic human relations. The persistent physical violence– "They took his servants and thrashed one, killed another, and stoned a third," "They did the same to [a larger number of servants]," "They took [the son], flung him out of the vineyard, and killed him"–is out of proportion to how one would imagine a quarrel over real estate. The scene of destruction with which the story ends contrasts drastically with the everyday setting–a landowner leases his vineyard to a group of tenants–with which the parable begins. The tension between the familiar world of business and the eruption of multiple beatings and killings seems to me to be "the extraordinary within the ordinary," which Ricoeur makes responsible for the metaphorical process. I find here the "element of extravagance" that, according to Ricoeur, lets the reader know that this story has an "outside referent," or in other words, that the story is not just a story, but a parable, and thus stands for something else (p. 130).

This referent in human reality is not just of any kind, if I follow Ricoeur. Rather, the referent of the parables of Jesus is determined by the specificity of religious language. Parables, according to Ricoeur, are *poetic* discourse insofar as they have the power to redescribe reality. But they are *religious* discourse insofar as they have the power to disclose a special dimension of reality. Here, again, Ricoeur takes recourse in the notion of extravagance. The surprising, outlandish, excessive, and eccentric traits, Ricoeur argues, constitute the religious moment of the parables. They are a religious kind of poetic discourse insofar as they transgress traditional forms of parabolic discourse and therefore disclose what Ricoeur calls limit-experiences of human life.[9] With reference to the philosophy of Karl Jaspers, Ricoeur describes the ultimate referent of the parables in the following way:

> The human condition as such includes experiences which baffle discourse and *praxis.* Jaspers names death, suffering, guilt and hatred as examples. But it is not just experiences of distress that have this power of rupture; culminatory experiences–"peak experiences"– especially experiences of creation and joy…are no less extreme than are the experiences of catastrophe. (p. 128)

In reading the parable of the Wicked Husbandmen, in being receptive to its strange traits, in letting myself be moved and irritated by the clash between

---

[9]At this point it should be noted that Ricoeur's theory has blind spots when it comes to the problem of anti-Judaism. Ricoeur suggests a contrast between the Jewish literary tradition and Jesus' parables. Jewish parables, to put it simply, illustrate general ethical truths, whereas the parables of Jesus, by transgressing the traditional Jewish form of parables, "exercise the power of 'disclosure.'" And on the basis of such binary opposition, Ricoeur defines the religious quality of the parables of Jesus. The moment of transgression, according to Ricoeur, not only alters the function and form of the Jesus-parables but also makes them "religious discourse." For readers who are sensitized to the problem of Christian anti-Judaism, this argument has odd implications. Is Ricoeur suggesting that Jewish parables at the time of Jesus lacked religious quality? Is Ricoeur suggesting that with Jesus the religious potential, the disclosive power, of parables is actualized?

a familiar setting and the subsequent scenes of savagery, I am supposed to make a transition from the world of the story to human limit-experiences. The accumulation of physical violence that I have claimed to be the element of extravagance within the parable should refer me to a boundary-situation of the human condition. In a very vague sense I could say that the parable somehow points to experiences of catastrophe and distress, to use Ricoeur's vocabulary. A little more specifically, I could say that the parable is pertinent to experiences of physical destruction caused by human hatred. Although Ricoeur claims that an interpretation will always be related to a particular situation, a parable's message is open, he says, to "fresh reinterpretation according to new contexts of discourse and of life" (p. 71). If this is the case, where do I find the extreme aspects of human life in our time?

When I read the parable in the German church I was reminded of the atrocities committed by Nazi Germany. The tenants' brutality seemed so exaggerated to me, the multiple killings so out of proportion to common sense, in fact, the whole outcome of the story so horrific that I did exactly what Ricoeur's theory suggests. I made a transfer from the world of the story to my own "context of discourse and of life"; I felt myself being powerfully referred to limit-experiences of "death, suffering, guilt and hatred" in my own time, memories of violence that shaped the particular context where I was at home.

One may object that Ricoeur's notion of "limit-experiences" is incompatible with my reference to Holocaust experiences, that my application does not take account of the kind of philosophical discourse that informs Ricoeur's reflections. An important source for these reflections is Karl Jaspers' *Philosophy* and particularly his notion of boundary situations. In contrast to situations that always change, that are contingent and historically unique, boundary situations are timeless:

> Situations like the following: that I am always in situations; that I cannot live without struggling and suffering; that I cannot avoid guilt; that I must die—these are what I call boundary situations. They *never change,* except in appearance. There is no way to survey them in existence, no way to see anything behind them. They are like a wall we run into, a wall on which we founder.[10]

Boundary situations, according to Jaspers, characterize human existence whether we are aware of them or not. Death, suffering, guilt, and hatred belong fundamentally and inevitably to human existence. Jaspers is interested in the foundations more than in the historical contingencies of human experiences— or so it seems.

Jaspers' *Philosophy* was first published in 1932. Three decades later the notion of limit-situation reappeared in his 1962 book *Philosophical Faith and Revelation.*[11] In a central part of this work Jaspers discusses how religious

---

[10]Karl Jaspers, *Philosophy,* trans. E. B. Ashton (Chicago: University of Chicago Press, 1969–71), 178.

[11]Karl Jaspers, *Philosophical Faith and Revelation,* trans. E. B. Ashton (London: Collins, 1967).

language, what he calls *"chiffre,"* is able to illuminate human existence, particularly the limit-situations of disaster and evil. What I find significant in this discussion is the fact that Jaspers offers concrete examples of such limit-situations. He starts his contemplation with a series of "facts" *(Tatbestände)* that illustrate disaster and evil in history. Human beings have always done violence to one another, Jaspers states, and he mentions human sacrifice, the Inquisition, the cruelties in wartime beyond political reason, or the murder of millions of people by totalitarian systems. And then he writes:

> Under the regime that ruled in Germany from 1933 to 1945 Jewish children were torn from their mothers' arms, exposed to the agonizing fear of death, and killed only after a time of hunger and torment. An occasional delight in cruelty and a more frequent obedience in looking the other way— "Orders are Orders"–showed how men could turn into imagination-free, thoughtlessly functioning "operators" of an extermination machinery that went from arrest to transport to the actual killing. There would be no end to a description of the horrors that fill human history and strike us as unprecedented only where we personally witnessed them or knew about them, and thus came to share the guilt.[12]

Holocaust experiences exemplify here the "facts of evil" that constitute human life in general. It is true, Jaspers integrates the German "extermination machinery" into a long history of human cruelty. But he also suggests that for those who witness an evil such as the crimes committed under the Nazi regime, the particular evil is experienced like an unprecedented horror (*nie dagewesenes Entsetzen*). After the war, Jaspers was one of the first Germans to publicly articulate a response to the Nazi atrocities.[13] I surmise that in writing about those who witnessed evil, who knew about it and therefore became guilty, Jaspers refers also to himself. Notwithstanding his universalizing approach to "disaster and evil," I suspect that for him the Holocaust is at the center of contemporary actualizations of limit-situations.

I do not know whether this is the case for Ricoeur as well. But Jaspers' historicizing gesture affirms my Ricoeurian reading of the Wicked Husbandmen. The "extravagance" of the parable, the tension between its ordinary setting and its extraordinary plot development, can initiate a metaphorical transfer to the extreme events of the Holocaust. This transfer will be made not by everybody, but by those readers whose cultural memory is informed by the Holocaust, by an audience such as the German congregation I was part of. German (and arguably American) culture of the 1990s is characterized by what Andreas Huyssen has called a "memory boom" with

---

[12]Jaspers, *Philosophy*, 205.
[13]Jaspers, *The Question of German Guilt*, trans. E. B. Ashton (Westport, Conn.: Greenwood Press, 1978).

regard to the Holocaust.[14] Photographs of Auschwitz, of the liberated camps, accounts of survivors published in books and displayed on video, have become part of and may even stand at the center of our cultural imagination. And since the Holocaust is so prominent in public memory, its figures of "hatred" or "suffering" are readily available for metaphorical connections such as the one to which I have been referring.[15]

I find my Ricoeurian reading valuable because it captures the resonances between the violent story and the events of the Holocaust and thereby articulates something that I suspect usually remains unspoken or less than conscious. I was uncomfortable reading the parable of the Wicked Husbandmen in the church because twentieth-century violence echoed uncannily in it, but I was unable to explicate these echoes. What would have been helpful in that church service was an interruption that spelled out the kind of association evoked by the parable's "extravagance." I envision here a critical intervention giving words to vague resonances, that moves from a fleeting thought about "Auschwitz and Buchenwald" to concrete accounts of Nazi violence. Karl Jaspers' description of the crimes committed under the Nazi regime could be a starting point.

To be clear, the intervention I am envisioning does not make our parable less unbearable. Quite the opposite, it increases the difficulty of reading the story in any meaningful way. The metaphorical process I have described does not result in what Ricoeur calls a "redescription of reality," in a reorientation of disconcerted readers who find themselves faced with the reality of Auschwitz. Rather, it leads to a new tension that no act of interpretation can resolve, namely the tension between an anti-Jewish canonical text and testimonies of recent Jewish catastrophe. In the end, a reader would have to cope with a layer of texts: with accounts of the Holocaust evoked by the story, with the Christian tale of supersessionism being unwittingly read into the story, and with the "original" pro-Jewish versions discovered beneath the story by Milavec and other critics.[16] In my opinion, these alternative versions belong to the parable's contemporary reception history, but they will save this text neither from its anti-Jewish history nor from the exaggerated violence of its plot. The parable will remain a tainted text and will continue to cause feelings of unease. In the meantime, as long as the Wicked Husbandmen appears in

---

[14]Huyssen, *Twilight Memories. Marking Time in a Culture of Amnesia* (New York: Routledge, 1994), 5. This "memory boom" manifested itself in what Huyssen calls "a never-ending sequence of Nazi related 40th and 50th anniversaries" as well as in the tireless effort to build museums and memorials. However, Huyssen points out that these efforts do not safeguard a population from forgetfulness. Huyssen writes that the "difficulty of the current conjuncture is to think memory and amnesia together rather than simply to oppose them" (7). Associating the parable with images of Nazi brutality does not necessarily engage a reader in a conscious act of remembrance.

[15]For a helpful discussion of Holocaust metaphors, see James Young, *Writing and Rewriting the Holocaust. Narrative and the Consequences of Interpretation* (Bloomington and Indianapolis: Indiana University Press, 1990), 117–33.

[16]For example, David Stern, "Jesus' Parables from the Perspective of Rabbinic Literature: The Example of the Wicked Husbandmen," in Thoma, *Parable and Story*, 42–80.

our various "contexts of discourse and of life," we might use the parable as a venue for exploring the complicated legacies that confront post-Holocaust audiences.

School's in Session

The Making and Unmaking of Docile Disciple Bodies in Mark

Deborah Krause

Prefa(s)tory: Seminary Days

It was the fall of 1986. I was a seminarian, and I sat with other seminarians and a professor around a seminar table. We were studying the gospel of Mark. Our main textbook, other than the gospel itself, was a 1982 publication entitled *Mark As Story* by David Rhoads and Donald Michie.[1] That title captured the project of our seminar: to read Mark as a story. On that particular day we were covering a portion of the story (Mk. 4:35–8:26) in which Jesus and the disciples travel around Galilee. We focused on the disciples. Who *were* these guys? In this section Jesus repeatedly tells and shows them who he is, and they just don't get it. Instead of faith, they are filled with fear. Then one of us shouted out... "These guys are more like DUH-sciples than di-sciples!" The class erupted in appreciative laughter. It was a group expression of the private giddy relief I have felt as a student when a fellow student gives the wrong answer. The disciples, not we, were "bad students." The ugly underbelly of our laughter was an uneasy awareness that in some way we were feeding on the failure of our own. As in a scene from Golding's *Lord of the Flies* we each glanced around the table as we laughed, wondering if one of us might be next.

Introduction

The history of Markan interpretation is so often told as a necessary tale in which the appreciation of the gospel as comprehensive narrative, a story, is

---

[1]David Rhoads and Donald Michie, *Mark As Story: An Introduction to the Narrative of the Gospel* (Philadelphia: Fortress Press, 1982).

the innocent and natural conclusion.[2] But what if it isn't that? What if there is no disembodied necessity driving our reading of this gospel as a whole story? What if instead we can discern this history as the construction of something–something like an institution that says as much about what we desire as it does about the gospel of Mark.

I want to read Markan interpretation and Mark itself as a tale of desire. Specifically, the desire to master and control bodies–the body of Mark's text and the bodies in Mark's text. In particular, I want to focus on the schoolmaster and teacher relationship in Mark, as it applies to readers in relationship to Mark's text, to Jesus in relationship to his disciples, and to some extent to the Father in relationship to the Son. I find the nexus of all these relationships in the interpretation of Mark to be bound up in the theme of discipleship in the gospel. Rather than an office or valued vocation, I want to investigate discipleship as it relates to its etymological root: to coercion and to power. As is clear from my prefa(s)tory, I find some personal historical connection with this theme and the ways in which it relates to the dynamics between teachers and students in the seminary classroom. At different points in my exploration, theorists Michel Foucault and Jane Gallop have helped me to examine Markan interpretation on the disciples as the disciplining of Mark's text and the making docile of his disciple bodies. Foucault helps me to ask what the cost of this project of narrative interpretation has been for Mark's disciples (and for our own work as teachers and students). Gallop then helps me to venture my own undisciplined reading of the disciple bodies in Mark–something along the lines of a Gallop through the gospel.

The Disciplining of Mark

For most of its existence, Mark's gospel has not been read as a story about discipleship. A review of the scriptural reference indexes of ante-Nicene, medieval, and Reformation exegetes offers no evidence that Mark's disciples were ever considered a problem. Texts throughout Mark that are understood by more contemporary exegetes to portray the disciples as faithless or confused

---

[2]There are many treatments of this subject. Some of the most influential are: Norman Perrin, *What Is Redaction Criticism?* (Philadelphia: Fortress Press, 1969); Sean P. Kealy, *Mark's Gospel: A History of Its Interpretation* (New York: Paulist Press, 1981), 90–237; Frank J. Matera, *What Are They Saying about Mark?* (New York: Paulist Press, 1987), 75–95. See also the recent treatment by Janice Capel Anderson and Stephen D. Moore, "The Lives of Mark," in *Mark and Method: New Approaches in Biblical Studies* (Minneapolis: Fortress Press, 1992), 1–22. The practice of "literary" and "narrative" criticism in the interpretation of the gospels has been challenged by Stephen D. Moore in his work *Literary Criticism and the Gospels: The Theoretical Challenge* (New Haven: Yale University Press, 1990). Moore's criticisms are primarily lodged on a theoretical front: Namely, what has "passed" for literary criticism in gospel interpretation has had a new critical emphasis and has not been reflective of the more recent structuralist, poststructuralist, deconstructive, and reader response critical approaches at work in larger academic theoretical discourse.

are either not addressed, or they are brought into larger doctrinal discussions.[3] Apparently, the fact that Mark presents the disciples as something we might call "bad students" has not always been evident. Perhaps this perspective is not as natural or as obvious as it seems. Perhaps it is the result of a more recent construction...something like a school.

In 1972 Foucault lectured on an element of his theory of power-knowledge in a study of social control and punitive systems in eighteenth- and nineteenth-century France. Foucault's purpose was not so much to study the period as to study a problem, namely that institutions are not the "necessary" results of social history, but rather are specific innovative responses to certain social circumstances.[4] These lectures were later developed into his 1975 publication translated into English as *Discipline and Punish: The Birth of the Prison*. In the work, Foucault delineates the practice of discipline as an innovation that "organizes an analytical space." It involves an overarching strategy of enclosure of items in space, but not rigid enclosure. Rather, disciplinary enclosure attempts to create functional space for the control and use of bodies,

> to be able at each moment to supervise the conduct of each individual, to assess it, to judge it, to calculate its qualities or merits. It (is) a procedure, therefore aimed at knowing, mastering, and using.[5]

Foucault illustrated such strategies at work in Jean Baptiste La Salle's conception of the elementary school classroom in the mid-eighteenth century. Instead of the prior system, in which the schoolmaster individually tutored students while others waited, LaSalle conceived the classroom to function as a whole system of *super*vision. The class would be so organized that each individual would have a space to make possible the observation of each and the simultaneous work of all. According to Foucault, La Salle's conception "made the educational space function like a learning machine, but also as a machine for supervising, hierarchizing, rewarding."[6]

In 1901, William Wrede catalogued a variety of texts in Mark that he saw as anomalous to the nature of historical narrative.[7] These texts included Mark

---

[3]See Origen, *De Principiis,* book 3, chap. 1, sec. 7 (Greek text) where Mark 4:11–12 is considered as a problematic text for the assertion of the doctrine of free will, because it seems to insinuate that God selects some (not all) for secret knowledge and salvation. See also Tertullian, *Contra Praxeas,* where the fear of Peter, James, and John at the transfiguration's revelation of the Son (Mk. 9:6) is contrasted with what would have been their certain death if they had seen the Father (i.e., Ex. 33:20). Unlike later redaction and narrative critical readings that disparage the three for their "fear," Tertullian seems to understand it as the obvious and appropriate reaction to the event.

[4]Barry Cooper, *Michel Foucault: An Introduction to the Study of His Thought* (New York and Toronto: Mellen, 1981), 81. Cooper notes that Foucault was studying a problem more than a historical period. He wanted to argue that the current practices of punitive and educational systems were not driven by a "mysterious necessity." Rather, such practices were a part of what Foucault understood as the system of "power-knowledge" in industrial society.

[5]Michel Foucault, *Discipline and Punish: The Birth of the Prison,* trans. Alan Sheridan (New York: Pantheon, 1977), 141–43.

[6]Ibid., 147.

[7]William Wrede, *The Messianic Secret,* trans. J. C. G. Greig (Greenwood, S.C.: Attic Press, 1971).

4:11–12 (referred to as the "parable theory"); various citations in Mark where Jesus enjoins demons, the recently healed, the disciples, and the crowd to silence after his miracles; and finally the reactions of Peter, James, and John to Jesus in the transfiguration scene (Mk. 9:2–9). Each of these texts he gathered under the whole idea of what he called Mark's "Messianic Secret." According to Wrede, this theme was a literary artifice, created by the evangelist Mark, to explain why Jesus had not been confessed as Messiah during his lifetime. With this assessment, Wrede challenged the previous treatment of the gospel as a disparate collection of historical reminiscences and posited that it had a unified dogmatic intent.

Wrede is often viewed by Markan scholars as a seminal figure in the interpretation of the gospel.[8] In him the insights of previous text critics (Lachmann, Wilke, Holtzmann) are seen to converge, and from him flower the form-, redaction-, and narrative-critical interpretations of the gospel. Read through Foucault's analysis of disciplinary practice, however, Wrede's catalogue can be seen less as an organic inevitability and more as a decisive act of power-knowledge–a specific innovation in which the elements of Mark's text are arranged into a unitary enclosure. Along the lines of LaSalle's eighteenth-century schoolroom, the gospel under Wrede's magnifying glass[9] functions as a whole unit for supervision. The elements have been so arranged as to comprehend the whole. Mark's book is no longer seen as loosely constructed history, but a unified curriculum set forth by Mark to teach us something.

Wrede's construction of the comprehensive nature of Mark's curriculum has not come without a price. If Mark has something comprehensive to teach and Mark's central character Jesus is the master teacher, why is the lesson so hard to get across? In the latter part of this century, readings of Mark that have attended to its unity have answered this question simply: The disciples are bad students.

In the readings of redaction and narrative critics, the disciples have been monitored as never before. These men, heretofore allowed to stand in combination with their presentations in the other canonical gospels and the broader traditions of the church, have been enclosed in Mark's text, supervised in their every word and deed and forced to march together through the school yard (or is it a prison yard?) of Mark's story. There they have been made docile. They are known, mastered, and used to offer Mark his message. In their poor comprehension and faithless behavior they are either stand-ins for the heretical Jerusalem church or examples of the fallibility of all followers of

---

[8]Kealy, *Mark's Gospel,* 90.

[9]Kealy translates Wrede's claim about the theological nature of Mark: "If one examines Mark through a magnifying glass (*Vergrößerungsglas*), then one finds a writing of the same kind as the gospel of John" (*Mark's Gospel,* 93). One could not find a more clear expression of Wrede's supervision of Mark's gospel as a comprehensive whole

Jesus.[10] Through them Mark is understood to be operating either as a polemicist or a pastor.[11] Under the construction of Mark's comprehensive curriculum, Mark's disciples are the vehicle through which Mark's readers are taught the "lesson" of the gospel.

Galloping against the Grain

But does Mark necessarily present such a comprehensive curriculum? Is there a way to read the gospel in which I might not supervise the disciples through the enclosed space of Mark's story? Is there a way to engage in an "un-disciplined" reading of Mark? Here is where I turn to Jane Gallop and her use of Jacques Lacan–Lacan who reads Sigmund Freud though Ferdinand de Saussure–Freud, in other words, rendered linguistically...deconstructively.

Many feminist theorists have engaged Lacan, some to argue with him, others to embrace him. But all acknowledge that he freed the study of the psyche from Freud's biological essentialism (namely, that boys have certain complexes because they are boys, and girls because they are girls) by placing the castration complex and the whole Oedipal drama in the realm of language... making castration an equal opportunity employer.

What I like about Gallop's appropriation of Lacan is that she applies the notion of the castrated self to the quest for power and comprehension. As a feminist, this means of analysis affords me the opportunity to challenge both traditional readings of biblical texts and biblical texts themselves for ways in which they have masked the problem of full comprehension/castration in the service of oppressing women, children, the two-thirds world, and the planet. Her way of reading gives me leverage to argue with what I have always been told a text means, to assess it as a domineering and oppressive reading, and to challenge that reading in favor of more diffuse, less domineering interpretations. Here's what Gallop says about Lacan:

> Lacan's major statement of ethical purpose and therapeutic goal as far as I am concerned is that one must assume one's "castration"... castration for Lacan is not only sexual; more important it is also linguistic: we...can only signify ourselves in a symbolic system that we do not command, that, rather, commands us...Only this realization, I believe, can release us from "phallocentrism," one of the effects of which is that one must constantly cover one's inevitable inadequacy in order to have the right to speak.[12]

Specifically, Gallop's work in her *Reading Lacan* and her collected essays, *Thinking through the Body,* help me to respond to the comprehensive and

---

[10]The two most striking examples of these alternative readings may be seen in Theodore Weeden's "The Heresy that Necessitated Mark's Gospel," *Zeitschrift für die Neuetestamentliche Wissenschaft* 59 (1968): 145–58, and Elizabeth Struthers Malbon, "Fallible Followers: Women and Men in the Gospel of Mark," *Semeia* 28 (1983): 29–48.

[11]Frank Matera, 33–55.

[12]Gallop, *Reading Lacan* (Ithaca, N.Y.: Cornell University Press, 1985), 20.

coercive curriculum that has become Mark.[13] I connect her appropriation of Lacan's insights about castration and her challenge to "phallocratic" comprehensive forms of knowledge with Foucault's unveiling of the apparent "mysterious necessity" of institutional development to reveal practices of power-knowledge.[14]

The assumption of one's castration or the limitation of one's will to comprehend, to master, announces something that Gallop refers to as "the bodily enigma."[15] There is no free body, free to will–at least without the employ or subjugation of other bodies. Bodies are, well, embodied in language. Phallocentric forms of knowledge attempt to deny this enigma through disembodied constructs of "mind over matter."[16] Castrated knowledge explores the enigma by intentionally sticking with the "matter" and thinking through the body.

The disciplined interpretations of Mark I have critiqued here tend to follow the disciples' minds. Assuming that Jesus' message is comprehensive and comprehensible, they place the blame for its failure squarely on the disciples' shoulders. The disciples don't comprehend Jesus' teaching, and, in the end, they fail by deserting him. Gallop might characterize such practices of reading Mark as participating in the "powerful narrative of mind over matter."[17]

My "Gallop" through Mark tugs at the edges of "mind over matter" interpretation to disclose that Mark's curriculum is neither comprehensive nor comprehensible. It is fragmentary. My Gallop through Mark dislocates me from the "meaningful order" of Mark's story to think through the disciples' bodies, and Jesus' will for their bodies.[18] It pays attention to "odd, marginal

---

[13]Gallop would not like to be paired with Foucault in a theoretical analysis. She considers him one father whose influence she most desires to repress. Yet she admits his work has been the scene of some of her work's conception; "The Female Body," in *Thinking through the Body* (New York: Columbia University Press, 1988), 88–89.

[14]Coincidentally, Barry Cooper notes that some theorists have compared Foucault to Freud in their comparable projects of exploring the uncharted regions of sexuality and power. Cf. Jacques Donzelot, "Misère de la Culture Politique," *Critique* 373–74 (1978): 575, cited in Cooper, 133.

[15]Gallop, "The Bodily Enigma," in *Thinking through the Body*, 11–20. For Lacan the problem of the self is that after she separates from the mother, and understands herself as autonomous, she is the subject of an illusion (hence, this is called the mirror stage). Specifically, the illusion–seen either in a mirror, the eyes of the mother, or the image of an older child–is that as an infant, she can stand, sit, or walk on her own when, in fact, all she has seen in the reflection is a lie. The rest of her life is spent *desiring* this illusion of autonomous self, endlessly trying to capture mastery of herself as a free, whole subject that she never really was. For Lacan, getting back to this illusion is the root of desire. And desire is never fulfilled or satisfied. Lacan understands this desire to drive what he calls the culture machine–applied to Markan studies, it seems to me to drive the interpretation machine.

[16]Gallop, *Thinking through the Body*, 8–9.

[17]Ibid., 8.

[18]Gallop's title to her collection comes from Adrienne Rich's reflection on her poetry in *Of Woman Born: Motherhood as Experience and Institution* (New York: Norton, 1986). Rich claims that she is asking "whether woman cannot, at last, *think through the body*, to connect what has been so cruelly disorganized." Gallop notes that for Rich, the philosophical problem is the "mind-body" split, and so practicing "body thinking" is not some romantic, earth mother experience, but rather, if we think the mind-body split through the body, it becomes an image of shocking violence; *Thinking through the Body*, 1.

moments," to slips in which, as Lacan noted of Freud, "the truth manifests itself in the letter rather than the spirit, that is, in the way things are actually said, than their intended meaning."[19] Thinking through the disicples' bodies is a project of joining the disciples under the constructed mind of Mark's text. What's it like down there?

Galloping through Galilee: Jesus' Curriculum Trouble (by Stephanie P. Lacks)

In standard treatments of Mark's teaching theme, the *locus classicus* of the problem is the so-called "parable theory" of Mark 4:10–12. Hardly a theory, it is a "hard saying." Interpreters have queried: Why would a teacher intentionally obfuscate his meaning? Wrede's construction of the master curriculum, the messianic secret, tried to explain this anomaly in Mark's narrative. But this is not the only point of curricular ambiguity in Mark. Before this, in the apparently private moment of Mark 3:13–15, when Jesus gathers his closest students, the Twelve, we are told that his primary objective is to call those whom he desires (θέλειν) to be with him (ὦσιν μετ᾽ αὐτους). In other words, this instruction from the beginning involves desire for their bodies, not just their minds.

Inherent in Jesus' plan is a tension that signals trouble in the integrity of his curriculum. He calls those whom he desires. He wants them to be with him, but in the same breath, we learn that they are also called in order to be sent away to preach (ἀποστέλλειν). As such, they are pulled close (to be with him), and they are pushed away (sent out). From here on, just what it is Jesus wants from the Twelve is not clear. His will is not comprehensive or comprehensible. And the disciples (or are they apostles?) are never really sure where they stand.

Nowhere in Mark does it seem as though Jesus has more of a lesson to teach the Twelve than in the feeding narrative cycle. This is the place in Mark's text where Jesus and the Twelve shuttle back and forth across the lake. The lake is trouble for them. There are storms. There are ghosts. They strain at the oars. Here we see the ambiguity of the curriculum of Mark 3:14 in action: In Mark 6:7ff. Jesus wants to be with the Twelve, yet he sends them away to preach; in Mark 6:31–37, he takes them away from the crowd to rest, yet he demands they give the crowd something to eat; in Mark 6:48, he comes toward them walking on the sea, but he intends (ἤθελεν) to pass them by.

To further unsettle the waters, the centerpiece of the section is not one, but two: a Markan doublet—two feedings. In Mark 6:30–44, the disciples assist as Jesus feeds 5,000 men. In Mark 8:1–10, it appears as though the lesson is repeated. Here narrative critical readings are hardest on the disciples, reading them as dense, dim-witted buffoons who—in spite of repeated tutorials—"just don't get it."

The classroom is a boat, a boat the disciples have learned not to trust. This is no solid ground for instruction. After the feedings and several trips

---

[19]Gallop, *Reading Lacan*, 22.

back and forth across the lake, Mark's narrator remarks that they had forgotten to bring bread, except for one loaf. Jesus warns them: "Beware of the leaven of the Pharisees and the leaven of Herod." They know the parables; Jesus' enigmatic speech has another dimension. "He's talking about our not having bread." Jesus chides them. "How can you talk of having no bread!!!! Do you not yet know or comprehend? Remember: When I broke five loaves for five thousand, how many baskets full of broken pieces did you take up?"

They answer: "Twelve."

"And the four for seven thousand, how many baskets full of broken pieces did you take up?"

They answer: "Seven."

"Do you not yet comprehend?"

But need the double lesson of the feedings be an indication of the disciples' dim-wittedness? Might there be something to this insistent–almost inane–repetition of different equations: 5+2=5,000 with a remainder of 12; 7+ a few =4,000 with a remainder of 7? Remember, we–in the Western tradition–have sent the Twelve to a Roman reform school and regimented them from the Greek term μαθηταί, into Latin *discipuli.* As μαθηταί, however, they remind us that they are in part about the comprehension of numbers, *mathematicians;* indeed, they are named "the Twelve." In the feedings cycle, Mark's Jesus presents the disciples with a veritable math book, yet it is a math book full of *word* problems. The final exam comes at the end of the cycle. It is a test of their comprehension, a comprehensive exam. It turns out that they have studied. He asks, "How many?" and they answer: "twelve"; they answer: "seven."

The μαθηταί know the numbers, but they cannot put them together in Jesus' comprehensive pattern. Throughout the section we are told that they are afraid. Perhaps they have math anxiety. Of late, this is always read as *their* problem. They are bad students, "duh-ciples." But might it just be *the* problem? Despite his frustration at their lack of comprehension, Jesus' own words seem to stumble over it. Twice he repeats the cumbersome phrase "How many baskets full of broken pieces did you take up?"–σπυρίδων πληρώματα κλασμάτων. Jesus wants the disciples to comprehend the lesson, to put it all together, but all he gives them is this enigma: baskets *full* of *broken pieces.* The Twelve, like the twelve baskets, are fragmented in their comprehension. Jesus' will for them to see, to understand, has rendered them fragmentary and broken. They are basket cases.

Galloping from Galilee to Jerusalem: The Phallic Will Unveiled

In the passion narrative, Jesus no longer teaches. Διδάσκω does not appear, except in reference to earlier teaching (Mk. 14:49). The three passion predictions have driven Jesus' teaching of the Twelve since the feeding cycle (8:31; 9:31; 10:32–34). This teaching is what has brought them here, to Jerusalem. Once *in* the passion, however, Jesus seems to embody his fragmented message, rather than profess it. He breaks bread, and he takes a cup and calls them his body and blood. He offers these fragments to his disciples, but this time there's no quiz, no numbers. These fragments are not part of some comprehensive curriculum; they are supper.

After the supper, Jesus and the Twelve gather for the last time in the garden of Gethsemane. Here Jesus does not gather them as students, but as bodyguards. He tells most of them to "sit here," while he prays. Then, as is his custom, he divides Peter, James, and John from the group, and a little farther on tells them to "remain here, and watch." The commands recall the initial curriculum of Mark 3:14, "He called those whom he desired (θέλειν) to be with him." "Stay," he seems to be saying, "be with me."

In the midst of this scene, as the disciples stay and sleep, Jesus explores the heart of the curriculum problem: His will and the Father's will are not one. To this point, Mark has veiled the will that has driven Jesus to Jerusalem, the disciples limping behind, within the passive constructions of Jesus' own speech: for example, "the Son of man *must suffer* many things," (8:31). Jesus' passivity makes the will behind these constructions appear to be a necessary (δεῖ), irresistible force.[20] Mark has been complicit in this project, portraying the divine voice at two occasions confirming Jesus' authority: "You are my beloved son with whom I am well pleased" (1:11) and "This is my beloved son, listen to him" (9:7). But in the garden, Jesus unmasks the Father's will as distinct from his and resists it—even as he submits to it. He prays: "Abba, Father, to you is all power, remove this cup from me; but not what *I will* but what *you will.*" Jesus has not mastered the Father's will; he does not comprehend it. Like the disciples, he is embodied and overpowered.

After his prayer, Jesus returns to find Peter asleep. Jesus cannot will Peter to "watch," only to "stay." What he says now to Peter is most often read as a rebuke: "The spirit is indeed willing (in Greek, not just "willing," but πρόθυμον, "zealous"), but the flesh is weak." It is read as something like "Peter, you pathetic slob, you're all good intentions and no follow-through!" But read through Peter's body, the claim is much different. His flesh is indeed steadfast. He has remained. But his spirit has not been one with Jesus. As he has shown throughout Galilee, he can follow in body, but he cannot conform in spirit. He can repeat formulae ("You are the Christ") and figures ("twelve," "seven"), but he cannot comprehend the whole of Jesus' will. Coming as it does after Jesus' own prayer, which uncovers the tension between his will and his Father's will, the remark to Peter has an undercurrent of *commiseration:* "The spirit is willing, but the flesh is weak." It reads as something like: "The flesh is no match for the overwhelming will of the phallic Father." Peter already knows this (and so he sleeps), and now so does Jesus. In Gethsemane, for a brief moment Jesus uncovers the story as a mind-over-matter narrative, and

---

[20]Additionally, Jesus' use of the Son of Man title functions to further distance this necessity from his own body and from the Father's will.

he unveils his own symbolic castration.[21] With this he is handed over for arrest. The seminar is cut short. The disciples disappear. Can there be such a thing as a castrated teacher?

Throughout the gospel, what makes the disciples "disciples" is the fact that they "follow" or try to follow Jesus. This is their distinctive mark. Jesus calls them to "follow" him. But in the passion narrative, the students get ahead of their teacher. Though they insist they will not (14:31), they disappear (14:50) before him (16:1–8). In 16:7, the young man in white conveys the phallic Father's will for order one more time. The women are told to tell the disciples and Peter: "He goes *before* you into Galilee (προάγει ὑμᾶς εἰς τὴν Γαλιλιανίαν); there you will find him." The message is: "Get back in line. Get back there and follow him again." Here is an attempt to get the curriculum back on track, to drive the story around to the beginning again, where Jesus' will and the Father's will appear as one. Is it no wonder that these women who cared for his body all along, who ministered to him in Galilee (15:40–41), remain silent and flee in fear? Unlike the Twelve, they are quick studies on the subject of castration and the phallic will to power.

Outer Story: Seminary Teaching Days

It was my first syllabus: for a required course already named "New Testament Foundations." I was filled with fear and very earnest. If ever there was a subject matter of baskets full of broken pieces, it was the New Testament—twenty-seven baskets to be exact. The big problem: Where to begin? Begin with Paul and choose a historical foundation? Begin with the gospels and choose a canonical-ecclesial foundation? Where was the true foundation? Ah! Eureka! Begin with the historical Jesus (believe it or not, for a few hours, I thought that was *the* answer!).

Trying to embody the problem, or more likely trying for some stylish postmodern posture of (un)mastery, I opened the class with a lecture on the various ways I could begin the course. What would it mean to start with Paul? the gospels? Jesus? After all, this was not "*the* critical introduction to the NT," it was "*a* critical introduction to the NT." The students just stared at me, bemused. Why didn't I just begin somewhere? I was furious with them. "Don't they see? Don't they comprehend?" I fumed. And I am left with these problems: Can our curricula ever resist the phallic drive for comprehensive mastery? Can there be such a thing as an openly castrated teacher?[22]

---

[21]Gallop begins her essay collection with some reflections on the cover photograph of her volume (a newborn's head emerging from its mother's vagina in a hospital delivery room) that seem appropriate for this moment in the garden. Thinking through the body–at this point in history–"only occurs in brief intervals, soon to be reabsorbed by the powerful narratives of mind over matter, like the photograph I wanted to catch hold of those moments when something else occurs."

[22]I wish to thank Vincent J. Miller of the theology faculty at Georgetown University who offered valuable comments on this paper delivered at the Linafelt Birthday Lectures at Georgetown University in the Spring of 1999. I also thank Mark George of the biblical faculty at Iliff School of Theology, who offered helpful critique on an earlier version of this paper.

The Power of the Dog

John Dominic Crossan

*[The proconsul Aegeates] commanded that Andrew be flogged
with seven whips. Then he sent him off to be crucified and
commanded the executioners not to impale him with nails but to
stretch him out tied up with ropes, and to leave his knees uncut...
for Aegeates intended to torment him by his being hung and his
being eaten by dogs if still alive at night.*

Acts of Andrew: The Passion of Andrew 5:1–54.

Dogs and crosses. Dogs beneath the cross. But not beneath the cross of
Jesus. There are no dogs in Mark where Jesus is buried in a rock-tomb, nor in
Matthew and Luke where Jesus is buried in a new rock-tomb, nor in John
where Jesus is buried in a new garden-tomb. They were always there, of course,
in Psalm 22, that powerful quarry for passion detail. The sufferer there cries
out that "dogs are all around me; a company of evildoers encircles me,"
(NRSV) in 22:16 and begs God to "deliver my soul from the sword, my life
from the power of the dog," in 22:20. Those parallels of dogs/evildoers and
sword/dog point toward canine metaphor as does the inclusion of the dog
verses in a chiasm of bull-lion-dog in 22:12–16 and dog-lion-bull in 22:20–21.
But no early Christian exegete historicized those particular items as they did
so many other ones in that sadly beautiful prayer. Recently, a journalist cited
Tom Wright's comment that, since I had argued for most passion details as
prophecy historicized, I had historicized those dogs as well. I felt sure that
was more an offhand crack than a serious criticism, so I told him it was better
to historicize dog than bull. Very clever, to be sure, but is cleverness enough?
Does our exegesis, especially in its postmodern readings, get a little too clever
at times? That is not a simple rhetorical question whose answer I know for
certain. Here, as a way of probing it, of sniffing around it (alternative verbs
optional), I look at two readings of Jesus' (non)burial in the gospels. One is
postmodern, one is not. But which is which?

Dogs in a Constructed Drama

In an article in the Society of Biblical Literature's 1992 *Seminar Papers*
Jeffrey Staley wrote this: "Inside my house we kept a dog as a pet, and it

187

would sleep at night, curled up at the foot of one our beds. But outside my front door dogs were called…'shit-eaters' and were starved, beaten, and kicked at every opportunity. One of my most vivid memories of childhood is of those dogs."[1] In adapting that paper for a book in 1995, he rewrote it slightly like this:

> Inside our house we kept a dog as a pet, and it usually slept at night curled up on our front doorstep. But beyond our front door the name for dog was…shit-eater, and I saw starving, cowering dogs kicked at every opportunity. Occasionally laughing Navajo children would throw live puppies into the mission's garbage dump fires. It was not unusual to find their small blackened bodies the next morning, mixed in among the empty cans and broken bottles. My most vivid childhood memories are of dogs. They haunt my dreams. Their silvery shadows flit across the moonlit edges of my unconscious.[2]

Staley began with living dogs and was forced, very early, to recognize the difference between the intradomestic dog-as-pet and the extradomestic dog-as-scavenger. Pictures in his text also include a rather terrible in-between category, the hunting dog turned against people as Spanish conquerors used them to attack native Americans.[3] In those engravings, the dogs are very prominent and quite unmistakable but only prior awareness or a specific search would discern a "slinking dog" near the cross in that Albrecht Durer woodcut.[4] But it's there, it's definitely there. An account of that very early experience in another society's alternative sociology of the dog reappeared as prelude to a five-act "postmortem passion play," involving three unidentified crucified corpses.[5]

Act 1 begins as a "Roman soldier begins to cut the leather thongs that hold the three bloodied bodies to their crosses. He rips the valuable iron nails from the still-warm flesh. They will be saved, straightened, and reused another day for another grim demonstration of Pax Romana. As he drops the first corpse on the ground, Death rattles their throats and the tale begins."[6] In Act 3 "a knot is cut and the second corpse drops to the ground beside the first."[7] In Act 5, "the last hanging corpse…is finally loosened from its cross and thrown down on the ground next to the other two."[8] The soldier is the only other protagonist present. As the second corpse puts it: "Everyone who cared about us has left, convinced that we're dead. The only one still here is this cursing

---

[1]Jeffrey Lloyd Staley, "Reading with a Passion: John 18:1–19:42 and the Erosion of the Reader," in *Society of Biblical Literature 1992 Seminar Papers,* ed. Eugene H. Lovering, Jr., (Atlanta: Scholars Press, 1992), 65–66.

[2]Staley, *Reading with a Passion: Rhetoric, Autobiography, and the American West in the Gospel of John* (New York: Continuum, 1995), 154–56.

[3]Ibid., 16–161.

[4]Ibid., 214.

[5]Staley, "Reading," 68–76 (= *Reading,* 204–28).

[6]Staley, *Reading,* 204.

[7]Staley, "Reading," 71 (= *Reading,* 216).

[8]Staley, "Reading," 75 (= *Reading,* 226).

Roman, trying to cut me down from my cross before sunset."[9] Those loosenings represent the only action in the play, the rest is dialogue, debate, discussion, talk, talk, talk. Except, maybe, for one other element. The dogs. But are they a nightmarish fear or a sniffing, prowling, gnawing reality? Are they protagonists in the play or dreams in the mind of a player?

The second and third corpses conduct an erudite and elegant discussion about the passion(less) story in John's gospel. They interweave multiple forms of contemporary criticism, from philological to theological viewpoints and from reader-response to social-world interpretations. I concentrate here on the first corpse's fascination with the dogs.

They are introduced by the first corpse at the very start of Act 2. "Dogs! Dogs! There are dogs all around me!" The first corpse, face in the dirt, screams out in the darkness. "Thin ones, with ribs protruding, ears down, and their tails between their legs. There are dogs in this story, hungrily sniffing and licking my dried sweat, blood, and excrement—just like Jezreel's dogs that gnawed Jezebel's bones (2 Kings 9:30–37). First come the dogs, then come the beady-eyed rats!" The second corpse says there are no such dogs in the story-world of John's gospel, but the third corpse counters that there would be in the social-world of Mediterranean expectations. They debate over those dogs, absent from story-world but present in social-world, metaphorically present in Psalm 22 but also realistically present beneath the crosses. At least for the first corpse, at the very end of Act 2, "So give the dogs to me! They're mine, and they're eating me alive."[10]

The first corpse's terror of the dogs reappears in each of the following acts. In Act 3 there is only a passing reference as the second corpse calls them "your ridiculous dogs."[11] But in Act 4 they are back much more emphatically. The first corpse asks, "Are the dogs gone yet? I'm sick of hearing them panting and sniffing around my head. Where did they go?" Then, almost immediately, "Damn it! The dogs are back. I think they're beginning to dig a hole to bury my bones."[12] In Act 5, just after the third corpse, "the last hanging corpse" is loosened to the ground, comes this: "Oh no, it's dogs! My God! It's the dogs. I can hear them sniffing around my face. They're here and they're gnawing my eyes! My eyes! They've eaten my eyes!"[13] The speaker-corpse is not identified but, in context, the second corpse now joins the first's focus on those scavenger dogs. The dogs are actual-protagonists and not dream-protagonists within the drama. This is confirmed by what follows immediately after that just-cited scream. "'Don't get so upset. It's all just part of erosion,' laughs one of the dogs, its mouth full of dirt, sinew, and bone." They are, besides the corpses, the only other speakers in the play and this is their only utterance. Nevertheless, the third corpse still dismisses them as "the dream dogs of a croaking corpse."

---

[9]Staley, *Reading*, 220.
[10]Staley, "Reading," 69–71 (= *Reading*, 208–15).
[11]Staley, "Reading," 72 (= *Reading*, 216).
[12]Staley, "Reading," 74 (= *Reading*, 223–24).
[13]Staley, "Reading," 75 (= *Reading*, 227).

A few lines later, the drama's last words are given to the first corpse's commentary on that eros-ion. "It's all about eros. 'The cravings for unity, for essence, for the total picture, for the real and the true, are primitive' [Bela Szabados], and eros will live on in readers regardless of what happens to us or the texts. No wine-sopped hyssop can ever quench the tanha-like thirst for completion, nor will a weighty mixture of myrrh and aloes silence its voice."[14]

Dogs in a Reconstructed History

When I was growing up, we did not have dogs as family pets, and my Irish background never knew those scavengers that Staley met on the Navaho reservation. But both of us, around the same time and independent of each other, brought dogs into association with the passion of Jesus. I did not, however, start with living dogs from childhood but with written texts from adulthood. This occurred in three steps, as clearly as I can reconstruct them.

A first step was in 1976, and it concerned only the empty-tomb story, not the preceding burial story. I concluded, to my own satisfaction, that Mark 16:1–8 was created by that author, was the only source for the other three gospel versions, and did not exist anywhere beforehand nor anywhere afterward except under Markan influence. It was produced, after the failure of apparitional deliverance during the First Roman War reflected in Mark 13, in order to replace risen apparitions and to end the gospel without them. That was, at least, the most economical explanation I could see then and still see now. But all I said about burial was this: "It is most probable that Jesus was buried by the same inimical forces that had crucified him and that on Easter Sunday morning those who knew the site did not care and those who cared did not know the site."[15]

A second step was in 1988, and this concerned the burial itself. I argued that the trajectory of that unit was from, first, a hoped-for burial by the authorities who had crucified Jesus as in *Gospel of Peter* 2:5a and 5:15, through, second, a hurried burial by their personification in Joseph of Arimathea as in Mark 15:42–47, and into, finally, an extravagantly magnificent burial by Joseph and Nicodemus as in John 19:38–42. All I could see at the start of that trajectory was hope, not history. That was exactly the same conclusion that I gave in *The Historical Jesus* in 1991. "*Nobody knew what had happened to Jesus' body.* And the best his followers could initially hope for was that he had been buried out of Jewish piety toward Deuteronomy 21:22–23."[16] There was nothing new there. In that analysis I was profoundly influenced by how the burial got better and better as you moved from Mark, through Matthew and Luke, into John. The burial not only got more descriptively grandiose, it got more historically

---

[14]Staley, "Reading," 75–76 (= *Reading,* 227–28, with the latter's "a tightly wrapped linen cloth" replacing the former's "a weighty mixture of myrrh and aloes).

[15]John Dominic Crossan, "Empty Tomb and Absent Lord," in *The Passion in Mark,* ed. Werner Kelber (Philadelphia: Fortress Press, 1976), 152.

[16]Crossan, *The Historical Jesus: The Life of a Mediterranean Jewish Peasant* (San Francisco: Harper San Francisco, 1991), 394.

credible. The earliest reader-response criticism on Mark was conducted by Matthew and Luke. They asked themselves: If Joseph was a "respected member of the council," how was he "looking for the kingdom of God," as Mark 15:43 put it? Mark already saw the problem and used "Sanhedrin" back in 14:55 and 15:1 but "Council" in 15:43, as if the two bodies were not the same. Matthew 27:57 solved it one way: Joseph *was not* in the Sanhedrin but simply a rich disciple of Jesus. Luke 23:50–51 chose the alternative option: Joseph *was* in the council-Sanhedrin but "was a good and righteous man who, though a member of the council, had not agreed to their plan and action." They asked themselves this too: If there were already other bodies in Joseph's tomb, how could Mark have his later empty-tomb story? They both agreed, independently but similarly, on the answer: It was, said Matthew 27:60, "his own new tomb"; it was, said Luke 23:53, one "in which no one had ever yet been laid." But, of course, one problem will always haunt that Markan creation. The more one insists on the plausibility of a pious Sanhedrist obedient to Deuteronomy 21:22–23, the more one must ask about those other two crucified bodies. Would he not have buried them all, buried them all together, even if all together in his own new and unused tomb? Where were they on Easter Sunday?

A third step was not taken and not even imagined by 1991. I had been concentrating exclusively on the negative by claiming that Mark's swift-burial and empty-tomb stories did not represent oral memory nor historical tradition but a self-creation for very specific theological reasons. I never asked the next question, but it happened to me unexpectedly. In late February of 1992, John Loudon, my Harper San Francisco editor, called to tell me that *The Historical Jesus* would appear as number 2 in the forthcoming *Publishers Weekly* on March 16. After some remedial education about what all that meant, he asked me to go on a promotional tour for the book in the two weeks before Easter. I said yes, as long as it could be worked around classes at DePaul. On that tour, somebody somewhere stopped me cold with this question: If Jesus was not buried by Joseph of Arimathea, what happened to his body? I am not surprised at forgetting the questioner because, though I thoroughly enjoyed the tour and loved the high-voltage, nonstop, give-and-take of the process, its details have all merged into a blur and only by checking my publicist's log could I discriminate even its general parameters. But I was and still am somewhat chagrined that I had not even thought about that obvious question before it was asked.

What do you think happened to the body of Jesus? If the gospel story was not history remembered but hope historicized, not a factual account of what Jesus' companions knew had happened but a fictional account of what they hoped had happened, the trajectory was most likely from horror to hope to "history." At the start of the trajectory was horror, the normal, expected, and terrible fate of a crucified person. Jesus had been left on the cross, had been kept on the cross, as carrion. The dogs below, the birds above, the flies in between. I was on an open mike, had to reply immediately, and that was what came immediately to my mind. It was my best historical reconstruction of what would have happened to any crucified body. It was, therefore, absent more explicit information, what most likely happened to Jesus. I knew from both text and tomb, from both literature and archeology, that a crucified body could be given to its family or friends. But that was not what was said about Jesus in Mark. If soldiers under Pilate's command obeyed Deuteronomy 21:22–23 (which I thought very unlikely), I could only imagine a speedily indifferent and necessarily shallow grave with lime at best to keep the digging dogs away. Or, if this is better, a charnel cave close by in which all such corpses were summarily dumped. Dogs. Lime. Dump. But as far as I remember, I only answered the first possibility: the dogs beneath the cross.

In 1991 I had not read, as I most surely should have, Martin Hengel's book *Crucifixion,* an exhaustive list of ancient texts that insists, again and again, that carrion was the ultimate and most terrible result of that supreme penalty.[17] Unable to get that question out of my mind, once it had been openly asked and honestly answered, I read *Crucifixion* in late 1992, took down its sources, and looked them all up. That is why, by the time *Jesus: A Revolutionary Biography* (note, by the way, the deliberate line separating/joining those last two words on the cover), the popular version of *The Historical Jesus,* was published in 1994, "The Dogs beneath the Cross" was the title for the chapter on Jesus' execution and (non)burial.

Fictional Dogs and Historical Dogs

My purpose in this article is to let Staley's reading and mine vibrate against each other. He began far before I ever did with actual and historical dogs on a Navajo reservation, and he learned, far before I ever did and much more experientially than I have ever done, the difference between the single dog as pet and the pack dog as scavenger. It was therefore maybe inevitable that he would end up with dogs beneath the cross. But, despite the triadic crucifixion, his dogs are not actual or historical ones that prowled beneath the crosses of Jesus and his co-crucifieds. He has a fascinating discussion of John's passionate nonpassion conducted by the *three* crucified corpses. He has a powerful dialectic between dogs and, above all others, *John's* account of the crucifixion.

My own reading, on the other hand, is almost classically traditional in form and content, style and substance. There is a transmissional analysis of the tradition from Mark through Matthew and Luke into John. Standard questions are asked. Is Mark itself all tradition, all redaction, or some in-between combination? Did Mark itself create that "tradition"? If yes, what, in one's best historical reconstruction happened to the body of Jesus? My answer to that came in response to a late questioner, not an early experience. I am relatively certain that Joseph of Arimathea is not pre-Markan tradition, let alone transmitted crucifixion history. I admit there could have been a swift

---

[17]Martin Hengel, *Crucifixion in the Ancient World and the Folly of the Message of the Cross* (Philadelphia: Fortress Press, 1977).

(because of soldiers) and shallow (because of location) burial in a limed pit and that maybe the lime would win out over those still-prowling dogs. Hope begot Joseph of Arimathea, but hope is not history. Horror, all too often, then and now, is history.

Here, then, is my concluding question and the point of this article. Which of those two readings, Staley's or mine, is a postmodern interpretation of the fate of Jesus' physical body? neither? either? both?

Son(s) Behaving Badly

The Prodigal in Foreign Hands

R. S. Sugirtharajah

Two critical categories that are causing turbulence in an already crowded and congested arena are postmodernism and postcolonialism. Judgments about critical theories have always been notably belligerent. In the case of these categories, the debate is still fierce because of the mixed and scattered nature of their origins. This is further complicated by a virtual absence of any irrefutably agreed-on precise understanding of what these terms stand for. On the face of it, both categories look as though they were made for each other and could well be natural partners in their mission to destabilize hegemonic hermeneutical practices. However, the alliance is not as unproblematic as it appears.[1] Those who work in the field have discerned two types of postmodernism: the postmodernism of complicity and the postmodernism of revolt. The first is exemplified by a cynical recovery of used-up modes and a compliance with predominant cultural agencies. The second is characterized by its irreproachable political agenda, theory, and agency, which unsettles various dominants like classism, racism, and sexism.[2] It is with the second—oppositional, critical, and praxiological activity—that postcolonialism wishes to be associated.

One of the emblematic marks of postmodernism has been its employment of irony as a counter-discursive practice. Basically, what irony does is to disrupt "the taken-for-granted meaningfulness of utterance and writing," [and] exposes its artificiality.[3] This discursive practice, as Linda Hutcheon has argued, is not

---

[1]For a discussion on the interface between postmodernism and postcolonialism, see Ian Adam and Helen Tiffin, *Past the Last Post: Theorizing Post-Colonialism and Post-Modernism* (Hemel Hempstead: Harvester Wheatsheaf, 1993), and Ato Quayson, *Postcolonialism: Theory, Practice or Process* (Cambridge: Polity Press, 2000), 132–55.

[2]Tim Woods, *Beginning Postmodernism* (Manchester: Manchester University Press, 1999), 131.

[3]Andrew Edgar, "Irony," in *Key Concepts in Cultural Theory,* ed. Andrew Edgar and Peter Sedgwick (London: Routledge, 1999), 199.

confined to postmodernism alone; "postcolonial and the feminist enterprises, among others, have also often turned to irony."[4] However, like many other tropes, when irony is put to use by practitioners of both postcolonialism and postmodernism, it assumes different incarnations and comes with its own diverse nuances and variations, reflecting different social and cultural contexts of production.

Having forged a critical but productive collocation between postmodernism and postcolonialism, let me spell out the aim of this paper. What I am proposing to do is to look at one of the iconic narratives of Luke recorded in chapter 15, universally known as the Prodigal Son, and to study its interpretive fate as it travels outside its natural Christian habitat and falls into the hands of interpreters—especially expositors who belong to other religious traditions and writers of secular fiction. These writers, who are conversant with the story, retell it to meet their own ideological and hermeneutical agendas. I will confine myself to the Indian literary landscape and look at Kiran Nagarkar's novel *Ravan and Eddie*,[5] where a character employs the Lucan parable to thwart its inherited centuries-old interpretation. A parable that is defined and circumscribed by its Christian and colonial association is now being used to harass the very people who first employed it for ideological and propagandistic purposes. The second example is a fiction, "The Serpent and the Master" by Thomas Palakeel,[6] where the writer attempts to rewrite and subvert the Lucan parable from the prism of the son's balked attempt to gain freedom from his father's emotional and material grip. In interrogating these writings, I will try to place them within the postcolonial/postmodern trope of irony and demonstrate how, in their appropriation of this trope, they end up falling prey to the very values they sought to unmask. I will also investigate the hermeneutical purposes and implications of such an appropriation of a Christian story.

The Prodigal Son in Khaki Shorts

The retelling of the Prodigal Son in Nagarkar's novel occurs when one of the eponymous heroes, Eddie Coutinho, a Christian, unwittingly enrolls himself as a member of a Hindu religious organization in his neighborhood. Although the parable is not pivotal to the plot, it is narrated at an important stage in the development of the character. Briefly, the novel is about sons of two Indian families—one is Hindu, the Pawars, and the other is Roman Catholic, the Coutinhos. It concerns their self-discovery in postcolonial India. They live on different floors of the same Central Work Department *chawl*[7] number 17 in

---

⁴Linda Hutcheon, "The Post Always Rings Twice: The Postmodern and Postcolonial," *Textual Practice* 8/2 (1994): 210.

⁵Kiran Nagarkar, *Ravan and Eddie* (New Delhi: Viking Penguin India, 1995).

⁶Thomas Palakeel, "The Serpent and the Master," *Yatra: Writings from the Indian Subcontinent* 4 (1994): 171–82.

⁷*Chawl* is a low-cost housing estate inhabited by the low-income families of bus conductors, peons, and petty government officials.

Bombay. Despite being thrown together in the congested housing estate, they might well have lived in parallel worlds. They come from different states in India, the Pawars from Maharashtra and the Coutinhos from Goa. They speak different languages at home and celebrate different religious festivals. Eddie goes to an English medium school run by Roman Catholics, and Ravan attends a municipal school where English is taught as a second language. They are not only separated by religion, culture, and language but also divided by a different colonial heritage—one British and the other Portuguese. To all intents and purposes, though Eddie was born and bred in India, as with all Indian Catholics, his "umbilical cord was stretched all the way to Lisbon."[8] Where the worlds of Eddie and Ravan collide is the most unlikely place of all, *sabha*—a hinduist organization involved both in educational and mobilizational work in the *chawl.* Its description "of white shirts and flared khaki half-pants fame,"[9] alludes to the Rashtriya Swayamsvek Sangh (RSS), a paramilitary and militant Hindu organization with strong nationalistic undercurrents. The *sabha* was active in the *chawl,* and under the leadership of Lele Guruji, it vigorously recruited members from all communities to save India from non-Hindus. In one of his rousing speeches to his sharply attentive *sabha* boys, Lele Guruji thunders:

> For centuries, Muslims, Catholics and Protestants have converted Hindus. It is time we turned the tide. What we need is a wild bushfire that spreads across the country and brings back the lost souls to Hinduism. Anyone who enrolls a non-Hindu in our Sabha will get a Wilson fountain pen. And the new member will be given not only a Wilson fountain pen and ball-point set but also a beautifully illustrated and abridged copy of the *Stories from the Mahabharata and Shri Krishna's Life* in Hindi, English or Marathi. Go into the world and light fires, the fires of Hinduism. Jai Hind[10]

Ravan was already a member of the *sabha,* but he did not join with a view to save India from non-Hindus. That was the last thing he had in his mind. He was forced into it by his mother, Parvathi, whose objective was purely pragmatic—to keep Ravan out of mischief. She did not have any inkling of the politics of the *sabha.* Enticed by the idea of getting a Wilson pen for bringing new members, Ravan embarked on a recruitment campaign. He had a couple of disasters initially. On one occasion he was thoroughly beaten up for associating with an outfit that was allegedly linked with the group that killed the father of the nation, Mahatma Gandhi. Then one fine day, he ran into Eddie and casually mentioned the *sabha.* This was the very first time they had spoken to each other. Eddie, to everyone's surprise, turned up at the founder's day of the *sabha.* Elated by Eddie's arrival, Appa Achrekar, the elderly firebrand

---

[8]Nagarkar, *Ravan and Eddie,* 16.
[9]Ibid., 17.
[10]Ibid., 20.

of the *sabha,* in celebration of a new catch and a Christian at that, told the story of the Prodigal Son in a perverse way. In a delightfully mischievous ironic reversal, Achrekar dubbed the Christian Eddie as the Prodigal who had now come back to his rightful home. After centuries of missionary preaching that branded Indians and those who were outside the Christian framework as prodigals, Achrekar ironically inflated and at the same time punctured the roles. Listen to the way the leader ended the story:

> Eddie Coutinho is our prodigal son. How many centuries have passed since he and his people were converted and left us? I have lost count. But he is back amongst his own and we rejoice at the return of our prodigal.[11]

What happened when Eddie's mother and his Catholic priest discovered his conversion (to their horror) and called him the prodigal a second time round is another matter and need not detain us here.

The Yielding Son

Palakeel's story, in keeping with the Indian way of storytelling, is full of plots and subplots and is inhabited by a whole host of characters. It is essentially a primordial parable that retells the tale of a young person's failed attempt to leave home and lead a life of his own, free from parental control and the pressures of the extended family. It is about a Christian family in Kerala in South India who fast and pray during Holy Week and brood about the death and resurrection of Jesus. It points out the futile effort of the son, Appu, to live literally and imaginatively away from home and his father's expectation. The son's desire is to study Malayalam literature and become a writer, but his father's plan is to send him to medical school and make him the first medical doctor in the family. As a way of counteracting the resistance of the son, the father sends him to spend time at a secular monastery run by a master whose fame included, among other things, producing a fake Bible. Eventually, when the father and the master urge him to undertake the self-quest he is pining for, and offer money, the son, unlike the son in the Lucan story, becomes frightened of the impending journey. When he thinks about the prospect of the hazardous long rail rides, deserts, and strange languages, he decides to return to the family, much to the joy of his father. Whereas, in the Lucan narrative, taking the money is seen as the son's right, in Palakeel's story it is seen as a failure. In the eyes of his granduncle, the moment Appu took the money, he had come a cropper: "You took money. You failed."[12] The son—egoistical, insecure, and underconfident—realizes that stargazing alone is not sufficient. He starts hearing voices: "Turn back. Go home. Return to your beginnings. Go home."[13]

---

[11]Ibid., 33.
[12]Palakeel, "The Serpent and the Master," 182.
[13]Ibid.

The Prodigal Going Native

These retellings acknowledge the background and the influence of Judeo-Christian elements, but, at the same time, they redirect that influence by opening and nativising or Hinduising it. Indigenization is achieved either through writing in additional materials or excising awkward elements in the texts. In Nagarkar's retelling, the elder son, who stood steadfast by the family, was aghast at the celebration, and he asked what was to be his reward. The father's reply was literally from the Bhagavad *Gita*: "Duty well done is its own reward, my son."[14] Unlike the Lucan father, who reminded the elder son that all that belonged to the father belonged to the son as well, the Indian retelling propounds the message of the *Bhagavad Gita*. Disinterested service, one of the spiritual tenets of the *Bhagavad Gita*, which has become the gospel of Hinduism, is injected into the text.

These accounts are more inclusive than the source-text in that they are gender inclusive. By contrast, in the Lucan parable, the narrative centers around the father, and the role of the mother is written out, inexplicably in a drama set in a West Asian context. These retellings restore the mother to the text and give her a part, however restricted it may be. In Nagarkar's narration, it is the mother, seeing a dot at the very edge of the horizon, who asks, "Who could it be?"[15] And unlike the Lucan story, where only the father embraces the son, here the mother, too, puts her arm around him. The mother is accommodated, though her role is circumscribed by patriarchal norms. For instance, in Palakeel's story, Appu, agonizing over his decision, shares it with his mother. Instead of understanding her son's dilemma, the mother identifies herself with patriarchal beliefs and disapproves of her son's quest. Along with others, she too laughs at his decision.[16]

The elements that do not translate well into the Indian context are edited out. The repentance speech, which the Lucan younger son prepared when he found himself impoverished, is effortlessly left out, whereas it is an essential component in the Christian story. In Achrekar's narration there is no pang of conscience, since personal guilt and sinning against God does not have the same theological valence in the Hindu way of thinking. The Hindu concept of sin ranges from the simple belief that associates sin with disease, to the most sophisticated one that holds that sin is a denial and betrayal of the soul and self. In-between these two, according to Dandekar, there are other perceptions that describe "sin as a debt, or a breach of caste rules, or a defiance of god, or absence of harmony with the spiritual environment, or lack of spiritual power."[17] Sin as personal guilt in the Christian sense does not have

---

[14]Nagarkar, *Ravan and Eddie*, 33.
[15]Ibid., 32.
[16]Palakeel, "The Serpent and the Master," 179.
[17]Ramchandra Narayan Dandekar, "The Role of Man in Hinduism," in *The Religion of the Hindus,* ed. Kenneth William Morgan (Delhi: Motilal Banarsidass, 1987), 152.

the same theological weightage in Hindu thought, and thus the son's speech that exemplifies this is absent from the Indian text.

Out also goes any reference to feasting on a fatted calf, which forms part of the Lucan celebration. In Nagarkar's version, the father orders "a feast such as the town, nay, that part of the world had never seen,"[18] and omits any reference to feasting on meat. In a culture that shares a symbolic belief in the sacredness of cows, killing and eating calf is viewed with repugnance. In a culture where dietary regulations are informed by caste norms and where strict vegetarianism is privileged and required as a way of maintaining the sense of purity, those who consume meat—Christians, Muslims, and dalits—are deemed and categorized as impure. Translating the term *fatted calf* caused considerable hermeneutical concern for missionaries. Newly converted, high-caste Christians were scandalized to read that their religion was being associated with lower-caste customs, and even urged the offending reference to a fatted calf be removed from the text.

Abbe Dubois, a Roman Catholic missionary, narrates an experience that he had in 1815. After he had preached on the parable of the Prodigal Son, about how the father had killed the fatted calf to entertain his friends in a welcoming home party for his son, some Christians afterward told him that his mention of "fatted calf" was very improper. Their worry was that Hindus, who were often present at such services, on hearing of the fatted calf would have their worst fears confirmed, namely that of "the Christian religion being a low or pariah religion." The caste Christians' practical advice to Dubois was that if he should ever give an "explanation of the same parable, to substitute a lamb instead of the *fatted calf*."[19]

It is not unusual for Indian Christians to resuscitate local referents from Hindu myths and *puranas* in order to bolster their theological enterprise. They incorporate them into Christianity by Christianizing them. Indian Christian literature is replete with such examples.[20] Based on the methodological presupposition of synthesization, these retellings employ local nuances to serve different agendas. They use the very same method, but this time to Hinduize the Christian story.

Textual Gestures

Playing on the Lucan parable, both these retellings illustrate their own postmodern and postcolonial status. Nagarkar's version takes into account

---

[18]Nagarkar, *Ravan and Eddie*, 32.

[19]Abbe Jean Antoine Dubois, *Letters on the State of Christianity in India* (New Delhi: Associated Publishing House, n.d.), 18 (italics in original). In a recent article in a Tamil literary journal, A. Sivasubramaniyan has shown how Roman Catholic literature produced in the 1920s often changed "fatted calf" to "lamb" to appease caste Christians and to make Christianity appear untainted with low-caste associations; "Fatted calf and fatted lamb," *Kanaiyazhi* (January 2000): 53–55.

[20]For examples of an earlier generation see Kaj Baago, *Pioneers of Indigenous Christianity*, Confessing the Faith in India Series no. 4 (Bangalore: The Christian Institute for the Study of Religion and Society, 1969); and for recent attempts, see Kalarikkal Poulose Aleaz, *The Gospel of Indian Culture* (Calcutta: Punti Pustak, 1994), and Michael Amaladoss, *Beyond Inculturation: Can the Many Be One?* (Delhi: ISPCK, 1998).

the text's missionary and colonial linkages and parodies them. By ironic repetition of a colonial textuality, it sets itself in opposition to the interpellative power of colonial homiletics. Nagarkar imitates the biblical parable but distances it critically by subverting the missionary ideology, which for centuries branded Indians and those outside the Christian framework as prodigals. Achrekar retells the Lucan parable from the perspective of those who have been at the receiving end of missionary propaganda, and he reverts and inverts the original text. His retelling provides an example of the ways in which the missionised turn the tables by simultaneously using and abusing the very material employed by the colonizers to mold and incorporate them. Ironically, the poignant moment in Nagarkar's retelling is when Eddie receives, as a conversion gift, a set of Hindu sacred texts—*Stories from the Mahabharata and Shri Krishna's Life*—thus overturning the age-old custom of Christian converts' receiving the King James Version as their proud possession. What these two retellings do is to dislodge Christian interpretation, otherwise regarded as uncontestable. Palakeel's story fictionalizes, exposes, and more importantly, mediates the tensions and pressures felt in extended families. The critical moment in Palakeel's story is when the son returns and observes the father's reaction. It provides a hermeneutical clue as to the inner workings and mind-sets of both, the observer and the observed: "I detested the frantic joy in my father's face. Fathers always rejoice when their prodigal sons return home, defeated. A father waits for the son's fall."[21]

What we see at work here is the postmodern use of irony—irony not as a counter-discourse, but sadly siding with normative constraints and reactionary values. These retellings are deconstructive in the postmodern sense of not relying too much on Christian polemics. They reframe the parable from the evangelized point of view. But they are not liberatory in the postcolonial sense of offering counter-models to prevailing hegemonic trends. The trope of irony is evoked, not to destabilize but to shore up the foundations of patriarchy, family values, and stability of home life. These retellings work to make the Lucan parable ambiguous and thereby subvert it from outside, whilst defending the establishment views from within. As Linda Hutcheon points out, irony is "transideologic" and malleable in the hands of those who use it. Irony, according to her, "can obviously be both political *and* apolitical, both conservative *and* radical, both repressive *and* democratizing."[22] These retellings engage in double-talk. While they assume a speaking position from within the colonial discourse, they simultaneously undermine the received reading and allow in ingredients that perpetuate oppressive and worn-out values.

The Indian retellings, though they appear to be dismantling the Lucan parable, in no way eradicate or erase the basic religious and theological tenets of the biblical story. They do open up the story and deviate from it, but in the

---

[21]Palakeel, "The Serpent and the Master," 182.
[22]Linda Hutcheon, *Irony's Edge: The Theory and Politics of Irony* (London: Routledge, 1994), 35 (italics in original).

end they reinstall the hierarchical tendencies of the Christian story. The fatherhood of God is restored and reconfigured as natural, given, and universal. The moral of the Lucan parable and Palakeel's story is that patriarchy should never be questioned. The narratives argue for a type of father (for "father" read "God") who is in a position to know what is right for all and act in a nurturing way so that his children either anticipate his wishes or accept them without question. The father effectively demands not only love but also obedience and unquestioning recognition of his authority. When we see Appu eventually returning home and accepting the father, we can see that the son, to use the Indian psychologist Sudhir Kakar's diagnosis, has internalized from childhood the authority of his father:

> [Y]ounger professionals have from childhood internalized the "hierarchical tradition," so any discrepancy between the criteria of professional performance and the prevailing mores of the organization does not produce either a confrontation with the older men or the persistent, critical questioning necessary to effect change. The aggression...in the younger generation is blocked from expression in outright anger; instead, the conflict between intellectual conviction and developmental "fate" manifests itself in a vague sense of helpless and impotent rage. The anxiety triggered by the mere possibility of losing the nurturing patronage of powerful figures usually prevents any deviation from the safer compliant stance.[23]

A digression. Interestingly, the bleak version of the reunion and uneasiness of the younger son's coming home comes through in a poem written by that colonial sage Rudyard Kipling. The poem brings to the fore the son's isolation, the expression of his personal interests, and the assertion of his individuality. Essentially, it is about sons and daughters wanting to be free from paternal pressures. Listen to the words of Kipling's "The Prodigal Son":

> Here come I to my own again,
> Fed, forgiven and known again,
> Claimed by bone of my bone again
> And cheered by flesh of my flesh.
> The fatted calf is dressed for me,
> But the husks have greater zest for me.
> I think my pigs will be best for me,
> So I'm off to the styes afresh.

> My father glooms and advises me,
> My brother sulks and despises me,
> and Mother catechises me
> Till I want to go out and swear.

---

[23]Sudhir Kakar, *The Inner World: A Psycho-Analytic Study of Childhood and Society in India* (Delhi: Oxford University Press, 1992 [1981]), 120.

Unnerved, the prodigal son sets off again.
I'm leaving, Pater. Good-bye to you!
God bless you, Mater, I will write to you...
I wouldn't be impolite to you,
But, Brother, you *are* a hound![24]

Now, reverting to these retellings: They are reluctant to shake loose from the strict demands of orthodoxy. Family (= patriarchy) and home are seen as valuable and secure sites. Family/home provides the stabilizing influence in a world disrupted by sweeping changes occurring all around. What one is looking for is not a modernist understanding of the family, in which the self-interest and desires of the individual run counter to the collective interests of the family, as Kipling's Prodigal Son desires and advocates. Rather, what is hoped for is the promotion of the family as an imaginative and egalitarian changed space. Kakar's observation comes closer to a postcolonial notion of family. In his view, a family should be "a more flexible, egalitarian structure in which the capacity for initiative as well as seniority governs role relationships, in which competence rather than age legitimates authority, and in which the organizational mode is non-coercive and fraternal."[25]

Central to these retellings is the idea of home or returning to home. It is conceptualized as a private place and as a public arena. In Palakeel's story, the home is presented as a stable, comfortable, settled, and familiar place to which everyone should eventually return. Bolshevik Kuttan, one of the characters in the story, advises Appu against undertaking such a rigorous journey to find the obvious truth and tells him a story from Hindu myths to extol the virtues of home. In this Puranic story, the Lord Shiva and his consort Parvathi offered a fruit as a prize to two of their sons, whoever first circumambulated the universe. Subramanya, the exuberant one, anxious to cover the earth, took off on his divine peacock, whereas Vinayaka, whose vehicle was a little mouse, circled around his parents and claimed the reward. When his parents told him that he hadn't even begun his journey, Vinayaka's reply was: "Yes, I've completed my journey around my universe. You're my universe."[26] In Palakeel's retelling, home is not the place one escapes from; it is renarrated and framed as a rightful, natural, and real space for all, including sons, to dwell.

In Nagarkar's story, the home stands for public arena, thus serving as a metaphor for nation. The "fold" to which Eddie returns is not the tolerant, inclusive home that India encouraged for so long. When Lele Guruji invites all to come back to the fold, "all" in his lexicon does not include Muslims. What he and his *sabha* imagine is a reinvigorated ethno-nationalist Hindu home. And if one takes the metaphor of Lele Guruji seriously—"But faith is a

---

[24]Rudyard Kipling, "The Prodigal Son," in *The Works of Rudyard Kipling* (Ware: Wordsworth Editions, 1994), 579–80 (italics original).

[25]Kakar, *The Inner World,* 120.

[26]Palakeel, "The Serpent and the Master," 181.

torch. Unless you light torches in the hearts and souls of others, our flame will waste and die"[27] –it is a home that produces arsonists for Hinduism. It is a home that stigmatizes all the minorities in India by promoting a hate-filled Hinduism that is intolerant. The home that is metonymic for India is not a shared space for different and diverse communities, nor is it accommodating enough to hold porous identities. Rather, it is a home of extreme religious nationalism. Home is presented as a seductive place of belonging and of living in community, but it is governed by the principle of inclusion and exclusion based on religious, caste, and communal identities.

As a way of concluding this section, let me reiterate what I said earlier in this essay. These retellings ironize the Lucan parable and, in the process, undoubtedly unsettle the Christian story and its received interpretation. The transideological nature of the trope allows a rerendering of value systems and cultural conventions. The retellings retain and reauthorize benevolent paternalism and the idealization of home, obedience, and family values in the biblical narrative, though not necessarily in their explicit Christian form. They do not actually displace the biblical story, but they replace some of its inherent features–responsibility, guilt, forgiveness–with those of patriotism and religious bigotry, and they legitimize them as local, traditional, and internal to the culture.

Appropriations, Reinscriptions

These two readings benefit from the current widespread sympathy for communities and their interpretive concerns. These concerns have to do with determining meaning as something not inherent in the texts but confected by and for the community to suit its hermeneutical aims.

Narratives will take on a life of their own outside their respective natural theological habitats. In their diasporic existence, they will be mined for different, even contrary, ideological purposes than those for which they were originally intended. Unlooped from the binds of Christian interpretative traditions, biblical narratives will keep on offering new complexities and dimensions to the story. It is safer to assume that interpretations propounded in the original contexts will not be consistent with the interpretations that emerge from the new exilic state. What these retellings do is to prevent any reemergence of one, single reading as the valid one. The proper hermeneutical response is to read them contrapuntally with the concurrent awareness of both Christian and non-Christian discourses. Such a contrapuntal reading will demystify the received and established framework and read against the grain. This means, in their attempts to understand not only the text but also its interpretation, Christian interpreters have to look beyond the traditional hermeneutical arenas, such as in the Christian West. What these new readings in foreign contexts do is to relativize the Christian text and invite and force

---

[27]Nagarkar, *Ravan and Eddie,* 19.

Christian interpreters to keep their eyes open to disruptive, even uncomfortable, readings. This means constantly rethinking Christian hermeneutical conclusions, accepting them as only provisional, and acknowledging their methods as tentative. Anything other than this will be a return to the exegetical imperialism that has often marked and marred Christian scholarship.

In a way, these two retellings are postmodern, for they take liberties with the narrative. There is a sense of postmodern playfulness about them, especially in Nagarkar's retelling. They emphasize the problem of textualized truth and the impossibility of retrieving one single meaning.

The old scholarly quest for the original meaning is now replaced by the search for a "good misreading." Paul de Man explains a misreading as "A text that produces another text which can itself be shown to be an interesting misreading, a text which engenders additional texts."[28] Misreading, in Paul de Man's sense, habitually manages to turn a narrative inside out, as it were. The willful/playful misreading of the writings of the colonized is a way of overcoming inferiority and regaining the voices and cultures that had been muted and denigrated.

These retellings do not deny the theological capital of the Prodigal Son within the Christian tradition, nor do they replace the Lucan narrative. The biblical parable retains its character and will continue to be mined for its polemical potency and for missionary preaching and propaganda. Indian reinscriptions function as hermeneutical palimpsests, where new readings, meanings, and texts are written, rewritten, and reworked. The idea of palimpsest is explained thus in *Key Concepts in Post-Colonial Studies:*

> The concept of the palimpsest is a useful way of understanding the developing complexity of a culture, as previous "inscriptions" are erased and overwritten, yet remain as traces within present consciousness. This confirms the dynamic, contestory and dialogic nature of linguistic, geographic and cultural spaces as it emerges in post-colonial experience.[29]

Nagarkar and Palakeel's reinscriptions do not attempt to dislodge or denigrate the Lucan version. It is a palimpsestic attempt to prevent a monopolistic reading of Christian homiletics. It teases out the vestigial features that surround the text and its interpretation, as a part of understanding the present.

Finally, I would like to end with the question every interpreter who deals with sacred stories wrestles with. Why are we so attracted to stories, especially religious stories, we often know? What prompts us to read and reread, tell

---

[28]I owe this quote to K. K. Ruthven, *Feminist Studies: An Introduction* (Cambridge: Cambridge University Press, 1990), 91.
[29]Bill Ashcroft, Gareth Griffiths, and Helen Tiffin, *Key Concepts in Post-Colonial Studies* (London: Routledge, 1998), 176.

and retell, hear and rehear, when we already know the end? What is so alluring about them? Arundhati Roy, the author of the award-winning novel *God of Small Things,* may have a clue. What one of her characters says about the great Hindu sacred stories may well be true for other religious narratives as well:

> [T]he secret of the Great Stories is that they *have* no secrets. The Great Stories are the ones you have heard and want to hear again. The ones you can enter anywhere and inhabit comfortably. They don't deceive you with thrills and trick endings. They don't surprise you with unforeseen. They are familiar as the house you live in. Or the smell of your lover's skin. You know how they end, yet you listen as though you don't...In the Great Stories you know who lives, who dies, who finds love, who doesn't. And yet you want to know again. *That* is their mystery and their magic.[30]

---

[30]Arundhati Roy, *The God of Small Things* (New Delhi: IndiaInk, 1997), 229 (italics in original).

Postmodern Pentecost

A Reading of Acts 2

David Jobling

Just before its dispersal, the Bible and Culture Collective (author of *The Postmodern Bible*) worked on the texts of Babel (Gen. 11:1–9) and Pentecost (Acts 2). That work culminated in a collective presentation at the annual meeting of the Society of Biblical Literature. The following reading, though in this form entirely my own, is generally inspired, and in some places specifically informed, by that collective work. Danna Fewell deserves more particular mention, since drafts she prepared provided me with the historical-literary line of thought that I use to connect Pentecost to Babel. My colleagues have given me permission to present this reading in my own name. They will relish, though, the irony that a reading of Pentecost beginning in dialogue should end in monologue.

What makes a postmodern reading postmodern? To offer a precise answer would not be very postmodern, as the variety of the essays in this and the companion volume attests! But for pedagogical reasons I shall take care to identify the postmodern moves that I make in this reading. Postmodernism, at least as I experience it and find it usable, obeys a pedagogical imperative and has an interest in undoing the distance between "academic" and "popular." It wants to expose to the scrutiny of readers who are not endowed with authority the ways in which "authoritative" readings are arrived at.

Acts 2 falls into three parts. Verses 1–13 recount the Pentecost event, the language miracle. There follows a speech given by Peter in the wake of this event, and the immediate consequences of the speech, a mass conversion and baptism (vv. 14–43). Finally, there is a brief account of the character of the believing community that emerged from Pentecost (vv. 44–47).

This reading will not overturn traditional, particularly Christian, readings. By a very different route I will arrive at a somewhat different place. I did not intend or anticipate this, but I am glad of it since it helps make a point:

Postmodernism is not about turning everything on its head, but about uncovering the assumptions that got us where we are.

1. My first postmodern strategy is *intertextuality.* This means reading a text through the lens of another text or texts. In its widest definition, intertextuality doesn't assume any particular relation between the texts. It simply explores how one text may open up another, regardless of any intentional links in the process of their production, regardless of whether or how anyone has linked them before.

I shall read Acts 2 primarily through the lens of the Babel story. This is not, you may feel, a strikingly original use of intertextuality. One doesn't need to be postmodern to read Pentecost in relation to Babel. Christians have been doing it for a long time. (In fact, not as long as we might suppose; there seems to be no evidence from before the fourth century. Acts 2, though it refers to a good many passages from the Jewish Bible, does not refer to Genesis 11.) Part of my strategy will be to problematize the links that have previously been made between these passages.

One powerful reason for reading Babel and Pentecost together is that they both have to do with the diversity of languages, an issue in which (though it is a major feature of human existence) neither the Jewish Bible nor the New Testament otherwise shows much interest. In this sense, the two stories seek each other out. But this begs the question, not only why Christians were slow to make the link, but why the remainder of Acts 2, after verses 1–13, is so little interested in the specifically *linguistic* character of the miracle.

The basic Christian mode of connecting Pentecost to Babel has been to see Pentecost as solving a problem that Babel creates. "Defeat our Babel with your Pentecost!" concludes a recent hymn.[1] I do not assume in advance that Babel creates a problem or that Pentecost is a response to Babel. An intertextual reading need not rely on one text's being a response to another. In fact, the only reason that I travel via Babel to Pentecost is that it is the Pentecost text that I am interested in reading here. A reading could as well move in the opposite direction. In fact, I will use intertexts other than Babel, and even the "Babel" that I use as intertext will not be precisely Genesis 11:1–9, but rather a new "text" constituted by a rereading of Babel.

2. Recently, there have been two general ways of interpreting the Babel story. The more traditional has been especially favored by a certain kind of Christian reader. It sees Babel as God's punishment of humanity for trying to breach the barrier between earth and heaven. Read this way, Babel becomes a repetition on a grander scale of the story of the garden and the fall (Gen. 2–3). When humans become discontent with the place allotted to them, they have to be "put in their place." This interpretation has begun to be less popular because of the unattractive light in which it places God. God becomes

[1]Fred Kahn, "We Turn to You" (1965, rev. 1993), in *Voices United: The Hymn and Worship Book of the United Church of Canada* (Etobicoke, Ontario: The United Church Publishing House, 1996), no. 685.

defensive: "This is only the beginning of what they will do" (Gen. 11:6). But why should God be worried when humans are simply striving to realize their potential? Doesn't God want "his" creatures to do that?

So an alternative reading has become popular (somewhat more among Jewish readers) in which Babel is a story of humans *failing* to realize their potential and having to be pushed by God into doing so. God wants humans to fill the whole earth, but the Babelians want safety through unity and geographical centeredness. God scatters them to get them back on the right track. God confuses human language to discourage any further attempt to centralize.

Different as these readings are, from the perspective of postmodernism they have a major problem in common: They are both "grand narratives." A grand narrative is one that pretends to give a *total* account of the world, to explain life, the universe, and everything. Religions characteristically deal in grand narratives, but they have no corner on this market. Political systems such as communism and liberal democracy also offer unified accounts of what happens in the world, and what should. *Suspicion of grand narratives,* regardless of where they come from, is one of the most important postmodern strategies. Truth is to be sought not at this exalted level, but at the level of local and specific issues.

Both interpretations of Babel, those that stress divine punishment and those that stress human opportunity, agree that it is a story about *all humanity.* Both see Babel as conveying a message that applies to everyone, equally to rich and poor, equally to men and women. Humanity as a whole, all people equally, deserve divine punishment or need to be reminded of their divine destiny. Babel is a story that, more than most others, has functioned in our consciousness as a grand narrative. From the viewpoint of postmodern suspicion, such a story may obscure—and exist precisely *to* obscure—specific differences among humans.

How can we read the Genesis account as a story of human difference rather than unity? One impulse to do so comes from the iconographic tradition that Babel has spawned, one of the richest of any biblical story. This introduces another postmodern strategy, to stress the *visual* as a way of undoing the supremacy of the word (this is one aspect of what is sometimes called the critique of *logocentrism*). In this essay I include only one visual illustration, but in our collective work, with a special contribution by Tina Pippin, we included many. Some of the artists of Babel lead us directly into a scene of human difference. Pictures of the building of the tower often contrast supervisors and planners (typically large, in the foreground) with those doing the actual labor (smaller, in the distance). The painter "knows" what the writer "forgets," that human building projects come typically from coerced labor in a system of class difference (think of the building of the pyramids). One modern portrayal of the Tower of Babel shows it as actually made out of human bodies!

A second clue lies in the name "Babel." Genesis 11 explains it etymologically as a reference to linguistic confusion, and our virtually identical word *babble* attunes us to this explanation. But "Babel" elsewhere in the Bible is not the name of an anonymous, mythic city where language got messed up, but of a specific historical city, well and bitterly known to the Israelites–Babylon. Within this *general* story of universal human pride lies, thinly disguised, a *local and specific* story out of Israel's experience.

The Bible is full of stories of Babylon, of its cruelty, its pride, and its fall. Israel experienced the Babylonians as imperialists, as conquerors. At the beginning of the sixth century B.C.E. they ruined Jerusalem and carried off its prominent people and treasures. Many biblical passages refer to these events. Several accounts single out "artisans and smiths" among those carried off (2 Kings 24:14, 16; Jer. 24:1; 29:2). No doubt they were put to work building the towers of Babylon.

The Israelites carried into exile, and maybe even those left behind, had to learn a strange language (Jer. 5:15; cf. Isa. 28:11–13, Zeph. 3:9). Imperialists often impose their language on the people they conquer. It is a legacy of modern imperialism that English has become a near-universal language. The innocent words of Genesis, "The whole earth had one language" (11:1, NRSV), mask, then, a *specific* oppression. Linguistic unity is an effect of power.

Later, the might of Babylon collapsed, and another group of biblical passages celebrates its fall. Think of the fall of Nebuchadnezzar's great statue in Daniel 2. My favorite is the "taunt against the king of Babylon" in Isaiah 14:

> How the oppressor has ceased!
> 　How his insolence has ceased!...
> How you are fallen from heaven,...
> How you are cut down to the ground,
> 　you who laid the nations low!
> You said in your heart,
> 　"I will ascend to heaven;
> 　I will raise my throne
> 　above the stars of God;...
> 　I will make myself like the Most High."
> But you are brought down to Sheol,
> 　to the depths of the Pit. (vv. 4, 12–15, NRSV)

Try reading Genesis 11 in the light of this!

After Babylon's fall, some of the exiles went home. We call this the Restoration. The irony is that they went home and created their own Babel! The exiles returned to Jerusalem, it seems, with official Persian sponsorship. They found there a population of fellow Jews, descendants of those who had not been exiled. As Persian agents, they were able to impose their power on these "people of the land." Their first priority was to rebuild the temple, not only as a center of religion but also as the provincial economic center. The temple was the hub of the tax system by which the ruling bureaucracy serviced its own needs and also met the demands of the Persian overlords for tribute.

These returning exiles dreamed not of a new and equal community saved from Babylonian domination, but rather of restoring Israel's old imperial glory under King David and King Solomon. Once again, Jerusalem (though in reality a backwater of Persian power) was to be cast ideologically as the supreme city, the center of the earth. Instead of rejecting Babylon's blasphemous pride, the rulers of Jerusalem pathetically imitated it, treading down their own people as Babylon had trodden them down.

It is even possible that the Babel story as we read it in Genesis was created in this setting. By retelling the Babel/Babylon story as a *universal* story of human pride, the elite can hide their own particular Babylonish guilt under a theological generality: "That's just the way everyone is!"

3. This intertextual path leads us now back to Pentecost. Our reading strategy here will be *deconstruction*. This means locating points where the text *unravels* itself through its inner contradictions, where it becomes unsure what it wants to say. In the work of deconstructing Acts 2 our rereading of Babel helps us.

In verses 1–13 the disciples, inspired by the Spirit, tell of "God's deeds of power" in foreign languages previously unknown to them. Diaspora Jews, from all over the world and with a great variety of native languages, hear all these languages spoken. They are perplexed. But others who are present apparently experience nothing remarkable, and they scoff.

Is this a reversal of Babel? Not in a literal sense. The world does not revert after Pentecost to a single language. Yet what occurs seems not unrelated to Babel. The Babelian scattering (Gen. 11:9) had two aspects: geographical separation and linguistic confusion. The Pentecost story deals in its own way with each aspect. Geographical separation has been reversed before the story begins, by the universal reach of *Judaism.* Those who experience the Pentecost miracle have previously gathered from the ends of the earth to Jerusalem. Now *Christianity* solves the confusion of language, in the sense that language difference ceases to be a barrier to communication.

Deconstruction of Acts 2 may begin by asking the question, In what language were the words in verses 7–13 spoken? Those who experience the miracle can hardly address "one another" (v. 12) in their various native languages, since they would not be understood. They must have some common language in which they can communicate. But if they already have a common language, what is the point of the miracle? These questions extend to the biblical telling of the story: Must not the text *assume* a common language in order to tell its story of language unification? They extend also to the following speech of Peter. His hearers must all have known the language (Greek?) in which he told them the "meaning" (v. 12) of their experience.

Essentially the same point can be made in a different, narratological way. No one, even an eyewitness, or a narrator assuming the place of an eyewitness, could be in a position to verify from his or her own knowledge the truth of the Pentecost account. To verify that the disciples really did speak all those languages one would have to know them all, which no one person could. Authority for what happened lies with the *multiple* hearers–to believe the story is to believe their *several* accounts of what they heard.

Given such narrative instabilities, it comes as no surprise that this story of unification ends with the creation of division. As well as the "ingroup" who experience and celebrate the miracle, there is an "outgroup" of skeptics who reject it. Who are these skeptics? Are they diaspora Jews who have somehow *not* heard a disciple speak their language? Or were there others present—but why in that case were we not told—in addition to diaspora Jews? To the deconstructive mind, it is also no surprise that the end of the story falls into a contradiction, between "all" (v. 12) and "others" (v. 13). "All" leaves no room for "others." The story seems to *desire* unification but to be forced at the end to admit division. It is in a bind. Its believability rests, as we saw, on the believability of many eyewitnesses; but in the end it must confess that the eyewitnesses did not agree about what happened.

The members of the Bible and Culture Collective were likewise unable to agree about the Pentecost story. Some of us read in it a story of Babelian difference collapsed into unity, and felt (as "postmoderns") very negative about this. Others of us thought that the Pentecost text could not be so easily tamed. If it evokes unity, it is a *diffuse* unity, a unity that resides only in the separate testimonies of many. The story of unity entails irreducible variety; the story of inclusion leads inevitably to exclusion.

4. The unraveling of the Pentecost story continues in a different way in the rest of Acts 2, which provides it with two different and even opposite sequels. Sequel one (vv. 14–43) consists mostly of an enormous speech by Peter (vv. 14–36). This speech takes its cue immediately from the mockery in verse 13, but more profoundly from the question in verse 12, "What does this mean?" Peter sets out to *explain* Pentecost.

He does so by reference to Joel 2, with its prediction of the outpouring of God's spirit. This certainly fits with the explosive activity of the Spirit at Pentecost. But it does not pick up on what is most *specific* to Pentecost, the language miracle. Peter does not accept the obvious invitation to refer to Babel! In fact, not only does he fail to mention language, he takes pains to avoid the subject. To the scoffers' reference to "new wine" (v. 13) he lamely responds that the disciples are not winos (v. 15), when he could have retorted by asking what kind of wine teaches you fluent Cappadocian. The miracle, he seems to suggest, was simply to get attention, and for this purpose any manifestation of the Spirit would have done as well. Language is not the important point.

Why this odd lack of interest in what his listeners had found so amazing? The reason, I suggest, is that the multiplicity of languages creates in the story an element of disorder, of the uncontrollable, which goes against the tenor of Peter's speech. It rests on the testimony of the many, whereas Peter offers a single testimony. He seems to imply that the words spoken by all the disciples in all the different languages were identical to the words he will now speak, which will contain the single gospel. He will give the authorized version of "God's deeds of power," which everyone previously heard about in their own languages. This, of course, raises difficult questions. How could this claim be verified? What is the point of repeating what everyone has already heard?

In both form and content the speech works to bring chaos back to unity. It is intensely monologic. It delivers a single compelling message that leads to mass repentance and baptism. It establishes Peter, among the apostles, as a single center of authority. Reading through the lens of Babel, we can see Peter rhetorically building a tower, a tower of biblical prooftexts, one on top of the other, to reach the heaven of general conviction. Enough of a gospel of chaos, an unverifiable gospel of multiple voices and multiple witnesses. Let one voice erect the true and single gospel! The opening words set the tone: *Statheis de ho Petros,* the rock standing up (v. 14)!

The content of the speech matches its monologic form. Speaking from Mount Zion, Peter employs exclusively the theology that makes this mountain the center of the world–the place where the nations will gather (e.g., Isa. 2:2–4), as the diaspora Jews have indeed gathered–and which makes Jerusalem's king (David) the king of the world (see esp. the use of Ps. 110 in Acts 2:34–35). The claims Peter puts forward for Jesus are imperialist, Davidic, ultimately Babelian claims. Just as the Babelians/Babylonians (Isa. 14:13 as well as Gen. 11) could not climb to heaven, so even the emperor David "did not ascend into the heavens" (Acts 2:34, NRSV). Jesus is the one who has climbed all the way up into heaven. God has said to him: "Sit at my right hand [in heaven], until I make your enemies your footstool."

This is Luke's main message, to be often repeated in Acts. The old imperialist dream has been baptized into Christ. We are on the road to Constantine. With the tacit help of Rome (the new Babylon) Christ will triumph. The unity of diverse peoples in the Pentecost miracle is already a reality in the *pax Romana,* and Christianity will "build" on this.

Most of the iconographic tradition of Pentecost falls in with this Petrine ideology. It tends to emphasize the vertical dimension of the miracle, the Spirit's coming *down* on the disciples. It very often makes the figure of Peter tall and central. But a different view is expressed in a Reformation picture of Babel. It shows Luther in the foreground and behind him a typical tower of Babel, which (via the understanding of the Roman Empire as the new Babylon) has now come to represent the Church of Rome!

Almost invisible in the shadow of Peter's towering rhetoric is the description of the formation of the Christian community in 2:44–47. "All who believed were together and had all things in common" (2:44, NRSV). These verses provide a very different, indeed an *alternative* sequel to Pentecost. Here, the community is not represented by a single powerful voice, but practices power-sharing. Like verses 1–13, verses 44–47 use the pronoun "they" for the community as a whole, rather than singling out particular leaders. This community grows steadily, but by example rather than by baptisms at mass meetings. Verses 1–13 and 44–47 evoke a miraculous unity in diversity in opposition to the monolithic unity of verses 14–43.

Which sequel does the Pentecost miracle "authorize"? Does it find its fulfillment in helping to prove the monolithic, universal gospel or in enabling the establishment of a sharing community that grows because of the quality of its common life? Acts 2 affirms the first answer at length, with considerable sound and fury. The second is a still, small voice. At least within this chapter, it has the last word, but its theme will be only once more repeated (4:32–37) and then dropped. If sequel one put us on the road to Constantine, on what road might sequel two have put us?

5. **We can begin to answer this question by exploring another postmodern strategy, *listening to the marginal voices*.** Voices are suppressed or marginalized both within the Bible and in biblical interpretation. When I evoked the "voice" of the laborers who did the actual building of Babel, and when I highlighted the brief account of the socialist community in Acts 2, I was listening for voices marginalized in the text. Now we turn to the interpretation or "reception" of the Bible.

The voices of some readers and interpreters of the Bible go unheard because of systems of political and social exclusion based on class, gender, race, and other lines of division.[2] But also the development of the discipline of "biblical studies" within traditional academics has silenced important voices. Writers from other fields who have not taken the course of studies that makes one a biblical scholar have, till recently, simply not been listened to when they spoke about the Bible. One of the major accomplishments of postmodern reading has been to question such boundaries. The following examples are of these two kinds of marginal voices, in reverse order.

In his book *The Parasite,* Michel Serres offers a reading of "Pentecost."[3] I can barely begin to describe the work of this extraordinary theorist, who inhabits the boundary between the humanities and the natural sciences as no one else does, and who brings the texts of ancient philosophy and religion into fruitful interchange with modern science (for example, Lucretius and fluid mechanics). The whole of *The Parasite* is an extended play on what "parasite" means in medicine, economics, and communication theory (it is the French term for "noise"), out of which Serres creates an entire theory of human development.

Capturing the sheer chaos and excitement of the scene in Acts 2:1–13 as few biblical commentators have, Serres reads Pentecost as inaugurating a "third system" of human communication. The first is that of Leibniz, in which no being communicates with another except through God as intermediary. The second is that of Hermes, in which one-way interpretations flow from an authorized interpreter (hence "hermeneutics"). The semiconductor, which allows current to pass in only one direction, stands as a symbol for this system. In the third system, that of the Paraclete, interpretations flow simultaneously in all directions. Serres makes the obvious link with the Internet. Here there is no externally imposed system of authority, but "the many regulate themselves."

---

[2]Fernando F. Segovia and Mary Ann Tolbert, eds., *Reading from This Place,* vol. 1, *Social Location and Biblical Interpretation in the United States* (Minneapolis: Fortress Press, 1995).

[3]Michel Serres, *The Parasite,* trans. Lawrence R. Schehr (Baltimore: Johns Hopkins University Press, 1982), 40–47.

What is particularly interesting is that Serres' reading completely ignores Peter's speech (which presumably would be a classic example of the hermeneutic system, with the single voice in charge of interpretation). He jumps directly from the miracle of Acts 2:1–13 to verses 44–47. What interests him is the *community* of the Paraclete system, those who "live together in the space in which the material and the logical are exchanged."

It is hard to think of two discourses more different than *The Parasite* and the World Council of Churches study guide that provides my second example.[4] In 1996 the WCC brought together in Brazil people who practice, in various ways, marginalized reading of the Bible (aboriginal and former colonial people). The study guide for the meeting was based on the Acts of the Apostles.

People like those who gathered in Brazil are caught up (as postcolonial theory teaches us) in a fundamental linguistic problem, what we might call a Babelian bind. In their local situations they usually employ and value their vernacular languages as means for maintaining cultural identity. They see European languages as a tool of colonialism and treasure the Babelian confusion of human language! But when they want to talk together about their common concerns, they have to do so in the only language they have in common, English, the most successful of all imperial languages.

The first study in the guide[5] is of Acts 2:1–13 and 42–47. Two features in particular of this study home in on issues that emerged in my postmodern reading. First, the study strikes a careful balance between unity and diversity, between instilling communal values and leaving room for individual expression. Second, it finds the appropriate sequel to the Pentecost miracle not in the imperial certainties of Peter's speech but in the sharing and growing community at the end of Acts 2. As Serres did, the study jumps right over Peter's speech. When the marginalized speak, the voice of power is silenced!

It is from this guide that I take the illustration on page 216.[6] In this medieval German painting, the Spirit comes to the disciples seated at a circular table. There is no emphasis on the vertical and no sense of leadership by one individual. And the gift the Spirit brings is the communion wafer! This accomplishes visually the direct link between Acts 2:1–13 and 44–47.

[4]World Council of Churches, *Spirit, Gospel, Cultures: Bible Studies on the Acts of the Apostles* (Geneva: WCC, 1995).
[5]Ibid., 10–14.
[6]Ibid., between pages 28 and 29.

6. Finally, postmodernism subverts the sharp division between text and interpretation. Texts are always already interpretations; interpretations are new texts to be interpreted. To turn this insistence into a reading strategy, I borrow the psychoanalytic category of *transference*. By this term I refer to the ways in which the dynamics within the text are repeated, often in uncanny ways, in its interpretation. Study of the dynamics of interpretation, conversely, often reveals unnoticed aspects of the text.

"Speaking in other tongues" readily stands as an allegory for the recent invasion of biblical studies by many new methods, methods of great and irreducible diversity. Fernando Segovia employs this allegory when he entitles an essay "'And they Began to Speak in Other Tongues': Competing Modes of Discourse in Contemporary Biblical Criticism."[7] The chapters of *The Postmodern*

[7]Segovia and Tolbert, *Reading from This Place*, 1–32.

Bible get their names from some of these "languages" that biblical scholars have begun to learn and speak ("poststructuralist," "ideological," "feminist and womanist"). A surprising variety of people tell us that they recognize these as their "own languages" (Acts 2:11).

In this allegory, Peter's speech stands for efforts to reduce methodological chaos to singleness and clarity. Just as Peter finds a single basic message in the Bible, so there are those who still hanker for a single authorized discourse of "biblical studies" (with themselves usually as the authority). Even pioneers of nontraditional methods sometimes want to cap the well. In this vein, Robert Alter and Frank Kermode specifically banish a whole range of literary methods from what they define as the proper literary study of the Bible.[8] Their exclusions mostly correspond to the chapter titles in *The Postmodern Bible!*

It is tempting to recall the very old days when the Society of Biblical Literature held most of its annual meetings at Union Theological Seminary in New York, with its "Bible tower" on the corner of Broadway and 120th Street. What a methodological scattering of the society there has been since then, what a reaching to the ends of the earth in both membership and perspective. As we see our numbers being "added to day by day" (Acts 2:47), what will be the nature of the new community of biblical studies? Are we, in a postmodern world, taking steps toward a varied, open, and sharing mode of professionalism?

---

[8]Robert Alter and Frank Kermode, eds., *The Literary Guide to the Bible* (Cambridge: Harvard University Press, 1987), 5–6.

Paul and the Remedies of Idolatry

Reading Romans 1:18–24 with Romans 7

Teresa J. Hornsby

The idea of a postmodern reading of a group of narratives, poems, and songs is hardly an innovative idea among literary critics. In fact, postmodernism is considered passé in many literary circles. But if one undertakes a reading of narratives, poems, and songs that make up one of the most authoritative and powerful texts in the Western world, and the lives of human beings depend on its interpretation, the approach is, and should be, slow and careful. The power of the Bible to influence and the authority that it commands as a result of its power cannot be denied, whether one approves of such authority or not. To my knowledge, no one has ever been beaten and hung on a cattle fence to die because of an interpretation of a Shakespearean sonnet. A postmodern reading of a biblical text may address specifically the foundations on which the authority rests. However, one of the assumptions about providing a postmodern critique of a biblical passage is that the critique would somehow seek to undermine or even deny that authority. Indeed, some postmodern interpretations do approach the biblical text in order to deconstruct it, that is, to show its internal inconsistencies in order to bring into question its worthiness to be such an influential text. But in this short piece, I propose that one can do postmodern interpretations of biblical pericopae and accept the fact of their authority whether one accepts the basis of that authority or not.

One possible way of thinking about the work of biblical interpretation is that it is not to undermine the power of scripture in the modern Western culture, but to use that power in an alternative way. A postmodern reading of scripture allows the biblical scholar to use "any means necessary" to first reveal what may be false foundations on which destructive and hateful interpretations rest, and second, to provide alternative readings that are just as arbitrary and just as constructed, but offer a positive and loving interpretation of the text.

219

As an example of the possibilities, I have chosen to reread one of the most foundational and controversial texts in the New Testament: Paul's only mention of female homoerotic behavior, Romans 1:18–24.[1] I propose that one can read this text in a way that affirms homosexuality.

This paper examines the relationship of the homoeroticism and idolatry in Romans 1:18–24 to the crucifixion and idolatry of Romans 7:3–8:3. Rather than argue that homoeroticism is perceived by Paul as punishment for idolatry, I want to suggest that one might see both homoeroticism and the crucifixion as remedies to human alienation from the Sacred; I will argue that one can read a parallel between the homoeroticism of chapter 1 and the crucifixion in chapter 7ff. By using the work of Georges Bataille, who emphasizes the chaotic, violent, and dangerous aspects of the Sacred, and using a model of the Sacred found in Near Eastern and in certain Rabbinic thought (as opposed to Hellenistic thought) I will reconsider Paul's notion of the Sacred.

Where Does God Live?

One of Paul's primary concerns in both Romans 1:18–24 and Romans 7 is idolatry. On Romans 1, Daniel Patte and Franz Leenhardt have convincingly argued that Paul understands that God may be known to an extent in God's creations. Leenhardt notes that humanity has the capacity to have knowledge of God but has refused the "real and valid knowledge which God offered them."[2] For Leenhardt, the result of human blindness to God is the inability to discern what is natural from what is perverse. Patte understands God's knowableness similarly. He writes, "What is knowable about God is manifest (or 'plain')...He makes himself known...In sum, God manifests himself in the world in such a way that any human being can clearly perceive and know him."[3] Patte and Leenhardt define idolatry as not knowing the real, the natural in God's creatures. Therefore, how can humanity know what is "natural" concerning anything else? "They corrupt the human body and human relations which were supposed to be manifestations of God's power and deity."[4] In other words, God may be known through the natural, which is a part of God's ordering of the universe, but God cannot be known in disorder and in those things that the human has rendered "unnatural." In addition to those unnatural and idolatrous images named in Romans 1:23, Patte also suggests that Paul views the Jewish understanding of Torah as idolatrous; it is the same type of misrecognition of God's presence as found in the images of chapter 1. He writes:

---

[1] It is questionable if Paul is indeed talking about homoeroticism in this passage. For the sake of argument, I will begin with the premise that he is.

[2] Franz Leenhardt, *The Epistle to the Romans* (London: Lutterworth Press, 1961), 64–65.

[3] Daniel Patte, *Paul's Faith and the Power of the Gospel* (Philadelphia: Fortress Press, 1983), 258–59.

[4] Ibid., 261–62.

This enslavement to the Law has the same effect upon the Jews' life that the enslavement to idolatry has on the pagans. The pagans follow the demands of their bodies–this part of the creation out of which they made an absolute–because they believe that in so doing they do good...Similarly, the Jews follow the demands of the Law–this revelation that they received from God and out of which they made an absolute–because they believe that in so doing they do good.[5]

The problem of human alienation from God for Paul, according to Patte, becomes one connected with the body.[6] In a near-Platonic reading, the body exists apart from the Sacred. When "the flesh" becomes mixed with the perfect revelations of God, those revelations become false. In 7:24b Paul cries, "Who will rescue me from this body of death?" His answer is, Jesus Christ: "For God has done what the law, weakened by the flesh, could not do: by sending his own Son in the likeness of sinful flesh, and to deal with sin, he condemned sin in the flesh" (8:3, NRSV). It is ironic that an image that has been rendered false by the flesh (the Torah) is remedied by another image of sinful flesh. The image offered here is one that is consistent with ideas within non-Hellenized, Near Eastern, and early Rabbinic thought.

Perhaps Paul is not responding to the problem of idolatry through a traditional Hellenistic way of thinking about the locus of the Sacred and its relationship to order. The Hellenistic or "platonic" model is only one of at least two prominent discourses in the first few centuries B.C.E. and C.E. on the relationship between the body and the spirit. According to Mary Douglas, for example, in the formation of any society, prohibitions are set up to separate the community from those things perceived to be dangerous. What is tacitly understood from Douglas is that in this system, encounter with God is elided through a human construction of order. Protection from chaos (the locus of the Sacred) lies within the confines of community and in the ability to delineate clear and distinct boundaries. The place of greatest danger lies in those areas that cannot be clearly defined. The assumption is that the safe place is the place of order, of community, and of civilization. The body, according to Douglas, signifies the community. If the body is whole, its boundaries intact, and its entrances and exits regulated, there can be such a thing as a "holy body." Conversely, in a Hellenistic way of thinking, the body (any body) represents disorder and is counter to spirit and to perfection. The unregulated or disorganized body in Douglas' model is dangerous because it allows the possibility of an encounter with the power and the danger of the Holy. The platonic body, on the other hand, can never be joined with the Sacred under any circumstance.

Various historians of religion have noted that in most mythologies of Near Eastern origin, the Sacred most often originates and remains in the realm of chaos, safely away from civilization. For example, Jonathan Z. Smith observes

---

[5]Ibid., 263.
[6]Ibid., 277.

that one of the most sacred points in many societies, including those known to us through ancient Near Eastern texts, is called the *omphalos,* or the navel. Mircea Eliade refers to this place as an Axis Mundi, or the center of the world. In myth, it is the place where the upper world joins with the lower world; it is the point of intersection between the sacred and profane. But Smith brings us back to the fact that it is called a navel nonetheless, and what is a navel but a scar? This particular symbol, the navel, is the scar "left behind when heaven and earth were forcibly [and violently] separated in creation."[7] After considering numerous creation myths from various cultures, Smith concludes that the locus of creative power is in the "disjunctive rather than conjunctive."[8] Counter to a Hellenistic understanding, which would perceive that the Sacred resides within perfect order, in some Near Eastern worldviews, those things considered Sacred occupy a place of violence and a place of disorder. An ambiguity of the locus of the Sacred surfaces, as we should suspect, in the letters of Paul, a man who is a Hellenized Jew, a Pharisee (Phil. 3:5) taught at the feet of Gamaliel (if we accept Acts 22:3), though well-educated, it seems, in Greek rhetoric and literature.[9]

Evidence of a tension in Paul's "body work" surfaces most noticeably in 1 Corinthians. With an underlying assumption that the human body is representative of one's community, Dale Martin separates two strands of conflicting body theory in 1 Corinthians.[10] One indicates an etiology in which the body is attacked by exterior agents; thus one should fortify the body (and therefore, community boundaries) against alien intrusion. The other etiology understands that the body (and the community) becomes unstable because of internal imbalances.

The former etiology is one that is quite similar to the model that Mary Douglas uses to talk about the community boundaries formed by the Levitical codes. If one assumes that the human body stands for "any bounded system," as Douglas argues, one must be extremely vigilant about what may enter and exit the body. Each break of the skin takes on new significance as it comes to symbolize a place of possible societal transgression.

Overall, Paul's understanding and use of the body and of sexuality is one that follows the Levitical model and one that occurs more often in Rabbinic writings.[11] Martin asserts that even though Paul employs both etiologies in

---

[7]Jonathan Z. Smith, "The Wobbling Pivot," *The Journal of Religion* 52 (1972): 134–49.

[8]Ibid., 145.

[9]On Paul's education, see Joseph Fitzmyer, *Romans,* The Anchor Bible 33 (New York: Doubleday, 1993), 40–42; Bruce Winter, *Philo and Paul Among the Sophists* (New York: Oxford University Press, 1997); Margaret M. Mitchell, *Paul and the Rhetoric of Reconciliation* (Tübingen: J. C. B. Mohr, 1991).

[10]Dale Martin, *The Corinthian Body* (New Haven: Yale University Press, 1995), 37.

[11]See Daniel Boyarin, *A Radical Jew: Paul and the Politics of Identity* (Berkeley: University of California Press, 1994); Boyarin, *Carnal Israel: Reading Sex in Talmudic Culture* (Berkeley: University of California Press, 1993); and Martin, *The Corinthian Body.*

1 Corinthians, Paul finds it necessary to switch models depending on the dominant social class of his audience. On the one hand, Paul seeks to build up strong barriers between the Christian community and those outside the confines of that community. But at the same time, Paul must produce a healthy Christian body by dissolving internal boundaries and by bringing the body into balance. Underlying Paul's "body work," according to Daniel Boyarin, are strong representations of the body and a positive rendering of sexual desire that parallel the models found in Rabbinic teachings, particularly the Babylonian Talmud. The Rabbinic understanding to which Boyarin refers accepts that the body and spirit are not separate and the encounter with God occurs within (rather than in opposition to) carnality.[12]

Perhaps because Paul's character is a product of both Greek and Jewish cultures, this also seems to be true about his hermeneutic on the body. Paul, as Boyarin remarks, is "not quite a platonist."[13] Paul seems to assume to some extent a body/soul split, but Paul's body is not the empty, meaningless carcass of pure platonism. He exhibits, in 1 Corinthians 15:42–50 for example, a positive comprehension of the body intermixed, as Boyarin points out, with a Hellenistic condemnation of the body.[14] Boyarin goes on to say, "This seems then to produce a moment of unresolved tension, or even incoherence in Christian platonism."[15] Boyarin recognizes this "unresolved tension" as it surfaces, for example, in the first letter to the Corinthians as Paul struggles to explain how Christians should value their bodies. Boyarin and Martin understand that Paul's ambiguity about the body is a result of his own saturation with diverse and often conflicting cultures. Paul's "body" cannot be kept entirely apart from the "spiritual," that is, the "Sacred," nor is it a body that can be wholly integrated into his community. Thus, if Paul uses the body as metaphor to talk about the relationship of a community to God, we should explore the possibility that the same influences that have shaped Paul's ideology of the body could also affect Paul's understanding of God (the Sacred).

Idolatry and the Crucifixion in Romans 7—8

Just as a tension arises in Paul's portrayal of the human body and its relationship to the Sacred, we should assume that the same tensions that erupt from Paul's writings about the body surface in Paul's perceptions of God. And they do. Paul's assertion that God was made manifest in an image of sinful flesh suggests that Paul believes that the body and the Sacred can indeed merge into one. Further, Paul's teaching that the sacrifice of that flesh was able to resolve the human alienation from the Sacred, that is, the sacrifice was able to dissolve the boundaries between the two, suggests that Paul assumes

---

[12]Boyarin, "Paul and the Genealogy of Gender," *Representations* 41 (1993): 1–33.
[13]Boyarin, *A Radical Jew*, 61.
[14]Ibid., 62.
[15]Ibid.

not only that the Sacred and the body can merge, but that the blending of the two occurs through violence and confusion.

The crucifixion, as Patte describes it, functions for Paul in much the same way as Georges Bataille describes a sacrifice: "Jesus' death plays the central and essential role of reconciling God and humankind, removing the wall which separated them."[16] There is an abundance of scholarship dedicated to sorting out how Paul thinks about the crucifixion, but here I will summarize just the dominant strands. I. Howard Marshall lists the four ways in which he sees how Jesus' death is interpreted in recent scholarship: redemption in a broad sense, redemption in a sacrificial context, in terms of justification, and in terms of reconciliation.[17] Marshall goes on to claim that even though sacrifice is scarcely mentioned, it is the most significant reading of Paul's on the crucifixion. Joseph Fitzmyer also says that Paul translates the crucifixion as an expiatory sacrifice, but he defines it in this case as a wiping away of human sin once and for all.[18] Patte sees expiation as another way of talking about justification and reconciliation. Concerning expiation, Patte writes:

> For Paul, this is an unusual way of speaking about the cross. Nonetheless, such statements can easily be understood as a theological/sacred historical explanation of his convictions which emphasize the correlation of the believers' experience with Christ's death. In the same theological/sacred historical perspective, justification is understood as the result of the reconciliation, that is, of forgiveness.[19]

Fitzmyer notes that Paul "hints" that Jesus' death was a type of sacrifice (1 Cor. 5:7; 11:24–25), but argues that Paul characteristically understood the crucifixion as a salvific event, a "wiping away of human transgressions" (cf. Rom. 4:25; Phil. 2:9–10; 1 Thess. 4:14). That Jesus' death functions as a reconciliation has been convincingly argued not only by Patte, but others as well.[20] Ultimately, I see no difference between how Christ's death operates as a sacrifice or as a reconciliation, that is, justification. Both reconcile God and humanity; both "designate the overcoming of the separation between God and humankind."[21] Paul, I think, sees in Jesus' death an act of reconciliation, of setting things in right relationship. While Patte understands that these two terms, justification and reconciliation, could be synonymous for Paul, Fitzmyer argues that they are distinct.[22] Although Fitzmyer seems to go out of his way

---

[16]Patte, *Paul's Faith*, 201.
[17]I. Howard Marshall, "The Death of Jesus in Recent New Testament Study," *Word and World* 3 (Winter 1983): 12–21.
[18]Patte, *Paul's Faith*, 205; Fitzmyer, *Romans*, 63.
[19]Patte, *Paul's Faith*, 205.
[20]Fitzmyer, *Romans*, 63. Cf. Leander Keck, "The Law of Sin and Death (Rom. 8:1–4): Reflections on the Spirit and Ethics in Paul," in *The Divine Helmsman: Studies on God's Control of Human Events, Presented to Lou H. Silberman*, ed. James L. Crenshaw and Samuel Sandmel (New York: KTAV, 1980); M. Dwaine Greene, "A Note on Romans 8:3," *Biblische Zeitschrift* 35 (1991): 103–6.
[21]Joseph Fitzmyer, *Pauline Theology* (Englewood Cliffs, N.J.: Prentice Hall, 1989), 55.
[22]Ibid., 54.

to avoid saying the word *sacrifice,* he writes, "If at times Paul seems to stress the death of Christ for human salvation without mentioning the resurrection, he does so to emphasize the cost that this experience on behalf of human beings demanded of Christ."[23] The phrase "the cost...on behalf of human beings" is, I think, just a circumlocution for the word *sacrifice.* I do not want to claim that the only way Paul understood the crucifixion was in terms of a sacrifice, but it is a valid and, in certain passages, a better reading.

One of these passages is certainly Romans 7. In Romans 7, Paul demonstrates a level of awareness concerning the interrelation of sin (transgression) and God. When Paul asks in 7:24, "Who will rescue me from this body of death?" he is also asking how to transform the lifelessness of the transgression (i.e., the tension between Law and Sin) into a relationship with God. And his answer comes in verse 25: "through Jesus Christ our Lord." The crucifixion as sacrifice is a response or remedy to idolatry, that is, the people's failure to connect with God through God's creation and through the Law. Paul, therefore, opens access to God through the sacrifice, that is, the crucifixion.[24] Through the sacrifice, boundaries between God and the human, between the sacred and the profane, are dissolved.[25]

The crucifixion for Paul comes about as a "rescue" from the alienation of idolatry. In one sense it is a physical manifestation of the sacred that occurs in order to remedy the separation of the physical and the Sacred. The crucifixion, with its fusion of flesh, spirit, and violence, arises as a consequence of not being able to let God be manifest in God's creations. Paul understands that the crucifixion has solved the problem of idolatry; God has produced an event that forever joins God, humanity, spirit, and flesh.

In Romans 1:18–24, on the other hand, the event of idolatry is countered by, according to nearly every interpretation of the passage, God's wrath and abandonment of those who are idolatrous and "unnatural." Although the conduct of the pagans in chapter 1 and of the Jews in 7–8 is the same (they are enslaved by the idols that were supposed to make God plain to them), God reacts differently, according to most interpretations. In 7:25 and 8:3, Paul writes that the crucifixion is an immediate remedy to "what the law could not do" (8:3), which is to rescue us from this body of death (7:24b). Here, Jesus' sacrifice is a direct response to the failure of the people to see God revealed in the Law, that is, according to Paul, the idolatry of the Torah. Yet in Romans 1, the direct consequence of idolatry is that God "hands them over (παρέδωκεν) to their desires (ἐπιθυμίαις)."

---

[23]Ibid.

[24]I do not think Paul is considering the resurrection here at all. For example, see also 1 Thessalonians 5:10; Galations 2:20; and especially Romans 3:24–25; 5:6, 9–10. Particularly with reference to the Romans citations, Paul clearly understands the death of Jesus as a kind of sacrifice. See Marshall above and also all essays in the section on "Reconciliation" in Robert Banks, ed., *Reconciliation and Hope: New Testament Essays on Atonement and Eschatology* (Grand Rapids: Eerdmans, 1975).

[25]Georges Bataille, *Theory of Religion* (New York: Zone Books, 1989), 43.

Event	⇒	Consequence/Remedy
Idolatry in Romans 7	⇒	Crucifixion
Idolatry in Romans 1	⇒	Homoeroticism

When Paul writes, "Therefore (διό), God handed them over," eroticism is set up as a direct consequence of idolatry, just as the crucifixion in Romans 7 is the consequence of idolatry. Since both function as direct responses to idolatrous relationships to God, it becomes necessary to examine any relationship between the homoeroticism of Romans 1 and the crucifixion in Romans 7ff.

Bernadette Brooten provides an excellent ingress into how homoeroticism functions for Paul in Romans 1. She acknowledges that first and foremost for Paul, homoeroticism is about breaking down boundaries.[26] Additionally, Brooten's in-depth encounter with past scholarship clears the way to get beyond what Paul "means," that is, to bypass the myriad arguments about Paul and homosexuality, arguments that are without the possibility of resolution: for example, did he understand homosexuality as in the modern sense, or did he mean pederasty, or something else entirely? Brooten more than adequately deals with these concerns and, as a consequence, I will move beyond her conclusions and delve into the complexities of Romans 1:18ff.

Homoeroticism in Romans

One of Brooten's primary theses in *Love Between Women* is that Paul's understanding of female eroticism in Romans 1:18–32 does not greatly differ from most writings of that era and geographical vicinity. Brooten has clearly shown that Paul's passage about homoerotic behavior cannot be explained away as merely opposing pederasty (counter to Scroggs), or explained by claiming, as Boswell does, that Paul does not condemn homosexuals engaging in homosexual acts, but heterosexuals engaging in homosexual acts.[27] Rather, Brooten works her way meticulously through classical and Hellenistic Greek literature, classical Latin literature, Greek authors of the Roman period, and postbiblical Judaism to demonstrate that Paul's main concern with homoerotic behavior was its boundary-blurring capabilities.

Precisely because of the chaotic potential of homoeroticism, Brooten suggests that it was no accident that Paul uses this example in Romans 1: "Paul's very selection of homoeroticism, in all of its boundary confusing aspects,

---

[26]I am fortunate to be writing this essay after Brooten's magnum opus on homoeroticism in early Christianity. Instead of spending time on aspects of the Roman letter that have been argued by scholars throughout the last few decades, arguments that have been summarized and critiqued by Brooten, I will merely recount some of her well-founded, soundly argued conclusions concerning the function of homoeroticism and idolatry in this text.

[27]Bernadette Brooten, *Love Between Women: Early Christian Responses to Female Homoeroticism* (Chicago: University of Chicago Press, 1996), 361. Detailed critiques of both Boswell's and Scroggs's arguments can be found in Mark D. Smith, "Ancient Bisexuality and the Interpretation of Romans 1:26–27," in *Journal of the American Academy of Religion* 64/2 (1996): 223–56.

is particularly suited to elucidate the chaos that results when people fail to observe proper religious practices."[28] Further, Brooten writes, "Homoeroticism is fundamentally about gender. Impurity applied to gender thus means that people are not maintaining clear gender polarity and complementarity."[29] In other words, homoerotic acts are perceived as uncontainable or excessive because they do not adhere to a particular sexual ethic, that is, they are not procreative; they (and some heterosexual acts) exist in the realm of pleasure only. This sexuality is effusive and breaks through the bounds of order and human control. Effusive sexuality, hetero- or homoerotic, reaches beyond the controlled and sanctioned sex of procreation into a place that cannot be controlled.

Brooten proposes that for Paul, both idolatry and homoeroticism represent a perversion of God's intention: The idols of Romans 1:23 are "impotent," lifeless copies of God's creation, and the homoeroticism of 1:24 is also "lifeless" in that it is sex beyond procreation.[30] Thus, Brooten maintains that Paul is relying on a tradition of setting up a "lifeless and impotent" sexuality as the antithesis to the Sacred.

I agree with Brooten that Paul uses homoeroticism because of its boundary-blurring potential. Brooten is right also in that Paul sees a connection between the homoeroticism of the pagans and their idolatry. But the connection may not simply be a "lifeless" response to lifeless gods. It is essential to recognize that impotence and lifelessness are distinct from each other. For example, the crucifixion for Paul may be "lifeless," but never impotent.

Further, Paul's reasons for choosing certain purity concerns (sexual ones and ones concerning idolatry) over others (food and circumcision) raise questions about his intentions. Brooten suggests that Paul avoids the issues of food and circumcision because these cause more schism within the Jewish/Gentile Christian community rather than solving already existing divisions: "[Paul] upholds sexual impurity in relation to gender differences but rejects [purity] in food issues because it divides Jews and Gentiles."[31] Thus, Paul uses homoeroticism because it blurs boundaries. But Paul's use of homoeroticism is much more complex than the maintenance of community boundaries. One could argue that Paul, on some level, recognizes a power in homoeroticism in the same way he understands the boundary-eradicating power of the crucifixion. Perhaps for Paul, homoeroticism dissolves not just the internal boundaries of community but those boundaries between God and the world as well.

Paul probably understands that same-sex intercourse blurs boundaries and puts the community in a state of impurity; he says as much in 1:24: "Therefore God handed them over in the desires of their hearts into impurity

---

[28] Brooten, *Love Between Women,* 298.
[29] Ibid., 235.
[30] Ibid., 295.
[31] Ibid., 233.

(ἀκαθαρσίαν)." But what exactly does being impure mean for Paul? Does being "unclean" mean that one is in opposition to God? If Paul is not thinking in purely platonic processes, as Martin and Boyarin suggest, then impurities, desires, blood, and so on may not necessarily be counter to the Sacred for Paul. For example, he refers to "sacrifice" as holy in Romans 12:1 as he implores the members of the Roman church to "present your bodies as a living sacrifice, holy and acceptable to God" (NRSV). In the Greek θυσίαν ζῶ'σαν ἁγίαν, it is clear that "holy" modifies "sacrifice," not "bodies." The antithetical relationship of holiness and impurity might seem clear in 1 Thessalonians 4:7: "God did not call us to impurity but in holiness" (NRSV). But the preposition ἐπί is followed by the dative, such that the verse could also read, "For God did not call us on account of impurity but in sanctification." This reading then becomes less a condemnation of impurity and even suggests that the sexual desires could be in a state of sanctification. Paul also writes that nothing in and of itself is unclean (Rom. 14:14). I am not claiming that Paul finds sexual desire to be a good thing; rather, I am arguing that one cannot claim that Paul's cosmology is firmly planted in platonic dualism and that God (or holiness) always remains apart from flesh, violence, and sex.

Paul, as we have noted, is ambiguous about how God and things associated with chaos relate. Impurities, sacrifices, and effusive sexuality all lie among disorder. In chapters 7ff. it is clear that Paul perceives the crucifixion, the sacrifice of Jesus Christ, as a bridge between humanity and the Sacred. It is also clear that Paul has various understandings of the body in his communities. It is certainly conceivable that Paul may also have various understandings about whether or not God may be found among chaos, impurities, and violence. Likewise, as we have seen in Romans 7ff., one encounters God through the corporeal and impure violence of a sacrifice. If Paul perceives in Romans 7–8 that God and human are brought together through unclean flesh, it is plausible that Paul also perceives the (unclean) sexuality of Romans 1 as remedy to the human alienation from the Sacred. The idea that the human and the Sacred may be joined through sexual and/or violent acts (as we have already seen in Paul's description of the crucifixion) is emphasized in the work of Bataille. A summary of the work in which Bataille accentuates the possibilities of drawing closer to the Sacred through disorder, filth, and/or violence should enhance our understanding of how Paul might have understood the eroticism in Romans 1.

Bataille and the Sacred

The anthropological/history-of-religions paradigm during the era of Mircea Eliade admits a primarily binary social structure of cosmos and chaos opposed.[32] In this worldview, taboos and prohibitions keep the world

---

[32]Mary Douglas, *Purity and Danger: An Analysis of Concepts of Pollution and Taboo* (Hammondworth: Penguin, 1970); Mircea Eliade, *Traité d'histoire des religions* (Paris: Payot, 1970), 15–45; Eliade, *The Sacred and the Profane: The Nature of Religion* (New York: Harcourt, Brace, 1959); Victor Turner, *The Ritual Process: Structure and Antistructure* (Chicago: Aldine, 1969).

structured by blocking out chaos and keeping hard and defined boundaries that separate order from disorder. Mary Douglas, Victor Turner, and others (following Levi-Strauss) note the danger that resides in the marginal or liminal places–those places neither "in" nor "out" and those places that provide a point vulnerable to confusion and mixing. The task of the Sacred, according to Eliade et al., is to impose order on the chaotic universe by setting up boundaries in the form of laws and taboos. If the taboos are transgressed, chaos and danger ensue. Eliade writes, "[The sacred] founds the world in the sense that it fixes the limits and establishes the order of the world."[33]

In Douglas' and Turner's work, more so than in Eliade's, one recognizes the inversion of both beneficence and danger into the Sacred. While the Sacred is desirable, it is at the same time repulsive; even as the Sacred is creative, it is also potentially fatal. The binary constructions of cosmos/chaos or civilization/ nature seek to bind up and contain the Sacred so that its danger and power may be rendered safe. However, the Sacred, as Bataille notes, defies any attempt at categorization because it is both/neither chaotic and/nor orderly; it is both/neither creative and/nor destructive. The binaries that humans propose dissolve in the proximity of a Sacred that manifests the qualities of everything and nothing. Although certain aspects of Bataille's understanding of the Sacred do not differ radically from those of Douglas and Turner, his work diverges from theirs in his particular emphasis. Bataille emphasizes the chaotic, violent, and destructive aspects of the Sacred–indeed, Bataille rarely addresses any other aspect.

Bataille forms his theory of religion on the foundation that God or all of the Sacred is found *only* among the places of chaos. He retains the binary oppositions of chaos and order, but the Sacred resides wholly within the realm of chaos, while order is a human construction; walls, both real and meta-phorical, are built to separate the human being from what is perceived to be harmful and chaotic. For Bataille, order is the feeble attempt to cordon off and restrain those things that threaten: things that are called filthy, or degenerate, or violent. While civilization constructs itself through its attempts to control the filth and violence, Bataille maintains that those things rendered filthy and degenerate and violent by "proper societies" are in fact the loci of the Sacred. By extension, Bataille asserts that the sacred lies in excess of the profane. A human being can approach the Sacred only by dissolving the boundaries that shield order from chaos. The dissolution of the (imposed) boundary occurs only through its repeated transgression. For Bataille, there are only two transgressions that allow one to approach the Sacred: the act of sacrifice and participation in effusive sex acts, that is, sex that moves beyond procreation, beyond what is "necessary" or "normal."

---

[33]Eliade, *The Sacred and the Profane*, 30.

The most important point of similitude between sacrifice and effusive sex, according to Bataille, is the quality of excess. The excess becomes manifest in both as each rejects categorization and spills over all attempts at containment. Effusive sex, for example, holds both life and death within itself: the erotic is "specifically the point of tension between the animal body [nature] and the civilized body [culture]."[34] Because it occupies a liminal place between nature and culture, according to Bataille, the erotic cannot be a part of that faction that maintains structure and order; it is "a revolt, a refusal of the proposed condition."[35] Bataille argues that "paradise is momentarily recovered and we merge into our surroundings as we interpenetrate with each other's bodies and so any distinction between nature and culture vanishes."[36] In the sacrifice, these distinctions vanish as well.

The thing sacrificed is profane; it exists only in the mundane. Through its sacrifice, its "thingness" disappears and it is "drawn out of the world of utility" into one of "unintelligible caprice."[37] And all those who sacrifice benefit, according to Bataille, because they become connected to "the sovereign world of the gods and myths, to the world of violent and uncalculated generosity... I withdraw you, victim, from the world in which you were and could only be reduced to the condition of a thing...I call you back to the intimacy of the divine world, of the profound immanence of all that is."[38]

In sum, Bataille seems to understand taboos and prohibitions as attempts to set up strict definitions between the world and the Sacred. In order to encounter the Sacred, to dissolve any separation between the human and God, boundaries, laws, taboos, and so on must be transgressed. But the primary distinction between Bataille and others lies in whether one values or condemns that chaotic place: the place of impurity and uncleanness. For Bataille, the chaotic violence we encounter when we defy boundaries is Sacred. Every human, Bataille argues, has an absolute propensity to break the bounds, to transgress. This transgression spends the self beyond all boundaries, and thus exceeds the self to communicate with the sacred, which is being beyond limits. Ritual sacrifice and sexual excess are the two most significant indications of this urge to break away from the mundane toward the Sacred, according to Bataille. By violating the interdiction, the ritualized transgression dissolves the boundaries between God and creation and fills the gaps so that the former distinctions evaporate.[39] With the categories of eroticism and sacrifice in mind, I return to the eroticism of Romans 1 and the sacrifice of Romans 7.

---

[34] Paul Smith, "Bataille's Erotic Writings and the Return of the Subject," in *On Bataille,* ed. Leslie Anne Boldt-Irons (Albany: State University of New York Press, 1995), 233.

[35] Bataille, "L'histoire de l'érotisme," in *Oeuvres Completes* 8 (Paris, 1976), trans. and quoted in Boldt-Irons, *on Bataille,* 234.

[36] Michael Richardson, *Georges Bataille* (London: Routledge, 1994), 104.

[37] Bataille, *Theory of Religion,* 43.

[38] Ibid., 44.

[39] Mark C. Taylor's chapter on Bataille in *Altarity* (Chicago: Chicago University Press, 1987), 115–48, is especially helpful for understanding Bataille's theories of the sacred, transgression, taboo, and sacrifice.

In Romans 7 and 8, Paul claims that through the death of Jesus, God is completely revealed to human beings. Paul evokes a sacrificial image of the crucifixion to remedy an alienation between the Sacred and the world of the human. Through the violent and filthy sacrifice, or at least through its invocation in his text as a response to idolatry, Paul sets up a way in which the Sacred and flesh are forever joined. In Romans 1:18–23, Paul tells us that humans neglected to see God in God's creations but, rather, chose to seek out the Sacred in their own creations that were lifeless copies of God's creatures. Thus, it was human agency that denied a sacred presence to God's creatures. In 24–32, Paul again uses images and language that are evocative of excess and of impurity; the images of "unnatural passions" and their power of boundary-dissolution erase all distinction between the human and God, according to Bataille.

Because humans could not comprehend God in creation, they are given over to the desire of their bodies. Through eroticism and through sacrifice, the categories of Bataille and of Paul, the Sacred may indeed be made known. The Sacred can be encountered by dissolving the boundaries that shield the rest of the world. The separation is diffused by physicality and sex that moves beyond procreation into ecstatic pleasure, such as the homoeroticism suggested in Romans 1:24–27, or by the sacrifice that joins the Creator with the creation, the crucifixion (7:25; 8:3). Paul understands that the idolatry of the pagans in chapter 1 and the Torah of the Jews in chapter 7 function in the same way: Both are set up as signifiers for God but neither is powerful enough to dissolve the boundaries in order to approach the Sacred. Thus, the eroticism functions just as the crucifixion; both images are invoked to repair the estrangement of God from the world.

What I propose then, is that the homoeroticism Paul infuses into the text parallels the crucifixion; just as the crucifixion reconciles humans who transgress the Law, the homoeroticism of chapter 1 reconciles those who have failed to approach the Sacred otherwise. As Brooten argues, Paul sees homoeroticism as bringing about impurity and chaos. But if we can understand that God resides within the impurity and is a part of the chaos, we can understand how the eroticism actually works here for Paul: Just as God allows the crucifixion to occur, God allows the pagans to let themselves be consumed with passion for one another. Through excessive sex, sex beyond procreative purposes, we break through the constraints of culture and become dangerous, transgressive, and unclean. As dirty and chaotic bodies, we finally encounter God. Paul brings both of Bataille's categories, eroticism and sacrifice, powerfully into play. Just by uttering the language of boundary dissolution, he invokes a power from the text that was not present before. It is a power that works through the erotic and through the nature of "things" to dissolve the boundaries between the world and the Sacred. Thus, he opens, in an unlimited way, the potential for communication with God without mediation.

In this discussion of the complex relationship of eroticism, the crucifixion, and idolatry, I have suggested that Romans 1:18–24, when read with Romans

7:3–8:3, exposes a tension in Pauline thought. While Paul struggles to maintain order within the Roman community, he also draws on a tradition that sought to reconcile God with those who do not or could not know him. Paul's awareness of a tradition that recognizes a corporeal and often chaotic relationship with God surfaces in his appeal to the crucifixion and his explanation for homoeroticism. Eroticism and the sacrifice are traditionally aligned with chaos, death, and violence, but these things are also sacred. Most interpreters of Paul see only a Hellenistic Paul; they have removed the divinity from the violent and chaotic and have made the Christian God one-dimensional. Thus, everything has the potential of being idolatrous, impotent, and other. The implications of this schism between the Creator and the creation are manifested in destruction that occurs only when people and objects are perceived as "things," devoid of God, and completely other. An alternative way of reading Romans 1:18–24 understands that God allows humans to be consumed with their passions so that they might find God in that sacred place of filth, of chaos, and of powerful lifelessness.

Inside Jokes

Community and Authority in the Corinthian Correspondence

Sandra Hack Polaski

The Corinthian correspondence, the New Testament's most intimate portrayal of the relationship of a missionary with the congregation he founded, describes a complex, dynamic, and shifting relationship, as Paul addresses various concerns and negotiates shifting alliances. These texts are polemical, written to correct the errors into which the members of the Corinthian church have been led by certain persons professing to preach the same gospel as Paul does—but who, according to Paul, have misled the congregation. Closer examination of the texts, though, reveals that the identification of these parties and their views is not easy. Indeed, the more we seek to look *through* these texts to describe with (presumed) historical objectivity the situation that gave rise to them, the more these texts, as texts, demand our attention. Events described in these letters are presented not only from the partial perspective of a single actor but also from a perspective that is highly ideologically loaded, as Paul tries to persuade the Corinthians to adopt his perspective. Attention to the interplay of ideology and rhetoric, as these shape the dynamics of community formation and authority structures, reveals a text that constructs rather than reflects a social fabric. Paul's description of events in Corinth, his repetition of the Corinthians' words, his appeals to mutually recognized texts and traditions, and his enigmatic description of the opponents function rhetorically to create community identity between Paul and the Corinthians and among the members of the Corinthian congregation.[1]

---

[1] It should be noted that though I speak of the "rhetorical" nature of these texts and recognize the importance of the systematic study of Greco-Roman rhetoric to the understanding of the impact of these texts on their first audience, I will not deal in detail with Greco-Roman rhetorical categories and terminology in this essay. For such resources, see, for example, Ben Witherington, *Conflict and Community in Corinth: A Socio-Rhetorical Commentary on 1 and 2 Corinthians* (Grand Rapids: Eerdmans, 1995), especially the bibliography cited on pp. 55–61. Witherington's approach differs from mine in that his focus on historical method leads him to reject understandings of rhetoric that do not derive from Greco-Roman models (see esp. pp. 57–58), while my interest in the literary function of the texts admits a wider variety of rhetorical models.

Situational References in Corinthians

The Corinthian correspondence is replete with references to the situation in Corinth and the relationship between Paul and the congregation there. Scholarship has generally read these as statements of fact, hard evidence for the Corinthian situation, and used them in attempts to reconstruct the history of the Corinthian church and the chronology of Paul's relationship with it. Yet the means by which Paul comes to have this information about the Corinthians and their behavior, the nature of his knowledge, and the factors that shape his presentation are not as transparent as scholars have commonly assumed. Attention to Paul's perspective, biases, and point of view encourages us to inquire into Paul's presuppositions regarding the Corinthian situation, the nature of the information he has received, and the direction of his agenda for the Corinthian church. All of these contribute to Paul's choice of wording in the Corinthian letters, particularly when they bear on the history of the Corinthian congregation or the experiences and beliefs Paul and the Corinthians share in common. If we read these texts with an eye toward the intertextual connections they create, we see that these various references are threads in a complex fabric that connects Paul with his Corinthian community.

What Paul Knows

Frequently Paul makes reference to events that have taken place in the Corinthian community in his absence, subtly asserting his right to oversee the congregation and implying, in good Panoptical fashion, that he knows even more than he lets on.[2] Paul claims that some of the oversight is invited, at least by those members of the community who have written to Paul (e.g., 1 Cor. 7:1). Paul's indefinite, second-person plural references, though, while making it clear that Paul does not think all his readers fit the categories he describes, invite readers to wear the shoe if it fits. Just after describing the Corinthians as "my beloved children" (1 Cor. 4:14), he warns that "some" have become arrogant in his absence (4:18) and promises discipline when he arrives for those who will not "imitate" their "father" (4:15–16). Arrogance among "you" (pl.) is also an issue regarding the member living with his father's wife (5:1ff.); Paul moves swiftly from the passive construction "it is reported" (lit. "it is heard") to a pronouncement of judgment that implies that he understands the situation clearly and intimately.[3] Our knowledge of Corinthian legal practices comes from research on the court systems of the Roman Empire, certainly not from the description Paul gives in 1 Corinthians 6; still, because

---

[2]See Michel Foucault, *Discipline and Punish: The Birth of the Prison,* trans. Alan Sheridan (New York: Pantheon, 1977), esp. 195–228. Foucault utilizes Jeremy Bentham's notion of the Panopticon, a prison designed so that a single guard can view any individual prisoner at any time, and prisoners have no way of knowing when or whether they are being watched.

[3]Commentators note that the precise situation is not clear to us, whether the father had died or divorced the stepmother, but agree that "the Corinthians of course knew the particulars of the matter" (Richard Hays, *First Corinthians,* Interpretation [Louisville: John Knox Press, 1997], 81). Paul's knowledge of the "particulars" is likewise generally assumed.

he speaks authoritatively on these practices, we as readers simply assume that Paul knows exactly what has been happening. Paul "hears" that there are divisions in the church regarding the Lord's Supper (11:18). Paul's responses to these reports, however, leave no room to question whether he has "heard" correctly or whether he has the authority to speak concerning these matters.

Frequently in the Corinthian correspondence, Paul does not mention the source of his information when he addresses a situation in Corinth–a practice that strengthens the reader's impression of Paul's (near-)omniscience. He addresses such matters as believers taking one another to court (1 Cor. 6:1ff.), women praying and prophesying with uncovered heads (11:4ff.), and so forth, without indicating how he got his information and with the implication that he is fully and accurately informed on every matter that affects the Corinthian church. The historical questions such statements raise have to do with the identity of messengers between Corinth and Paul; the rhetorical effect of such statements is to bolster Paul's authority by enhancing the impression of his knowledge. In a context in which "knowledge" (γνῶσις) (1 Cor. 8:1ff.) and "wisdom" (σοφία) (1 Cor. 1:17ff.) are at the center of the dispute, Paul overtly disclaims "wisdom" (1:17) but subtly bolsters his authority by demonstrating just how much he knows.

Not only does Paul know what has been happening in Corinth in his absence, he also appears to know exactly what the Corinthians have been saying. Again, some of these quotations are supplied, apparently, by a text to which Paul has access: "Now concerning the things about which you wrote..." (1 Cor. 7:1; cf. 8:1, 10:23). Sometimes the speech is transmitted to Paul by report: "For it has been reported to me concerning you, my brothers [and sisters], by Chloe's people that there are quarrels among you. I mean this, that each of you says, 'I am Paul's,' or 'I am Apollos's,' or 'I am Cephas's,' or 'I am Christ's'" (1 Cor. 1:11–12).[4] Other quotations, however, imply Paul's ability to overhear: "How can some of you say that there is no resurrection of the dead?" (1 Cor. 15:12). Paul not only knows what the Corinthians are saying, but under what influence they say it: "No one speaking by the Spirit of God ever says, 'Let Jesus be cursed!' and no one can say 'Jesus is Lord' except by the Holy Spirit" (1 Cor. 12:3, NRSV). He even knows what his opponents are saying about him, namely: "His letters are weighty and strong, but his bodily presence is weak, and his speech contemptible" (2 Cor. 10:10, NRSV).

The presence of so many clear quotations in the Corinthian correspondence has led scholars to consider whether Paul is also quoting the Corinthians even where the text does not indicate so as clearly. When Paul says, in 1 Corinthians 4:8, "Already you are filled! Already you have become rich! Apart from us you have become kings!" is this merely sarcastic language, or is Paul using terminology that the Corinthians have already used and turning

[4]The literature on the identity of the "parties" in 1 Corinthians, and whether there was in fact a "Christ party," is extensive: see, for example, the excursus and bibliographic references in Hans Conzelmann, *1 Corinthians,* Hermeneia (Philadelphia: Fortress Press, 1975), 33–34; and the discussion in James D. G. Dunn, *1 Corinthians,* New Testament Guides (Sheffield: Sheffield Academic Press, 1995), 31–34.

it on them?[5] Some commentators have suggested that 1 Corinthians 14:34–36, the requirement of women's silence, is neither Paul's view nor a later interpolation, but a quotation of a perspective in the Corinthian church that Paul then refutes.[6] Although we may not be able to isolate every instance of Paul's use of terminology and phrases originally from the Corinthians, it seems likely that Paul does quote the Corinthians more often than he indicates formally; such quotations reinforce the illusion that Paul is present with his Corinthian congregation.

Paul also seems to know what the Corinthians have been saying about him and answers their accusations. Although these statements are not so clearly tagged in the text as some of the statements reported to Paul, they may be yet more important markers of Paul's relationship with the community, since they suggest Paul's ability to monitor the ideas of those who disagree with him. In 1 Corinthians 9:3 he announces his "defense to those who examine me," citing rights to companionship and financial support—although these are the very "rights" of which Paul says he has chosen not to make use for the Corinthians' sake (and apparently which lie at the root of some of Paul's conflict with members of the Corinthian church). The more polemic 2 Corinthians suggests that Paul is responding to accusations regarding his reliability (2 Cor. 1:17), his mental stability (5:13), his ministerial trustworthiness (7:2), and his financial scruples (8:20). In the bitterly sarcastic last section of 2 Corinthians (chaps. 10–13), Paul pretends to acknowledge his opponents' arguments: "even if I am unskilled in speech" (11:6); "but being crafty, I took you in by deceit" (12:16). The cumulative effect of these quotations of his opponents is an impression that Paul has an uncanny knowledge of the Corinthians' thoughts.

"If Someone Comes and Proclaims Another Jesus..."

It is also important to note the indirect, but highly allusive, ways that Paul refers to his opponents. Paul is arguing against other points of view in both 1 and 2 Corinthians; but in 2 Corinthians in particular, and most especially in 2 Corinthians 10–13, it is interesting to note how Paul speaks of those who oppose him. Paul is careful to describe his opponents in his own terms rather than theirs—a time-honored political strategy.[7] There are hints that allow us to sleuth out the controversies that stand behind Paul's references: When Paul refers in 2 Corinthians 2:17 to "peddlers of the word of God," he is likely

---

[5]The phrases recall Stoic and Cynic philosophical claims; see discussions in Conzelmann, 87–88; Hays, 70; Richard A. Horsley, *1 Corinthians,* Abingdon New Testament Commentaries (Nashville: Abingdon Press, 1998), 69.

[6]See Charles H. Talbert, *Reading Corinthians: A Literary and Theological Commentary on 1 and 2 Corinthians* (New York: Crossroad, 1987), 93; David W. Odell-Scott, "Let the Women Speak in Church: An Egalitarian Interpretation of 1 Cor. 14:33b–36," *Biblical Theology Bulletin* 13 (1983): 90–93.

[7]Dieter Georgi, in his classic study *The Opponents of Paul in Second Corinthians* (Philadelphia: Fortress Press, 1986), argues that Paul's opponents' self-designations can be simply extracted from what Paul says about them, either directly or ironically (27). The present study takes a very different point of view, namely, that Paul reveals only selected bits of information about his opponents, pieces chosen to present them in a partial and unflattering light.

referring not only to the sincerity with which he claims to proclaim the message, but also to the crisis (alluded to elsewhere) caused by his refusal to accept payment from the Corinthians. When he speaks of "those who commend themselves" and "compare themselves with one another" (10:12), the context suggests that Paul considers Corinth his missionary "territory" and the other preachers interlopers in his region. Apparently the credentials the other preachers claim have to do with Hebrew heritage:

> But whatever anyone dares to boast of–I am speaking as a fool–I also dare to boast of that. Are they Hebrews? So am I. Are they Israelites? So am I. Are they descendants of Abraham? So am I. (2 Cor. 11:21–22, NRSV)

Historically speaking, it is not altogether clear what distinction is intended between "Hebrews," "Israelites," and "descendants of Abraham" in this text. Rhetorically, though, it is important that Paul claims *all* these categories, refuting the claims to superiority apparently being made by others.

Often, though, Paul's references to his opponents are famously vague. In 2 Corinthians 2:2–10 and 7:12 we learn that a member of the Corinthian church has wronged another, that Paul has urged discipline, and that the church has carried out that discipline. The gravity Paul seems to assign to the incident, and the fact that he refers to it more than once, suggests that it was a serious issue; yet we know nothing more about what happened, or if the wrong was against Paul directly, perhaps an attempt to supplant his place in the Corinthian congregation, or against another member or group with whom Paul sides. This manner of discussing the incident makes it possible for Paul to speak of it at some length without bringing up the messy details of the actual controversy, which might encourage consideration of the merits of the other side of the debate.

Shared Traditions

The Corinthian correspondence is also replete with intertextual references of the ordinary sort, that is, written texts and verbal traditions that Paul and the Corinthians presumably shared in common. The indices of the ABS Greek New Testament list twenty-seven quotations of the Hebrew Bible in 1 and 2 Corinthians, as well as more than 125 allusions and verbal parallels.[8] Sometimes these quotations lead into highly original exegesis, as with the experience of the wilderness ancestors ("they drank from the spiritual rock that followed them, and the rock was Christ," 1 Cor. 10:4, NRSV) or the veil of Moses (2 Cor. 3:7–16) that hid not the brilliance of divine glory, but its fading. Although it is no longer widely held that 1 Corinthians 13 is a preexisting hymn borrowed by Paul for his argument,[9] its elevated and elegant

---

[8]4th revised edition, ed. Barbara Aland et al. (Stuttgart: United Bible Societies/Deutsche Bibelgesellschaft, 1983, 1994).

[9]See Margaret M. Mitchell, *Paul and the Rhetoric of Reconciliation: An Exegetical Investigation of the Language and Composition of 1 Corinthians* (Louisville: Westminster/John Knox Press, 1991), 272, n. 483.

style almost certainly incorporates phrases and images that would have been familiar to the Corinthian congregation. Paul cites Jesus' words (1 Cor. 7:1) and example (11:1) as authoritative. The existence of these clear instances of intertextuality should cause us to inquire further how Paul uses shared language to foster a sense of community with the recipients of his letters and interprets shared traditions so as to emphasize his role as the community's signal interpreter.

Clearly, Paul is concerned to show that he and the Corinthian congregation stand in the same tradition. He also takes care to let his Corinthian readers know that he understands the details of goings-on among them, sometimes by citing quite specific details, sometimes by allusive language, the epistolary equivalent of a wink and a nod and a "You and I both know..." Again and again we, as modern readers, find ourselves frustrated by our lack of historical knowledge that, we feel sure, would illuminate Paul's precise but unclear statements. This strangeness is a clue to us to suspect that more is going on in Paul's references to the Corinthian situation than we, as "outsiders," are able to discern.

The "Inside Joke"

In *Lake Wobegon Days,* storyteller Garrison Keillor describes the predicament of a man who, having married a Lake Wobegon woman, is spending Thanksgiving with her family:

> At the in-laws', Bill felt as if he had walked into the wrong class, medieval history instead of civics which he had studied for, and everyone but him knew the right answers. Names, dates, stories of which they only used the punch line ("I didn't know that was your horse!" "*Svensk*"), obscure references. If his wife had been offered a brandy, she'd say, "Just up to the first bird," referring to a childhood tumbler with four painted chickens down the side. *The whole town is like this,* he thought. *A cult.*[10]

In Keillor's story, Bill's strong sense of outsider status, which he describes in religious terms *("A cult"),* is created not only by the existence of a set of community intertexts but by the inscrutability of those intertexts and the fact that everyone else *does* "know the answers." Not only the existence but also, and importantly, the inscrutability of the intertextual references reinforces the perception of community boundaries for one who lacks knowledge of the "right answers."

Bill's wife, Barbara Ann, on the other hand, knows the right answers without recognizing that there are questions:

> Everything in the kitchen was the same except the mixer was moved to the counter by the stove. Barbara Ann found, to her not very great surprise, that she knew it by heart; she got the colander out and rinsed

---

[10]Garrison Keillor, *Lake Wobegon Days* (New York: Viking, 1985), 215.

strawberries; the meat platter was on top of the fridge, the gravy boat down behind the cereal, the sieve was nesting in the mixing bowls.[11]

The kitchen layout, even the out-of-the-way storage places for rarely used serving pieces, is a text she knows by heart, and that she hardly notices that she is being called on to recite.

The contrast Keillor depicts illustrates the community-reinforcing function of shared information, from intimate knowledge of a certain space to obscure names and dates to inside jokes, referenced only by their punch lines. Indeed, the notion of the "inside joke" is a useful one to consider how intertextuality shapes and reinforces community identity.

What, then, is an "inside joke"? First, it is important to acknowledge that the inside joke may or may not actually be funny. Indeed, Keillor's designation of "stories" may be a more accurate one, except that such stories generally have a jokelike "punch line" or "tag line" by which they are referenced by those who know the story. Even if the original story is not a particularly funny one, though, the mention of the punch line or tag line often raises a laugh or at least a knowing smile from those who understand it–a response created less by amusement at the story than by the sheer pleasurable sense of understanding (and, perhaps, gladness at being part of the group to which the inside joke belongs). Sometimes an inside joke may not even be noticeable to the outsider. Obviously, such references do not function to demarcate community boundaries, but they are very effective in reinforcing community identity for insiders, since not only the joke's esoteric meaning but the very existence of an esoteric meaning is an insider's secret. The best inside jokes–"best" meaning those that most effectively reinforce community identity–are those whose meaning can least likely be guessed by someone outside the community, precisely because they call to mind more of the community's shared story.[12] Thus, an enigmatic or innocuous statement, from the outsider's perspective, may not only be particularly meaningful from the viewpoint of the community member, but it may also function to remind the community member that he or she "belongs," to make that individual "feel at home," and thus, implicitly, to encourage the member to agree with or acquiesce to what is being said or directed, since it comes from "one of us."

The Inside Joke and Community Identity in Corinthians

The evidence of the Corinthian correspondence suggests that precisely this sort of insider rhetoric, some of which is strange to, or completely overlooked by, modern readers, is at work in these texts. Who ever said,

---

[11]Ibid.

[12]In a debate preceding the 1994 Florida gubernatorial election, Republican candidate Jeb Bush answered a question in Spanish to show his solidarity with Florida's Spanish-speaking community. Democratic candidate Lawton Chiles replied, "Well, you may speak Spanish, but I speak Cracker, and let me tell you, the he-coon walks just before dawn." Bush was clearly baffled; Chiles won the election largely by carrying the Panhandle region, heavy in native Floridians who recognized Chiles as one of their own.

"Jesus be cursed!" (1 Cor. 12:3)? Where, and in what context? While some argue that this is a hypothetical example,[13] I suggest that it is much more likely the "tag line" that references a story known to the Corinthians—perhaps a single occurrence, but also likely a series of incidents or a long-running debate, the convoluted narrative of which the community recalls from the tag line, so that Paul's use of the phrase enmeshes his teachings into the community's ongoing life.

In 1 Corinthians 11:10, Paul advises that women praying or prophesying should do so with covered heads "because of the angels" or "messengers" (διὰ τοὺς ἀγγέλους). This odd, enigmatic statement is virtually overlooked by many interpreters, and those who tackle it must go beyond the surface evidence of the text to shape a satisfactory explanation.[14] Yet it is highly unlikely that the meaning of this phrase, whatever it may have been, was lost on the Corinthians. Rather, it is possible that the Corinthians' "insider" understanding of the role of the ἀγγέλοι made Paul's oblique reference all the more persuasive, since it would have raised a knowing smile of agreement within the congregation.

Clearly these examples could be multiplied ad infinitum, particularly since there may be references that have particular meaning only for those knowledgeable to recognize it. Just as clearly, it is impossible to prove that any particular Pauline phrase is, in fact, an example of insider rhetoric. The preponderance of the evidence, though, argues that the search for "inside jokes" is at least on the right track. Paul clearly has a good deal of information about the Corinthian community and is at pains to communicate that he understands their situation. He is concerned to represent himself as one of them, not an interloper. He recalls their shared history. He seeks to ground his authority for the instructions he gives them. And in so doing, he frequently writes statements that are difficult for "outsider" readers to interpret.[15] All suggests the strong likelihood that Paul is, indeed, employing the rhetorical tool of insider rhetoric or the "inside joke" to reinforce his place and standing within the Corinthian community.

We, the Outsiders

From this perspective, then, the inability of historical critics to nail down references to events in the Corinthian correspondence is not simply a function of Paul's single-mindedness or writing style. Rather, the letters function more effectively, rhetorically, precisely because they are laced with "inside jokes," references to people and situations that were understandable only within the community to which they were written. Yet this observation should be taken as more than just a statement about the limits, weaknesses, or lacunae of the

---

[13]Cf. Conzelmann, 204–5.

[14]See the careful and wide-ranging study of Dale Martin, *The Corinthian Body* (New Haven: Yale University Press, 1995), esp. chap. 9, "Prophylactic Veils."

[15]As evidenced, for example, by the seemingly never-ending flood of monographs on the Corinthian correspondence.

historical-critical method of New Testament study. Indeed, for all this essay's references to "Paul" and "the Corinthians" as if they were living, flesh-and-blood people, it is important to recognize that they exist for us as characters in a text, an "implied author" and "implied readers" whose relationship to the "real author" and "historical audience" is impossible to precisely ascertain.

Quite apart from historical speculation, though, we can investigate the Corinthian correspondence as documents that explore the relationship of ideology, authority, and community identity, particularly in light of the relative lack of more formal authority structures. Paul's churches apparently have in common a lack of the ecclesiastical structures that developed in the later church, and the congregation at Corinth is, if anything, more "charismatic" than most. Yet Paul, who is not even able to be present with the Corinthians regularly or predictably, nonetheless seeks to direct certain aspects of their congregational life and belief by creating an epistolary presence, a cozy sense of shared history and shared ideology.

Perhaps it is, after all, Paul's best shot, since we hear that "his letters are weighty and strong, but his bodily presence is weak, and his speech contemptible" (2 Cor. 10:10, NRSV). Yet it is also interesting to note that Paul's efforts to bolster his authority by the rhetoric of community identity compete, at Corinth, with other means of establishing authority. Various members, apparently, possess impressive spiritual gifts, though Paul tries to corral these charismatic leaders by alternately channeling the exercise of their gifts and claiming to "speak in tongues more than all of you" (1 Cor. 14:18, NRSV). Too, while the ecclesiastical hierarchy of later years may not yet be in place, the routinization of charisma[16] has already begun to set in, at least to the extent that some individuals request, and other individuals write, letters of recommendation, which some see as necessary for recognizing true prophets (2 Cor. 3:1; cf. 3 Jn. 12). The firestorm begun by Paul's refusal to accept payment from the Corinthians (1 Cor. 9:12, 15) suggests that there existed a notion of the authority of the paid expert.[17] Paul's self-definition of his authority, then, competes with other models of authority for the Corinthians' allegiance. The Corinthian correspondence in the New Testament documents that struggle.

[16]The phrase comes, of course, from sociologist Max Weber.
[17]A similar psychology seems to be in place today with the phenomenon of the modern corporate consultant.

Paul's Riposte to Fr. Rodrigues

Conceptions of Martyrdom in Philippians and Endo's Silence

Stephen Fowl

In his 1930 commentary on Philippians, Ernst Lohmeyer read the entire epistle in terms of the theme of martyrdom.[1] That is, in writing Philippians, Paul was writing a manual of martyrdom. There are numerous reasons for modern scholarship's comprehensive rejection of Lohmeyer's account. The most obvious are found in Lohmeyer's rather heavy-handed attempts to find references to martyrdom under every exegetical stone. As a result, very few contemporary commentators are willing to find any consideration of martyrdom in Philippians. This position is further solidified when one compares Philippians with second- and third-century martyrological texts. Philippians is very different. Nevertheless, in Philippians, Paul pays rather persistent attention to his own disposition toward his imprisonment, trial, and possible death (1:12–26; 2:17). He is concerned that the Philippians manifest a common life worthy of the gospel of Christ in the face of opposition. He goes so far as to say that he and the Philippians have been granted the chance not only to believe in Christ but to suffer for his sake (1:29). Paul presents the story of Christ in terms that are very similar to the suffering servant of Isaiah (2:6–11), and he desires to know "the power of [Christ's] resurrection, the fellowship of his sufferings and to be conformed to his death" (3:10).

If it is the case that Philippians is not explicitly a manual of martyrdom, I think one can claim that one of the aims of the epistle is to display and help form habits of perception, attention, and action necessary for life as a faithful Christian in a world hostile to Christianity. If this is right, it is also fair to claim that such habits are those necessary for forming people to be martyrs. This is because being a martyr is not an end in itself; steadfast obedience and fidelity

---

[1]Ernst Lohmeyer, *Die Briefe and die Philipper, an die Kolosser, und an Philemon* (Göttingen: Vandenhoeck and Ruprecht, 1930).

243

are appropriate ends of Christian living. Whether or not faithful Christians become martyrs is, in large part, out of their hands. It depends on the acts and responses of a hostile world. Hence, while Lohmeyer might be wrong in thinking Philippians is directly about martyrdom, he was on the right track to the extent that Philippians is about the habits and dispositions needed to be a people capable of offering their lives back to God in the face of intense hostility.

Given this perspective on Philippians, I would like to put Paul's approach to martyrdom (or, at least its possibility) into an intertextual conversation with Shusaku Endo's novel *Silence*.[2] Endo sets his novel in seventeenth-century Japan during a time of state-sponsored persecution of Christians. After Saint Francis Xavier, S.J., brought Christianity to Japan in 1549, there was a period of fairly rapid growth. Within thirty years there was a flourishing community of 150,000 Japanese Catholic Christians within a politically fragmented Japan.[3]

As the sixteenth century ended, however, power in Japan became increasingly centralized. At first, the Portuguese Jesuits enjoyed access to the halls of power. This was in part due to Japanese desire for increased silk trade with the Portuguese colony of Macao. As time passed, however, the Japanese ruling class became increasingly suspicious of the Jesuit missionaries. This suspicion was partly fueled by the arrival of English and Dutch (Protestant) traders who spoke ill of the missionaries. In addition, the rulers noted that the Japanese Christians had a much stronger allegiance to their priests than they had to the newly forming central government. In 1614, an edict expelling the foreign missionaries from Japan was issued. At this time there were about 300,000 Christians in Japan out of a population of 20 million.

In light of the expulsion order, missionary activity went underground. The order also signaled a period of direct persecution. Between 1614 and 1640, some 5,000 to 6,000 Christians were killed by the state in Japan. Public execution of Christians (usually by burning), as Tertullian noted, simply led to the growth of the church. Frustrated by this result, the Japanese rulers shifted their focus. Understanding that persecution and martyrdom was much less a threat to the church than apostasy, they instituted sustained periods of torture, designed to produce apostasy prior to execution. The most effective form was called "ana-tsurushi" or "the pit." In this torture, the victim was suspended upside down in a pit of excrement. To prolong survival and increase pain, a small slit was cut in the victim's forehead.

It was in such a pit that in 1632, the Portuguese Jesuit Provincial, Christovao Ferreira, leader of the now-underground mission in Japan, became the first apostate among the missionaries. This historical event becomes the impetus for Endo's fictional Jesuit, Sebastian Rodrigues, and two of his brother Jesuits to leave Portugal and to try to enter Japan. Ferreira had been their teacher

---

[2]Shusaku Endo, *Silence*, trans. and intro. William Johnston (New York: Taplinger Publishing, 1980).

[3]For the following historical background I am indebted to William Johnston's preface to his translation of *Silence*.

and friend. His apostasy shook them deeply. They journey to Japan to find out the truth about Ferreira and attempt to atone for his apostasy through their own martyrdom. As he departs Portugal, Rodrigues is filled with zeal, passion, and courage.

Endo leads us, with Rodrigues and his fellow Jesuits, through the difficult journey to Macao. After some time in Macao it becomes clear that one of the Jesuits, Juan de Santa Marta, is too sick to continue. After convincing their superior in Macao, Fr. Valignano, to let them try to enter Japan, Rodrigues and his other companion, Garrpe, are smuggled into Japan. There they are received and hidden near Tomogi, a small village of Japanese Christians. From their hiding place in the hills above Tomogi, Rodrigues and Garrpe witness the execution of two of the villagers for aiding them. To Rodrigues, there is nothing glorious about this martyrdom. While the martyrs cry out in agony, God remains silent. In his subsequent wanderings about the Japanese countryside Rodrigues is plagued by doubts. He worries that his own desire to atone for Ferreira's apostasy has put Japanese peasants at risk and even cost some of them their lives. Interestingly, Rodrigues never questions whether one can atone for the apostasy of another. Moreover, even if the answer to this is yes, he never pauses to ask why Japanese martyrs cannot atone for Ferreira's apostasy.

Rodrigues is eventually arrested. A substantial part of the novel is set in prison. By this point, God's silence and the doubts and questions this poses consume Rodrigues. While in prison, Rodrigues is brought face-to-face with Ferreira, who has been given a Japanese name and is now working for the Japanese authorities.

In conversation Ferreira relates the reasons for his apostasy. Several peasants had been subjected to the pit. Ferreira was told that they would not be released until he apostatized by stepping on an image of the face of Christ, the *fumie*. Ferreira offers two related reasons for his apostasy. First, he became convinced that the Japanese are not and cannot be real Christians. He tells Rodrigues that twenty years of missionary work has convinced him that, "The one thing I know is that our religion does not take root in this country" (147). The Japanese Christians confess belief in the God of Jesus Christ; they pray to this God using standard Christian language; they perform all the practices constitutive of Christian identity—including martyrdom when called for; yet Ferreira is convinced that they do not actually believe in the Christian God and never will. No doubt there is a large measure of self-justification here. Nevertheless, on these grounds Ferreira argued that he could not continue the suffering of these people, since it was the result of a misunderstanding.

Ferreira gives his second reason during his next meeting with Rodrigues, when it is clear that Rodrigues is to be given the same choice as Ferreira— apostatize to free others from the pit. Ferreira is convinced that in this situation apostasy is the option Christ himself would have taken. He tells Rodrigues, "A priest should live in imitation of Christ...Certainly Christ would have apostatized for these peasants" (169).

As Rodrigues is then led outside into the breaking dawn, he approaches the *fumie*. Throughout the novel we have been told that Rodrigues has always considered the face of Christ to be an object of great beauty. "This face is deeply ingrained in my soul–the most beautiful, the most precious thing in the world has been living in my heart. And now with this foot I am going to trample on it" (171). As he is about to step on the *fumie,* the image of Christ speaks to him (or so he imagines), breaking God's long silence, "Trample! Trample! It was to be trampled on by men that I was born into this world. It was to share men's pain that I carried my cross" (171).

Endo's novel probes some of the deepest crevices of Christian doctrine. He offers no answers, no tidy endings, no finally reliable narrator, no fixed ground from which one might decisively argue for or against Rodrigues' actions.[4] Hence, in bringing the issues of martyrdom in *Silence* into conversation with Philippians, I am not claiming to offer Endo's own views on these matters. Neither is mine the only defensible reading of *Silence.*[5] Rather, I am seeking to create a conversation between these two texts for the purpose of sharpening issues that have not and really cannot be addressed in the standard modern commentaries and monographs on Philippians.

Although it might seem improbable, in several respects the prospects for an examination of Paul's views and Rodrigues' are quite good. They share enough in common to be put in conversation; yet they differ enough to suggest that their interaction might point to some interesting aspects of martyrdom. When Paul writes to the Philippians, he himself is in prison. Moreover, he is writing to a congregation that is facing some form of opposition. Indeed, he suggests that the Philippians are engaged in the same struggle he is (1:30). A large portion of *Silence* is set with Rodrigues in prison. He, too, is in a pastoral relationship with persecuted Christians. Indeed, the horrors of Rodrigues' imprisonment (and they are mild compared with those suffered by the Japanese Christians) should remind biblical scholars that prisons in the Roman Empire were not directed toward the rehabilitation of offenders. Prison was a holding pen until the authorities figured out what to do with/to them.[6] The mental strains and physical deprivations of prison life would have been as real for Paul as they were for Rodrigues and the Japanese Christians.

Yet, in the end, Paul's tone in Philippians is both cordial and hopeful. Rodrigues is filled with doubt and despair, which ultimately contributes to his apostasy. How does the Rodrigues who leaves Portugal with such zeal and anticipation of martyrdom come to trample on the *fumie?*

---

[4]I have not even mentioned the striking character of Kichijiro, who hounds Rodrigues from the moment he leaves Macao, whose ugliness repels Rodrigues as much as the face of Christ attracts him.

[5]For a compelling reading that puts *Silence* into conversation with John Paul II's *Veritatis Splendor,* see W. T. Cavanaugh's "The God of Silence," *Commonweal* (March 13, 1998): 10–12.

[6]For a discussion of Paul and ancient Roman prisons see Craig Wansink, *Chained in Christ* (Sheffield: Sheffield Academic Press, 1996).

Without attempting to account fully for Rodrigues' apostasy, I will identify two significant respects in which he differs from Paul. These crucial differences might contribute to their different courses of action. The first concerns Rodrigues' reading of the divine economy and how he fits into that ongoing drama of God's saving purposes. The second, related, issue has to do with the sort of ecclesial polity from which Rodrigues approaches Japanese Christians.

We get a glimpse of how Rodrigues and other Portuguese Jesuits view the divine economy early in the novel. When speaking of an initial group of priests desiring to sneak into Japan to carry on missionary work in the aftermath of Ferreira's apostasy, Endo writes that they wish to "atone for the apostasy of Ferreira which had so wounded the honour of the Church…Furthermore, in the Europe of that time the fact that Ferreira had been forced to abandon his faith in this remote country at the periphery of the world was not simply the failure of one individual but a humiliating defeat for the faith itself and for the whole of Europe" (7). In addition to this group, we meet a group of three Portuguese Jesuits, of whom Rodrigues is one. The three had been Ferreira's students, and they want to find out the truth about Ferreira. "It was impossible to believe that their much admired teacher Ferreira, faced with the possibility of a glorious martyrdom, had groveled like a dog before the infidel" (8).

As the story progresses, we learn of other reasons for the journey Rodrigues and his friends make. Here at the outset, however, their mission is a chivalrous quest. They will either redeem the honor of the church, or bring back the truth about Ferreira and thus restore his honor. The assumptions here are strongly shaped by the desire to make history turn out right. The ongoing drama of God's salvation is seen with comedic, almost triumphalist, eyes. Moreover, it is clear that the central character in God's drama of salvation is the European church. That is, on their reading of God's economy, the church will not only triumph but must always be seen to triumph. Any besmirching of her honor must be answered directly and at once. On this sort of reading of the divine economy, almost any action could be (and has been) justified as long as one could argue that it serves to move the drama of salvation toward its inexorable end. To the extent that they continue in this view, these Jesuits play a dual role of both priest and knight. This situation fundamentally shapes Rogrigues' relationship to the Japanese Christians, their suffering, and his own eventual apostasy. Knights must protect those within their care, not cause them to suffer.

As priest, Rodrigues sees himself and his partner Garrpe as essential components to the survival of Christianity in Japan. When they can no longer remain in the village of Tomogi, they decide to separate.

> For a long time we talked the thing over wondering if we should flee together or separate. Finally we decided that even if one became a prey of the gentiles it was better that the other should remain. In other words, we would part company. And yet why on earth do we remain in this country at all? We did not make that long journey

around Africa, across the Indian Ocean, on to Macao and then to Japan just to flee like this from one hiding place to another. It was not to hide in the mountains like fieldmice, to receive a lump of food from destitute peasants and to be confined in a charcoal hut without being able even to meet the Christians. What had happened to our glorious dream?

Yet one priest remaining in this country has the same significance as a single candle burning in the catacombs. So Garrpe and I vowed to one another that after our separation we should strive might and main to stay alive. (61)

Here Rodrigues expresses the numerous tensions in the position he and Garrpe occupy. On the one hand, they are leaders in the church, lights in the catacombs. On the other hand, they are hunted like prey, victims unable to control their own destiny. According to them, the Japanese church depends on them for its very survival. Yet the Japanese are unwilling and unable to have them around because of the danger their presence entails. Their dreams were of glory; the reality is brutal and ugly. These tensions are only exacerbated to the extent that Rodrigues adopts the posture of a knight on a chivalrous quest to defend the honor of the church (or Ferreira), to win glory or die trying.

As knight, Rodrigues views the Japanese Christians as vehicles for finding information about Ferreira. He seems to feel an obligation to keep them from harm, if not protect them. From the time the two peasants of Tomogi are martyred because of his presence in Japan, Rodrigues begins both to question God and to feel a measure of guilt and responsibility for the peasants' suffering. Their deaths were not glorious; Rodrigues cannot hear or see God's presence in these martyrdoms. He views their deaths from a distance, both spatially and spiritually. He and they are not fellow members of Christ's body, members who all suffer when one of them is in pain (1 Cor. 12:26). On this view, Rodrigues and the Japanese Christians are not engaged in a common project. They suffer in parallel, not together. He cannot read their suffering and his suffering as their shared role in God's ongoing drama of redemption. Because of this, he is unable to require them to suffer for his beliefs. Indeed, under Ferreira's influence, he questions whether he and they even share a common belief, despite all the signs that they do. Hence, he tramples on the *fumie*.

While Philippians is temporally prior to *Silence*, I want to take Paul as offering a riposte to Rodrigues. In Philippians Paul manifests habits of mind and heart that would allow him to resist following in Rodrigues' footsteps. This is not because Paul is self-evidently more pious or even tougher than Rodrigues. Rather, Paul has cultivated a set of dispositions and outlooks that make it difficult or impossible for him to conceive apostatizing in order to save the Christians in Philippi from suffering.

One of the key dispositions Paul displays in Philippians is his emphasis on the *koinonia* he shares with the Philippians. It is not so much the case that Paul and the Philippians share things with one another (although they do), it is the fact that Paul and the Philippians are fellow sharers in the gospel (1:5).

Paul sees that he and the Philippians are engaged in a project independent of themselves. This project is nothing less than participation in the economy of God's salvation. Because they are fellow participants in the divine economy of salvation, Paul's sufferings and the Philippians' sufferings can be narrated within the scope of that common project. As a result, it is not Paul's beliefs that might require the Philippians to suffer nor the Philippians' beliefs that might require Paul to suffer. Rather, it is common convictions about God's work in the world, most particularly in and through the story of Christ narrated in 2:5–11, that lead Paul to claim that the Philippians have been given the opportunity "not only to believe in Christ, but to suffer for his sake" (1:29).

Given this resource, it is crucial for Paul to help the Philippians develop the skills of being able to so interpret the movement of God's economy and to so situate themselves within the movements of that story that they, as a community, can remain as a faithful witness to the gospel in the midst of suffering. This point is brought home in 1:27, where Paul urges them to conduct their common life[7] in a manner worthy of the gospel of Christ.

Nevertheless, as Rodrigues, Paul, and the Philippians well know, the movements of the divine economy can sometimes be difficult to trace. One's eye has to be trained so as to discern both the ways in which the economy of salvation moves and the particular ways in which Christians might fit themselves into that economy in the light of their particular circumstances. To help train the Philippians' eyes for the divine economy, Paul relates the story of God's activity in Christ in 2:6–11. Although these are some of the most exegetically contested verses in the New Testament, the basic structure of the story is relatively clear.[8] That measure of clarity will suffice for my purposes. In 2:6–11 Paul narrates the story of the exalted Christ, who willingly takes on the form of a slave. This manifests itself in a human life dedicated to obedience to God, obedience that ultimately results in death on the cross. God vindicates the obedient suffering one, exalting Christ and bestowing on Christ the name above all names. There is a deeply ironic structure to this story. That is, the initial result of Christ's obedience and suffering appears to be death. God overcomes death, reversing one's initial reading of the human Christ's self-emptying.

In 2:5 Paul claims that he wants this story to shape the common life of the Philippian congregation. More precisely, he wants this story to shape their common life by allowing it to form their practical reasoning.[9] Thus, Paul is trying to form in the Philippians the intellectual and moral abilities to be able

---

[7] I take this to be the force of the verb πολιτεύεσθε in 1:27.

[8] For a good survey of the current state of the various exegetical issues related to this passage, see the essays in *Where Christology Began,* ed. R. P. Martin and B. Dodd (Louisville: Westminster John Knox Press, 1998).

[9] This is the position I argued for in *The Story of Christ in the Ethics of Paul* (Sheffield: JSOT Press, 1990). Around this same time Wayne Meeks argued similarly in "The Man From Heaven in Paul's Letter to the Philippians" in *The Future of Early Christianity: Essays in Honor of Helmut Koester* (Minneapolis: Fortress Press, 1991), where he states, "This letter's most comprehensive purpose is the shaping of a Christian *phronesis,* a practical moral reasoning that is 'conformed to [Christ's] death' in hope of his resurrection" (333).

to deploy their understanding of this story in the concrete situations in which they find themselves. To do this, they need to be able to understand the way the divine economy works. Hence the account offered in 2:6–11. From such an understanding they can then fit their own lives into the unfolding story of God's salvation. This is also an acquired skill. It demands an ability to see one's own circumstances in the ironic light of God's work in Christ. Paul helps the Philippians develop these skills in two particular ways.

First, he offers accounts of his own life and his own particular situation in prison. Second, he offers an account of the Philippians' situation, in which he argues that they are engaged in precisely the same struggle he is. Therefore, they should "read" their situation the same way he reads his and act accordingly. Paul offers two distinct accounts of himself in Philippians. The more well known is the short autobiographical section in 3:4–11. In the beginning of this passage Paul narrates his life prior to Christ as a story of unrelenting achievement within Judaism. The irony is that now, from the perspective of being in Christ, he regards all those things as "crap."[10] Instead, he now aims to know the power of Christ's resurrection, to share in his sufferings, and to become conformed to his death in order that he might attain the resurrection from the dead (3:10–11). Here Paul is able both to account for his past and to articulate the telos of his life by fitting it into the economy of God's saving purposes.

At the beginning of the epistle, Paul also provides an account of himself. In this case, he is speaking about his immediate circumstances in prison. As with Philippians 3, he adopts an ironic perspective. In 1:12 he begins by claiming that, despite what one might expect, his circumstances have worked to advance the gospel. He then goes on to explain how this has happened. His account reaches its climax when he confidently asserts that now, as always, he plans "to magnify Christ in his body" (1:20). A Roman prison would be the last place in which one would be expected to have any control over one's own body. In the context of imperial imprisonment, the prisoner's body becomes the text on which the empire's power is inscribed.[11] In the one situation where the Roman Empire would be expected to have complete control over Paul's body, Paul asserts that Christ will be magnified. Ironically, Paul's body will become Christ's text rather than the Empire's. As the rest of the passage makes clear, this will be true whether Paul lives or dies, whether he is released from prison or martyred. Again, Paul manifests this ironic perspective because he has been formed by the story of God's work in Christ.

Because the Philippians have fellowship with Paul in the gospel (1:3–11; 4:10–20), because they are participating in the "same struggle" as he does (1:30), Paul wants the Philippians to have the same perspective that he does. Such a perspective will require that they manifest the practices of 2:1–4. That

---

[10] This translation of σκύβαλα in 3:8 was offered by Richard Hays in *Echoes of Scripture in the Letters of Paul* (New Haven: Yale University Press, 1989), 122.

[11] This general point in regard to imprisonment and punishment was first made by Michel Foucault in *Discipline and Punish,* trans A. Sheridan (New York: Vintage Books, 1979).

is, their common life must manifest a Christ-focused unity, sharing the same love, participating in a common pattern of practical reasoning, and seeking the benefit of others before their own.

Moreover, in a situation where their convictions about Christ bring them into public disfavor, they must remain steadfast, united in one Spirit in the face of their adversaries (1:28). From their adversaries' perspective, this signals the destruction of the Philippians. As Paul ironically sees it, however, such an attitude will result in their salvation (1:29).[12] In fact, it accords well with God's economy of salvation as exemplified in the story of Christ in 2:5–11.

Philippians then displays two crucial elements for a Pauline account of martyrdom. First, one must be able to narrate, to understand, and to be formed by God's economy of salvation. Such formation enables followers of Christ to fit the story of their own lives into that ongoing narrative of God's saving work. No doubt there are a variety of points of view one might adopt to narrate both the story of God's saving work and how one fits into that story. In the face of sharp and powerful opposition to the gospel, Paul manifests an ironic point of view. In several respects, however, Paul's ironic point of view is markedly different from the perpetual irony of postmodernity, an irony that infinitely defers judgment and commitment, an irony that cannot but lapse into cynicism. Rather, Paul's irony is christologically dense. It is an ironic perspective that is decisively shaped by a particular narrative, the narrative of God's economy of salvation that reaches its climax in the life, death, and resurrection of Jesus. Like the irony of postmodernity, Paul's ironic perspective allows him to see the temporal contingency of present circumstances and current configurations of power. Unlike the postmodern ironist, Paul comports himself in the midst of adverse circumstances in the knowledge that these circumstances are ultimately ordered by God's providential will. Moreover, this ordering ensures that ultimately all things will be subject to Christ.

While one can easily imagine isolated individuals adopting postmodern forms of irony, Paul's ironic perspective cannot really be sustained by isolated individuals. This is in part due to the fact that certain specific commitments underwrite Paul's irony. Moreover, these commitments might require the suffering of oneself or others. In the face of such suffering, the ironic perspective of the isolated individual of postmodernity appears deluded, irrational, insane. Why suffer or, more importantly, cause others who don't share your views to suffer for a set of utterly contingent beliefs that might just as easily be changed? This is very much like the question the Japanese and Ferreira posed to Rodrigues. For Paul and the Philippians this particular question does not arise because of their *koinonia,* their joint participation in the project known as God's economy of salvation. While there are diverse ways of narrating this project and a variety of points of view one might adopt in fitting oneself into this story, it is recognizably a common story, generating a common set of

---

[12]A version of this reading of the obscure syntax of 1:29 can be found in Gerald Hawthorne, *Philippians* (Waco, Tex.: Word, 1987), 58–60.

practices regulated by the story of Christ. Because Rodrigues cannot recognize that he and the Japanese Christians participate in that same project, he is unable to sustain the ironic perspective needed to endure the sufferings of his circumstances. Because he does not have any sort of *koinonia* with the Japanese Christians, he comes to see himself as the cause of their suffering. He is thereby responsible to stop that suffering by trampling on the *fumie*.

I am not arguing here that it was impossible for Paul or any particular Philippian to have apostatized. Such a claim would underestimate the power of torture. For the same reasons, I am not claiming that had Rodrigues heard the riposte of Philippians rather than the urgings of Ferreira he would have *not* apostatized. Rather, my point is that the specific contours of Rodrigues' apostasy–the perspectives, promptings, and concerns that shape his practice– are inconceivable in the light of the ways Paul addresses these matters in Philippians.

Eyeing the Apocalypse

Catherine Keller

Around the throne were four living creatures full of eyes before
them and behind them: the first like a lion, the second like an ox,
the third with a face of a man, and the fourth like a flying
eagle…and the four living creatures, each of them had six wings,
they were full of eyes around and within, and day and night they
never cease to sing…

Revelation 4:6ff.

i

The four creatures arrayed around the bejeweled, shining, flashing, thundering throne, standing on "something like a sea of glass, like crystal," return the glitter with open eyes, mirroring back the lightning glories of the deity. John of Patmos displays the highest destination of Jewish mystical apocalypticism, the divine throne room, as surrounded by the four mythic creatures *(Chayyot)* driving Ezekiel's fiery chariot of half a millennium prior. But while Ezekiel had spread only the rim of the wheels with ocular organs, John outdoes him. The creatures "were full of eyes around and within." He saturates the creatures' bodies with eyes. So has John's vision of visions saturated the body of Christ—its churches, its cultures, its countercultures—with its views? Not with a single one. Has there ever been a single apocalypse?

Vision within the vision, vision of visions: eyes proliferate over the four bodily surfaces; eyes line their innards, merging inside and out, day and night. Already in Ezekiel these creatures disorder the divisions of human, animal, angel, and monster. In John they break into polyoptic perversity. The android— "like a human face"– offers no familiar point of view, no humanistic privilege. He blends into theriomorphic harmony, merely the third member of the animal quartet that relentlessly sings and stares. Do these eyes ever blink? Do they portend the nightless neon of the final day? Then, in the culminating biblical trope of total Presence, the One on the throne will replace the sun and shine continuously. Do these omniocular bodies not prepare the way for the single, eternally switched-on Lamb-Lamp (Rev. 22:3–5)? Certainly they never sleep.

253

They are wakefulness itself. Watch–it comes in the twinkling of an eye. The apocalypse. *The Apocalypse.* Keep your eyes open.

Or at least the book. Could we close it by now even if we tried, as have so many? A casual sampling: "My spirit cannot abide this text" –Martin Luther; "ravings of a lunatic"– Thomas Jefferson; "a curious record of the vision of a drug addict"–George Bernard Shaw; "repellant because it resounds with the dangerous snarl of the frustrated, suppressed collective self, the frustrated power-spirit in man, vengeful"–D. H. Lawrence. "There are many monsters in the Apocalypse, but the real bad-ass monster sits on the heavenly throne"– Tina Pippin.[1] "Congested with vision...a postmodern monstrosity"–Catherine Keller.[2]

Nonetheless, I still am unable not to return, to rerun; I still try to slow down the hyperspeed of John's vision, flashing like MTV to the next image, and the next, and–his sentences are grammatically gorged with "and"–the images multiply like the eyes. Something in this text keeps winking at me, something still trying, for all the hallucinogenic overexposure of *The Apocalypse,* to get some attention. Pssst, here, look. Amidst this prooftext of the most exclusively, the most fundamentally, singular gaze, might these creatures be silently sending signals invisible to the author himself? In their eye-studded bodies might they signify multiplicity itself–quite precisely the endless plurality of viewpoints? This would be a poignant condition, given their context. What views of the Apocalypse itself would such plurivision open up? What views of its legacy of exclusive, once for all, all for One, one and only truth-claims? If we (postmodern by default or by desire) gaze into the ancient kaleidoscope of this text, do we see anything but eyes eyeing us? How many of them are our own mirrored back?

ii. Apocalypse In and Out

I raise these questions this way, trying to demonstrate, not merely to adumbrate, a style of reading that proceeds for now under the cover of the "postmodern." It might pass as a response to David Tracy's recent call for theology to heal the split between its form and content. By this last moment in this anthology, with the one biblical text inevitably to be discussed "post" the others, you may have read a number of balanced and daring assessments of narrative, rhetorical, queer, poststructuralist, or postcolonial strategies of interpretation, all of which, especially perhaps the poststructuralist, have bearing in this essay. But rather than mobilizing another methodological apparatus, or recapitulating the work of Apocalypse commentaries (which proliferated at the millennium like the eyes), rather than "arguing the apocalypse"[3] within the rapidly fading context of "the millennium," rather

---

[1]Tina Pippin, *Apocalyptic Bodies: The Biblical End of the World in Text and Image* (London and New York: Routledge, 1999), 91.

[2]Catherine Keller, *Apocalypse Now and Then: A Feminist Guide to the End of the World* (Boston: Beacon, 1996), 35.

[3]Stephen D. O'Leary, *Arguing the Apocalypse: A Theory of Millennial Rhetoric* (New York and Oxford: Oxford University Press, 1994), offers a sophisticated analysis of the function of apoca-lyptic language within multiple contexts of doomsday politics.

even than developing my own categories of antiapocalypse, retroapocalypse, neoapocalypse, counterapocalypse, I am staging a hermeneutical encounter with its four creatures.

Such an encounter cannot take place without borrowing the poetic license with which these chauffeur-creatures first operated. But then I would make the same claim about theology in general: It cannot encounter its originative texts unless it enters into the form, not merely into an abstraction of the content, of the artful imagery of scripture. To the extent that theology has instead merely extracted a supposed "biblical" meaning, it has practiced a hermeneutic of control. The alternative is not to be controlled by the text. If we seek instead a theological hermeneutic of relation, that is, of indeterminacy—rather on the model of quantum theory, in which the relation of observer and observed evinces an uncontrollable and irreducible mutuality—it is not in the rather transparently self-authorizing guise of merely subordinating ourselves to the text.

This hermeneutical indeterminacy admits at once its kinship to deconstruction. That is, it presumes that the rhetorical constructs of Revelation reveal much more about its writers and readers than about any One sitting on a throne. I assume that Derrida's poorly understood slogan "*pas de hors texte*" illumines the way in which we are always-already in this text—in apocalypse, in its "tone," in its forcefield of effects, its culture, its aftermath.[4] Yet such an intra-apocalyptic position might lock us into a temporality that dissolves every moment into a prelude to the end. An end framed by an author who certainly intended to capture all time and space within the net of his text. "Nothing outside of the text," no exit? Yet the end does not come, but continuously generates new beginnings that rush toward it. And what closure does such a text threaten/promise, that does not dissolve into relativity as we approach it? The end of death, of time, of history, of the Roman church, of the aristocracy, of the bourgeoisie, of patriarchy—which single goal stands still, stands there as The End, the final goalpost, outpost of all known perspectives? Or am I asking *merely* postmodern questions, meaninglessly multiplicative, not yet interpretative, a post signifying that there is no significance?

One writes about Apocalypse after the millennium with a redoubled sense of posteriority, of postapocalypse. Yet commentators on John's Apocalypse have always been constrained by the grammar of a peculiar afterward, by the throne room temporality of that future that John witnessed *(martyrein)* in advance, as though the future lies already in the past: "and I saw a star that had fallen from heaven to earth" (Rev. 9:1). Interpretation takes place always as afterword, in the afterward of a perpetual not yet, not quite, soon and very soon.

How would we step altogether outside the agonized time pretzel of apocalypticized Western history? Perhaps we return to the text—the text of no return, of pure destruction and New Creation—in order to discern the trace of an alternative space-time; of a *dis/closure* even here in this revelation of ultimate

---

⁴Jacques Derrida, *Of Grammatology*, trans. Gayatri Chakravorty Spivak (Baltimore: Johns Hopkins, 1976), 158.

closure. "Trace" here echoes Derrida's sense of the differance that haunts the same, that defers closure. "Without a retention in the minimal unit of temporal experience, without a trace retaining the other as other in the same, no difference would do its work and no meaning would appear."[5] The Derridian *differance* still (unlike many of its adherents) insists on "meaning." The deconstruction of the classical assumption of a pure "transcendental Signified" should never have been confused with some nihilist abolition of significance. Nor does it negate the world in and toward which language signifies. Deconstruction meditates on time, indeed on the spacing of time and the temporizing of space, and therefore on a world in which the text lives, which it permeates, which it effects. If there is nothing outside it, this is because *no fixed boundary can be drawn between the text and its context,* between, for instance, our text's interpretation of Ezekiel and of later Jewish apocalypses, and the history of Christian interpretations of the text, and our own late, very late, version of and within that history.

Nonetheless, I do not "apply" Derridian method to the Bible, rendering the text a pretext for poststructuralist performance. It is more true to say that prior struggle with this particular text, with all that it protects and ignores and assaults and hopes, all that it closes and dis/closes, sent me after the fact, after "the book" (too late) to Derrida. This text has done a lot of sending. Its endtime missionaries are everywhere on the planet. Derrida has also sent his *Carte Postale,* his postcard (mass mailings to the U.S. academy), further deferring the arrival of the parousia: "within every sign already, every mark,...there is distancing, the post, what there has to be so that it is legible for another."[6] It seems, then, only fair to read the text through one or two Derridian eyes, but then also, inevitably and at the same time, Derrida through the eyes of this text. Derrida clarifies precisely what a theologian might need from a deconstructive reading:

> Operating necessarily from the inside, borrowing all the strategic and economic resources of subversion from the old structure, borrowing them structurally, that is to say without being able to isolate their elements and atoms, the enterprise of deconstruction always in a certain way falls prey to its own work.[7]

Thus, we enter a space that we have never quite left, beginning on the inside—itself full of eyes. The encounter can only be intimate, therefore, risking proximity to the mythopoeic vortex of the imagery. The encounter cannot then remain bounded within the disciplines of history or literary analysis. The distance collapses along with the familiarity of the canonized text. In

---

⁵Derrida, 62.

⁶Derrida, *The Post Card: From Socrates to Freud and Beyond,* trans. Alan Bass (Chicago: University of Chicago Press, 1987), 29. Cf. Stephen Moore's brilliant redirecting of the "postal principle" to the gospel of Mark, in *Mark and Luke in Poststructuralist Perspectives: Jesus Begins to Write* (New Haven: Yale University Press, 1992), 38ff.

⁷Derrida, *Of Grammatology,* 41.

other words—admittedly not in the words of the philosopher himself—deconstruction exposes us to the theological force field of the text. Once sucked into its whirlwind, we may only move gracefully by making intentional theological gestures of our own. Or is that the bias of a theologian?

Only in its apophatic and apocalyptic moments has theology learned to reflect on how it falls prey to its own work: how it voices doctrinal certainties only by silencing competitors, how otherwise it dissolves at its own boundaries, how it stutters at the edge of speech. This element of predation should not come as a surprise, given Revelation's cosmic bestiary of predators—animal, divine, demonic—playing their roles within a theater that serves as the prototype for Western revolution and reaction; and arguably already mimicking the structures it subverts. Deconstruction recognizes that it operates always within its text, since the text has no final boundaries. Such an interior position eschews any parasitical spirit of negation, which would only destroy its own host.[8] It is also the case that in all its forms, theology (in distinction from other religious studies, perhaps even biblical studies) presupposes and cultivates this interiority. It may defend violently or rigidly against all deconstructive gestures. But it at least recognizes that it operates always within a tradition and a community derived from the interpretation of a text. The text of texts, to be sure—whose status as the canonized and closed Book surely inspired the Derridian call for "The End of the Book and the Beginning of Writing."[9]

Reentering a text within the Final Book within the Book, we may find ourselves, however unpleasantly, already mirrored, fragmented, diffracted in its gaze. We may not emerge with critical singularity of vision, with a monoperspectival clarity "about" it, as though we had finally gotten outside it and could look on. I hope we can read without either the aching apologetics of most progressive Christianity, straining its good news from Revelation's toxins, or the seamless sarcasm of a particular tone of deconstruction, for which good news is no news. I have found serviceable instead (as a feminist theologian who cannot afford the luxuries of justification or of dismissal) a certain *methodological ambivalence.* According to this hermeneutical uncertainty principle, our relativity as interpreters enmeshed in an endless process of interpretation—Nietzsche's "infinite interpretation"—does not absolve us of specific ethical and ecological responsibilities. Rather, it holds us accountable to definite relations to and within our world. In other words, it always—does a theologian more than a biblical critic bear this cross?—obliges itself to a constructive re/vision.

---

[8]"I have constantly insisted on the fact that the movement of deconstruction was first of all affirmative—not positive, but affirmative. Deconstruction, let's say it one more time, is not demolition or destruction" (Derrida, *Points,* ed. Elisabeth Weber, trans. Peggy Kamuf et al. [Stanford: Stanford University Press, 1995], 211).

[9]Although he aims his critique not at the biblical corpus but at the entire tradition of "ontotheology," which emerges in force from the confluence of Greek metaphysics with scriptural authority; Derrida, *Of Grammatology,* 6ff.

iii. Reading as Preying

Of the four "living creatures," the eagle and the lion represent beasts of prey, sated here by the vision of God. The third, the humanoid, represents the most aggressive predator on the planet, the one who has posed its culture against nature. The ox, a creation of domestication, pulls the weight of human culture. The four pray continuously. Engorged with eyes, eyes that we might imagine look out pitilessly, blankly, like royal Assyrian statuary. Or do they strain, bloodshot, with infinite insomnia? Or gaze in hallucinogenic hallelujah at what is forbidden to human eyes? We see these eyes seeing. Unlike the eye of God, which sees but is not seen, these eyes are spread out before our vision, through John's vision, mirroring his mystical throne room voyeurism back to him, to us, in an endless—if textually fleeting—refraction. Unlike the single point of view of the God's-eye view, which is therefore no point of view but mere omniscience, these eyes would appear to stare back at us in extravagant multiplicity. Traditionally, the covering of divine beings or demons with eyes connoted their inhuman vision, their omnivorous sight, their all-seeing and all-knowing consciousness. Or if not know-it-all—most commentaries reserve omniscience for the deity, with whom they do not want to identify these creatures—at least their inescapable attention. We cannot see what the eyes see, and the eye-bearers are eternally singing. So one cannot read the text as an uncharacteristically Hellenistic privilege of vision over audition, as the stillness of theoria, as dispassionate speculation/speculum. Rather, it offers the tableau of a harmoniously monstrous little menagerie, singing their Sanctus day and night.

Still, Revelation makes quite a spectacle of itself. What are we to say back to Nietzsche when he, tormented prophet against Christian cruelty, cites at length Tertullian's promise? For our present purpose, gazing at Tertullian's vision through Nietzsche's furiously apostate eye seems all too apposite:

> "We have martyrs instead of athletes. If we crave blood, we have the blood of Christ…But think what awaits us on the day of his triumph!" And the rapt visionary continues: "Yes, and there are still to come other spectacles—that last, that eternal Day of Judgment, that Day which the Gentiles never believed would come,…when this old world and all its generations shall be consumed in one fire. How vast the spectacle that day, and how wide! What sight shall wake my wonder"…*Per fidem:* so it is written.[10]

Perhaps one can say back: The power of Nietzsche's fiery denunciation emanates from his mimesis of the apocalyptic tone. When he later dubs himself Antichrist, he surely reveals his own implication in its reverberating intertextuality. The choice of Zarathustra, a reference to Zoroaster, the likeliest candidate for progenitor of all apocalyptic discourse, reflects the mirroring of many ancient eyes.[11] Infinite interpretation. After The Book.

---

[10]Friedrich Nietzsche, *Genealogy* 1.15, in *The Birth of Tragedy and The Genealogy of Morals*, trans. Francis Golffing (New York: Doubleday Anchor, 1887/1956), 184f.

[11]On the origins of eschatology in the Zoroastrian combat myth, cf. Norman Cohn, *Cosmos, Chaos and the World to Come: The Ancient Roots of Apocalyptic Faith* (New Haven and London: Yale University Press), 1993.

"Whoever's name was not found in the book of life, he was thrown into the lake of fire" (20:15). Christians have lived by the hope that their names have been inscribed in that final book, reservations in the splendid New Jerusalem confirmed. Progressive Christianity, of course, wants the hope without the hell. We invoke the social architecture of the New Creation without the torture chambers in the basement; liberation without the final exteriorization of our particular oppressors, our Other, as damned or demon; justice for the Others of history, not vengeance. Indeed, I can no longer deny solidarity with certain aspects of this text—its wish for "no more tears," for "water free for all," hopes desperately dear to the growing majority of the present earth.

Yet to claim the liberating without the damning seems perilous: Do we not then "take away from the words of the book of this prophecy?" In which case, "God will take away his share in the tree of life and in the holy city, which are described in this book" (Rev. 22:19). At any rate, our selective readings had better make their ambivalence clear, had better admit when they read against the grain of the text, had better thus relativize the authority of this author to the moral claims of variously oppressed publics. For some of these publics read it, hope and pray through it; masses of others will remain outside Christianity, if not outside its effects. Thus, if we do not want to transmit the greatest binary closure in all literature, if we do not want to absorb the damnation along with the salvation, liberation hermeneutics may wish to consider admitting the moral limits of this book—even and especially while recognizing the virtual illimitability of its effects: *pas de hors texte.*

This book of books, indeed, makes a spectacle of scrolls, of text, of itself *as* book, of its own bookishness. *Text,* after all, distinguishes itself from *voice* by virtue of its visibility. John is writing feverishly at the angel's command, of course, and along the way swallows a book—textuality itself?—whole: "bitter to your stomach, but sweet as honey in your mouth." Any postmodernism that joins Derrida in privileging the text over orality should recognize its risky continuity with John's book, whose preoccupation with writing is unprecedented in the Bible. Far be it from the present writer to suggest any link between writing and hell. But when we celebrate the sweetness of "writing" —indeed Derrida set a "pure writing" apart from the logocentric authority of voice and book—we may want to remember the Apocalypse.

"Write!" commands the angel. Indeed, "in a book," the ultimate in closure. Yet the operative contrast in Revelation is not between book and text, but between speech and writing.[12]

We may wish to recall the bitter belly and the unprecedented hell that accompany this early assertion of the privilege of writing. With its hell, it at

---

[12]Granted that Derrida wishes precisely to identify the two contrasts, his assimilation of writing to the freedom of the text over and against his identification of Book with the oral authority of its "transcendental Signified" is pivotal to his critique of logocentrism. However, the resulting illusion of a convergence of Book with orality seems to me to emanate from one of his shakier arguments; cf. Derrida, *Of Grammatology,* pt. 1. Mark C. Taylor's dissemination of the a/ theological version of Derrida's distinction of Book and Text highlights the contrast of the closure of apocalyptic writ with an open *scriptura,* writing in *Erring* (Albany: Suny University Press), 1990. But it begs the question of the apocalyptic privilege of writing itself.

once disposes of its Others and reinscribes them in its margins. John's vision of the New Creation requires that the damned pile up against the gates of the holy city, even in the end. Perhaps this irresolvable divide communicates that the New Jerusalem—in which trees produce leaves "for the healing of the nations"—does not stand outside of history, outside of struggle and opposition after all. Yet the bitter, damning rage does not even aspire toward a wider redemption, let alone a salvation of the whole—as to Jonah before the whale, the concept of God still trying to redeem the idolaters remains intolerable to John. The sweetness of salvation is textually enhanced by the contrasting hell. Writing may be a bitter pill, but it promises the final healing.

The surface of the New Jerusalem sparkles with myriad gems. In its architecture of pure culture, the natural elements reappear as park, purged of all wilderness—rivers are canals, trees are planted in geometries and yielding useful fruits. The sun has no more use; "there will be no more sea." In my own affinity to poststructuralist projects of "denaturalization," I cannot miss the apocalyptic anticipation of the radical denaturalization of the universe, in which the elements are melted down as in a cosmic forge: the primordial chaos, waste and wild, the predatory animals, and the wild bodies have no place at all in this apotheosis of pure culture. As temple complex, it magnifies, indeed it now in some sense takes the place of, the glittering throne of God, who will in the end inhabit His creation fully. Yet only the Lamb, most domesticated of all creatures, appears in that end, shining as the twenty-four-hour lamp of the pure light of YHWH. A tired set of neon-blasted eyes might read here the worst of the postmodern, the Disney-topia of pure artifice.

iv. Animal Dreams

Our beastly quartet, however, stands a bit to the side of all this horror and hope. They have seen it all. And perhaps because they stand off, seeing too much, seeing from innumerable perspectives, they soon get adopted as the supreme mascots of textuality. Through patristic allegory, they would be typologized as the four gospels. If there is "good news" for postmodernity in this textual polyoptic, it lies in the unlikely ancient protection of an irreducible plurality: For all the massive subsequent success of the Christian imperial mononarrative, the multiplicity of perspectives itself got fixed within its canon. (Psst: look, not two eyes and a single view; not a single story; not a single gospel.) The need for four, still dangling their loose ends and mutual contradictions, rather than a compression into one, remains neither trivial nor explicable. Indeed, under the circumstances of an aggressively domesticated and monocultured Christianity, it remains a little wild.

And how hungrily the visual artists of the Middle Ages would pounce on this little bestiary. In this exegesis, I find myself standing with one foot in this nonlinguistic subculture, within a long lineage of anonymous iconographers grateful for this animating animality. Authorized to lift these four supreme authors into relief from the text, the sculptor of a tympanum on a cathedral could slow the vision down to granite. Celtic manuscript illuminators caressed and complicated these images, enmeshing them in twining beasts and vines, bringing their own ancient cosmological symbolism to new fruition as it reframed the missionary culture of the Book. I easily project myself into their eyes, into the visual artists' and their people's appetite for all that could be saved from the new dualism of God as the supernatural, the church as the pure culture of the Logos: the elemental presences, the creaturely images, wild things, monsters, gargoyles, indeed even lambs, Mary, the baby. Anything but more men, more beards, more stiffened desensualized bodies. Anything for relief from the droning, dematerialized andromorphism and anthropomorphism—which was after all hardly getting off the ground in the rich sensorium of the biblical visions. Anything to postpone that apocalypse that never gave the first creation its chance. (I said I project.)

Scholars recognize a "capacity to see that vastly exceeds the human."[13] A recent commentary oriented to social justice joins in this old tradition of hungry hermeneutics, reaching for support into the more flesh-friendly Jewish tradition: "These four living creatures probably represent all living beings, for there was a rabbinic tradition that the greatest of wild animals was the lion, the greatest of domestic animals was the ox, the greatest of birds was the eagle, and the greatest of all was the human creature. Thus, the four living creatures bring to the throne the worship of the entire creation."[14] This is a hopeful reading, and I share the hope, if not the reading. Yet even the Gonzaleses do not, unfortunately, problematize their ecosensitive exegesis in terms of Revelation's anticipation of virtual geocide as the presupposition for the New Creation. They appropriately link John's New Creation to the Isaianic eschatology it cites, but then simply affirm the New Creation as the end of death ("it is eternal life") and as the proper Christian expectation. One might want at least a struggle, an acknowledgment, of some cognitive dissonance between the emerging vision of the end of all mortality and the Jewish eschatological one of a renewal of creation, this creation, in which life cannot be abstracted from death. The failure to acknowledge such biblical tensions illustrates the problem with liberation apologetics mentioned earlier. Moreover, the traditional left commitment to social justice has until recently been won at the expense of care for the nonhuman creatures, who have been fair game for exploitation. Indeed "dominion" (Hebrew *kabash*! Gen. 1) has been exercised with violent anthropocentrism on both the right and left sides of Christianity. Yet by the same token it illustrates the rhetorical power of having the Bible on your side in order to advance a progressive agenda, a strategic situation I share. But we must beware of inadvertently betraying the material context for the vitality both symbolized and embodied in "all living beings."[15]

[13]Johann Michl, *Die Engelvorstellungen in der Apokalypse Des Hl. Johannes* (Munich: Max Hueber Verlag, 1937), 70, auth. trans. Michl's view typically avoids attributing divine omniscience to the creatures, while granting them more than human "*Sehvermoegen.*"

[14]Catherine Gunsalus Gonzales and Justo L. Gonzales, *Revelation,* Westminster Bible Companion (Louisville: Westminster John Knox Press, 1997), 40.

[15]Cf. Keller, "The Heat is On: Apocalyptic Rhetoric and Climate Change," *Ecotheology* (July 1999): 40–58. Also see Anne Primavesi, *From Apocalypse to Genesis: Ecology, Feminism and Christianity* (Minneapolis: Fortress Press, 1991).

Yet neither should I expect sympathy for my animalization of text from many poststructuralists. They are just as likely to have disregarded the nonhuman earth. They are less likely than the biblical writers to include the multiplicity of creatures within paeans to the plural (Michel Serres is a wonderful exception). Indeed, postmodernists may anthropomorphize faster than the Apocalypse, anxious to root out the conceptual residues of "nature." They rightly expose the sort of fixed, conservative, logocentric "nature" that has been dubbed in where, instead, "culture" should be made to acknowledge its own construction. Yet while "culture" remains, within poststructuralist writing, a concept larded with rich complexities, "nature" is left in the dust of its deconstruction.[16]

Yet I find an intriguing corroboration of my own concern in Derrida's formulation of the "trace":

> If the trace, arche-phenomenon of "memory," which must be thought before the opposition of nature and culture, animality and humanity, etc., belongs to the very movement of signification then signification is *a priori* written, whether inscribed or not, in one form or another, in a "sensible" and "spatial" element that is called "exterior."[17]

Here Derrida makes clear that his metaphor of text should not be reduced to any graphic medium, or read as lacking reference to the material universe. Might we consider the pericope of the four polyoptic, polymorphic creatures to bear just such a trace of the sensible-spatial exterior, in which all living creatures become and pass away? But this exterior has leaked precisely into the text, before it is even written, in such a way as to dissolve the dualisms of nature/culture and animal/human.

"Trace" is equivalent to "differance," when "differance, in a certain and very strange way, (is) older than the ontological differance or than the truth of Being" ("When it has this age it can be called the play of the trace").[18] Certainly, John's Hebrew throne room vision, and even his early Christianization of its context, recalls a faith older than its revision by Greek ontological categories. The beasts in their celestial gaminess mark an even older moment, at the very least prior to the conquest of the biblical paradigm by what Heidegger first called "ontotheology"–the identification of God with an immutable, self-knowing Being. Their iconographic citation, however, of even older, mythological imagery of the ancient world can hardly be missed. And the ancient Middle East sits on a neolithic theriomorphology, in which the lines between nature and culture, animality and humanity, seem to have been drawn only sufficiently to allow their mutant and hybrid recombinations.

Perhaps the signifying movement of the beasts, precisely as they include a human not as "greatest" but as so pointedly just third of four, marks its

---

[16]Cf. the helpful discussions of *FutureNatural: Nature/Science/Culture,* ed. G. Robertson, M. Mash, et al., esp. Kate Soper, "Nature/'nature'" (London: Routledge, 1996), 22–34.

[17]Derrida, *Of Grammatology,* 42.

[18]Jacques Derrida, *Margins of Philosophy* (Chicago: University of Chicago Press, 1982), 22.

difference from the anthropomorphism that had been gathering momentum along the biblical trajectory as well. This bestial reading may not seem capricious when linked to other wild traces, such as preeminently the whirlwind epiphany of Job 39–43. That text, if interpreted out of the commentary commonplace of a divine bully declaring supremacy over creation, grants only the untameable bodies of the cosmos and of feral animals the honor of appearing in the restorative creation vision. This whirling, distinctly noneschatological vision, undermines the supremacy of the human to great ecological effect.[19] The "carnival of creation" mocks the domesticating anthropocentrism of human cultural presumption.[20] I am not conflating Job with Revelation. *Au contraire*, everything that YHWH offers as creation from the whirlwind gets eliminated in John's New Creation. Moreover, no purely theriocentric or ecotheological perspective can obtain these or any other biblical beasts. I do wish to register, however, the improbable possibility of an *ecotheologically poststructuralist* set of eyes with which to re-view them. From such perspective(s), the consonance of the four animals with Job's vision hints, perhaps at most, at a residual countertradition that might signify something quite beside the author's point.

v. Bloody Deconstruction

Within a few verses the lens will shift to the supreme beast, the object of this prayer, the Lion of Judah who appears as the Lamb: "the good old lion in sheep's clothing," quips D. H. Lawrence.[21] The Lion-Lamb also has too many eyes: seven, one presumably for each of the seals that he alone is worthy to break, open, and read; he the predator who has fallen prey, the better to read? Slaughtered in order to conquer; there it comes: "by your blood you ransomed," the gory heart of the coming Christian metanarrative, the predator become prey to whom we pray in hopes of–the apocalyptic feast? The book's climactic moments of eating include eating a scroll, the Beasts (unlike our good ones) who strip and cook and eat the juicy whore, and the parodic eucharistic feast for the birds of prey at Armageddon: "Come, gather for the great supper of God, to eat the flesh of kings, the flesh of captains,...flesh of all, both free and slave, both small and great" (19:17f., NRSV).

Or as one New Testament commentator, who confesses "My Father Was a Butcher," has written:

> In truth, however, Jesus' throat was cut from the moment that he first strayed, bleating, into [John's] Gospel: "here is the Lamb of God who taketh away the sin of the world!"...The next day, Jesus staggers by again, still bleeding profusely [cf. Rev. 5:6]...The trail leads straight

---

[19]Cf. the unique and accessible exegesis of ecologist Bill McKibben, *The Comforting Whirlwind: God, Job and the Scale of Creation* (Grand Rapids: Eerdmans, 1994).

[20]J. William Whedbee, *The Bible and the Comic Vision* (Cambridge: Cambridge University Press, 1998), 221–62.

[21]D. H. Lawrence, *Apocalypse* (New York: Viking, 1980), 51; cf. my *Apocalypse Now and Then*, 50.

to the cross, which is also a spit, for it is as roast lamb that Jesus must fulfill his destiny (cf. 6:52–57): "How can this man give us his flesh to eat?"[22]

Thus, Stephen Moore, himself prey to poststructuralism, traces the trail of blood between the Johns. He obstructs any tidy opposition of the loving martyrdom of the gospels versus the butcher shop of the Apocalypse. Through the macabre account of the Maccabee brothers' iterative self-sacrifice (2 and 4 Macc), through Paul's echoing call to imitate Christ's sufferings, Moore performs a stunning deconstruction of the entire apocalyptically charged pattern of martyrology. Holding his gut (having already autobiographically vomited on the threshold of *God's Gym*), he traces a "mimetic chain, slick with blood," as it "snakes out of the text and seeks to coil itself around the audience."[23]

Of course, I am reading deconstruction apocalyptically, or vice versa, which is to say that, recoil as we may, we as Christians and Westerners have that blood on our hands. And if we are still *in* the text, *in* apocalypse, there is no ready escape from this coiling. Another poststructuralist, science critic Donna Haraway, has captured this interiority nicely. She writes of a particular extension of the living text of the Apocalypse, which she recognizes as such, that is, the technoscientific salvation-history narrative of what she likes to call the "second christian millennium." Her wider hermeneutical project, that of a "modest witness," resonates to our exegesis. While she herself does not reflect on the martyriological associations of "witness," the modesty she calls for directly counteracts the ferocious single vision of classical apocalypse:

> We might learn to live without the bracing discourses of salvation history. We exist in a sea of powerful stories:…but no matter what the One-Eyed Father says, there are many possible structures, not to mention contents, of narration. Changing the stories, in both material and semiotic senses, is a modest intervention worth making.[24]

I presume we do indeed wish to change the received metanarrative of apocalypse. I presume also that the ambiguity of the grammar of "changing the stories" remains irresolvable: Are we to transform this story or change to a different one? Indeed, anyone reading this anthology who has not dismissed John's text for its vengeful, omnicidal, misogynist potencies is at least disturbed by the toxicity of its "*Wirkungsgeschicte*," indeed, of its "*wirkliche Geschichte*," that is, of its hermeneutical effects in history.[25] This history of effects can

---

[22]Moore, *God's Gym* (New York and London: Routledge, 96), 3.

[23]Ibid., 27.

[24]Donna J. Haraway, *Modest_Witness@Second_Millennium. FemaleMan_Meets_OncoMouse: Feminism and Technoscience* (New York and London: Routledge, 1997), 45.

[25]*Apocalypse Now and Then* can be read as a meditation on the "*Wirkungsgeschichte*," history-of-effects in a quasi-Gadamerian sense, of Revelation (p. 89). One might now wind such a hermeneutical approach around Foucault's reading of Nietzsche's "*wirkliche Geschichte*," by which the former pries open a space within history, or the discipline of history, for the "insurrection of subjugated knowledges." Most apocalyptic movements would count as such insurrections, while their suppression normally depends on conservative apocalypticisms.

always be written off to bad interpretations–fundamentalist, dispensationalist, millennialist, crusading, demonizing, pacifying, Stalinizing, Nazifying, Y2K, Hollywood...Not the new age, not the *reich*, not the utopia John had in mind! But if for a moment we bracket the clumsy question of whether we should blame the text itself or only its interpretations for all the man-made apocalypses of 2,000 years of biblical citation, we may at least agree that the story needs changing. Then perhaps we can read the deconstructive trope of the many eyes as signalling inside opposition to "the One-eyed Father."

Moore hopes to free the reader from the snaking blood (an avatar of the red serpent of Rev. 12?), not to redeem the Bible from its own effects. To join him in this freedom, must we identify the complex coil of the biblical text with the straight line of Christian imperial theology? I hope not. The bloody flesh may have served as pulp for the Book: "This now, is my body: take it– and read it."[26] But none of it had yet, in either apocalypse or gospel, been sanitized and wrapped as the sacrificial climax–the Cross–of salvation history. The linearity that originates as The Creation and ends in The Second Coming and New Creation emerges with, and only with, the baptism of Hellenistic ontotheology. Far from such a metanarrative, the Revelation can barely even muster a narrative: Schüssler Fiorenza has compared its structure to Sonya Delaunay's multicolored spiral abstractions–coils of form as well as content.[27] Far from the coherent salvation history that will be cooked up from its raw mythemes, these are bloody remains, nonrepresentational shreds and splashes, violent flashes and ephemeral blinks of story. Perhaps for this reason it has inspired the earnest attempts of generations of premillennialists and millennialists to explicate, in meticulous detail, the secret linearity of the sequence of dispensations. But for this reason it also inspires some of us to continue to liberate it from the mononarrative.

vi. Flashes of Intertext

Does this qualify Revelation as at least an original–the raw, meaty vision to be processed and packaged by later traditions? We need only to check out the oracles of warning in Ezekiel 1–24, or–as I would urge the present reader– only just the vision of the first chapter, to grasp how unoriginal is, for instance, the mytheme of the four creatures. Christian commentators tend merely to note the dependency in passing, as though Jewish texts exist to resource the New Testament. Of course, biblical authors are all stubbornly premodern in their indifference to individual authorship, to the distinction of original and derivate, of citation and plagiarism. But Ezekiel's chariot vision makes John's version read like a hacked-up, butchered, overcooked quote.

Ezekiel elaborates the creatures in a poetically beautiful Hebrew, with the sustained attention of one who has seen something that has riveted him to

---

[26]"Doubled over in pain, folded like a stack of leaves, Jesus is bound to a hard wooden spine. He is leafing his body in order to read/turn as a book...But in death his voice will acquire the volume that it lacked in life," Stephen Moore, Matriculation Address, September 1999, printed in *New@Drew: A Publication of Drew University Theological School,* vol. 1. no. 1 (Winter 2000): 2.

[27]Elisabeth Schüssler Fiorenza, *Revelation: Vision of a Just World* (Minneapolis: Fortress Press, 1991), 36.

its every detail. The four creatures each have four faces (and only four wings, unlike the six that John took from Isaiah)—a multiplication of fours suggesting the self-similar complexity of fractal iteration. These creatures, far from fixed at the foot of a throne, "darted to and fro, like flashes of lightning." As to the eyes, these are not indiscriminately plastered all over and inside the creatures, but rather cover the rims of the mysterious wheels within wheels—one pair for each—by which the collective animal/human/angel/mechanical hybrid travels in any direction. Indeed, through Haraway we may recognize such a compound of biological and machine intelligence as an early cyborg.[28] No wonder UFO enthusiasts prize such evidence of early terrestrial visitations! But setting aside Ezekiel's aeronautical premonitions, the prophet's more immediate concern lay with the historical cataclysm his people were about to suffer in the form of the destruction of Jerusalem by Babylon. John encoded a similar sense of dread before the colonial power of the Roman Empire, with the symbol of Babylon, the Great Whore. Of course, Ezekiel actually outdoes and prepares the way for the book of Revelation in the scale of its raging misogynist imagery, taking mainly the form of tantrums against various "whores," tropes for unfaithful cities.[29]

A postmodern reading recognizes John's use of the fragment left over from Ezekiel's chariot not as secondary but as intertextual. As Daniel Boyarin deploys Kristeva's concept of the intertext in the interpretation of Jewish midrash, "The text is always made up of a mosaic of conscious and unconscious citation of earlier discourse."[30] So it is not that in Ezekiel we have "the original"; his more lively, imaginative chariot itself draws from Canaanite theophanies and local throne iconographies. It would inspire the entire Jewish mystical Merkhava tradition of chariot descent, which would merge with Jewish apocalypticism, to form another stream of influence for John. Indeed, as the Bible and Culture Collective avers: "Deconstruction rejects the notion that the origin *(archê)* whatever its form (the author, God, the signified), should be given any sort of priority; it denies that there is an origin in any substantial sense."[31] Of course, such denial of absolute origin emits disturbing theological resonances. It begins to unravel at the literary level the very time line on which the master narrative of *Heilsgeschichte* has depended.

As Boyarin further suggests, "Intertextuality is, in a sense, the way that history, understood as cultural and ideological change and conflict, records itself within textuality."[32] John's recognition of the need for a new rhetoric of theodicy in the face of ongoing persecution, for a public response to a threat

---

[28]Cf. Haraway, *Modest_Witness.*

[29]Keller, "Eyewheels and Arboricide," response to David L. Petersen, "Creation in Ezekiel: Methodological Perspectives and Theological Prospects," unpublished paper, Society of Biblical Literature Annual Meeting, 1999.

[30]Daniel Boyarin, *Intertextuality and the Reading of Midrash* (Bloomington and Indianapolis: Indiana University Press, 1990), 12.

[31]The Bible and Culture Collective, *The Postmodern Bible* (New Haven: Yale University Press, 1995), 130.

[32]Boyarin, *Intertextuality and Midrash,* 94.

experienced as economic, ecological, spiritual, and global certainly deserves the liberation reading it has received so strongly across the world, especially in Latin America and Africa. Like Ezekiel, John faced up to the crushing power of imperial injustice. Ezekiel would work to help his people retain a sense of hope, indeed to craft a postexilic Judaism. John would work from Jewish themes and communities to interpret the specific sense of disappointment and threat felt by many followers of Jesus. Both prophets would adjudicate between destruction by and accomodation to the Empire. These Empires were cosmopolitan and pluralistic, not unlike the neoimperium of the postmodernity, as we shall see.

One needs many eyes indeed to survive with integrity in the urban centers of Empire or neo-Empire. But if that integrity is not to rigidify into a defensive identity formation, one might also need Ezekiel's wondrous vehicle, which flies in the face of despair. Why has John dispensed with the magic chariot? Does the deity no longer motor about? Did "He" get glued to the throne of an unmoving transcendence? In terms of traditional history, John represents the tendency to replace Merkhava with Hekhalot, or throne room mysticism.[33] Yet he has–characteristic of other Hekhalot narratives (cf. Akhiva)–retained elements of the chariot symbolism. John's polyopsis thus exemplifies Boyarin's notion of intertext as "the more or less untransformed detritus of the previous system." We do not read the loss of the multidirectional mobility of the chariot and the metastasis of its eyes on to and into the four creatures as good news.

vii. Liberating Apocalypse

The crisis in the early Christian signifying system, registered in Revelation 4 as the fragment or trace of a prior rupture, suggests to me something more than most current interpretive models suggest. They treat the rupture in terms of religious or cultural persecution brought on by resistance to assimilation in the economies of paganism. John of Patmos' hysterical effort to delegitimate the prophetess of Thyatyta ("Jezebel," in his name-calling) and to lay down clear lines of control and exclusion between communities, suggest that the "conflictual dynamics" do not operate only in relation to imperial oppression. John's text offers meager alternatives for female figuration–arrogant whore, suffering mother, virgin bride. Among them, the coalescence of the "whore Jezebel," clearly a competitor for leadership among influential Christians, with the "Great Whore," Rome herself, seems especially cagey.

Misogny mixes–as it has so often, in so many revolutionary communities– with courageous resistance to economic and cultural injustice. So the crises of the early Christian context in relation to empire and internal conflict may well mirror the rupture among relatively like-minded (feminist, anti-imperialist, deconstructive) readers of Apocalypse two millennia later. "Would that you were either cold or hot," complains John to the church at Laodicea. He certainly

---

[33]Cf. Rachel Elior, "The Concept of God in Hekhalot Literature," in *Studies in Jewish Thought, Binah,* vol. 2, ed. Joseph Dan (New York: Praeger, 1989), 97–120.

gets heat from the progressive and revolutionary traditions of readers, unlike the lukewarmth of a mainstream Christian embarrassment with his excesses.

On one side, we hear the hot revolutionary discourse of liberation theology, which almost invariably and transnationally recognizes John of Patmos as a compadre in the struggle. Boesak's brilliant commentary *Comfort and Protest,* much of which was written from a South African prison cell, presents not a vengeful or violent, but certainly a radical and militant vision of resistance to the apartheid systems, as client of the current superpower and its Babylonian system of power and commerce.[34] More current, Nestor Miguez's analysis of the allegory of the Whore of Babylon deploys its full rhetorical power to expose late capitalist global economics. Given the economic intricacy of John's trope of the obscenity of the global trade in luxury items (hence his lengthy diatribe against the merchants and the sea captains, by which Roman trade and rule extended throughout the known world), such an economic hermeneutic seems fitting and effective. Miguez argues that "the mythopoetic language of apocalyptic and revelatory polysemy of Scripture makes it possible to read this text from the perspective of the victims of the neoliberal capitalist marketplace and its imposed instrumental logic."[35] This is no naive identity politics, but an apocalyptic representation of the economics of the current global imperium:

> Babylon...stands for whatever system enthrones the marketplace,... For whatever turns the human body and soul into merchandise for trade. Within such a system the only need that exists is the need of those who have the ability to pay; consequently the basic needs of all human beings yield to the luxury markets of great merchants and traders. Wherever such luxury goods are piled up, the sounds and lights of creative activity, of the everyday life of all human beings, are excluded.[36]

Martyrdom then gets read not as repulsive addiction to butchery, but as a sometimes inevitable strategy and effect of subversion:

> As in the case of John, the system condemns those who expose the fetishistic nature of the marketplace. Its claim to uniformity, its constant presentation of itself as the only way (and where is the discussion of an alternative to GNP orthodoxy and free trade?)...its conviction that any other alternative is bound to fail also form part of this logic of death. In the end, such logic also includes self-destruction.[37]

---

[34]Allan Aubrey Boesak, *Comfort and Protest: Reflections on the Apocalypse of John of Patmos* (Philadelphia: Westminster Press, 1987).

[35]Nestor Miguez, "Apocalyptic and the Economy: A Reading of Revelation 18 from the Experience of Economic Exclusion," in *Reading from This Place: Social Location and Biblical Interpretation in Global Perspective,* ed. Fernando F. Segovia and Mary Ann Tolbert (Minneapolis: Fortress Press, 1995), 250–52. Cf. Pablo Richard, *Apocalypse: A People's Commentary on the Book of Revelation* (Maryknoll, N. Y.: Orbis, 1995).

[36]Ibid., 261.

[37]Ibid., 262.

Miguez straightforwardly names his hermeneutic apocalyptic: "apocalyptic literature stands out as the place par excellence for the expression of such a perspective."[38] Justo Gonzalez's *For the Healing of the Nations* situates the Apocalypse within the parallelism between the situation of the colonized world in the first two centuries of the Christian era and the postcolonial circumstances of today. The cultural pluralism within a circumstance of a widening gap between the wealth of the global elites and the poverty of the colonized majority shows startling resemblances to situations being constituted by global "free trade" today.[39]

This progressive apocalyptic hermeneutic stands in intertextual solidarity with the entire Western revolutionary tradition. As Ernst Bloch, the socialist philosopher, has argued in the *Philosophy of Hope,* this tradition derives its radical futurity, its utopian hope for the fullness of justice for the poor, from the revived medieval apocalyptic tradition that runs from Joachim of Fiore through the Radical Franciscans to the Radical Reformation.[40]

viii. Antiapocalypse

Characteristically, such liberation theologians as Miguez, Boesak, Gonzalez, and even Schüssler Fiorenza do not worry about the violence of the vision itself, apparently justified by the prior violence of empire. Thus, they do not criticize the radical misogyny of apocalypse and its heirs. They do not question the spiritual machismo energizing itself from the cunning icon of the Great Whore's titillating demise. Certainly, feminist perspectives can smite traditional left politics with an especially distracting case of cross-eyes. Out of a laudable if doctrinaire interest in keeping "the eye on the prize," that is, focusing Christian energy on the single goal of struggle for social justice, it avoids interpretive ambiguity and ambivalence. It does not, for instance, consider the problem, which postcolonial theorist Homi Bhabha has dubbed "colonial mimicry"–the reinscription of the structures of power in the very act of resistance. It does not problematize the mutual mirroring of "whore" and YHWH, both on their thrones. Feminist readings–prone to our own monofocal gaze, of course–constitute only one means of exposing the oppressive patriarchal models operative within the revolutionary vision.

So then on the other side, we have those feminists and deconstructivists chilled by the bloody misogynist martyr's cult of apocalyptic lords and warriors. The title of Lee Quinby's Foucaultian feminist analysis of American culture as ridden with apocalyptic masculinity, *Anti-Apocalypse,* well summarizes this position, further elaborated in *Millennial Seduction.*[41] Here she performs

---

[38]Ibid., 253.

[39]Justo L. Gonzalez, *For the Healing of the Nations: The Book for Revolution in an Age of Cultural Conflict* (Maryknoll: Orbis, 1999).

[40]"Joachim was cogently the spirit of revolutionary Christian social utopianism;" Ernst Bloch, *The Principle of Hope,* vol. 2 (Cambridge, Mass: MIT Press, 1986; German ed., 1959), 515. Cf. Keller, *Apocalypse Now and Then* for extended discussions of the revolutionary political effects of Revelation, esp. chapters 2, "Temporizing Tales," and 5, "Congregating Conflagrations."

[41]Lee Quinby, *Millennial Seduction: A Skeptic Confronts Apocalyptic Culture* (Ithaca, N.Y.: Cornell University Press, 1999), 35–58. See also Quinby, *Anti-Apocalypse: Exercises in Genealogical Criticism* (Minneapolis: University of Minnesota Press, 1994).

insightful genealogies of the "apocalyptic gender panic" of the Promise Keepers, of the "programmed perfection" through bioengineering–staged as "skeptical revelations of an American feminist on Patmos." Tina Pippin offers vibrant feminist deconstructions of Revelation from within New Testament studies proper. "What remains," she concludes of John's Apocalypse, "is the misogyny and exclusion by a powerful, wrathful deity. In the Apocalypse, the Kingdom of God is the kingdom of perversity."[42]

Also navigating convergent feminist poststructuralist streams, Stephen Moore challenges atonement theology in its relation to apocalypse. Here he takes his cue from feminist theological work on the relationship between child abuse and the image of God as a father who requires the stripping, humiliation, torture, and death of his Son.[43] Moore indeed zooms right in on our visionary creatures, who are singing and worshiping along with twenty-four elders, to reveal that "the heavenly throne room in Revelation as a whole (in which it functions as the principal setting) mirrors the Roman imperial court." For the emperor Domitian was constantly surrounded by twenty-four lictors, officials bearing fasces; Nero by elite young men functioning as "an imperial cheerleading squad."[44]

Unbeknownst to themselves, such gendered deconstructions follow the lead of the feminist whom feminist poststructuralists love to dismiss as "essentialist"–Mary Daly. She it is who satirically decried the apocalyptic return of the Lord:

> This "Word" is doublespeak…preparing the way for a phallotechnic Second Coming. It is the announcement of the ultimate Armageddon, where armies of cloned Jesus Freaks (christian and/or nonchristian) will range themselves against Hags/Crones, attempting the Final Solution to the "problem" of Female Force.[45]

Daly, the most radical feminist apocalypse of anti-apocalypse, messianically declares her own final Armageddon: "The ultimate contest was wrongly described in the Book of Revelation…The author in his vision failed to note the Holy War waged by Wholly Haggard Whores casting off the bonds of whoredom."[46]

While I may have been more swayed than the above feminists by the largely nonwhite voices of the liberation tradition who read Revelation sympathetically, I too cast my lot with John's Jezebel. A rival Christian prophet, she provokes in John a misogynist tantrum: "Beware, I am throwing her on a bed, and those who commit adultery with her I am throwing into great distress, unless they repent…I will strike her children dead"(2:22–23, NRSV). The

---

[42]Pippin, *Apocalyptic Bodies,* 125; see also Pippin's *Death and Desire: The Rhetoric of Gender in the Apocalypse of John* (Louisville: Westminster/John Knox Press, 1992).

[43]Moore, *God's Gym,* 12.

[44]Ibid., 125.

[45]Quoted in Keller, *Apocalypse Now and Then,* 264.

[46]Ibid., 247.

poetics of power, of conquest, of swords and iron rods pitted against female bodies, none too subtly symbolized as "earthen pots" (2:26), penetrate the significatory field of the Apocalypse. A feminist ethic surely cannot in the long run re/veil the misogyny of its revelation.[47]

Whether essentialist or antiessentialist, however, the repudiations of apocalypse tend to ignore the powerful religious, countercultural, and then secular millennialism stimulating progressive social movements in general, and in particular the women's movement in the nineteenth century and each stage of its further development.[48] To the extent that such postmodern feminisms cannot take seriously the liberation hermeneutic, which can be dismissed as an essentialist knockoff of the Marxist metanarrative, to that extent they do not account for the economic, ethnic, and coalitional implications of their own indignant antiapocalypse.

ix. Double-edged S/Word

Both the liberation neoapocalypse and the feminist antiapocalypse remain pure. Hotly mimicking the warrior hierarchy of the domination to be resisted; or in the feminist case, coldly mirroring in its antiapocalypse the dualism of all apocalyptic demonization. Both modes of progressive thought suffer from unacknowledged binary strategies, which endanger the potential for creative new coalitions. The apocalypse reinscribes that which it opposes; the antiapocalyptic stance reinscribes the apocalypse.

Yet any attempts to resist mere liberal lukewarmth, mere postmodern relativism, may produce such dualistic emissions as an inevitable by-product. A Foucaultian sense of power, liable to discursive rearrangements rather than final triumph, should prepare one to expect as much. As with the Derridian text, so with Foucaultian power: "one is always 'inside' power, there is no 'escaping' it, there is no absolute outside where it is concerned."[49] At least, however, we can recognize the dead ends of such willful or inadvertent apocalyptic politics; we might learn to recognize our ejaculations of unambiguous purity as the leakage of our own uncertainties. We can at least open a few more of our own eyes.

On the particular theological rim *(eschaton)* where I perch, I need as a feminist both an honest sense of my own precedents in the Christian tradition and a working coalition with those ethnic groups and liberation movements who will for the foreseeable future (which has already extended much further than John could foresee or could have tolerated) find their plight mirrored in John's radical antiimperialism. One risks on this boundary being spit out as lukewarm, though actually the temperature feels more variant, subject to chills

---

[47]Despite even a great feminist New Testament scholar's love of this text as the primary New Testament text of justice; cf. my discussion of Schüssler Fiorenza in *Apocalyspe Now and Then*, 44–46.

[48]Keller, *Apocalypse Now and Then*, documents this extensively in its chapter on gender.

[49]The Bible and Culture Collective, *The Postmodern Bible*, 141.

and fevers.[50] This has led me to inhabit what I had called *counter-apocalypse:* a critical edge—perhaps the two-edged tongue after all—that shares much of antiapocalyptic critique. But it acknowledges the debt of all radical political traditions to that very apocalypse. Therefore, it recognizes the counter-apocalypse as itself a form of apocalypse: hopefully one of dis/closure rather than final closure.

x. Apocalypse Without Apocalypse

But then it turns out that Derrida had *come* already. I would not mention the peculiar sensation of postapocalypse: of an unveiling of that which had been veiled precisely in its prior apocalypse; now, having written my way through to the counterapocalypse, wanting to be done—it is finished—with the texts and topics of the End, upon rereading "Of an Apocalyptic Tone" and finding the pivotal insight of my counterapocalypse folded into his "apocalyptic *pli* (fold, envelope, letter, habit, message)."[51] I would not mention this postapocalyptic (cha)grin, did I not suspect that my "I" here mirrors something of the postmillennial moment. I do not gaze at all these winking eyes alone. A cloud, indeed a crowd of witnesses—prominent among them those who have built their reputations on the shifting sands of the ever-receding Endtimes—share the varieties and intensities of postapocalyptic perturbation. Sometime in the last millennium, I had read the following sentence as closure:

> Now here, precisely, is announced—as promise or threat—an apocalypse without apocalypse, an apocalypse without vision, without truth, without revelation, envois (for the "come" is plural in itself, in oneself), addresses without message and without destination, without sender or decidable addressee, without last judgment, without any other eschatology than the tone of the "Come," its very differance, an apocalypse beyond good and evil.[52]

Worst of both worlds, I had thought: granting the status of a transcendent "beyond" to its own demystification, we are left with a facile Nietzsche, finality without discovery, "without" with no remainder, "Come" with no content—the empty gesture without the zen of emptiness. I had perhaps held out not for this erasure of vision, truth, disclosure, message, destination—but rather for the proliferation of visions and truths that becomes possible when the "last" is subtracted from the judgment, when the single, the One, the Only, the Final is taken away from the truth—leaving not nothing, but a liberating proliferation that, after all, resonates with other deconstructive tones, with the

---

[50]I am pleased to be criticized by Pippin as "submitting to the authority of the biblical text" (*Apocalyptic Bodies,* 8) and by Ted Peters as scorning it: no "positive appropriation of this biblical text for today…no guiding exegesis of a text 'that proves nothing'" (review, *Theology Today* [July 1997]: 243–46).

[51]Derrida, "Of an Apocalyptic Tone Newly Adapted in Philosophy," in *Derrida and Negative Theology,* trans. John P. Leavy, ed. Harold Coward and Toby Foshay (Albany: State University of New York Press, 1992), 58.

[52]Ibid., 66.

polytonalities of dissemination and the multiple. And I still hold out. I still see the people perishing without a vision. And I am still trying to tell some truth—all the more so because of negotiating the mendacious reassurances, the sincere (white?) lies to which even the most progressive theology is always tempted, the confusion of faith with belief, of metaphor with proposition. As Derrida caricatures the apocalyptic message—thinking more perhaps of its echo in politics, philosophy, psychoanalysis:

> "We're alone in the world, I'm the only one able to reveal to you the truth or the destination, I tell you it, I give it to you, come, let us be for a moment, we who don't yet know who we are, a moment before the end the sole survivors, the only ones to stay awake, it will be so much better."[53]

Not truth but its monotone, what Nietzsche called "monotonotheism" *(The Antichrist),* poses as the "only one." So in the name of the multitonality of truths and the multiplication of visions, I confess to my unveiling (after the fact, after the book) within that same almost antiapocalyptic essay the key to counterapocalypse:

> Everything that can now inspire a de-mystifying desire regarding the apocalyptic tone, namely a desire for light, for lucid vigilance, for the elucidating vigil, for truth...it is already a citation or a recitation of John.[54]

Ah, then he mirrors in John the very impulse with which we might deconstruct the apocalypse itself: "You have tested those who call themselves envoys and are not, you find them liars" (2:2). Bringing to light the circularity of the "*Aufklärer* of modern times," of the enlightened critics of all the false apocalypses—among whom must ipso facto belong true antiapocalypticists—he asks the question from which there may be no exit: "Shall we thus continue in the best apocalyptic tradition to denounce false apocalypses?"[55] In other words, the denunciation of the apocalypse always mirrors the apocalypse. Derrida makes clear the political risk of his own denunciation: "Nothing is less conservative than the apocalyptic genre."[56] It is not a matter of reaching some more enlightened, more progressive vantage point—some saturation of eyes—from which to unmask the conservatism of the apocalyptic ends. Now Derrida folds the question into itself, asking it in its famous form:

> Since the habit [*pli*] has already been acquired, I am not going to multiply the examples; the end approaches, but the apocalypse is long-lived. The question remains and comes back: what can be the limits of a demystification?[57]

---

[53]Ibid., 54.
[54]Ibid., 58.
[55]Ibid., 59.
[56]Ibid.
[57]Ibid.

By asking this question, Derrida steps off the track of an apocalyticism all the more relentless for its ability to mask itself as deconstruction–as the ultimate, the final, strategy of unmasking. Yet he precisely does not step outside the text of Revelation. "And what if this outside of apocalypse were *inside* the apocalypse?"[58] Rather, he lets it yield up its own opening. He cites its last chapter, in his preferred translation: "Do not seal up the words of the inspiration of this volume" (22:10). He remains faithful to the radical interiority of the work of deconstruction–prey to itself. It took my own long and clumsy struggle within the radicalisms of the apocalyptic tradition to hear, to see, the grace of that double opening. It does not seem like much, perhaps. Perhaps as a theologian, denizen of an archaic discipline, one is grateful for a mere crumb from the Parisian table. I think, rather, that our own eucharistic banquet loses its taste without some analogue to the Derridian predation.

The Postmodern Bible had read, via Mark C. Taylor, the Derridian "apocalypse without apocalypse" as "an/apocalypse": a felicitous rendition, undeveloped yet almost parallel to the apocalypse retained in counterapocalypse. For this an/apocalypse, "the text does not reveal but is revealed–as text, writing, scripture."[59] We have already noted Revelation's core imperative: "Write!" Yet we are reading differently here: We are failing to deny the text's capacity to reveal. In this, the "counter" remains after all more active, more engaged in an ironic mimicry, than the prefix *an,* a simple negation, can support. We are only denying the text's–this text, any text's–claim to an ultimate or certain truth, for a revelation of the one and only good.

We are allowing the "Come!" some content that Derrida might well want purged. But then he surely recognizes the provenance of all purges. John Caputo has read this *"Viens"*in a fresh "tone": The apocalypse that the apocalypse is without, comes into its own. "For inasmuch as apocalypticism is the call of this 'come,' a hymn and recitative of *viens,* then deconstruction is apocalyptic through and through, *grace à Dieu,* and Derrida would never think of shedding his apocalyptic tone."[60] Moreover, Caputo reads in this tone Derrida's debt to the messianism of Walter Benjamin, as well as to the alterity of Levinas, both translated into Derrida's own "Jewishness without Judaism":

> Viens, oui, oui, is an upbeat and affirmative tone of passionate affirmation, maybe even a slightly Jewish tone, by which we open ourselves to the event and shift into messianic time. The passion of Derrida's apocalyptic tone is not dire fire and brimstone, not a wild-eyed declamation of imminent doom, nor is he trying to terrorize his critics with a forecast of eternal damnation…The apocalyptic tone recently adapted in deconstruction is upbeat and affirmative, expectant and hopeful, positively dreamy, dreaming of the impossible.[61]

---

[58]Ibid., 67.
[59]The Bible and Culture Collective, *The Postmodern Bible,* 138.
[60]John Caputo, *The Tears and Prayers of Jacques Derrida* (Bloomington: Indiana University Press, 1997), 95.
[61]Ibid., 98.

Caputo returns fervently to the convergence of John's final "Come!" with Derrida's *Viens:*

> Can John keep his Apocalypse absolutely safe and sealed tight from deconstruction?...What could "seal" John's message off? There, *la,* is the opening for which Derrida, on cat-soft paws, was searching. The Lord told John expressly not to seal it off (Rev. 22:10), to keep it open![62]

A cat prowling among the stranger apocalyptic creatures, finding the crack, keeping it open? For if apocalypse, which translates as "un/veiling," "dis/closure," stays open–the threat of omnicidal closure may begin to dissipate into the crack. In the face of the bitter closures of John's unequaled dualisms of good and evil, now and then, old and new, we and they, keeping it open seems almost enough. It spares us the apocalyptic reruns of pro and con. It gives respite from the habit of renewal through revenge. But, of course, undecidability remains a necessary but not sufficient cause of any renewal worth singing about.

Not that the opening now should be (again) reinscribed as a mere means to some End–as of full gender/sex/race/culture equality and differance. But in order for the very process of opening to sustain itself, there may need to be some content, some commitment, some decision to open. A hermeneutic of uncertainty is not identical to a theory of undecidability: We decide in favor of the multiple and in favor of some pluralities more than others. Theology need not now return to fill the deconstructive void, to plug the opening, and in effect to close it up again. Rather, it has been operating (if somewhat between the lines, as befits a modest witness) all along, pleading, praying, winking, hosting a polyperspectival view.

xi. Apoca/Lips

As for the apocalyptic *Viens,* it will keep coming. Even Luce Irigaray, no later than Derrida, was waiting for what is to "come." There in the early '80s she also and just as startlingly, just as irreducibly, had recourse to the apocalypse: "Waiting for parousia would require keeping all one's senses alert. Not destroyed, not covered, not 'dirtied,' our senses would be open."[63]

Without her we might not find the *body* of deconstruction. Why does it take a woman to call us to our senses? Yet this lost body is not female only. But it is nobody without the female. The opening of the senses requires more than the opening of a text–even as her text opens into the senses. But here virtually alone among poststructuralist Parisians, she invokes pneumatology: "Keeping the senses alert means being attentive in flesh and in spirit."[64] That is most intensively a theological proposition, no mere opening, but the opening

---

[62]Ibid., 100.
[63]Luce Irigaray, *An Ethics of Sexual Difference,* trans. Carolyn Burke and Gillian C. Gill (Ithaca, N.Y.: Cornell University Press, 1991), 148.
[64]Ibid.

by and in which I unveil myself as woman, by which my senses and even perhaps, even, again, my eyes open. To wit: "If God and the other are to be unveiled," she writes then, full throttle apocalyptic, "I too must unveil myself (I should not expect God to do this for me. Not this time...)."[65]

She then startles the reader by a quite unmistakable allusion to Joachim and his third epoch, the potent intertext of all European discourses of millennial hope, of revolution, or of new age: "The third era of the West might, at last, be the era of the couple: of the spirit and the bride?"[66] So here she has turned like Derrida to the end of the book of the end of the Book—the verse she seems to allude to without citing is Revelation 22:17: "The Spirit and the bride say, 'Come'" (NRSV).

The great feminist prophet of the "lips," the body parable of a subjectivity that is "neither one nor two" but multiple, has unexpectedly unveiled an apoca/liptic orifice for French feminism. "With father and son summoned for the coming of this third stage in the parousia," not shortchanging the Joachite heritage, she states apodictically: "The spirit and the bride invite beyond genealogical destiny to the era of the wedding and the festival of the world. To the time of a theology of the breath in its horizontal and vertical becoming, with no murders."[67] This is no coy literary device. Irigaray has joined the choir of feminist theologians.[68] She seeks no mere apophatic nothingness, but a sensuous incarnation of God as female. The aim would be unlimited incarnation, not the single incarnation of a son, not even the dyadic one of a couple, but of all that is "drawn into the mystery of a word that seeks its incarnation."[69] I pray that her pneumatology of the couple, because it chooses the gender-ambiguous Spirit rather than the couple actually celebrated in John's pericope, the Lamb and the New Jerusalem, his Bride, may not serve the displaced cause of heterosexist renewal. Certainly, it sidesteps the slaughterhouse atonement. Still, here too we need to keep our eyes open. Apocalyptic invocation does run the risk of the binaries always again, from which we will always again need an opening. Before it comes to murder.

xii. Kissing God's Body

What comes, matters. It materializes. It makes a differance. Wounded and wondrous, reading and read, animal/vegetable/mineral/mechanical/divine, the eyes see kaleidoscopically. Seeing perhaps Irigaray's *infini,* the unfinished? A counterapocalypse reveals that revelation is not *one,* not that it is *not.* Derrida proposed the "fiction" of a single apocalyptic tone, "that the

---

[65]Ibid.

[66]Ibid.

[67]Ibid.

[68]Most of her later works confirm this constructive theological interest; cf. most powerfully the concluding christological construction of *The Marine Lover of Friedrich Nietzsche* (New York: Columbia University Press, 1991), also *Sexes and Genealogies* (New York: Columbia University Press, 1993), and most readably, *I Love To You* (New York: Routledge, 1996).

[69]Irigaray, *The Forgetting of Air in Martin Heidegger,* trans. Mary Beth Mader (Austin: University of Texas Press, 1999), 178.

apocalyptic tone is not the effect of a generalized derailment, of a *Verstimmung* multiplying the voices and making the tones shift, opening each word to the haunting memory of the other in an unmasterable polytonality."[70] We might now reverse the fiction, invite the derailment, and welcome the multiplicative polytonality. This untoward quartet of creatures is noisy; they see and sing. Their harmonies might shriek dissonantly to our hearing; yet they do sing *together.* A theologian at least can invoke the carnival of creatures, the festival of the world.

The carnivalesque delight of our scene—despite John's general grimness—suggests itself in the midrash of the Hekhalot Rabbati (13:4), which describes how the *Chayyot* sport with YHWH in his heavenly throne room, kissing and caressing him, flapping their wings ecstatically, playing music, and dancing about. Then we are told: "They reveal their faces (to Him), but the King of Glory hides His face, lest the expanses of heaven burst before the King of Beauty, Splendor, Loveliness, Comeliness, Fairness, Radiance, Attractiveness, Brilliance."[71]

Long before the stunning scales and photos of the currently observable universe, the beauty *(yofi)* of the "body of God," which it was the special privilege of the Hekhalot mystics to perceive in sensory ecstacy, had so far manifested itself through cosmic luminaries.[72] Some recent theologies, such as process theology and the ecotheology of Sallie McFague, have developed a metaphor of the universe as the "body of God." If we keep the metaphor light enough for fiction, weighty enough to matter—invoking the poetic license for constructive theology—the creatures' polyopticon might suggest a certain playful panentheism. Most commentators would not agree to the tradition of reading the eyes as a displacement of the divine omniscience.[73] However, the creatures immediately surrounding the throne do embody theriomorphically the holiness of the inner sanctum. Perhaps as word-free animals, dangerously inaudible to Christians and postmodernists, they incarnate nonetheless the sacred sentience of all creatures. If divine awareness disseminates through their irreducible differance, their eyes belong neither properly to themselves nor to God. Eyes, stars, gems twinkle in a Morse code illegible within logocentric eschatology, signaling a future in which we humanoids sing along, just third of four.

[70]Derrida, "Of an Apocalyptic Tone," 52.

[71]The translation is from Martin S. Cohen's "The Song of Songs and the Shicur Qomah" (9), an unpublished paper that Stephen Moore has generously passed on to me.

[72]"The ascription of form and beauty to God are apparently daring; nonetheless, a careful analysis of the concept of beauty in Hekhalot literature reveals that the descriptions are based on cosmic beauty, on the majesty of the universe, and on the power of universal natural forces" (Elior, "The Concept of God," 107). The attempt to perceive and measure a Body of God, does in this early Jewish mysticism seem to anticipate the beauty and dimensionality discernible through the Hubble telescope and other quite nonmystical tools of the current golden age in astronomy. "God put his hand on me and blessed me…I was raised the height and breadth of the world and given 72 wings…each wing the size of the world, and on each wing there were 365 eyes, each eye the size of the sun. No luminescence or brightness was omitted *(Synopse,* paragraph 12)" (Elior, "The Concept of God," 107–8).

[73]Michl, *Die Engelverstellungen in der Apokalypse,* 71.